Pandanus Online Publ
web site, presents add

BITTERSWEET

Love is a splendid thing
... A Promise to keep
... A Dream to fulfil
... and many miles to go....

To Yogesh Bhai

from ... Anup Kumar SYDNEY
19th FEB 2007

BITTERSWEET

the Indo-Fijian experience

EDITED BY BRIJ V. LAL

Photographs by Peter Hendrie

PANDANUS BOOKS
Research School of Pacific and Asian Studies
THE AUSTRALIAN NATIONAL UNIVERSITY

Cover: *An Indo-Fijian girl, Nadi market, 1999*. Photograph by Peter Hendrie.

Typeset in Goudy 11pt on 14pt and printed by New Millennium Print, Canberra

National Library of Australia Cataloguing-in-Publication entry

Bittersweet : the Indo-Fijian experience.

ISBN 1 74076 117 0.

1. East Indians — Fiji — History. 2. Fiji — History. I. Lal, Brij V.

996.11

Editorial inquiries please contact Pandanus Books on 02 6125 3269

www.pandanusbooks.com.au

Published by Pandanus Books, Research School of Pacific and Asian Studies, The Australian National University, Canberra ACT 0200 Australia

Pandanus Books are distributed by UNIREPS, University of New South Wales, Sydney NSW 2052 Telephone 02 9664 0999 Fax 02 9664 5420

Production: Ian Templeman, Justine Molony and Emily Brissenden

For Indo-Fijians
At home and abroad

This is my mother country. The same place you live in,
the same place I live in. You must think about that. My
mother and father came to this country. They work hard
here. Where can we go? Tell me. We must stay here and
die here. No other place. That's the important part. We
must remember that.

'Babuji' Bechu Prasad, Indo-Fijian, Sabeto, 102 years old

GREETINGS
NAMASKAR

Every inheritance is alike beneficial and baneful; every historically conscious society has had to reassess that balance for itself.

David Lowenthal

ANNIVERSARIES mark milestones and measure the passage of time. Whether they celebrate some event of personal or collective significance — a birthday, wedding, national independence, the end of a conflict; or remember a loss — the death of a friend, family member or public figure (or the ravages of a natural disaster) — they provide an opportunity for reflection and introspection. We often remember the way things were nostalgically: how we dressed then, how slim we looked, the friends we had, the pranks we played, the things that gave us joy and hope or created fear and anxiety. We recall false prophets, false steps and false dawns. We talk wistfully about what might have been, why and how things turned out the way they did, the role we might have played in shaping our destiny. And, from the myriad images and impressions that cloud our minds and compete for our attention, we construct meanings and models to confront the future. For intensely personal moments, memory is often all we have with which to contemplate the meaning and purpose of our time on Earth.

This collection marks the 125th anniversary of the arrival of the Indian people in Fiji. The experience and the predicaments of the Indo-Fijian community have been well chronicled. Even so, much work remains to be done, especially on its inner social, cultural and spiritual experience, its symbols, rituals and ceremonies, which impart coherence and continuity; the way its people see themselves and their place on the national stage. We attempt to capture not the totality of the Indo-Fijian experience — an impossible task — but diverse and scattered fragments which illuminate its broad patterns through essays, memoirs and recollections. They are about personal journeys and transformations, chance encounters, individual discoveries, private moments, unexpected revelations as well as overarching themes and concerns that touch some aspect of the community's life but which, as a general rule, do not find a place in conventional historical narratives. Each contribution has its own unique character, its own distinctive voice, but collectively they throw a sharper beam of light on to a troubled people caught in a world at once complex and conflicted, with its fair share of benevolence and violence, greed and generosity, curiosity and nonchalance, ambition and despair, purpose and powerlessness, emptiness and anticipation.

It remains for me to thank the contributors – some of them writing for publication for the first time — for responding so readily to my request to write. Without them, of course, this book would not exist. I am delighted in niggling middle-age to include in the collection representatives of a younger generation who were school-age children, not much more, when the centenary celebrations took place in 1979. Among them are Indo-Fijians living in Fiji and in the diaspora as well as 'outsiders' who have become honoured 'insiders' through their enduring cross-cultural relationships, deep cultural affinity and imaginative sympathy. I hope that their creative spirit will not be sapped by the exigencies of earning a living in a brutally competitive world. More power to their pen — or word processor. Donald Denoon and Hank Nelson, my colleagues in Pacific and Asian History at

The Australian National University for more than a decade now, have earned my warm gratitude for their inspiring (but also utterly daunting) example of eloquent creativity and their sharp editorial pen, wielded invariably with collegial care and understanding. Mr Aubrey Parke, my District Commissioner in Labasa in the 1960s, went through the text with painstaking care and saved me from many embarrassing errors. Ian Templeman, my publisher, works miracles when it comes to coaxing creative things from people who never thought they had any. His staff at Pandanus Books, especially Emily Brissenden and my editor Justine Molony, have been exemplary in their professionalism and have earned my deep gratitude, as has Oanh Collins of my own department in the care with which she prepared the manuscript for publication. Jan Borrie's critical eye has improved the book's readability immeasurably. My friend, Peter Hendrie, whose photographs grace the book, is a rare gem — gracious and giving — and so good: his pictures do not need my words.

And to you, the reader: I hope that you will find something of interest and value in what we have to offer on a people about whom much has been assumed, often cruelly unflattering, but whose deeper fears and fractured hopes are less well understood. The Indo-Fijian experience is full of strange peculiarities and tragic ironies. It is the story of a people brought to work under conditions of extreme servitude to spare the indigenous people the fate of dispossession and violence at the hands of European settlers, but who somehow ended up as their *bête noire*. It is about the odyssey of a people who have made something of themselves, all on their own, often against great odds, without a helping hand, but who still feel uprooted and unwanted. And it is an experience that raises troubling questions. For how many generations does one have to live in a place to be allowed to call it home? As more and more of them migrate to settle elsewhere, will future generations see Indo-Fijian presence in Fiji — once half the population — as a nightmarish aberration in the history of that Pacific Island nation? Will they see Fiji as a temporary stopover for a people condemned by fate to wander the world? *Dekhi ye duniya ki yāri, bichde sabhi bāri bāri.* I have seen the ways of this world: they all depart, one by one. Immigration to emigration: will that be the epitaph for Fiji's Indo-Fijian community? If this volume enlarges your awareness of their predicaments, we will have achieved our objective. *Dhanyabad.*

Brij V. Lal

Pandanus Books gratefully acknowledges the support of the Reddy Group, Corporate Office, 35 Ravouvou Street, Lautoku, Fiji, in the publication of this book.

CONTENTS

Market vendor, Nadi. True son of the soil, a descendant of the girmitiyas.

CHAPTER ONE

Girmit, *History*, *Memory*

Brij V. Lal

The past is in its grave
Though its ghost haunts us
Browning

TWENTY-FIVE YEARS can be a long time in a community
or a nation's life. It has certainly been a long and troubled time
in the life of the Indo-Fijians. Twenty-five years ago — 1979 —
marked the 100th anniversary of the arrival of the Indian people
in Fiji. The event was celebrated nationally. High Chief
and Deputy Prime Minister, Ratu Sir Penaia Ganilau, headed
a distinguished multiracial national committee to plan and
supervise the two-day celebrations.[1] That kind of gesture, so
generous and inclusive and accommodating, would be unthinkable
now. At Albert Park on 13 May, the Royal Military Forces Band
played a selection of religious music, and an inter-faith service of
thanksgiving and dedication was attended by representatives of
all the major religions. Fittingly, the next day, young school
children assembled in the park, and a *meke* (Fijian action-song)
was performed along with a ballet by the Indian Cultural Centre

depicting the arrival of Indian immigrants and their indenture experience. Rugby, basketball and soccer competitions were held in the afternoon and trophies were awarded to the winning teams. And, bathed in a rainbow of colours on the field, the military band played on.

The Prime Minister, Ratu Sir Kamisese Mara, presented commemorative coins to a small group of surviving *girmitiyas*,[2] all in their late twilight, partially deaf or blind or both, visibly ill at ease in the limelight, perplexed about all the fuss being made over them. In his message, the Prime Minister acknowledged the nation's debt 'to these pioneers who, with others in our multiracial society, have played a notable role in building a free, prosperous and independent Fiji'. The Governor-General, Ratu Sir George Cakobau, agreed. 'Our Indian friends and their forefathers have worked hard for themselves and for Fiji — they have had a big hand in shaping what we see in this country today. I sincerely pray that they enjoy living in their adopted home and that peace and prosperity will prevail in this country of ours in the next hundred years.'

Torika Baleimali, a Form Four student from Nabala Junior Secondary School in Labasa, wrote in an essay for a national competition on how children would see themselves in 2000: 'I am a Fijian. My parents feel that the Indians are a menace to our race but I feel otherwise. My mind is more flexible. I am able to see both the disadvantages and advantages of having the Indians in the country.' Fiji, she wrote, was a multiracial country, and 'will remain so'. 'I feel that it is useless to drive people out because we dislike them. We must adjust ourselves to social change and this is a challenge in itself.' Shahmaag Munam, from Form Six at Xavier College in Ba, wrote about *her own* children in 2000 'growing up with other youngsters who are not aware of racial discord, who have no qualms about sharing lunch with either an Indian or a non-Indian'. 'It gives me immense pride and satisfaction to be a part of Fiji's community,' she continued. It was her home. Whatever happened, 'I would not leave Fiji for any other place. The overall atmosphere is one of tranquillity and amiability.'

These haunting words of youthful optimism speak to a different past, a past now vanished beyond recall. For the intervening 25 years have seen not 'tranquillity' and 'amiability', but violence and rupture, the pride of an Indo-Fijian being a part of Fiji replaced by despair and dejection, the sense of being at 'home' in the islands overtaken by a desperate desire to leave for some place else at the earliest possible opportunity. Since the coups of 1987, which deposed a government in which Indo-Fijians had appropriate representation for the first time in their history, some 80,000 people have left, the best and the brightest, taking with them skills and talents the country can ill-afford to lose. Emotionally uprooted, trapped and terrorised, more would leave if they could. The expiration of agricultural leases on native land is pushing people out and endangering the future of an industry — sugar — for which the Indians were brought to Fiji in the first place. And the glass ceiling stares back at them mercilessly in many areas of public life. One hundred and twenty-five years after arriving in the islands, the future for the Indo-Fijians looks almost as bleak as it did for their forebears when they embarked on their unpredictable journeys from Calcutta and Madras to destinations unheard of or unknown.

An important by-product of the 1979 centennial celebrations was the re-introduction of the word '*girmit*' into the general vocabulary of Fiji, especially Fiji Hindi.[3] For the first time, many people learned that the word derived from 'agreement', under which the indentured labourers had contracted to come to Fiji, that it covered the whole gamut of the indenture experience. Until then — and for some even now — the word was synonymous with shame. People recalled *girmit* — when they recalled the past at all — as a period of brutality and violence and debauchery, of poverty and degradation, of moral disintegration and cultural and social chaos, altogether a dark period best left unexplored to the obscure pages of a fading history. The *girmitiyas* were said to have no agency, no individuality, nothing, other than being disposable cogs in the heartless wheel of a profit-driven plantation system. They had not come to Fiji of their own accord, but were tricked into migrating by wily recruiters — *arkatis* — preying on the gullible, the greedy and the desperate. And they were the children of the lesser gods, the flotsam and jetsam of humanity picked up from the streets of Indian towns and shipped like cattle to Fiji. In short, indenture was slavery.[4] The words of Browning's dying Paracelsus could well sum up their feelings:

> *I saw no use in the past: only a scene*
> *Of degradation, ugliness, and tears*
> *The record of disgraces best forgotten*
> *A sullen page in human chronicles*
> *Fit to erase.*[5]

This *girmit*-as-slavery thesis has long been the dominant, popular rendition of the indenture experience in Fiji. And there is undeniable truth in it. Many were broken by work, claimed by disease or wrecked by human violence and greed. Suffering and pain and violence were an integral part of the *girmit* experience. All this is abundantly clear from the historical record. But it is not the whole story. Hindsight should not hound history nor the present prosecute the past. Nor is it wise to press a complex and contested past into a serviceable ideology to fight contemporary battles, however depressing the present might be. It is possible to acknowledge hardship while granting the *girmitiyas* agency. I have elsewhere sought to demonstrate that *girmit* was a complex, multi-layered experience that lends itself to multiple readings; that it was a limited detention of five or ten years, not a life sentence; that there was change over time; that the *girmitiyas* were not devoid of will and agency; that the plantation system was not a 'total institution' everywhere; that the grip of the plantation hierarchy varied over time and place; that, for some, migration and indenture could well have been a liberating experience from a vicious cycle of poverty and degradation at home, with no possibility of improvement in either this life or the next; that painting the *girmitiyas* as helpless victims does them and their legacy a grave injustice.[6] I shall not rehearse that debate here but provide readers unfamiliar with the Indian indenture experience with a broad survey of its main features.

Origins of a Journey

The introduction of Indian indentured labour into Fiji in 1879 was a direct result of the cession of the islands to Queen Victoria five years earlier. The new colony, remote and reluctantly acquired, needed rapid economic development to sustain itself, but the conditions for it were lacking. Local capital was unavailable, with the European planters reeling from the collapse of the cotton boom of the previous decade after the end of the American civil war. And Fijian labour had been effectively prohibited from commercial employment by Fiji's first governor, Sir Arthur Gordon, whose native policy required the Fijians to remain in their own traditional surroundings under the leadership of their chiefs, protected from the harmful effects of external contact.[7] Bold and imaginative and impressively connected to London, Gordon decided on a line of action that was to set the foundations of modern Fiji. Having settled on the plantation system as his preferred mode of economic development and sugar as the main crop, he invited the Australian-owned Colonial Sugar Refining Company (CSR) to establish the industry. The CSR arrived in Fiji in 1882 and left in 1973, effectively running the colony's economy for nearly a century.[8] To work on the plantations, Gordon chose Indian indentured labour whose success he had seen in Trinidad and Mauritius, where he had been governor before his Fiji assignment. European capital, Indian labour and Fijian land underpinned the Fijian economy in the century between cession and independence.

Indentured emigration was government controlled. The conditions of employment were stated on a form of agreement — *girmit* — in English, Hindi and Urdu in north India and in Tamil, Telugu and Malayalam in the south. The terms varied in detail according to time and place, but they all specified the conditions of work, pay, accommodation and provision of basic facilities. Typical conditions offered to the Fiji migrants stated that they would be engaged in work related to the cultivation and manufacture of agricultural products; that they would work for nine hours each week day and five on Saturdays, with Sundays and public holidays being free; that men would be paid one shilling daily and women nine pennies for time as well as task work. The labourers could return to India at their own expense after five years or at the Government's after 10 years of 'industrial residence'. There were gaps between what was promised and the practice on the ground, between the rhetoric and the reality of contractual obligation. The exploration of the gap has been the main thrust of modern indenture historiography.

Forty-five thousand of Fiji's indentured labourers were recruited from north India and 15,000 from the south when recruitment began there in 1903. For the southern Indians, neighbouring Malaya and Ceylon were the favoured destinations. Most of the southern indentured *girmitiyas* came from such poor and migration-prone districts as Vizagapatnam, North and South Arcot, Chittoor, Trichnipoly, Chingleput and Kistna.[9] In the north, United Provinces (UP) was the main recruiting ground in the late 19th century, replacing Bihar, whose migrants went to local destinations. The province, once the 'garden of India', had by the late 19th century become its 'moth-eaten' basketcase. Within the UP, the majority of the recruits came from the impoverished, desolate districts in the east: Basti, Gonda,

Faizabad, Azamgarh, Bahraich and others like them.[10] The emigrants in the colonies, however, mythologised the province's cultural and historical importance as a land littered with the ruins of great vanished empires ruled by noble kings and nobler emperors, home to great, glittering cities and the place of great pilgrimage sites; in short, a land flowing with milk and honey.

In the late 19th century, rural India was unhinged by increasing British revenue demands. The introduction of notions of private ownership of land caused large-scale subdivision of holdings and property rights, making them agriculturally uneconomic.[11] The traditional bases of agrarian relationships were undermined, removing the cushions which had once protected people against abrupt change. Landlords demanded more rent more promptly, deepening poverty and indebtedness in a rapidly growing population. Famines and droughts wrought their own havoc on a people already in distress.[12] With local employment prospects waning, people moved about in search of jobs. Ghazipur's experience was typical, where 'immense numbers of people leave their homes every year to find employment in or near Calcutta and in the various centres of industry in Bengal and Assam, while many weavers and others report to the mills of Bombay. The extent of this migration is astonishing and its economic influence is of the highest importance since these labourers earn high wages and remit or bring back with them large sums of money to their homes.'[13]

Indentured labourers to Fiji and other sugar colonies came from this desperate mass of uprooted peasants. Most of them registered for emigration in the province itself rather than in large distant cities such as Calcutta. Within the province, most enlisted in their own districts rather than in large provincial cities such as Kanpur or Lucknow. But not all who registered emigrated. In Gonda, for example, 52.4 per cent did not emigrate to Fiji and in Basti 48.5 per cent remained. In most other places, about one-third of those who registered were left behind either

because they were rejected or because they refused to go.[14] The
high failure rate gives some agency to the recruited. This is not to
say by any means that the unscrupulous *arkatis* did not ply their
trade and snare the gullible and the timid into their net. They
did, but perhaps not to the extent often uncritically assumed.

The movement within India was seasonal and circulatory.
Perhaps emigration to the colonies was viewed this way. For
peasants already uprooted from their homes and out and about in
search of jobs, going to the *tapus*, the islands, was like going to
Assam or some other similarly distant place. Many probably had
not heard of Demerara or Trinidad or Fiji before, but they all
knew — or hoped — that they would return. Most did not. Much
has been made of the notion of *kala pani*, the dark dreaded seas, as
an impediment to emigration because it brought contact with
mlecchas, polluting barbarians, and imperilled caste purity. Its
importance is exaggerated. The injunction against sea travel
applied only to the twice-born (*dvija*) and then only to the elite
of the highest castes; and it was often obeyed more in the breach
than in observance.[15] *Kala pani* was in truth more a metaphor
for a hard journey to a distant or dangerous place, a journey of
pain and permanent separation, than a strict prohibition against
foreign travel.

The indentured recruits were a much maligned lot,
disrespected by their contemporaries and despised by their
employers. They were assumed by everyone to be an unrepre-
sentative sample or, alternatively, a rotten sample, of rural India.
If men were bad enough, women were assumed to be worse:
individuals with light morals from broken homes, cast adrift by
society, beyond the pale of salvation. Indians were often
reminded of their lowly origins by the colonial officialdom as part
of the ideological underpinning of European dominance in Fiji.
The situation was, of course, much more complex.[16] The recruits
were, in fact, a representative sample of rural India, comprising
all castes and social groups, not only the lowly ones. More

importantly, most of the migrants were dispossessed cultivators or labourers, down on their luck or down and out, looking for a better future. Migration provided a way out.

Women probably migrated for economic as well as social reasons. More than 36 per cent of the women from north India came as members of families, three-quarters accompanied by their husbands only, 15 per cent by their husbands and children and 12 per cent with their children only. Smaller numbers came in the company of cousins, brothers or other relatives.[17] Most women migrating as members of families had left as part of a family unit from their own villages, which contradicts the conventional wisdom about fraudulent depot marriages arranged by the recruiters to expedite registration. Perhaps among the women were widows with children, women whose husbands had left for service abroad and did not return, young brides who had not brought sufficient dowry with them and were taunted and punished. Perhaps there were domestic hands who had never married. Kept during times of prosperity, they were tossed out when things became difficult. The recruiters' consoling voice sealed their fate: they left. The fact that the women were prepared to leave the familiar for the completely unknown suggests that they must have been individuals of remarkable courage and self-respect. These were certainly the values they nurtured in Fiji and other colonies.

From their local sub-depots, the recruits who had passed medical tests and interrogation by officials were taken to the ports of embarkation. There, they were once again questioned about the terms of the contract which they were signing or affixing their thumb prints to and were admitted when the Surgeon Superintendent and the Depot Surgeon certified that the recruit was 'free from all bodily and mental disease and has been vaccinated'. By the time they finally left for the colonies, a remarkable 40 per cent of the original recruits had not embarked: official inspection was not a formality. Cleaned, inspected, and

numbered — on a tin circle worn around the neck — the
emigrants boarded the ship, in parties of six at a time, single
women first, followed by married people with children and finally
the bachelors, all 'pleased and amused by the novel experience',
'decked out in their brightest corals, beads and ornaments'.[18]
Some wept and wailed as the reality of rupture dawned on them.
But calm soon returned as the ship was tugged out to sea and
duties were assigned: sweeping the deck, cleaning toilets, washing
clothes and utensils, preparing food.

In the 19th century, sailing ships took up to three months
to reach Fiji, a month with the advent of steamships after 1904.
Whether one month or three, the voyage was traumatic for a
land-locked people, most of whom probably had never seen the
sea before. In the crowded confines of the ship's cabins, old rituals
and ways of doing things could no longer be sustained. People
ate, cleaned, washed and played cards or *kabaddi* together, bound
by a shared destiny and a common destination. From the
fragments of a common past and a mutual predicament, other
bonds emerged. The most notable and enduring of these was
jahajibhai, the brotherhood of the crossing, as emotionally
powerful and intimate as real blood kinship, which men
cherished well into their twilight as a memory of a shared ordeal
and as a bond of solidarity against the alienations and asperities
of a hostile new world.

On the Plantations

Once in Fiji, and after quarantine on Nukulau — where, in sweet
irony, 2000 coup leader George Speight is serving his life
imprisonment — the labourers were allocated to plantations
around the country, the majority of which were owned by the
CSR. Care was taken not to separate families, but men from the
same village or district or having some other distinctive common
attribute were separated to prevent trouble – 'ganging up'. The
earliest areas of Indian settlement were Rewa and Navua in

south-eastern Viti Levu and Ba and Rakiraki in the north-west, but, as cane settlements spread, so did the Indian population. Conditions varied across the colony. The wet and humid areas of southern Viti Levu took a heavy toll on the workers' health, with hookworm, dysentery, diarrhoea and anaemic fever wreaking havoc on a new and unsuspecting population. Disease was, in fact, the worst enemy of indentured labour in Fiji, its greatest source of misery and mortality, far more than anything inflicted by the human hand.

The working experience of the *girmitiyas* on the plantations in all its excruciating detail — absence from work due to infirmity or illness, punishment for the breaches of the contract or insubordination, the heart-rending infant mortality rates, the accidental deaths, the men the *girmitiyas* murdered in revenge — all these are preserved in the records.[19] The routine was quickly mastered. After a hasty breakfast, the workers gathered their knives, forks and hoes and marched off to plough and weed the fields, dig drains, feed the horses and milch cows, cut and transport the cane to the mills, keep the road and bridges and tramlines serviceable. This was the routine for five years. In the early years, the tasks were excessive and were rarely completed on time. Nor did labourers always achieve the minimum statutory wage. Underpaid workers lived on inadequate diets, which caused sickness, which led to absence from work, which in turn led to reduced pay. Disease and violence extracted their own price. Still, the *girmitiyas* understood the constraints under which they worked and the reality of power relations on the plantations. They learned early from ill-fated strikes in Koronivia and Rewa in the mid-1880s that an open challenge to authority was futile. And so they chose to express their grievances through a variety of everyday resistance techniques and through the strategy of accommodation. They understood indenture not as a life sentence but as a limited detention.[20]

The plantation was a peculiar cultural institution, with its own complex set of rituals, routines, demands and expectations.

For five years, in some cases more, it defined the purposes and limits of the *girmitiyas'* lives. It was also the site of massive social transformation. Men and women of different ages, different social, economic and religious backgrounds, often speaking a variety of mutually incomprehensible tongues, with contrasting expectations of life, met and mingled. Out of that enforced interaction in the confined and constricting space emerged a new culture. In that new environment, old habits, patterns of thought and association, and understandings about the world and their place in it were shaken. The trauma had started much earlier, but the plantation experience etched the reality of the new world on the *girmitiyas* more sharply. Plantation work did not respect social boundaries or divinely sanctioned hierarchies. It rewarded personal initiative and enterprise. The plantation management saw the *girmitiyas* as 'coolies', little more. The absence of social and spiritual leaders compounded the problem. The *girmitiyas* seemed, then, to be caught in a barren, disorienting cul-de-sac of cultural fragmentation.

Things collapsed, but not abruptly. Fragments of old institutions and practices which fractured during migration and indenture were restored in a variety of ways and imbued with novel meanings incorporating the old and the new. The process of retrieval and reconstruction was vital for the immigrant community, as an instrument of survival as well as a tool of resistance. The new culture that was forged during indenture was complex and dynamic. Let me illustrate the patterns and processes of change by focusing on the caste system, marriage and gender relations.

Indenture dealt a mortal blow to the caste system as a social institution of practical relevance in the everyday life of the migrants, although vague notions of distinction and difference survived. Each *girmitiya* was individually contracted to the plantation, and was paid according to the amount of work he or she accomplished, not according to social status. People lived and worked together, slept under the same roof in the lines, shared the same well and toilet facilities. Even if they wanted to, they did not have the cultural resources to sustain the caste system. Most immigrants were young and illiterate and ignorant of the rituals and ceremonies associated with the caste system. The disproportionate sex ratio on the plantations produced cross-caste marriages. Breaches of caste rules could not be punished. As Chandra Jayawardena puts it: 'Since everyone had the same rights and duties, co-ordination of behaviour in matters of common concern was achieved by voluntary co-operation and the recognition of the self-interest of equal and free agents.'[21] Culture and religion rather than caste became the basis of identity in the new community.

The institution of marriage also suffered during indenture. Marriage for Hindus and Muslims was (and still is) more than a simple contractual matter. Traditionally, marriages took place within a narrow, restricted circle prescribed by custom. These were difficult to maintain on the plantations. But the most important cause of the havoc was the paucity of women, which led to inter-caste marriages of a type unthinkable in India. The crowded conditions in the lines created their own problem. There was no privacy, and close proximity between the houses of the unmarried and the married encouraged illicit relationships. Furthermore, marriages conducted according to Hindu and Muslim customs — the only ones the immigrants knew — were not recognised in colonial law.[22] This encouraged the unscrupulous and the criminally opportunistic to exploit the situation to their advantage, disavowing relationships and obligations when it suited them. Officials commented on the practice of some fathers 'selling' their daughters to several prospective husbands for financial gain.

Men devised means to deal with the shortage of women. Some, out of pity or greed, agreed to their wives providing sexual services to a small number of men. In some places, casual polyandry became a major source of tension in the lines, the cause, officials believed, of many suicides. Sometimes, several men 'kept' a single woman for domestic help. After a while, she attached herself to, or was taken over by, one of the men, to whom she was eventually married and bore children. On the whole, the plantation system undermined a stable family life — but not completely, for marriages continued to take place and families were raised. The symbolic importance and the comforting effect of the family during a time of turmoil in the life of the community cannot be overstated. Joint families were revived after indenture to meet agricultural needs, but eventually gave way to the new realities of greater individualism, independent incomes, and occupational and educational mobility. Its gradual disappearance was welcomed as a sign of changing times.[23]

Women everywhere were blamed for murders and suicides on the plantations and sometimes even for the high infant mortality rates. To the overseers and planters, the women were 'immoral' and 'socially unredeemable'.[24] Indeed, so low was their esteem for the indentured women they met in Fiji, some men regarded marriage with them as a temporary convenience to be discarded on returning to India. The difficulty of understanding the predicament of women is compounded by the absence of their voice in the records.[25] Men evaluated women's roles on the plantations in stereotypes. Some measured them against the ideal of Sita, the paragon of Hindu womanhood, who gave up everything to accompany her husband, Lord Rama, into exile. The ideal Indian woman accepted her fate without complaint, glorified the virtues of motherhood, deferred to male authority and, above all, worshipped her husband. On the plantations, men sought to reassert the patriarchal structure of agrarian Indian society, wanting to own the means of production as well as the labour of the women. When they failed, they blamed the women for their own misfortunes.

Indian men failed to appreciate that emigration and indenture had dramatically restructured the women's positions and thence their relationship with men. The institutions that sanctioned and enforced women's subjection had little jurisdiction in the domestic sphere of the indentured population. Indenture promoted a new egalitarian ethos and a freer society, which respected individual initiative. Women were employed on the plantations as individuals in their own right. Control over their own hard-earned income gave them a measure of power and economic and social independence. So, if circumstances demanded, they left their husbands when their life became constantly embroiled in tension and torment or was otherwise endangered.

Contrary to conventional wisdom, women were not disrespectful of marriage and family and other institutions of Indian society. They were themselves at the mercy of the overseers and Indian *sirdars* (foremen), who allocated and supervised their daily work, harassing, even assaulting, those who refused their sexual advances. The women could not refuse partners chosen for them by the overseers, nor the solicitations of influential men on the plantations. Powerless and vulnerable, they had little choice in the matter of morality. Their world was turned upside-down, and they were caught in confusion about roles and obligations. The new experience and new opportunities widened their horizons. They wanted greater respect and recognition within the parameters of recognised cultural and social institutions, not outside or in breach of them. They, too, wanted the security and the comforting cushion of culture – minus its excessive patriarchal prerogatives.

Life in the Lines

'One of the saddest and most depressing sights, if a man has any soul at all, is a coolie "line" in Fiji. Vice, wickedness, and abjectness abound. Personal filth is ever in evidence, and life seems to have turned rancid. Coarse, evil-looking women throw their jibes at criminal-faced men, or else quarrel with one another in high, strident voices, accompanied by angry gestures. Little children, naked save for a sacred piece of string, sores, and flies, play cheerlessly in the squalid places. The beholder turns from the scene debating whether disgust or pity is uppermost in his mind.'[27] This is culturally conditioned, self-interested missionary talk. Nonetheless, a mixture of disgust and pity informs virtually all outside accounts of plantation life.

Girmitiyas lived in basic accommodation provided by their employers. The wooden and iron buildings in the lines were divided into rooms of 12 square feet, each separated from the other by a partition topped by a gauze wire to allow for ventilation, and housing three single males or a family of husband, wife and two children. Cooking was done inside on an earthen *chulha* (stove). The room contained all the worldly possessions of the *girmitiyas*: their clothes, cooking utensils, firewood, farm implements. Cramped and sooty at the best of times, they became worse in the rainy season, dimly lit by *dhibri*, wick lamps, the earthen floor becoming soggy and the air damp. There was little privacy in the rooms, and not much more outside. Close to the dwellings were open trenches where people defecated. Many used the neighbouring fields for toilet as well, which bred deadly diseases such as hookworm and contaminated water for cooking and bathing.

Amid all the drudgery of the daily routine, though, the *girmitiyas* found time for rest and recreation. During weekends the *girmitiyas* could visit their friends on neighbouring plantations or seek the permission of the overseers to visit free Indians with whom they might have worked in the past. They could go to the bazaars. Or they could entertain themselves in a variety of ways. There was a plentiful supply of tobacco, *paan* (betel nut) and even *ganja*. Wrestling (*kushti*) was a favourite pastime, especially if it involved wrestlers from other plantations. Some managers encouraged inter-plantation competitions to maintain the morale of their workers. Sports was played, especially *kabaddi* and football.

In the lines, people played *bujhauni*, the Indian game of riddles. In the evenings, or on special occasions, they would play music and sing. The people prepared simple musical instruments such as *dholak* and *khajadi* from local wood and leather, and *dandtaal* and *tambura* from local iron and wires.[28] Special occasions for celebrations included pivotal moments in the life cycle. The birth of children, especially boys, brought great joy not only to the parents but to the community. The sixth day after birth held special significance. If a child survived its first few days, its chances of survival were good. So, on the sixth day, the *chattai*, the child was introduced to the world amid great celebration, singing and feasting. Later, a similarly joyous celebration would accompany the head-shaving ceremony, *moodan*.

Migration and indenture disrupted the *girmitiyas'* religious and cultural life. There were few shrines and sacred places, few *murtis* or images, few learned men, *pandits*, *sadhus* or *maulvis*, versed in the scriptures to impart moral and spiritual instruction. Their absence facilitated an essentially emotional, egalitarian and non-intellectual moral order among the *girmitiyas*. Nonetheless, as Jayawardena has observed, 'Religion was an important mechanism in promoting social solidarity among the plantation coolies [during indenture]. The powerlessness of the coolies made it necessary for them, in order to protect their interests, to form a tightly knit group which, as far as possible, spoke and acted as one united and unanimous body.'[29]

Most northern Hindus were followers of the orthodox Sanatan Dharam, the eternal religion (without beginning or end).[30] For them, the *Ramayana* of Tulsidas (1532–1623), written in 10,000 lines of verse, became the 'primary written source for standards of social and personal morality'.[31] Many *girmitiyas* came from Rama's birthplace — in Ayodhya near Faizabad. They knew the story. And it was a wonderful story full of drama and pathos and tragedy. Sung to the accompaniment of elementary music, the recital provided spiritual enlightenment as well as social entertainment. The *Ramayana* addressed themes of enduring human significance: the importance of righteous conduct in the face of the sternest adversity, the obligations of duty and loyalty and honour. To the *girmitiyas*, cut off from the source, their cultural fabric threatened by the violence and vagaries of the plantation system, the *Ramayana* must have represented eternal truths and certainties in times of crisis and uncertainty. The message of hope and redemption was unmistakable.

Sanatanis were not the only Hindus in Fiji. There were also smaller numbers of Arya Samajis, followers of a reformist branch of Hinduism, founded by Swami Dayananda Saraswati. They rejected the more ritualistic aspects of the faith and revered the *Vedas* as the principal texts of Hinduism. The Samajis' great contribution to Indian education came later.[32] At the beginning of the 20th century, a number of smaller sects dominated the main areas of Indian settlement — Kabir Panth, Ramnadi, Dadu Nath.[33] They were popular because they rejected the hierarchical system of Brahminical Hinduism, stressing the importance of devotion and the equality of human beings, which appealed to people from a non-literate background.

We know about the 'higher forms' of Hinduism, but little about the 'lower forms', which were probably more important in assisting people to make sense of their lives in an alien place. Most castes had their own deity or a set of deities — Dhi, Bhavani, Phulmati — which had to be appeased through animal sacrifice.[34] I vividly recall being told by old-timers of this practice being in existence well into the post-indenture period. An element of shame and secrecy surrounded animal sacrifice. For instance, the animal was always slaughtered at night and the meat eaten only after the chanting of some mysterious verses in incomprehensible Indian dialects. The practice was discontinued as *girmitiyas* died, the caste system disintegrated, knowledge of specialist rituals was forgotten and 'sanskritised' Hinduism with its established body of literature and inclusive ritual infrastructure took root.

Unlike Hinduism, which is amorphous and un-prescriptive, Islam, the other significant faith on the plantations, has a book, the Koran, a prophet, Mohammed, and a well-defined creed.[35] Every devout Muslim is required to observe them whenever possible. The five pillars of Islam are: a public declaration of faith — 'La Ilaha illa Allah, Mohammed bin Rasool Allah' — that is, 'There is no god but God and Mohammed is the Messenger of God'; the prescribed five prayers a day; the giving of *zakat*, alms, to the poor; fasting during the month of Ramadan; and the *hajj*, pilgrimage, to Mecca at least once in a lifetime. A[8]singular code and creed gave Muslims cohesiveness and unity of purpose. Most Muslims in Fiji were (and still are) Sunnis, who believe in Mohammed as the last prophet of Allah and the Koran as the revealed word of God. There were also a small number of Sufi Sunnis, a mystical sect of Islam, most of whom came from southern India. They held *Milad* to celebrate the life and teachings of the Prophet Mohammed and observed *Ratib*, a quasi-mystical ceremony, in which devotees cut themselves with a knife late at night without spilling blood, and with the *maulvi* promising a healed wound before the next morning as a demonstration of God's power.[36]

A minority of Muslims also belonged to Shia sects which, while recognising the supreme authority of Mohammed, also acknowledged the legitimacy of later messengers. The two sects also disputed who should have succeeded the Prophet, the caliphs or members of his own family. Sometimes, these differences caused friction (even violence) in the community, just as the debates between the more reform-minded Arya Samajis and the orthodox Sanatanis did among Hindus. During indenture, there were occasional conflicts between Hindus and Muslims in Rewa and Navua. These occurred when Muslims slaughtered cattle in the vicinity of Hindu homes or when

Hindus played loud music near mosques during Ramadan. But these were localised affairs brought quickly under control by community leaders and the colonial administration. Religious harmony rather than discord marked the indenture period. And that remained the pattern for the 20th century.

The *girmitiyas* came from a land full of festivals. Virtually every month had some festive occasion. The plantation regime did not permit the celebration of all the festivals the *girmitiyas* knew as children, but some were regularly celebrated in the colonies, especially those which involved group activity. Among the most popular was *Ramlila*, play-acting the life of Lord Rama. *Diwali* was also celebrated, although it gained its present popularity much later.[37] It was the same with fire-walking performed by south Indian *girmitiyas*. Perhaps the most popular Hindu festival during indenture in all the colonies was *Holi*, or *Phagwa* (named after the last day of the lunar month of Phagun), which celebrated the defiant deeds of god-fearing Prahalad over his power-drunk father, Hirana Kashyap. The following song, a specially composed *chautal*, indicates the spring festival's joyous mood:

> The sweet spring has come, in the month of Phagun
> The beautiful festival of Holi has come today;
> To love everyone is the wish of all,
> And every house is filled with happiness,
> Give hospitality to everyone, it is the month of Phagun.
> The fragrant gardens are today blossoming everywhere,
> Now we sing together the Phag of the virtues
> Of all patriotic leaders,
> May their fame spread! It is the month of Phagun.
> In each village pleasant gatherings occur
> And every brother sings praise of the country;
> In the intoxicating month of Phagun.
> All watch the gay colours; it is the month of Phagun.
> The drums and cymbals play today in every house,
> Today all sing with a united voice,

Ram Lakhan requests this,
To call Jai Hind. It is the month of Phagun.[38]

One celebration, which has now all but disappeared among overseas Indians, but which was popular with Hindus and Muslims during indenture, was *Tazia*, variously known as *Tajdah* or *Hosse* in the different colonies. On the 10th of Mohurram 61 AH (10 October, 1680), Hussain, the son of Ali and the grandson of the Prophet, was killed in a skirmish between government troops and a small body of supporters accompanying him to Kufa in Iraq, where his followers had invited him to lead them in a revolt against the Ummayyad caliphs of Damascus. His death was regarded by his supporters as an act of self-sacrifice in the cause of the faith, and the lesson was drawn that only through patient suffering and sacrifice was it possible to enter paradise. *Tazia*, or passion play, reached its climax on the 10th day when a procession designed as a funeral parade carried a structure representing Hussain's tomb to the accompaniment of drums and sad, mournful songs, such as this one:

What rains down? Blood! Who? The eye! How?
  Day and night! Why?
From grief! What grief? The grief of the monarch of Kerbela!
What was his name? Hussain! Of whose race? Ali's!
Who was his mother? Fatima! Who was his grandsire?
Mustafa!
How was it with him? He fell a martyr! Where?
  In the plain of Mariya!
When? On the 10th of Muharram! Secretly? No, in public!
Was he slain by night? No, by day! At what time? Noontide!
Was his head severed from the throat? No, from the nape
  of the neck!
Was he slain unthirsting? No! Did none give him to drink?
They did!
Who? Shimr! From the source of death![39]

There was something mysterious about the festival. People thought they saw blood in the tinsel mausoleum and heard soft wailing noises at night. A chicken or goat was ritually slaughtered to appease the spirits as men danced around the *tazia*, working themselves into a trance, while women took vows and gave donations in anticipation of some blessing (the birth of a son, removal of some affliction). The festival petered out as the old-timers passed away, other forms of entertainment reached the people, and the Sunni orthodoxy asserted its dominance.

The Free or the 'Khula'

By 1920, when the indenture system was abolished, four years after all indentured shipments had ceased, the Fiji Indian community had come a long way from modest and uncertain beginnings. The most visible change was the increasing ratio of Fiji-born to India-born. In 1911, only 27 per cent of the 40,286 Indians were Fiji-born; in 1921, 44 per cent of the 60,634 were locally born. By 1946, the local-born constituted 85 per cent of the population. In physical appearance, social behaviour, thinking and world view, the local-born were different. Few wore *pagri* or *dhoti* — the typical dress of rural India — they had more wide ranging friendships across caste and religion, enjoyed a more relaxed lifestyle, were egalitarian in their outlook and ethos and were unconstrained by the ritual protocols and procedures so dear to the India-born.

Most Indians settled in the sugar cane-growing areas. In 1905, of the 15,997 free Indians, 4,926 were in Navua, 4,500 in Rewa, 1,460 in Suva, 1,270 in Ba, 1,250 in Lautoka (on Viti Levu) and 2,000 in Macuata on Vanua Levu. In time, western Viti Levu would claim the largest concentration of Indo-Fijians. More than 75 per cent of the Indian population was engaged in agriculture, mostly sugar cane and to a lesser extent rice cultivation, but small numbers were making a living as hawkers, mechanics, domestic servants, stable-hands and the like. This pattern would persist for much of the 20th century. Trade and commerce in the Indo-Fijian community came to be dominated by free migrants from Gujarat (principally Surat and Navasari), who began arriving in small numbers from 1904 onwards. The urban-based Gujaratis remained a largely self-contained and self-absorbed community throughout the 20th century. The other significant group of free migrants was Sikhs from the Punjab (Jullundar, Hoshiarpur, Ludhiana), who excelled in agriculture. Many of their descendants migrated to Canada and the United States after independence in 1970.

The free Indian community developed early.[40] By the early 1880s, ex-indentured labourers were settling on land leased from Fijians around the sugar mills. The gradual development of free settlement was symbolically important as a beacon of hope and freedom to those still on the plantations. It also played a decisive role in defining the unique character of the Indian community in Fiji in contrast with, for example, the Indian communities in the Caribbean, where generations depended on the plantation system for their livelihood and were thus unable to recreate Indian cultural and social institutions to keep themselves together as a cohesive cultural and linguistic community. In Fiji, the free settlements kept the community intact. Out of necessity as much as choice, Indians cooperated in agricultural and social tasks, reviving festivals, building temples and mosques and roads and bridges, arranging marriages and sports and singing competitions, burying the dead, and making representations to the Government. Colonial indifference to the social and cultural welfare of the community forced people to rely on their own resources and on each other.

By the early 1900s, a cadre of leadership had developed of whom Totaram Sanadhya, Badri Maharaj and Manilal Maganlal Doctor were the most well known. Manilal, a lawyer, had come from Mauritius at the request of the local Indians to provide leadership to the community.[41] But there were others — 'educated members of that [Indian immigrant] class' — whose names I mention only because they lie in faded memory: S. Mastapha, M. S. Buksh, Ramroop, Ganpath, Tribhuvan, Raghunath, Umrao Maharaj, George Suchit, Ratu Ram Samujh and Manoharananda Saraswati. They formed the British Indian Association (later the Indian Imperial Association) and made representations to Suva as well as to London. Badri Maharaj was chosen by the Colonial Government as the first Indian-nominated member of the Legislative Council in 1915, although many Indians preferred the educated and articulate Manilal. The Indo-Fijian demand for elected representation on the basis of a common, non-racial roll would begin in the 1920s and continue throughout the 20th century.

Within the community, social and religious organisations began to emerge in the major areas of free settlements: mosques and temples, community rest houses (*dharmashala*). The Arya Samaj was formed in 1904, the Anjuman-I-Hidayat Islam in 1915, Anjuman Ishait El Islam in 1916 and Anjum-E-Islam (1919). Then India Sanmārgyā Ikyā Sangam, the umbrella organisation of the southern Indians, came in 1926 under the inspiring leadership of the great mystic, Sadhu Kuppuswami. Religious leaders — Totaram Sanadhaya and Maulvi Murtza Khan — provided moral and spiritual guidance. After the 1920s, religious leaders from India came to preach. Some of them introduced disputes which were then racking the Indian subcontinent: conflict between the Shia and Sunni Muslims, and between Arya Samaj and Sanatan Dharam Hindus. But these eruptions, though intense and bitter at the time, were largely contained and left few permanent scars.

The Indian community grew in complete isolation from the indigenous Fijians. This was deliberate government policy. In 1893, Abdoon, an Afghan, lived in Deuba, dressing and wearing his hair Fijian-style.[42] He got annoyed when called a '*Kai Idia*', a pejorative term for a person of Indian descent. Roko Tui Nadroga said he did not object to the man living in the village, but Governor J. B.

Thurston, the self-styled champion of the Fijians, who regarded Indian indentured labourers as 'working men and nothing more', overruled him. 'I am quite sure that an idle renegade Indian will do the people of Sigatoka very considerable harm,' he said and asked the Colonial Secretary to order the man to leave. In 1895, an Indian man on the Rewa delta applied for a retail store licence which was refused by the Stipendiary Magistrate: 'These Indians speak good Fijian and are very undesirable persons to throw into the society of the natives inland and I wish they could be kept out entirely.' In another instance, a sandalwood paste-covered Hindu priest in Nadurulolo, Rewa, was threatened with prosecution for practising 'witchcraft' when he tried to preach to the Fijians. In Ra, Sulieman — Solomone to Fijians — was refused residence in the village by the Government even though he had married a chiefly lady and the villagers wanted him to remain. In 1887, Buli Sabeto was fined for 'harbouring' an Indian immigrant and the chief of the village (Natumuku) also fined six pounds for the same 'offence'. No doubt, there are many more such stories of thwarted intermingling in the sugar cane belts of Fiji.

Government policy hindered ethnic interaction, but ignorance and prejudice also kept the two communities apart. The Stipendiary Magistrate of Rewa, in his September report of 1884, said: 'In all the colonies where the coolies have been introduced, I think I am near the truth when I say that in landing they found the land destitute or practically so of any coloured race with whom they are likely to be brought into contact. Here on the contrary a very different state of affairs exists. Here they find a proud and arrogant race professing to be owners of the soil, regarding all others as on sufferance, merely as *vulagis*. The Fijians and Indians regard each other with unconcealed contempt and disgust. The Indians never by any chance speak of the Fijians other than as "*jungalis*" the meaning of which is understood and deeply resented by them all to a man.'[43] The Fijians genuinely feared about their future, especially the future of their land as the number of Indian immigrants increased. They had no comprehension of who the Indians were, why they were coming to Fiji, whether they would return to India or settle in the colony when their contracts expired. The fear of dispossession, the Stipendiary Magistrate of Ba wrote in 1888, 'is probably at the bottom of the native dislike of the coolies'. So government policy as well as popular prejudice kept the two communities apart, with what tragic consequences we all know. Only if ...

> Footfalls echo in the memory
> Down the passage we did not take
> Towards the door we never opened
> Into the rose-garden.

— T. S. Eliot

The world of the *girmitiyas* was a complex one, full of turmoil and tension and uncertainty, goodness, greed and curiosity. Old habits had to be discarded and unfamiliar challenges faced. New experiences posed problems requiring creative responses. A new vocabulary had to be learnt, an unfamiliar geography explored, a new terrain mastered, new pragmatic social relationships established. The *girmitiyas* dealt with the challenges in their own way, modifying thought and behaviour, incorporating resilient threads from an old and frayed fabric into a new and unique garment. They were ordinary men and women whose accomplishments were extraordinary. It was a difficult journey. Many perished along the way, but most survived: not only survived, but conquered the odds and triumphed. The triumph of the human spirit over limitless adversities: that is — as it has to be — the ultimate meaning and legacy of *girmit*. In that stupendous struggle, to use the words of Matthew Arnold, the *girmitiya*

> Pursued a lonely road,
> His eyes on Nature's plan;
> Neither made man too much a God,
> Nor God too much a man.

NOTES

1   Discussion of the 1979 celebrations is based on Ministry of Information. 1979. *Girmit: A Centenary of Anthology 1879–1979*. Government of Fiji.

2   *Girmit* comes from the word agreement under which Indian indentured labourers were brought to Fiji. Those who served *girmit* were called *girmitiyas*.

3   Two anthologies marking the occasion were Mishra, Vijay (ed.). 1979. *Rama's Banishment: A centenary tribute to the Fiji Indians*. Auckland. And, Subramani (ed.). 1979. *Indo-Fijian Experience*. St Lucia, Queensland.

4   See, among others: Ali, Ahmed (ed.). 1979. *The Indenture Experience in Fiji*. Suva. For an application of the slavery thesis derived from Tinker, Hugh. 1974. *A New System of Slavery: The export of Indian labour abroad, 1830-1920*. London.

5   Quoted in Lowenthal, David. 1985. *The Past is a Foreign Country*. Cambridge. p. 64.

6   See Lal, Brij V. 2000. *Chalo Jahaji: On a journey through indenture in Fiji*. Suva and Canberra. An early and, in some respects dated, account is Gillion, K. L. 1973, 2nd rep. *Fiji's Indian Migrants. A history to the end of indenture in 1920*. Melbourne.

7   See Legge, J. D. 1958. *Britain in Fiji, 1858-1880*. London.

8   See Moynagh, Michael. 1981. *Brown or White? A history of the Fiji sugar industry, 1873–1973*. Canberra. Also, Narsey, Wadan Lal. 1979. 'Monopoly Capital, White Racism and Superprofits in Fiji: A Case Study of the CSR.' In *Journal of Pacific Studies*, 5. pp. 66–146.

9   See studies in Brennan, Lance and Brij V. Lal (eds). 1998. *Across the Kala Pani: Indian Overseas Migration and Settlement*. Special issue of *South Asia: A Journal of South Asian Studies*, vol. xxi. The history of the south Indian indentured migration is desperately in need of scholarly study.

10   For north India, see Lal, Brij V. 1983. *Girmitiyas: The origins of the Fiji Indians*. Canberra.

11   See Whitcombe, Elizabeth. 1972. *Agrarian Conditions in Northern India*. Vol. 1: *The United Provinces Under British Rule, 1860–1900*. Berkeley. The best sources are the Settlement Reports, which contain reliable information about society, economy and civil administration.

12   See Robinson, Francis. 1973. 'Municipal Government and Muslim Separatism in the United Provinces, 1883–1916.' In *Modern Asian Studies*, vol. vii: 3. pp. 389–441.

13   For these, see the Settlement Reports. Also Gupta, Ranajit Das. 1973. 'Factory Labour in Eastern India: sources of supply, 1885–1946.' In *Indian Economic and Social History Review*, vol. xiii: 3. pp. 277–329.

14   For further discussion, see Lal, Brij V. *Girmitiyas*.

[15] See Basham, A. L. 1964. 'Notes on Seafaring in Ancient India.' In Basham, A. L., *Studies in Indian History and Culture*, Calcutta. pp. 146–66.

[16] See Lal, Brij V. *Girmitiyas*. pp. 68–90.

[17] Ibid., pp. 97–116.

[18] For an eyewitness account, see 'Bound for the Colonies in 1905: A view of Indian indentured emigration.' Reproduced in *Journal of Pacific History*, 34: 3, 1999. pp. 306–9.

[19] These are in the Agent-General of Immigration Annual Reports published as *Legislative Council Papers*. They are available in Suva in hard copy and in Canberra and other places on microfilm.

[20] For further discussion, see Lal, Brij V. *Chalo Jahaji*. pp. 167–94, where these arguments are elaborated.

[21] See Jayawardena, Chandra. 1971. 'The Disintegration of Caste in Fiji Indian Rural Society.' In Hiatt, L. R. and C. Jayawardena (eds), *Anthropology in Oceania*, Sydney. pp. 89–199 at p. 94. See also Schwartz, Barton. 1967. *Caste in Overseas Indian Communities*. San Francisco.

[22] For a discussion of this, see Kelly, John D. 1991. *A Politics of Virtue: Hinduism, Sexuality and Countercolonial Discourse in Fiji*. Chicago.

[23] See Mayer, A. C. 1954. 'Fiji Indian Kin-Group: An Aspect of Change in an Immigrant Community.' In *Oceania*, xxiv: 3. pp. 161–71. Also, Jayawardena, Chandra. 1983. 'Farm, Household and Family in Fiji Indian Rural Society.' In Kurien, George and Ram P. Srivastva (eds), *Overseas Indians: A Study in Adaptation*, New Delhi. pp. 141–79. For a comparative discussion, see Nevadomsky, Joseph. 1983. 'Changes Over Time and Space in the East Indian Family in Rural Trinidad.' In ibid. pp. 180–214.

[24] Gill, Walter. 1970. *Turn North-East at the Tombstone*. Adelaide. p. 73.

[25] The lone book-length exception is Carter, Marina. 1994. *Lakshmi's Legacy: The Testimonies of Indian Women in 19th Century Mauritius*. Rose Hill: Stanley.

[26] For more discussion, see Lal, Brij V. 1985. 'Kunti's Cry: Indentured Women on Fiji Plantations.' In *Indian Economic and Social History Review*, 22. pp. 55–71. And Lal, Brij V. 1985. 'Veil of Dishonour: Sexual Jealousy and Suicide on Fiji Plantations.' In *Journal of Pacific History*, 20. pp. 135–55.

[27] Burton, J. W. 1912. *Call of the Pacific*. London. p. 108.

[28] See generally Mayer, Adrian C. 1973, 2nd ed. *Peasants in the Pacific: A Study of Fiji Indian Rural Society*. Berkeley. For a comparative-specific case study, see Akal, Suky. 1998. 'Beauty is God's Smile, Music His Voice: Indian Music and its Influence in Surinam and the West Indies.' Paper presented to the International Indian Diaspora Conference: 'Charting New Perspectives.' Stardust Hotel, Paramaribo, 30–31 May, 1998.

29 See Jayawardena, Chandra. 1965-66. 'Religious Belief and Social Change: Aspects of the Development of Hinduism in British Guiana.' In *Comparative Studies in Society and History*, vol. viii. pp. 211–40 at p. 230.

30 For an account, see Wilson, Jim. 1979. 'Fiji Hinduism.' In Mishra (ed.), *Rama's Banishment*. pp. 86–111.

31 See Barz, R. K. 1986. 'Indian Immigration and Hindu Literature in Mauritius.' In *Journal of Mauritian Studies*, 1: 1. pp. 57–89 at pp. 62–3.

32 See Billimoria, Purusottama. 1985. 'The Arya Samaj in Fiji.' In *Religion*, 15. pp. 103–30.

33 See Lal, Brij V. 2000. 'Hinduism Under Indenture.' In Lal, Brij V. *Chalo Jahaji*. pp. 239–60.

34 Jayawardena. 'Religious Belief and Social Change.' p. 228.

35 For a study of Fiji Muslims, see Ali, Ahmed. 1980. *Plantation to Politics: Studies on Fiji Indians*. Suva. pp. 107–29.

36 See Sandwith, George and Helen. 1954. 'Sufi Ratib.' In their *Research in Fiji, Tonga and Samoa*. Surrey. pp. 12–13. Also Ali, Ahmed. 2003. 'In the name of Allah.' *Fiji Daily Post*, 3 November, 2003.

37 See Kelly, John D. 'From Holi to Diwali in Fiji: An Essay on Ritual and History.' In *Man* (ns), 23. pp. 40–55.

38 See Mayer, Adrian C. 1952. 'The Holi Festival Among the Indians of Fiji.' In *The Eastern Anthropologist*, vi: 1, September. pp. 3–17.

39 From von Grunebaum, G. E. 1958. *Muhammadan Festivals*. London. p. 88.

40 For a general survey of the free community, see Mayer, *Peasants in the Pacific*. pp. 13-34. And Gillion, *Fiji's Indian Migrants*. pp. 136-63.

41 For further discussion, see Lal, Brij V. *Broken Waves*. pp. 46–8. Also Ali, Ahmed. 1978. 'Political Awareness Among Fiji Indians, 1879–1919.' In *Asian Profile*, 6: 5. pp. 477–91.

42 These quotations are from the files of the Colonial Secretary's Office, National Archives of Fiji.

43 Colonial Secretary's Office File 84/2140, National Archives of Fiji.

Typical cane settlement, interior of Viti Levu.
The unpaved road is a characteristic feature of rural Fiji.

CHAPTER TWO

Voices From the Past

Praveen Chandra and Saras Chandra

THE HOT MORNING sun filtered through the dusty humid
Suva air as I parked the rental car opposite the Fiji Broadcasting
Commission building in Carnavon Street. Walking down the
street at 8:30am on Monday 8 January, 2001, was like a
homecoming. I had spent a number of years working in Suva and
had many a fond memory of this once bubbling city. But on this
day the city looked almost alien, ruptured and bleeding from
the turbulence of the past 14 years. The people walked along
the street silent and resigned. Had Suva changed so much?
Perhaps I had been away too long, having migrated to Brisbane,
Australia, on 14 June, 1987 — exactly one month after the first
military coup in Fiji. I walked towards the old parliament
building in search of the National Archives, only to be told by a
civil servant that I was headed in the wrong direction. I turned
back and, leaving my car behind, walked to the city end of
Carnavon Street and found the white concrete, double-storey
building so typical of government offices in Fiji.

A strange feeling of anticipation overwhelmed me as
I entered the building. At last, I, of all my relatives, was doing
something concrete about tracing my ancestry back to India.
What would I find? Would I find anything? The thought of trying
to find records relating to family long departed was itself

astounding. Records written and forms filled by officials for people standing silently before them. The person I would start with was my paternal great-grandfather, Baijnath.

All I knew for certain was that my great-grandfather had come from India as an indentured labourer and was living in Vitogo, Lautoka, when he was convicted and hanged for a murder he may not have committed. I was not even certain of any dates. I knew that my father was born in 1919. Also, it was generally believed that my grandfather was born in Fiji in 1900 or 1899 and was about 13 years old when his father was hanged. That was all we knew about my great-grandfather's short life in Fiji.

At the archives, I told the girl on the ground floor the reason for my visit. She asked if I knew Baijnath's father's name, the year of his emigration and the name of the ship he came to Fiji on. No, I did not, I told her. Then it would be extremely difficult to find anything, she said. Was this the end of my journey? The girl must have noticed my distress; she went away and returned with a book. It was about 2.5cm thick, A4 size and had the letter 'B' written on its spine. She then asked me to complete an application to do research and took me to the main library upstairs before handing me the book she had brought. This book, she told me, contained a list of all the people whose names started with the letter 'B' who came to Fiji from India under the indenture system.

I sat down at a desk. At least the office was air-conditioned — the morning heat of the city had begun to choke me. There were a few other people engaged in research in addition to two very lethargic-looking clerks.

I thumbed through the pages of the book I had been given until finally — Baijnath! But there were 44 Baijnaths! Each had his father's name, the name of the ship and date of arrival against his name. All but two also had their emigration pass numbers listed. A cold sweat broke out on my face. Forty-four Baijnaths! How was I to find out which one was my ancestor? I went to ask the clerk if I could see the 42 emigration passes, only to find that the offices were closing for lunch. Despite the sweltering heat outside, I went out to do some shopping.

I returned an hour later, my shirt wet with perspiration and my mind almost numb at the prospect of the task ahead. At my request, the clerk brought about 22 emigration passes. I sat down and started looking through the sheets of names of people, places, ships and ports. I felt a sense of sadness going through the passes. The passes before me had belonged to people who long ago had left their motherland and ventured into the unknown. My mind conjured up images of their faces and the hardships they suffered in exile and in virtual slavery in a remote and hostile corner of the Earth. But which one of these was my great-grandfather? What meagre information I had about my ancestor was of no help. I started by eliminating those who had arrived in Fiji after 1900. This left me with about four names and a sinking feeling that I had reached the end of my so far unfruitful journey.

It was now past four in the afternoon and, as I waited for the remainder of the emigration passes to be brought to me, a man came up and spoke to me. I had noticed him doing research since the morning. A slightly older, but fit-looking man with a fair complexion, wearing black plastic-framed spectacles, he asked me if I was searching for the records of my ancestors. I said yes and briefly told him what little I had been able to find. He said that the history of the indentured labourers was one of the fields he had done a lot of work on. Then it dawned on me! 'You are Dr Ahmed Ali, the historian and former politician!' I said. He smiled. 'Do not lose heart, we will find the records, but firstly do not rely solely on this alphabetical list that you are consulting, it has a lot of errors.'

I was overjoyed. Dr Ali told me that he had come to know the system as well as any of the staff at the archives. He asked the clerks to bring the first volumes of the ships' registers and the death registers. The first column of the pages of the death

registers would have the name of the person and the last column
would have the cause of death of the person. Our first task would
be to find a Baijnath whose cause of death was hanging. The
ships' registers, on the other hand, gave lists of all people who
came from India, in chronological order. At his suggestion,
I started with the first volume of the death registers. The office
closed at 4:30 in the afternoon. Dr Ali said he was going to be in
the office after 11 the next day. He seemed as interested in my
search as I was.

The next day, Tuesday 9 January, I went to Nausori to do
some shopping before going into the archives library in Suva.
It was about 10:30 in the morning. I continued perusing the first
volume of the death registers and also asked the clerk for the
second volume. Dr Ali came in about 11 and inquired after my
efforts. I told him I had not found any Baijnath who had been
hanged. He encouraged me to persevere as we had not finished
looking at all the available documents. It had started to rain and,
as I sat at the desk, I felt tired and disheartened. And yet, as I ran
my fingers across the pages of the death register, a strange feeling
descended on me. The large registers with entries beautifully
handwritten in red and black ink told of events of long ago.
Again, I started thinking about the lives of people who had come
to work and die in a strange, hostile land. I finished the first
volume and, with the hope of success slowly fading away, started
on the second.

About midday I found it. Baijnath — judicial hanging —
hanged at Suva Jail — 17 March, 1913. The next three entries
had the same comment in the last column of the records.
Rajkumar Singh, Kallu and Houba also had judicial hanging
against their names. A sudden bolt of electric thrill shot through
my whole body. I was overjoyed. At last, I was looking at records
of my great-grandfather. I called Dr Ali, who was equally excited.
I noted the emigration pass numbers of the four and asked the
clerks to get them for me. There was also a file reference number

on the last column, 1720/1913. Dr Ali said that would be the reference number for the files of the court case. He asked the clerks for these files as well. The office closed for lunch. I came back about 2:30 soaked by the rain and sweat. Good and bad news awaited me. The emigration passes were available but the case files were not. I put in a request for the emigration passes to be photocopied. Dr Ali came up with another scheme for finding out more about the case. He asked for the *Fiji Times* of 1913 to be brought out and asked me to go through the thick folder. I went through the volumes laboriously looking for reports of a murder and hanging, but did not have any success. When the office closed at 4:30, Dr Ali told me that he would be in again at 8:30 the next morning.

On Wednesday 10 January I came in early. When Dr Ali came in a little later, he told me that there were in fact two newspapers in 1913, the other being the *Western Pacific Herald*. He had the 1913 volume of these brought for me to search through. About 10am, I struck gold again. I could not believe my luck and silently thanked the Government for establishing the archives. The edition of Monday 24 February, 1913, carried a story about the case and the sentencing. Dr Ali and I were both excited. I had already obtained copies of the four emigration passes, now I requested a photocopy of the newspaper article. There was something that puzzled me: the case in the newspaper mentioned only three people, Baijnath, Rajkumar Singh and Kallu. Who was Houba and why was he hanged? I had been so excited by my find that I had failed to notice the report of a second murder case on the same page of the old newspaper. Had I done so I would have found out that, although the four were hanged at the same time, the fourth person was hanged for a different murder, which took place in Rakiraki.

I decided that I would be happy with the emigration passes and the newspaper article and would leave for Lautoka after lunch. Dr Ali also left for home, but said that he would try to get the case

file for me. I gave him my Brisbane address, got copies of the
emigration passes and the newspaper cutting and, about noon, went
downstairs to say goodbye to the girl who had helped me. When
she saw me, she said, 'I have found the case files for you.' I was
overjoyed; a person could take only so much good fortune in a day.
She gave me three files, which I took up to the library to study.

The files contained all the relevant details of the case:
names, statements, a sketch of the crime scene, three death
warrants and a petition signed by a number of villagers requesting
a pardon for the accused men. The murdered man was
Ramsamujh and the three men hanged for his murder were
Baijnath, Rājkumar Singh and Kallu. Most importantly, I found a
copy of a submission made to the Governor of Fiji by one of the
defence lawyers, Reginald Berkeley, in which he claimed that the
guilty verdict was reached on circumstantial and fabricated
evidence from unreliable witnesses.

I postponed my decision to leave for Lautoka the next day
and asked for photocopies of the files. I also extracted the
emigration passes of the murdered man, his father and his mother.
He had come to Fiji with his parents in 1900 at the age of eight.

And so, after about $15 in parking fees, a few dollars in
photocopying fees, almost three full days of research and a lot of
help from Dr Ahmed Ali, my search in Fiji for records of one of
my ancestors had ended. Or had it? I still had to study the case
files in detail to determine the fairness of the trial and to ascertain
whether the people executed were in fact guilty of the murder.

In the next few months I read and re-read the case files and
tried to recall what little had been discussed at home and in our
village during the 1950s and 1960s about the fate of my great-
grandfather. At home, the topic was mentioned occasionally —
not with any sense of shame or disdain, but with the feeling that a
great injustice had been done. The real murderer had escaped
justice. My paternal grandmother was the person most willing to
share her knowledge of the affair with us. She would have been in

her early teens at the time of the execution. The culprit, everyone seemed to believe without doubt, was a person named Bahraichi, who had lived in our village of Vitogo in Lautoka. Bahraichi had killed, as he had on a few other occasions, purely for the money Ramsamujh was carrying with him on that fateful night.

As children in the 1950s, we were petrified at the mere mention of Bahraichi's name; nothing struck more fear in our hearts than his name. 'I will give you away to Bahraichi,' children who misbehaved were told by their mothers. 'Bahraichi passed this way today,' people, especially women, would tell one another — relieved that a potential danger had passed. The very name 'Bahraichi' to us came to mean a cold-blooded killer who, for some mysterious reason, seemed immune from prosecution no matter how solid the evidence was against him. Whether he got his alias because he was from Bahraich in India or because of an epithet became immaterial. His real name is still a mystery.

I remember seeing Bahraichi on a few occasions. During an Indian wedding once I saw a short, slim grey-haired man in khaki trousers and a light-coloured shirt sitting alone on a chair. He looked to be in his sixties, quiet, and seemed unaffected by the festive atmosphere around him. A small group of young boys came to me and said, 'Do you see that man? He is Bahraichi. He has killed many people!' One of the boys even dared another to go up and touch the man. On other occasions, people pointed out Bahraichi to us as he went on his way at a distance. An element of silent mystery surrounded the man. By the time we reached our adolescent years, Bahraichi seemed to have moved away from Vitogo. Out of sight, out of mind. People now talked even less about him. His murderous exploits became topics discussed only on rare occasions.

Information on Bahraichi therefore remained sketchy. A lot of what is known is supposed to have come from Bahraichi himself. People recounted how in the earlier days, the killer would tell to his friends in great detail how he carried out his crimes. He

would recount his plan and its execution after each case was
closed. Whether this was due to a secret urge in him to tell the
truth because the authorities could not find the killer and
sometimes ended up prosecuting innocent people, or simply due to
his arrogance, is difficult to tell. Based on these stories, as well as
her own knowledge, my grandmother once told me brief details of
each man Bahraichi had killed. It added up to four or five murders.

One was the murder of a poor farmer, Butru, and his wife.
As a sideline business, Butru used to produce coconut oil and sell
the bottled oil in the market. He would spend months collecting
coconuts and then go through the laborious task of producing the
oil and, when he had made a dozen or so bottles, he would sell
them at the Lautoka market. The story of these two murders
spread around the village because of Bahraichi's own confession
to his few close mates long after the deed. It so happened that
Bahraichi was at the market that fateful Saturday when Butru was
selling his oil. Business was good that day and Butru had made
quite a profit. Bahraichi noticed this and in the evening went to
Butru's house. Butru, being a simple, hospitable fellow, invited
Bahraichi to stay for dinner not knowing that he was inviting his
own death and the death of his wife. The couple had no children.
After dinner, Bahraichi and the couple talked until it was quite
late and Bahraichi was given bedding in the corner of the small
house and invited to sleep over. In the early hours of the morning
Bahraichi got up, took Butru's axe from its usual place of storage
and killed the sleeping couple in cold blood. He then calmly took
all the money and any other possessions of value the couple had
and quietly slipped out of the house. No one was ever arrested
and prosecuted for the crime.

The other murder that Bahraichi may have committed
wa the murder of Ramsamujh for which my great-grandfather,
Baijnath, and two of his friends were hanged.

———

The year was 1912. A large number of *girmitiyas* lived in Vitogo and Vakabuli, two villages outside Lautoka town. In Vitogo, sharing the border with Vakabuli, lived Baijnath, Yaro, Chotkai, Samdhani, Rajkumar Singh, Kallu and Janki. Samdhani was living on Baijnath's land. Seorattan lived in Vakabuli. He had a 20-year-old son, Ramsamujh, who worked for the CSR. Rajkumar Singh's sister, Lachminia, was married to Yaro. Ramsamujh had recently run away with Lachminia to the neighbouring town of Ba, but soon afterwards, Lachminia's husband Yaro and Seorattan went to Ba and persuaded the couple to return to Lautoka.

Ramsamujh now lived in the CSR lines in Lautoka town. On Tuesday 26 November, he went to see his parents in Vakabuli, a weekly routine he performed with some conviction. The journey on foot took him across two rivers and along the winding hilly land on Baijnath's farm. He slept at his father's house and returned to work the next day, promising his father that he would return on Thursday evening. On Thursday night Seorattan waited for his son till 11 o'clock and, when there was no sign of Ramsamujh, his father set out to look for him.

He found his son's battered, lifeless body at five in the morning on Friday 29 November. It was lying near a track on the border of Baijnath's and Rajkumar Singh's land, a few kilometres from Seorattan's own house. It seemed that the body had been dragged a few metres to its final resting place. There was blood on the ground; a blood-stained axe and the victim's lunch billycan lay nearby. Shocked and distressed, Seorattan reported the grizzly find to the overseer, who called the police. The body was taken to Lautoka Hospital where Frank Smart, the District Medical Officer, performed the post mortem on Saturday 30 November. He wrote in his report: 'Several serious injuries to head, face and neck – eight incised wounds. Large wound on left side of head, from top to level of ear, exposing [the] brain. Death was due to injury at [the] back of neck severing [the] spinal cord.' Ramsamujh had been brutally murdered.

The colonial justice system was set in motion. On Saturday 30 November most adult males living in the vicinity of the murder scene were taken into custody for questioning. They included Baijnath, Rajkumar Singh, Kallu, Yaro, Chotkai, Samdhani and at least two others. About 11 days later, all but Baijnath, Rajkumar Singh and Kallu were released. Chotkai, Yaro and Samdhani had collaborated on stories alleging that Baijnath, Rajkumar Singh and Kallu had committed the murder. The case against the three accused commenced on 11 February, 1913. The lawyers for the defendants were Dr Manilal and Reginald Berkeley. Yaro was the first to give evidence for the prosecution.

Yaro: 'On the Thursday before Ramsamujh's body was found I saw him towards dusk going in the direction of his father's house. I was outside my house for a call of nature. Ramsamujh was about two chains [40 metres] off. He was alone. At [the] same time I saw Baijnath, Rajkumar Singh and Kallu going along another track leading towards Seorattan's house, converging on Ramsamujh's track. Accused Rajkumar Singh had [an] axe on [his] shoulder. Ramsamujh was not carrying anything.'

Not so, according to the scaled sketch drawn by George Heimbrod, a registered surveyor commissioned by the Crown. From the sketch, the closest distance between Yaro's house and the track on which Ramsamujh was travelling was five chains [100 metres], so how could Ramsamujh have been 40 metres off? Also, there is a similar distance, if not more, depending where on the track the three accused were, between Yaro's house and the track on which the three accused were alleged to have been travelling. Furthermore, giving evidence, Heimbrod states that the area between Yaro's house and the two tracks was covered with thick bush and a person standing even 40 metres towards the tracks from Yaro's house could hardly have seen anyone on either track at dusk. Yaro further stated that he had not seen Ramsamujh carrying anything on the fatal evening. However,

Ramsamujh's lunch billycan and stick (*lathi*) were found near the body. It is evident that Yaro was lying.

Chotkai was next to testify: 'On Thursday I went to bathe in the creek near Baijnath's land. About after eight [pm] I got up to urinate and I heard a voice cry "that will do, I am killed now, let me go now, Baijnath, Rajkumar Singh and Kallu".'

Chotkai, in his initial statement noted in the deposition, had said that he had heard a cry '*Nahi maro*', ie, 'do not beat', but later changed it to the more naïve but incriminating one in the witness stand. The unbelievable thing about this statement is that a dying man would hardly cry out the full names of his murderers. Besides, the next witness, Samdhani, said that it was difficult to distinguish sounds near the creek due to the noise of the running water, thus casting further doubt on Chotkai's testimony.

The last to testify was Samdhani: '[I] remember the night before Ramsamujh's body was found. I was at home. Baijnath's wife called me — I was working for Baijnath at that time — and told me to take Rajkumar Singh's horse, which I did, to his house. He was not home. It was getting dark. [I] left the horse and was returning home. There is a creek on the way. I crossed it and heard a noise but could not distinguish it on account of running water. I came suddenly on Rajkumar Singh who turned quickly and asked, "Who is that?" "It is I, Samdhani," I replied. "Where are you going?" he asked. "I have been to your house to return your horse," I replied. Kallu said, "Strike this bastard two blows. He will give evidence." Baijnath said, "No, this is my man. Do not strike him." Only the three accused were there. Kallu was on the bank close to the creek apparently dragging something. [It was] too dark to see what it was. I moved away and started for home. When I got a little away, Rajkumar Singh called after me, "Bastard, if you say anything about this I will kill you." The next day I went with Constable Manoa to see the body. It was lying close to the spot where I had seen Kallu dragging something.

An axe, a billycan and two sticks I saw there. It was the same axe that I had used at Rajkumar Singh's house to cut coconuts. I have known it for a long time.'

This must have been the crucial testimony that sealed the fate of the three accused, an eyewitness just after the fact. Was Samdhani telling the truth? The defence contended that Samdhani did not work for Baijnath but for Baijnath's son-in-law Ramkissun, that Samdhani was not instructed to take any horse to Rajkumar Singh's house and that Rajkumar Singh's horse was at his house the whole day. It was also stated by a defence witness that coconuts were not cut with axes but with knives, a practice prevalent even today. The prosecution found nothing amiss in these statements.

The police had also taken stained clothes from the three accused, but tests by the District Medical Officer showed no signs of blood on any item. The accused had always maintained that the stains were from the sap of banana and wiriwiri (*bakrera*) trees on their farms.

The case was closed on 15 February and the Chief Justice, Charles Major, passed a guilty verdict on the three accused. On 24 February, 1913, the defence counsel, Reginald Berkeley, in a six-page submission to the Governor, cited gross inconsistencies in the evidence given by the three key witnesses. He concluded:

> *Observations hereof contained suffice to render quite incredible the evidence of Chotkai, Samdhani and Yaro. A motive for fabricating evidence (namely to be freed from arrest) is shown to have existed in the case of Samdhani and Yaro, and I ask you to disbelieve their evidence. I submit that upon the evidence called for the prosecution, and upon the evidence of the defence, in so far as it destroys the credibility of the Crown's witnesses (quite apart from the alibi proved by each accused man — alibis uncontradicted, except so far as the Crown has sought to confuse the witnesses as to the Thursday on which the crime took place) the case against the prisoners should have failed. If the evidence*

of Yaro, Chotkai and Samdhani were to be disposed of then the case for the prosecution must fall to the ground.

A petition for clemency was signed by about 100 residents of the village and sent to the Governor, but to no avail. On 11 March, 1913, the Governor ordered the hanging of the three accused to take place at Suva Jail on 17 March, 1913, at eight in the morning. Death warrants were issued and the sentences were carried out.

Exiled and in virtual slavery in a strange land, Baijnath's family eventually accepted their fate. There was nothing else they could do. The colonial oppressors had delivered their form of justice — '*Kala* [black] justice'. A murder had been committed, scapegoats found and justice was seen to be done. The swift and final form of justice was handed out also to remind the 'coolies' of their purpose in life in their new homeland.

As time passed, life in the area returned to normal and people started talking more freely without fear of persecution by the authorities. If the three accused had not committed the crime, then who had? Gradually, talk surfaced about the movements of one Bahraichi on the fateful night. In years to come, Bahraichi himself would boast about getting away with a number of murders. It seemed that Bahraichi killed only for money and jewellery. Gold sovereigns were his prized acquisitions. He would rob or kill for even small booties and had acquired a reputation as a master criminal who planned his crimes and escape with great ingenuity.

There is one mention of Bahraichi in this case. It is in a statement by Ilahi: 'I knew Ramsamujh. He lived in the upper lines of Lautoka. I last saw him Thursday at 6pm [on the night of the murder] in the Lautoka lines. [I] heard him called by Bahraichi, "your father wants you [to go to his house]." He went away. The men had been paid that week.'

This seemingly innocent and insignificant statement by Ilahi serves to bear out a scenario of what may have happened on the day of the murder. Bahraichi knew that the CSR workers had been paid that week and knew that Ramsamujh would have saved the money to give to his father. He also knew of the bitter enmity between Ramsamujh and the three accused. Bahraichi now tells Ramsamujh to go to his father's house. It is late in the afternoon. He would later accompany Ramsamujh to Vitogo, carrying with him an axe. He kills Ramsamujh near Baijnath's and Rajkumar Singh's land and leaves the axe behind. The axe, similar to hundreds more in the village, would be claimed by police to belong to either Baijnath or Rajkumar Singh. Bahraichi makes a quick exit.

Although the absolute truth of the murder of Ramsamujh will never be known, there is still doubt as to whether the three people hanged were guilty of murder or not.

———————

On 19 November, 2003, more than 90 years after my great-grandfather's hanging, my brother and I were driving from Chakia towards Bhatwari (my great-grandfather's village) in Uttar Pradesh. A multitude of emotions overwhelmed me. Had Baijnath walked these roads and tracks more than a century ago? Had he looked up and seen the range of hills that we were looking at? We had travelled from Delhi across Uttar Pradesh to Banaras – virtually following the holy Ganga, across the land of Ram and the line of Raghu, of Tulsidas and Kabir. We had met the Bhojpuri-speaking people and the smartly dressed, cheerful schoolchildren who reminded us of our childhood in Fiji. We had seen people and places from the pages of Premchand's novels and from the stories and fables we had grown up with.

But, as I approached the home of Anand Singh, the village *Pradhan* of Bhatwari Kalan, I knew that our search for our relatives was in vain. Our investigations within the past two years had identified names we could not verify. Unlike many other villages we had visited, it was obvious that Bhatwari had changed a lot in the past 100 years. There were fertile crops of rice and sugar cane as far as the eye could see, no mud or grass houses met our gaze. '*Jagriti* has come to this place,' our driver from Delhi commented. Conversation with the *Pradhan* helped us little in our search for our relatives. As I got up to go to our hotel in Banaras, I touched the bright soil at my feet and wondered if there was an old tree or rock I could touch in the hope that my great-grandfather had done the same more than a century ago. I took a long breath and got into our car. I felt that some part of Baijnath had returned to the motherland. It was like a homecoming.

A Hindu procession. The statue of a goddess, covered with
a necklace of flowers, is carried on its way to a fire walking ceremony.

CHAPTER THREE

Jaikumari

John Kelly

MUCH HAS BEEN written about Manilal Maganlal Doctor, the
first Indian barrister to practice law in Fiji. Less has been written
about his wife, Jaikumari. Manilal was a flamboyant and in some
ways tragic figure. He deserves his place in Fiji's history and in
the history of the British Empire. But Jaikumari deserves her
place, too. Observers at the time credited Jaikumari with leading
the strike in Fiji in 1920. Beyond any doubt, she led a key
delegation to the Governor. But many among Fiji's leading
Europeans of the time did not want to believe that the strike was
her doing, preferring to believe that behind her public acts lay
her husband's hidden hand. Yet Jaikumari had far more thorough
training as a Gandhian protest leader, a *satyagrahi*, than did her
husband.

  We will probably never know for sure how much of a
leader Jaikumari really was, or exactly how independent a force
were the women who attended her meetings and accompanied
her in public protests. To understand the story of Jaikumari's
strike, we have to understand European fears as well as Gandhian
tactics, and a quickly changing late-indenture and post-indenture
world, in which, especially in the Fiji Europeans' imaginations,
rituals, protests, strikes and riots all merged together in imagery of
chaos and threat. Confronting that imagery without apology,

Jaikumari, along with Manilal, Totaram Sanadhya and other early leaders, began the work of creating viable anti-colonial political voices and institutions, beginning the long struggle for rights that has constituted Indo-Fijian political history.

Fear of Riots

All sorts of crowds and meetings of *girmitiyas* made the Fiji Europeans nervous. They were unable to reconcile themselves to any sort of political organisation for the *girmitiyas*. Several plans were proposed for delimiting Indian 'customary law', or empowering Indian *panchayats*, councils of elders, to resolve disputes, but each was turned down by the authorities. The Indians constituted informal *panchayats* anyway, armed mainly with the power to declare people unwilling to abide by dispute resolutions to be outcast, not *satsang* or good company; those respecting the *panchayat* members would then refuse social contact with the person deemed not *satsang*, often resulting in the creation of disputing factions. When a police sub-inspector learned of unofficial *panchayats* arbitrating local disputes in Rewa in 1910, he notified the Government of 'Secret Meetings Amongst Free Indians',[1] and sought approval to take 'active measures to put a stop to it'. He wrote, 'This practice amounts to nothing more or less than sedition.' Cooler heads in government disagreed. Still, the sub-inspector was allowed to round up *panchayat* leaders and warn them not to conduct mock courts or levy fines, which he did with satisfaction.

In the mid-1880s, at a time when low world sugar prices pressured planter and company, and CSR was pushing its managers to cut costs by increasing the size of the workers' tasks,[2] Fiji faced its first large-scale Indian protests. Crowds of labourers refused to continue to work on their plantations. Twice crowds marched to Suva to make clear their complaints about over-tasking, once carrying with them knives, axes, hoes and sticks. The Agent-General of Immigration, Henry Anson, was sympathetic, but Governor J. B. Thurston accepted planter claims that the labourers 'had become idle, insubordinate, and even dangerous', and passed an ordinance making it illegal for groups of more than five immigrants to gather to make complaints and for them to carry work tools when doing so.[3] In all instances of large-scale protest, then and thereafter, 'ringleaders' were singled out and punished.

In fact, Fiji saw few large-scale strikes or riots by indentured *girmitiyas* for the rest of the period of indenture.[4] But, imagining 'coolie' nature as they did, the Fiji Europeans never lost their fear of Indian riot. The official judgments about when to inquire into and prosecute in cases of violence against Indians were directed largely by worry about 'exciting' the Indians. If a case was known, they acted quickly, and sought less to punish than to remove the Europeans who went too far. If an estate seemed to be running smoothly, they resisted poking around under the surface. What, if not actual riots and strikes, fed the imagination of the Europeans of 'coolies' out of control? A major clue comes in the wake of one of the marches on Suva: not only did the planters tell Governor Thurston that the workers had become lazy and dangerous, Gillion[5] reports, 'Some of the employers even imagined that they were about to be massacred at the *Moharram* celebration.'

Moharram

When Fiji set up its plantations it adopted regulations and practices from other Indian indentured-labour colonies, and one element adopted was recognition of two Indian festivals as work holidays: *Holi* and *Moharram*. Only *Holi* and *Moharram* were regulated by the ordinance on 'Festivals and Processions of Indian Immigrants', and only these gained holiday status by ordinance. In Fiji, as in other colonies, these became the principal yearly Indian ritual events. The choice, among all the Hindu and Muslim rituals and festivals celebrated in India, was surely not arbitrary, and I doubt it was originally made by employers. *Moharram*, or 'the *Tazia*' as it was more generally called, at least by the Europeans in Fiji, was a *tamasa* (festival and spectacle) of fabled scale, in Fiji and before Fiji in other indentured-labour colonies. I have never found a detailed description of 'the *Tazia*' as practised in indenture-period Fiji, but fragments of description and photographic evidence suggest that enormous and elaborate models were constructed of the tombs of the Shi'a martyrs, Hassan and Hussein. They were carried in parades, accompanied by devotees whose prayers and preparations raised them to a state of possession by the martyrs themselves.

On such occasions, stick fighting resembling sword combat could break out. The Indians of different plantations and free areas competed to build larger and better constructs. In the final parade, all the *tazias* of a given locale were paraded together. The parades ended at the riverside or seaside, where, in conclusion of the festival, the *tazias* were thrown into the water. Ali's *girmitiya* interviewees reported that the *tazia* was celebrated by everyone, Hindu and Muslim, and was occasionally the scene of real violence.[6] The other feature often mentioned in connection with the *tazia* was of songs eulogising the martyrs, apparently sung during the processions themselves. A surviving *girmitiya* told Prasad: 'I remember very well how my songs based on Tajia [*Moharram*] often made the women cry.'[7]

It is easy to understand how wild swordplay by ritually possessed men could intimidate their 'masters'. Government officials in Fiji and elsewhere feared the violence, symbolic and real, connected with the processions. In Fiji, the ordinance regulating the festival, like the anti-riot ordinance, forbade the participants to carry sticks with them on the parades. Missionary observers had deep distrust, and condemned the ritual as demoralising.[8] But what were the women crying about? The Shi'ite festival was a commemoration of tragedy, a narration of heroic martyrdom and an explanation of a world in which divine will was temporarily thwarted by corrupt worldly powers, in which true virtue existed against the grain of the apparent order of the world.

Holi

Holi as practised in indenture days was, similarly, a ritual of reversals, negation and comment on the social realities of its time. *Holi* is intrinsically a ritual of reversals and of breaking with the past, but in practice, it can vary tremendously in the intensity of its rule-flaunting play. None of the recorded *girmitiya* descriptions describes its practice in indenture Fiji in great detail. Overseer Walter Gill, however, wrote the following:

> On the day of Holi or Phagua, bands of women roamed the countryside until noon, showering men with a red fluid meant to represent blood. It was a rite associated with the goddess Khali [sic], and being their only period of license during the long year, the women made the most of it. By midday, unpopular overseers looked like what happened on St Bartholomew's day; the popular were drenched in cheap perfume. From the glimmer of dawn, Lautoka and the estates were overrun by gaggles of excited women and girls out for a good time. With male control absent for the time being, things happened which staggered the godly. The afternoon and evening were different. Lautoka with its hair down, thronged the Indian fair to risk maiming and worse on rickety merrygorounds, swingboats and ferris wheels. And if they were sufficiently uninhibited by raceconsciousness, and could laugh at themselves as well as others, people found that they were having an astonishingly good time. [9]

Gill describes here a considerably more brazen, rule-flaunting *Holi* celebration than that of later years in Fiji. My own experience of *Holi* in 1984 was closely in accord with Mayer's description of *Holi* there in 1950–51: 'Freedom from normal restraint was carefully regulated in Fiji — it did not extend to women, nor to those men who did not wish to join in.'[10] *Holi* by 1950, and likely even more so by the 1970s and 1980s, became a careful, formal, negotiated abandonment of social roles. Brenneis reported similar restraint in *Holi* as he observed it in Vanua Levu in the 1970s:

> In Fiji both holi and the cautal-singing associated with it seem initially quite polite, if not bowdlerized ... On the day of holi itself men and women gather together in the temple, participate in a ritual offering of clarified butter and sweetsmelling wood and in a program of songs and speeches. Holi is then 'played', not by the spraying of brilliant dyes and the tossing of urine, cow dung and garbage as in India but by the sprinkling of talcum powder, women dusting other women, men other men ... Fiji clearly lacks the insult, ribaldry and apparent release that it affords in India.[11]

Just as clearly, this wasn't always so. The surviving *girmitiyas* who note its popularity in indenture time were perhaps reticent to describe it in detail. One man told Prasad, 'We celebrated *Holi* with coloured water and always looked for the opportunity to pour water, powder and other things on women.'[12] What other things? When, as Gill reported, the indentured women were running wild, what did they do that 'staggered the godly'? Likely, as in more serious attacks on overseers reported in several sources, and akin to *Holi* celebrations in parts of India, they were throwing faeces and urine.[13]

Gill, who knew little about Hinduism, may have been confused in associating the festival with 'Khali' (Kali), a major form of the Goddess (though ritual worship of and songs devoted to various forms of the Goddess, especially Sakti, are often part of *Holi* in India).[14] Forms of the Goddess play little role in accounts of *Holi* I heard and read about in Fiji. Indo-Fijians today relate the festival to two primary religious contexts, both well-known in association with *Holi* in India. The first is the story of Prahalad, a virtuous devotee of Vishnu, whose devotion saves him from torture and death and leads to the destruction of an evil king. From this story come most of the symbolic vehicles of the ritual, including the throwing of red dye (which is not generally associated with blood in India, although it is still in Fiji). Second, *Holi* is related to Krishna, and his own celebrations of *Holi* with his *gopis*, his female devotees. The *Holi* I saw celebrated in 1984 could be called ribald only in its waning hours, as male singers who had been singing all day and drinking for the final hours began to intimately serenade each other with love songs explicitly related to Krishna and the *gopis* on *Holi*. Regardless of whether such songs of Krishna were part of the *Holi* of the indenture lines, two things should be stressed about the *Holi* of indenture.

First, in indenture times, *Holi* was almost certainly a ritual of social disintegration, role abandonment or reversal. It was probably an expression of a devotionally defined equality among all people, a statement, through red dye, that all people are equal, as all blood is red. This exegesis of the meaning of the dye is now well known in Fiji. As such, it was an acceptance of, and a refashioning of, the formal, legal equality and individualism that the indenture contract had made of aspects of *girmitiya* identity. A real equality did exist between people and it was their real nature, but it was found underneath the social impositions of an oppressive social formation, not within them.

Second, women played a much bolder and more autonomous role in the indenture *Holi* than in its later Fiji versions. An aggressive, refuse-flinging role for women in *Holi* is well known in parts of India. This part of *Holi* was used in Fiji, at least according to Gill, to fashion a reply, and a differentiated one, to the European overseers. As the style of devotion oriented to the Tulsi Das *Ramayan* became predominant over time in Fiji, this type of autonomous agency for women, which negated in ritual space her attachment to her husband, disappeared.

Holi and the *Moharram* commemoration set the practitioners against the structures of the world. In *Holi*, the aggressive acts of 'play' negated social relations and controls; in the *Tazia*, aggressive identification with the martyrs transformed people and sparked violence. Similarly, the Ram Lilas of indenture days focused on a confrontation with and triumph over evil.

Ram Lilas

Even before 'Sanatan Dharm' missionaries made the Tulsi Das *Ramcaritmanas* the focus of their effort to counter the reformist Hindu missionaries of the Arya Samaj, the story of Ram was well known and had great salience for Fiji's *girmitiyas* as a story of banishment and exile. This identification was promoted by Sanadhya and Chaturvedi and other critics of indenture, but was also, by many reports, part of attitudes in the lines before the articulation of the nationalist rhetoric. If the *girmitiyas* were, like Ram, innocent victims of circumstance and the sins of others, then their pollution and degradation in Fiji was not their own *karma*, a fault to search for in themselves, but rather a part of an epic struggle between uplifting and polluting, divine and evil forces.

Quite unlike the *Ram Lilas* of later days, such as those I saw and heard about in Fiji in 1984–85, the *Ram Lilas* of early last century climaxed around the destruction of giant effigies of the demon-king Ravan. The effigies could be nine metres tall or taller. In 1985, informants told me they 'no longer had the time' to build the towering figures; the final days of the *Lilas* dwelled on events connected with Ram's victorious return to Ayodhya, his capital. In indenture days, however, the focus of the *Lila* was the victorious struggle against evil itself, depictions of Ram's army fighting Ravan's, with the torching of Ravan as the climax. Depictions of Ravan from *Ram Lilas* in Trinidad,[15] make explicit what I think is fairly clear allegorically in the Fiji celebrations: Ravan dressed unmistakably in European clothes, even dressed as a plantation manager.

Bhakti *and European Incomprehension*

The colonial Europeans had little comprehension of, or patience for, the Indian religious *tamasas*, ritual festivals, of indenture days. They saw heathen, ungodly lewdness, dangerous tumult and disorder, and all the more evidence, they thought, of the Indians' 'bad character'. Even sympathetic observers of indenture days later tended to denigrate the morality of the earlier practices in praise of the very different religious practices that followed. Dr I. Hamilton Beattie was the Fiji European who was perhaps most sympathetic to the Fiji Indians' political causes, or at least the 'moderate' ones. Beattie founded a trilingual newspaper. He hosted meetings and events in his house in Toorak. He conveyed petitions to the Governor. And Beattie made reform of the rituals a particular personal cause. He was particularly pleased when the Government, in coordination with the Fiji Muslim League, made it all but impossible for any further major *tazia* processions to be held in the late 1920s. Many other observers shared his incomprehension and distaste. Even the astute historian, K. L. Gillion, praised the Arya Samaj reformers for their 'concern with more than the outward show of religion'.[16]

What the later observers grasped less than the European observers of the indenture days, was that the colonial Europeans were themselves a key referent of the great symbols of the indenture period rituals. The *girmitiyas* cast themselves as the soldiers of the martyrs, the supporters of Prahalad, the army of Ram, doomed but perhaps reborn, exiled but perhaps victorious. On May 15, 1929, while the Fiji Government held official celebrations, reluctantly and ambivalently planned, of the 50th anniversary of the arrival of the first *girmitiyas* in Fiji, the Arya Samaj Modern Youth Society burned indenture in effigy. It wasn't the first time.

Here precisely is a good point to recall some of subaltern studies historian Ranajit Guha's advice, 'acknowledge the insurgent as the subject of his own history' and find 'the

specificity of rebel consciousness'.[17] If we understand powerful
anti-colonial statements to be enmeshed in the popular rituals of
indenture days, is this to portray them merely as disguised
political arguments garbed in protective religious clothing? The
rituals *did* embrace the colonial sign of disorder and participants,
surely in such events as the bloody, filthy, gendered attacks on
Holi, took great pleasure in exploiting Europeans' fears and
anxieties. But, if we review more theology, we can see that there
was more than cheap thrill and particular revenge available from
these rituals in this context.

Bhakti, the devotional stream of Hinduism, has been
described by A. K. Ramanujan as 'a great, many-sided shift in
Hindu culture and sensibility'.[18] Hinduism itself, of course, is not
a unitary religion but a universe of religious discourse, a vague,
grand label encompassing highly variant identities and practices.
Bhakti has plural historical roots within Hinduism (and outside it;
for instance, Jains and Parsis may have had great influence on
bhakti in Gujarat). If, to begin to grasp what *bhakti* is, we seek
essential elements, we might go two ways. *Bhakti*, a word from
Sanskrit meaning devotional faith, is built from a root, *bhaj*,
which means 'to share, divide or share in'. *Bhakti* traditions share
a commitment to realise divine form in self and world. It is the
search, by means of passionate personal commitment, to find
the divine share in the self, the self as a part of the divine.[19]
A separated soul or self longs for the divine, with all love
relationships, including sexual ones, possible metaphors for the
soul's feelings for divinity. If this seems too abstract, for a religious
stream that tends to emphasise extremely vivid narratives and
imagery, the other way to begin to grasp *bhakti* is by what it is not:
bhakti traditions are generally sceptical of the practical, ritual and
knowledge-oriented paths authorised by Hindu discourses
preceding *bhakti*. In most *bhakti* theologies, ritual proprieties,
proprieties in all actions, or even disciplined control of the body,
all forms of *karma yoga*, will not by themselves lead the soul to

God, nor will all the forms of knowledge (*jnana yoga*) by themselves, for the universe is, after all, not simply a law-governed machinery, not simply the outcome of an inexorable *dharma*. This is a mere appearance. It is actually God's *lila*, God's play, a vast divine sport that does not bind God as it appears to bind people.

Most of the *bhakti* theologies and practices that began to spread in various parts of India from the ninth to the 15th centuries found ways to coexist with caste and other 'Hindu' social institutions and practices. But *bhakti* theologies tended rather to emphasise the similarity of all human beings, as souls separated from God, and *bhakti* theology was the foundation of many anti-caste ideologies and movements. The egalitarian premise of *bhakti* theology made it especially salient to the polluted, levelled situation of indentured overseas Indians, as proponents in India pointed out.

Not all Hindu missions that came to places such as Fiji were *bhakti*-oriented. The Arya Samaj, for example, the first Hindu society to send large numbers of missionaries to Fiji, was committed primarily to *jnana yoga*, the path of knowledge, and interpreted the world not as God's play, *lila*, but as a real materiality governed by laws, *dharma*. The *bhakti*-oriented missions ultimately won over more followers, but which form of *bhakti* was to be taught?

In many *bhakti* traditions, erotic love becomes a metaphor of longing for the realisation of divine form. A major debate between *bhakti* traditions concerns whether or how this imagery is truly metaphorical. Should one imagine one's love for God as if one was God's wife or consort, as if one was Radha for Krishna, or Sita to Ram? Or should one long to find God oneself; in fact, Krishna as a lover waiting in the forest? Should the divine be sought outside and beyond all known relations, or within known relations, by means of perfection in given roles? Some devotional writers argued that true love was possible only outside marriage, just as realisation of divine form depended on disintegration of the given, binding relations of the world. Others, notably Tulsi Das in his *Ramcaritmanas*, his 'Ramayan', found proper expressions of love and devotion in the perfect carrying out of worldly duty. Ram, following his father's word, enduring exile and struggling to defeat evil Ravan, was object and exemplar of a proper devotional attitude; Sita, his wife, was an exemplar of devotion in marriage. For this and many other *bhakti* traditions, the proper gender relations of husband and wife begin with a very simple devotional principle: that the wife should worship her husband as her lord.

Girmitiya accounts, such as Totaram Sanadhya's *Story of the Haunted Line*, make it clear that *bhakti* devotionalism was important for many, but not for all, of the indentured labourers in the lines. *The Story of the Haunted Line* theologically was an account of Sanadhya's efforts to rely on God, in the form of Krishna, for shelter from his problems while enduring his indenture. He framed the story as an illustration of a Vaisnavite *sloka* (verse), which he quotes near its outset, a verse which promises that God will meet all the needs of those who abandon themselves to His care. In the story, Sanadhya was unable to stop thinking about his problems, oppressed by overseer abuse and near-starvation and, despite efforts to pursue a proper devotional attitude, was tempted to commit suicide. Just in time, however — when he asked God, 'Oh God, take me. Away from You I am disinclined. I do not wish to live now' — a rat bite distracted him, and then the knock on his door turned his thoughts toward courage, and then to his duty to his mother, home in India. He realised that he had to go on, do his duty and rely on God to take care of him and rescue him from his problems. Then arrived his rescue, as surely arranged by God as the rat-bite. By realising that he should do his duty, and trust in God to take care of his needs, he was saved from starvation, despair and suicide. This story, like most of the Sanadhya/Chaturvedi writings, is a polemic for a duty-oriented *bhakti*, and also for aid to the indentured Indians.

The devotionalism of duty, however, and of seeking perfection in worldly affairs, was not alone and dominant in the social field of indenture-period Hinduism. It seems to have coexisted with and, further, been secondary to a devotionalism based on negation of worldly relations. The principal rituals of the Indians were not the set connected with Ram and the Ramayan, and the Tulsi Das rendition of devotionalism in duty and perfection, which rose to prominence later in Fiji history. The *Ram Lilas* were major events since at least 1902, a date Sanadhya cites. But the *Ram Naumi* (birth of Ram) and *Diwali*, associated with Ram's triumphant return, which later became rituals of the greatest importance in the Fiji Hindu calendar, were not holidays of principal importance during indenture. *Moharram* was not intrinsically a *bhakti* ritual, of course, but it resonated easily with the themes of world-disintegrating *bhakti*. *Holi* and the *Tazia*, as practised in the lines, not only villainised the exploitative, denigrating, polluting masters of the *girmit*, but defined a self outside the social roles of that world. They founded moral relations with God that not only injected new strength or licensed immediate cathartic reversal, but made real an alternative, disintegrating understanding of the 'coolie' situation. They were rituals of resistance, and more. They did not merely open a temporary communitas (a feeling of collective well-being), but proffered the vision of a self on different terms of order, a permanent new start beyond the *girmit*. Therefore, they rightly disquieted their European observers. Beaton, in Mauritius, was convinced that the *Tazia* undermined plantation discipline. Gill, in Fiji, was well aware that the *Holi* festival, even after its wild morning, was only for those 'sufficiently uninhibited by race-consciousness'.

Not all the *girmitiyas* were religious in any particular way. One of Ali's *girmitiya* interviewees, Gafur, reported that 'There was no talk of religion at all on my estate'.[20] And one of the witnesses in a trial in 1907 could not be sworn in: 'She says she does not know whether she is a Musulamani or a Hindu and does not know the meaning of religion having been born in Fiji.' But *Holi*, the *Tazia* and the dramatic *Ram Lilas* effloresced in the last decades of indenture, when there was more Indian money to sponsor the expenses and a larger free population to join in with those still indentured. Hinduism and Islam had their new vitality, as Burton complained, at precisely the time that the Christian mission made its largest, still failing efforts at inroads into the Indian community, and when the missions for the more chaste forms of 'Hinduism', explicit rivals to the Christian missions, were just getting started.

In sum, the *girmitiyas*, on their way to becoming Indo-Fijians, had their own reasons for being deliberately disorderly. Many did realise, and enjoy, the disquiet it provoked and the revenge it afforded, but also, for some, the whole point was that it took them outside their place in Fiji's social structure altogether — a very good idea on political and religious grounds. And, in any case, clearly the Indian riots best known to the Fiji Europeans were their most important rituals.

The Major Strikes

In the 1910s, massive and building protests in India caused the empire to shut down the indenture system. The last new *girmitiyas* arrived in 1916, and all contracts were cancelled at the start of 1920. CSR's upper management saw it coming a few years ahead of official Fiji, but Fiji European settlers had difficulty accepting the news even after it was fact and demanded new negotiations for some form of 'assisted' immigration of new labourers. Then, precisely, Fiji's Europeans faced the major upheavals they had long feared, and largely because of their resistance to adjusting to a world without 'coolies'.

In 1920 and again in 1921, Fiji Indian workers went on strike. The first strike was in the capital, Suva, and the second in the cane-growing areas. Both strikes were, first and foremost, about wages. Europeans apprehensive at the end of indenture were trying to hold wages down, despite high wartime inflation from the years of World War I. The season-long cane strike in particular turned the labour market for European cane planters from inadequate to non-existent, with dramatic consequences for the structure of cane production. CSR had already been experimentally leasing land to Indians and buying cane direct. After the strike, this system massively expanded, the labour supply for white planters dried up and, by 1925, there were no independent white sugar planters left in Fiji.[21]

Both strikes were led by Gandhian nationalists arrived from India on missions. The first was led by Jaikumari, a *satyagraha* activist trained at Gandhi's *ashram*, and by Manilal Maganlal Doctor, her husband, Fiji's first Indian barrister, who came to Fiji with Gandhi's blessing. The second was led by 'the *Sadhu*', Bashisht Muni, a religious mendicant who presented himself as a follower of Gandhi. The 1920 strike began with a deputation to the Governor asking for a rise in wages and a commission to investigate food shortages and high prices. The commission was appointed. But the Indians went out on strike anyway, and the Governor telegraphed London 'that the Indian unrest was assuming the character of a racial outbreak rather than a strike, that bloodshed was inevitable, and that Indian agitators were trying to disaffect the Fijians'.[22] The prediction was self-fulfilling in part, as the Governor deployed troops who shot into a crowd of striking workers, killing one and wounding several.

Eventually, the commission determined that the cost of living 'for Indians' had risen 86 per cent since before the war, and the Government chose to cut Indians' taxes, subsidise rice imports and give Indians working for the Government temporary food rations, all to avoid raising their wages. Straining economic reason, the Government sought any means to avoid giving the strikers what they asked for. But the shocked strikers had gone back to work shortly after the violence. The Government presumed that Manilal was the secret force behind the strike, that Jaikumari was apparently only the strike leader, as if Manilal could not have found a better blind if he had wished to operate secretly. But it forced Jaikumari and the 'disaffected' Manilal to leave Fiji.

The cane strike the next year was longer and more costly for colonial Fiji. More explicitly than Manilal, 'the *Sadhu*' articulated Fiji Indian interests and grievances in the terms of Gandhi's developing critique of colonial capitalism: the colonial capitalists were greedy and deluded, Indians' dignity was violated by racially unequal wage systems, he argued, and Indians should therefore avoid working for Europeans as long as the wage systems were unequal. The striking workers presented 16 demands, calling for much higher wages, better workers' housing, a five-day working week, Indian schools, the return of Manilal, lower prices, repeal of a law requiring one month's notice from labourers, and an end to racial distinctions in the railways. The Governor saw the demands as Bashisht Muni's work. Fiji's Colonial Secretary later explained in a despatch to Winston Churchill in the Colonial Office that the demands 'were couched in such extravagant terms, and involved political issues of so serious a character', that their object 'was to bar deliberately the door to any settlement and to create a deadlock'.[23] In reply, the Governor appointed a commission to inquire into the circumstances of the strike and to advise on measures 'to prevent such situations from arising in the future'. The Governor arranged for the announcement of the commission appointment to be read at a meeting chaired by Bashisht Muni on March 20, 1921. In the announcement, the Governor had two warnings issued:

> *Failing an early resumption of work the Commission may be compelled to suspend its sittings. Finally the Governor warns Indians against paying heed to the advices or threats of men who have no stake in the Colony, and are using them for tools for political purposes which have nothing to do with Fiji and can*

bring no benefit to Indians here. The Governor's authority is
paramount in the Colony and he will deal severely with any
person who attempts to undermine it or holds out to Indians
false expectations of what they may gain by persisting in
extravagant demands.

The Indians at the meeting voted unanimously not to
return to work. Three days later, Bashisht Muni was arrested and
deported for inciting disaffection and, on 29 May, the Governor's
reasons were explained in an extraordinary number of the *Fiji
Royal Gazette*:

> *The Governor has the welfare of the people at heart. Knowing*
> *these things, His Excellency would be failing in his duty if he did*
> *not take action. He cannot watch, unmoved, a man, who has no*
> *stake in the Colony and therefore nothing to lose, deluding and*
> *misleading people who have made their homes here, and whose*
> *welfare is bound up with the welfare of Fiji … Indians have been*
> *persuaded to put forward a series of demands which, as they*
> *themselves know, do not even afford grounds for discussion. It is*
> *not to be expected that employers will discuss terms at which it is*
> *known that the Indians themselves are laughing in their hearts …*
> *The Governor again urges Indians on strike to return to work*
> *and to remodel their requests on reasonable lines for presentation*
> *to their employers. He advises Indians to state their troubles fully*
> *to the Commission at which they may be assured of an impartial*
> *hearing. A Commission is the recognised method of finding out*
> *the truth of things. His Excellency's earnest desire is to learn the*
> *full truth in order that he may know what should be done to put*
> *right what may be wrong.*

The strikers did not respond to the Governor's new
approach, his critique of their hearts and invocation of his own.
They did not have much chance to, because the Government
used an ordinance passed during the previous strike to forbid
Indian public meetings without written permits. The meetings

that were allowed affirmed the strike and the commission
boycott. The Governor withdrew the commission and later
proposed another one if workers would return to work. They did
not.

The strike ended gradually in July and August, without a
moment of clear resolution. On 3 June, the milling company
unilaterally announced concessions, mainly in the form of
reduced prices for goods. But on 27 June, perhaps the more
important announcement came: a committee was coming from
India to investigate and report to the Government of India about
the conditions under which Indians lived in Fiji. What to the
Europeans was a chance to appeal for further immigration, was to
the Indians a hope of being heard.

The committee came in 1922 and wrote in its report,
'Wherever we have gone we have been welcomed with cries of
"Mahatma Gandhi kijai" ["Hail Mahatma Gandhi"], a piquant
experience for a deputation from the Government of India.'[xxiv]
But the Fiji Europeans also became uncertain about the political
identity of their visitors, starting when they learned that it had
more Indian than European members. Controversy erupted after
a press report that a member of the committee had told Indian
farmers to burn the sugar company in effigy.[25] What he had really
done, the committee chairman told the *Fiji Times* (15 March,
1922), was tell farmers on the occasion of *Holi*, a New Year
Festival, to cast the company and their troubles with it on to the
fire to be burned away before the New Year, 'so that nothing but
happiness and contentment remain ... The Company evidently
did not want them, so they should put the Company out of their
minds, and turn to farming for themselves'. In the same issue, the
Fiji Times editors argued that these remarks were 'a breach of
faith', violating the 'bond, so to speak, under whose terms he and
his colleagues came to Fiji'. Coming to Fiji 'under false colours',
this delegate had 'defied the covenances of honourable men', and
he and his colleagues 'in no way respected their position as

trusted guests of the Government'. With the *Fiji Times* attacking them as being somehow in violation of some implied covenant, as if in violation of some kind of indenture themselves, the committee members carried on their inquiry. On return to India, the committee wrote a report critical of Fiji's treatment of its Indians. In deference to Fiji, the Colonial Office in London saw to it that the committee report was never published, but appearances were all that official Fiji could save.[26] Official India abandoned all plans for further labour immigration to Fiji.

The strikes and the rituals clearly intertwined in the thematics of the Fiji Indians' agency as well as in the Europeans' fears. Whether it was the Gandhian *sadhu* or the official commission chairman, whether the reference was to seeking *swaraj*, 'self-rule', in the individual sense of self-respect, or to throwing the disrespectful company and the troubles with it on to the *Holi* fire, the advice of strike leaders used powerful combinations of religious and political imagery to articulate the Indians' push for substantive freedom. Finally, in the official treatment of the 'agitators', Manilal was not only forced from Fiji, but ruthlessly hounded out of the empire itself — and more especially in the testimony used against one of them, we can also get a feeling for how homogenising the fear of perceived disorder could be for Fiji's Europeans.

It was Jaikumari, leading a deputation of women, who presented the original 1920 strike demands to the Governor, demands for a higher wage and official inquiry into high prices. But the 'evidence' gathered by the Government, the sort they needed to justify expelling her, alleged that Jaikumari was connected to a quite different organisation of women in the strike:

> Mrs Manilal advised us to prevent the men from working, and if anyone did they would be beaten and filthy water would be poured ... We were all put on oath to assist in this matter ... Mrs Manilal cried at the meeting. Mrs Manilal said that if there was any trouble and if anyone was to be arrested she would be

the first to be taken, and as long as the women followed her and listened to what she had to say there would be no trouble. (Etwari, 'a married woman', 17 February, 1920)

Mrs Manilal said if the men go back to work she would get hold of them and beat them. ('One Chandkuar', 13 February, 1920)

Mrs Manilal said: if any husbands go, beat them too, and the Inspector too. ('One Fulquhar', 28 February, 1920)

At her own house [on 11 February] Mrs Manilal said, 'As to any men who go to work, stop them, and if they go gather all the women and beat the men and put dirty water ...' ('One Rachell', 13 February, 1920)[27]

Witnesses connected Jaikumari to 'dirty water' protests more graphically than I care to repeat. It seems highly unlikely that it would take a trained and experienced *satyagraha* activist, the sort who would weep publicly and insist on oaths to God as political statements and tactics, to organise this form of protest attack. Instead, let us recall the powerful arguments of subaltern studies historians that scholars should investigate the active, transforming reception of Gandhian messages by subalterns, and also that we should investigate the subalterns' independent, interested politics. And let us recall also the best point in Gayatri Spivak's critique of subaltern studies, that we should not generally expect to find a 'subaltern' alternative discourse of the style used to actually contend with elite, authoritative voices. Perhaps, we can here reconsider the image of the confused, inarticulate and inert, apolitical mass led by unstable agitators, without imagining a polished, articulate 'voice' always already part of subaltern political initiatives. All of these witnesses knew about attack by 'dirty water' or 'night soil', urine and faeces, a weapon of the weak extremely effective in plantation situations, humiliating, punishing, revenging against and often driving away specific enemies among the overseers and others with power. Without neglecting the fact that the protest form had a history in specific rituals as well as an affinity to plantation circumstances, I find it implausible that Jaikumari from Gandhi's ashram had anything to teach about this tactic to the *girmitiya* women and men who had endured the pressures and politics of indenture.

Perhaps, then, this 'evidence' from the trial of Jaikumari is instead a trace of the struggle of this Gandhian to reorganise and reconfigure the women's already quite definite political will, and to turn them from tactics that worked against individuals towards the building of a new society. The evidence is no doubt distorted by the official drive to blame her for all events. And yet something of her intentions shines through. 'As long as the women followed her and listened to what she had to say there would be no trouble.' The women were already ready to keep the strike disciplined, which by all accounts, it was. And, under Jaikumari's leadership, they were learning new tactics, such as the petition, publication, the public oath to God, and insistence on official inquiry. Here lay the agency of Jaikumari that truly threatened the colonial Europeans. Removing her from Fiji could not stop Fiji's *girmitiyas* and their descendants from finding political voices.

NOTES

[1] Colonial Secretary's Office File 6937/10, National Archives of Fiji.

[2] Gillion, K. L. 1962. *Fiji's Indian Migrants. A history to the end of indenture in 1920.* Melbourne. p. 89.

[3] Ibid., p. 83.

[4] See also Lal, Brij V. 1992. *Broken Waves. A history of the Fiji Islands in the Twentieth Century.* Honolulu.

[5] Gillion, K. L. *Fiji's Indian Migrants.* p. 83.

[6] Ali, Ahmed (ed.). 1979. *Girmit. The Indian Indenture Experience in Fiji.* Suva. pp. 41, 44.

[7] Prasad, Shiu. 1974. *Indian Indentured Workers in Fiji.* Suva. p. 29.

[8] Beaton, a missionary in Mauritius, provides the most detailed firsthand description I have ever read of *Moharram* in an indenture colony; see Beaton, 1859, pp. 182–9. His view is negative on strictly religious grounds, appalled that an 'exhibition of heathenism is tolerated' by the Government. He was also acutely aware of a threat to ordinary social relations: 'It unhinges and unsettles their minds, and makes them averse to their usual employments. It often leads them to desert their employment.'

[9] Gill, Walter. 1970. *Turn North-East at the Tombstone*. Adelaide. p. 121.

[10] Mayer, Adrian C. 1973, 2nd ed. *Peasants in the Pacific. A Study of Fiji Indian Rural Society*. London. p. 87.

[11] Brenneis, Don. 1987. 'Performing Passions: Aesthetics and politics in an occasionally egalitarian community.' In *American Ethnologist*, 14. pp. 236–50 at p. 245.

[12] Prasad, Shiu. *Indian Indentured Workers in Fiji*. p. 28.

[13] There are also many accounts of this kind of attack outside of ritual play. It was clearly a 'weapon of the weak' used effectively on rare occasions in the indenture lines. The elderly *girmitiyas* interviewed by Ali reported attacks on overseers, including one rapist, by bombardment with faeces (Ali 1979: 55). Gill claims that during his stint as overseer of a women's gang, at a time of trouble in the lines, he himself narrowly escaped having urine thrown on him, and that other overseers had resigned after similar attacks (Gill 1970: 37).

[14] For example, Mayer, Adrian C. 1960. *Caste and Kinship in Central India*. London. p. 107.

[15] Aisha Khan, personal communication.

[16] Gillion, K. L. *Fiji's Indian Migrants*. p. 148.

[17] Guha, Ranajit. 1983. 'The Prose of Counter-Insurgency.' In Guha (ed.), *Subaltern Studies II: Writings on South Asian History and Society*. Delhi. pp. 1–42.

[18] Ramanujan, A. K. 1981. *Hymns for the Drowning: Poems for Visnu*. Princeton. p. 103.

[19] One might say that *bhakti* is an effort to participate in the divine, to participate in something like Levy-Bruhl's sense, except that *bhakti* is not prelogical but rather postlogical, a deliberate and articulate rejection of the elaborate Hindu and other systems stressing knowledge (*jnana*) as a path to enlightenment or release (*moksha, nirvana*).

[20] Ali, Ahmed (ed.). *Girmit*. p. 35.

[21] For the best accounts of these strikes, see Gillion, G. L. 1977. *The Fiji Indians. Challenge to European Dominance, 1920–1946*. Canberra. And, Lal, Brij V. *Broken Waves*. For the demise of the white planters, see Knapman, Bruce. 1987. *Fiji's Economic History, 1874–1939. Studies of Capitalist Colonial Development*. Canberra.

22 Summarised in Gillion, K. L. *The Fiji Indians*. p. 30.

23 For this and other documents quoted on the 1921 strikes, see Colonial Secretary's Office File 5718/21.

24 Gillion, K. L. *The Fiji Indians*. p. 56.

25 Here we read over the shoulder of Benarsidas Chaturvedi, from his collected papers in the National Archives of India in New Delhi (especially section II/C of his papers, 'press clippings'). Chaturvedi was a Gandhian journalist and publisher, who monitored overseas Indian affairs and wrote books and articles about problems in Fiji and elsewhere. Chaturvedi also corresponded with the committee members, and probably influenced their judgment of the situation in Fiji, precisely as the Fiji Europeans feared. For new clippings on this commission to Fiji, see the Benarsidas Chaturvedi papers, especially II/C-484 to II/C-492.

26 Fiji's Governor was sent a copy of the report, and he wrote to the Colonial Office that it confirmed his view of the committee. '[T]he enthusiastic cries of "Mahatma Gandhi kijai" presents to my mind a contemptible rather than a "piquant" picture' (quoted in Gillion 1977: 97). Official India learned to respect Gandhi and the Indian National Congress; official Fiji was contemptuous for far longer.

27 Colonial Secretary's Office File C76/20.

A typical mosque in western Viti Levu, a cultural and religious centre for Muslims who gather regularly for the Friday prayer.

CHAPTER FOUR

Remembering

Ahmed Ali

TWENTY-FIVE YEARS ago we celebrated the 100th anniversary of the arrival in 1879 of the *Leonidas*, bringing to Fiji the first boatload of our *girmitiya* forebears. As we think of May 2004, the 125th anniversary, the mood is distinctly different from that of 1979. Then we were still basking in the euphoria of our freedom from colonial rule in 1970, even momentarily forgetting the intra-cultural and religious tensions of just a few years previously. We celebrated in May 1979 with enthusiasm, brimming with hope and optimism. A quarter of a century later, we look ahead with caution and uncertainty, the clouds of *coups d'état* in 1987 and 2000 not completely dispelled, and the sounds of indigenous ethno-nationalism no longer muffled but clear and insistent. The world beyond Fiji's shores, too, is different and we are more aware of its fickleness, of unending strife. Besides, we are all older as communities, more aware of the hypocrisies of international decision-making, more cognisant of the realities of national, communal and ethnic self-interest and of our puny pleas before the steamrolling steps of emerging and established giants.

In 1979, I was completing my research on the indenture system and the celebration in May offered me an opportunity to publish a monograph of my interviews with some of the few surviving *girmitiyas*. Then I left the field only to return to it recently out of revived interest, to be immersed again in its fascinations. This time, my concern was to fill the gaps in my knowledge of my own *girmitiya* origins. That mission is nearly complete. I hope to share it soon in the hope that it might encourage others to do the same. Discoveries on that path are exhilarating; they come unexpectedly, sometimes elusive and frustrating, turning up occasionally, after years of persistence.

My other reason for returning to our *girmitiya* past is my attempt to write a history of Muslims in Fiji. I finished a draft a decade ago. When I was intending to revise it, my son Hashim offered to help. With the liberties afforded a younger son, he returned the manuscript a week later telling me to rewrite with additional material. That has proved to be a useful but difficult direction.

My increased involvement with the Fiji Muslim League after my return from Malaysia in 1995 gave me access to written sources unavailable to outsiders, as well as to additional information from Muslims knowledgeable about their community's past and forthright about its aspirations and needs. This continuous dialogue, based on mutual trust, provides invaluable insights, and instills the sensitivity essential for history writing. I have also had considerable encouragement from Muslims concerning my research, writing and speeches on the subject. Muslims in Fiji want their history in Fiji's multicultural context written. They contend that theirs is a significant contribution to Fiji and to the Muslim *ummah* (community). As those of the faith of Gazali, Rushd, Khaldun and, lately, Iqbal, Jinnah, Qutb and Khomeni, they perceive their history, which traverses colour, languages, ethnicities and class, as an inspiration towards justice and universalism, not as a burden imposed by the communalism of the small-minded or the internal colonialism of those obsessed by self-created parochialisms of race and religion. That has influenced my choice of topic for this occasion; reminiscing on the survival of Islam and the Muslim identity during *girmit*.

What intrigues Muslims in Fiji has been the survival of their religious community without loss of the essential features of their faith despite the horrendous social and cultural experience of *girmit*. They consider the success of their forefathers especially remarkable as they were a minority among the *girmitiyas*. Of the Muslims who embarked at Calcutta between 1879 and 1916, there were 4,294 males and 2,263 females. From Madras, from 1903 to 1916, came another 816 males and 275 females. The northern Muslims constituted 14 per cent of the *girmitiyas* out of Calcutta and the southerners 7 per cent of their group. Those from the north were followers of the Hannafi law school of Islam, and the southerners of the Shafi legal tradition, but both were orthodox Sunnis.

Muslims emigrated for the same reasons others did, but there were also some specific circumstances which propelled Muslim emigration, among them the hostility of the British towards Muslims after 1857, and the sporadic outbursts of Hindu communalism against cow-slaughter and the Urdu language. Proportionally more Muslim women than men emigrated, reflecting the harsher impact of adverse conditions on women, especially those who had lost their fathers or their husbands from early marriages or who came from families too impoverished to provide for them. Islam permits emigration from environments inimical to it to one where its followers might practise their faith without harassment. Unfortunately, life in the *girmit* lines did not augur well for any spiritual values; the endless fortitude of individuals provided the only protection.

Traumatic as *girmit* life was, the *girmitiyas* clung tenaciously to those inherited values they deemed essential for their identity. Significantly for them, their religion distinguished them from others. The *girmitiyas* brought with them their way of life, which had been with their families for tens of generations. Hinduism was, of course, indigenous to the land of their birth; Islam arrived much later. In Uttar Pradesh, the Hindu heartland, *Arya-Varta*, in the north, Muslims were about 14 per cent of the population, and in the southern parts even less. Thus the Muslims who came to Fiji already knew the vagaries of being a minority, even when kinsmen of faith ruled India for long periods until 1857. They already possessed the knowledge of preserving their faith in environments and situations of continuous hostility. Strategies for survival were ingrained in their existence. They emigrated knowing the necessity of principled accommodation and reasoned flexibility for co-existence to maintain cultural continuity.

Islam had come to India early after its emergence in Arabia. It arrived with marauding conquerors and fortune-hunters and with seafarers and merchants who spread Islam while engaging in lucrative trade. Muslim missionaries, too, played their part, the Sufis being perhaps the most significant, for, by the 13th century, Sufism had become the movement in India that took Islam to the masses. Muslim *girmitiyas* in Fiji and elsewhere had Islam in their families for about 20 to 30 generations before emigrating. It was a deeply embedded heritage, of many trials, tribulations and triumphs, before appearing in the Pacific. These Muslims and their forefathers had already withstood onslaughts on their faith. Still, they did not relinquish Islam, and those few who strayed temporarily returned later for succour. The *narak*, or hell, of *girmit* was certainly persecution, but it was not an unknown or insurmountable adversity.

Girmit, with its cramped barracks, where women were perpetually insecure and moral values were under assault, with oppressive plantations where over-tasking and physical violence were frequent, where the *sirdars'* greed and the overseers' whips were the rule of law, was branded *narak* by the *girmitiyas*. It was slavery, but not for life; it was an oppressive contract for five years. The impact on human lives of its brutality, its anguish and emotional scarring cannot be underestimated even if its legal servitude and bondage was not for life. The *girmitiyas*, whether Hindu or Muslim, possessed sufficient cultural resources of their own to overcome it, though some, given their individual frailty, succumbed to disease or resorted to suicide. All the evils of plantation capitalism and colonial racism could not destroy the indomitable spirit of Hinduism and Islam, for the *girmitiyas* and their forebears had encountered similar injustices in their homes, mosques and temples for centuries. Five years was a small, albeit important, part of an individual's life, and the years 1879 to 1920, the period of indenture, were a mere passing phase, a transitory moment, in the long history of their faiths and traditions. And, after 1884, in Fiji, having completed their indenture, *girmitiyas* formed free settlements which each year thereafter spread and grew in size, accommodating new ex-*girmitiyas*, thus allowing for the emergence and establishment of Hindu and Muslim communities in which one's religion and its rites and festivals could be followed without obstruction.

Faith, however, was not left to chance. Teaching and socialisation might by force of circumstances be neglected, but they were never abandoned. In the traditional Muslim society of India in the 19th and early 20th centuries, the origins of the *girmitiyas*, Muslims learned enough Arabic to recite *suras* of the holy Koran to pray five times a day, and attend their Friday prayers. Furthermore, in their homes, they were taught key rituals and festivals which sustained Islam in the family and drew Muslims together as a community in their locality. The reality that they prayed in the same way, facing the same direction, gave allegiance to the same holy book, proclaimed Mohammed as the seal of the prophets, and insisted upon the Oneness of God, all made for a faith that could be practised consistently by all community members and this could be done without fanfare, in the home without mosques, if necessary.

Learning could be transmitted orally, and reading and writing could be taught by any knowledgeable faithful. Learning was desired and shared. For instance, in Rewa in 1887, Waleyat Hussein gave free lodging to Mokdum Buksh so that the latter could teach him Arabic. My maternal grandfather, Rustam Khan, born probably in 1885 in Rewa, knew Arabic sufficiently to recite the *suras* of the holy Koran and the *duas* (supplications to Allah). He and his brother, Nure Abdul Khan, knew English; the latter was among the founding members of the Fiji Muslim League. It was my grandfather who first read me English stories, and the simplified version of Defoe's *Robinson Crusoe* seems for ever etched in my mind. I did not know then, as I do now, that the tale owes its origins to Ibn Tufail's story of Hai bin Yagzan, translated as *The Journey of the Soul* (The Octagon Press, London, 1982). I do not think that source was known to my grandfather, otherwise he would have told me. Interestingly, it was my son, Hashim, who enlightened me and gave me a copy of the translation.

There were some Muslim *girmitiyas* who were educated, as evidenced by letters they wrote in Urdu to the local authorities and to families in India. My paternal grandfather, Nawab Ali, an intrepid Pathan, apparently corresponded in Urdu with his mother. His eldest son, Nur Ali, born in Fiji in 1903, became a *moulvi* (Muslim priest/teacher), fluent in Urdu and Arabic, enabling him to do extensive missionary work among Muslims in Tavua. My grandfather was also making arrangements for his younger son, Rahmat Ali, to go to India to train as a *moulvi* to propagate Islam in Fiji when the hardy *girmitiya* died unexpectedly in 1937. As for my uncle, he went on to serve Fiji with distinction in another endeavour. When, in the 1960s, golf courses in Fiji removed their whites-only membership rules, my uncle Rahmat, by then a skilled plumber, became one of Fiji's outstanding golfers, winning several championships and successfully representing Fiji at the South Pacific Games. He went to India in 1973 to play golf, and used his mother's *girmit* pass to get a contribution from the Fiji Government for his air fares. He shared his passion for sports generously, teaching his sons and nephews skills in cricket and golf. And he could read the Arabic of the holy Koran, which he learnt in Suva.

Learning about Islam, its prayers and its values, celebrating its festivals, reciting the holy Koran and reading it in Arabic, were all part of a Muslim's educational experience. He or she began learning through the socialising process at home and in a mosque school, which in the early days, as in Suva in 1898, was a clean room in a house, or even under the shade of a tree. This obligation of the *girmitiyas* to their children was considered a religious duty, hence the emphasis on education from the very beginning. Knowledge of one's faith perpetuated one's faith and one's primary identity, which was for Muslims their religious identity. Budhan Khan and Salar Bux from the *Leonidas* (1879) believed in this as much as Abdul Karim from the *Poonah* (1883) and those who came after them. And, in all this, the women *girmitiyas*, as wives and mothers, from northern as well as southern India, played their indispensable role. Without the unwavering devotion of these women to Islam, their inculcating of the initial religious learning and their subsequent supervision and encouragement in the home and in the family, there would have been no Islam or Islamic culture in Fiji today. In the formal learning agenda, it was not just Arabic and Islamiyat that Muslim *girmitiyas* considered essential. They wanted Urdu to be taught to all Muslim children, and in its Persian script. Urdu was their heritage, indistinguishable from their Islamic culture. The Muslim *girmitiyas* tenaciously held that, in Professor Mohammed Mujeeb's words, 'survival of the Indian Muslims in a culturally recognisable form is directly linked up with Urdu'.[1] Hence the persistent plea of Fiji's Muslims for Urdu taught in the Persian script, a demand emphasised to Fiji's first Education Commission in 1909, and repeated ever since. This pressure has ensured the availability of Urdu in our schools to this day and for all our public examinations — a considerable achievement for a minority. It is taught in all schools run by the Fiji Muslim League. To this day, Urdu is used in meetings of the Fiji Muslim League; there is social pressure on participants to speak it, even if they

have to intersperse their comments with words from English.
Urdu remains for many Muslims in Fiji their language, separating
them from other communities which trace their origins to India.

Life was not all work and learning. Festivity and celebration
were also present. The realities of existence dictated some
interaction and exchange for satisfying social and economic
needs. The observance of religious festivals and participation in
them became important facilitators of social contact. In August
1882, Fiji's Acting Agent-General of Immigration, Henry Anson,
visiting Taveuni, was told by Hindu and Muslim *girmitiyas* that
they wanted to celebrate their religious festivals as holidays.
Muslims asked for three: a day for Prophet Mohammed or *uemon
nabi*, or *milad-un-nabi*, *milad* as it became popularly known; *eid ul
zoha* or *bakr'id*, and *Mohurram*.

Mohurram and *Holi* were public holidays on all the
plantations of the British Empire. *Mohurram* was celebrated with
gusto in Fiji by Hindus and Muslims alike, as in the Indian
countryside. It is a Shi'a festival, adopted by Sunnis but without
Shi'a rituals. Celebrations in Fiji involved music and building tall
paper edifices, called *tazias*, taken in processions to the seaside. In
1887, it was reported that Indians in Rewa enjoyed three days of
feasting during *Mohurram*. There were boisterous celebrations in
Penang and Ba in 1901, and Labasa in 1902. In January 1914, the
Governor, garlanded with frangipani flowers, and from under a
canopy, briefly graced *Mohurram* revelry in Suva, on the swampy
Muanivatu flats. *Mohurram* aroused and sustained Islamic
consciousness among Muslims, but when it became a non-
religious commercial carnival, Muslim objections had it
discontinued. Other festivals were not officially recognised, but
Muslims observed them as time and resources permitted initially,
and with religious regularity subsequently. *Bakr'id* was at first
celebrated quietly as it involved animal sacrifice, then openly as
in Navua by 1894 and earlier in Nausori and Suva. From 1900
onwards, it was common practice among those who could afford

it to buy an appropriate sacrificial goat or even cattle; the sacrifice was performed individually or within an extended family, preceded by congregational prayers.

Uemon nabi or *milad* was initially confined to families, performed outside the *girmit* lines in the open, and in small groups. It fostered community bonds and kept alive the spirit of Islam. With the arrival of Muslims from Malabar after 1903, *milad* received added impetus. By 1912, the southern Muslims had a *Rateeb Ghar* in Wairuru, Ra, and *milad's* permanence was established in Fiji. The significance of *milad* is best captured in the words of the late Haji Moidean Ahmed, formerly President of the Maunatul Association of Fiji, the national organisation of our southern Muslims, when he said: 'Milad gatherings were the most important events in the history of Islam in Fiji because this was the only activity which collected the Muslims together and kept their *iman* [faith] in place.'

Muslims are also required to observe the Ramadan fast. This was near impossible for those serving *girmit*, but some Muslims did fast, as oral evidence from later *girmitiyas* suggests. Individual observance occurred well before it was possible to hold community prayers of *eid-ul-fitr*, the feast which marks the end of fasting. But that came when, on Sunday 12 January, 1902, Mulla Mirza Khan led the *eid-ul-fitr* prayer in the Nausori mosque, filled with 500 Muslims from Rewa. As the 20th century came on Fiji, Muslims and Islam were already comfortable in their new island home.

The celebration of these festivals allowed Muslims to take an annual census of their community members, which was useful for socio-religious visits and invitations, and for arranging marriages and taking collections for religious projects. The role of observing these festivals was critical in sustaining Islamic consciousness among Muslims in a new environment in which there was no previous tradition of Islam and where outward signs and symbols of Islam took time to emerge. These celebrations,

however, were confined to Muslims, though on occasions they
involved some social contact with Hindus. Islam in Fiji existed in
the ethnically compartmentalised world of colonialism.
Ironically, this enforced separation and isolation might even have
protected it from the hostility and interference of others. There
was no interaction with the sizeable and vigorous indigenous
community, who neither favoured nor welcomed the indentured
labourers, viewing them as a colonial imposition.

The world of *girmit* was generally an unexpected, strange
and traumatic one for the new arrivals and the first-time
girmitiyas tended to be inward-looking and absorbed with their
own ordeals. The predicament of single mothers provides apt
illustration. The ship, *Hereford*, which arrived in Fiji on 24 April,
1888, landed 538 immigrants, among them 44 Muslims — 28
males and 16 females. Of the females, two were single mothers
from Bihar, one with two children, another with three. Dawlatea,
aged 30, from Shahabad, came with her daughter Etwarea, aged
12 years, son Khedaroo, aged eight years, and another daughter,
Joomia, aged three, all fathered by Boolaki. The other single
mother, Nasibiya, aged 32, came from Gaya, with two daughters,
Ajmi, aged seven years, and another, aged two years, both
fathered by Chulkon. Two other Muslim women, aged 20 and 25,
were accompanied by their husbands. Of the remaining eight,
three claimed to have no next of kin, one gave her nephew and
the other a cousin as next of kin. It might be concluded that of
the 16 Muslim women who came on the *Hereford* only the two
with their husbands were part of an intact family; the rest came
from homes without husbands or fathers, thus without male
income-earners. Dawlatea and Nasibiya returned to India with
their children; Dawlatea on 14 May, 1895, and Nasibiya on 29
June, 1891, without completing her initial contract of five years.

On arrival in Fiji, Dawlatea had her daughter Etwarea
married off to Kallaim, who, then aged 13, had come earlier to
Fiji with his mother Shahula (aged 30 years) and his younger

brother Phell Khan, aged five years, on the *Bayard* (1883). When Dawlatea left Fiji in 1895, she took Etwarea, by then 19 years old, to India with her. Etwarea's husband Kallaim (now aged 24 years) remained in Fiji with his mother and brother. Dawlatea's and Etwarea's decision indicates that Dawlatea was unwilling to abandon her daughter without any family in Fiji. Etwarea's willingness to leave her husband and accompany her mother suggests that she felt the security her mother offered was greater than that her husband might have been able to provide in Fiji. Further, what became a temporary marriage was obviously arranged to protect Etwarea by providing her with a husband rather than leaving her prey to other men. This story reflects the precariousness of relationships during *girmit*, of acute uncertainty and insecurity. But not all the Muslim women who came on the *Hereford* returned. Some stayed and made Fiji their new home, and there is evidence of two of them marrying and remaining and raising families there.

The pattern, however, of single-mother families was not set with the *Hereford*. It was apparent from the outset, with the arrival of the very first indenture ship, the *Leonidas*, on 15 May, 1879, which had 104 Muslims (63 males, 41 females) out of the 498 who embarked at Calcutta; the Muslims being nearly 21 per cent of that shipload, much higher than their overall proportion in the total. Among the *Leonidas* passengers was 30-year-old Azimiah from Azamghar, who came with three sons and returned home on the *Hereford* with only one of them. Her infant son of 14 months barely survived a year and died in June 1880, while she was serving her *girmit* on Taveuni. Her eldest son, Jehangir, remained in Fiji when she left only to be killed in unusual circumstances in February 1899. At the time, he was in Suva, apparently unemployed and died of his injuries after being beaten or run over by a sulky. Three men were charged with his murder but were acquitted. Only Ozeer, who was too young to be indentured when he came, returned with his mother.

For single mothers, life in the indenture system was precarious. The experience of the Muslim woman, Montoorni, provides an apt example. Aged 24 years and from Ghazipur, she came with her brother Bootun (aged 30 years) and his wife Bhogmonea, on the *Berar*, the second indenture ship, in June 1882, along with her son Sookai, nine years old, and seven-year-old daughter Jomuni. Jomuni died before Montoorni, who herself fell victim to phitisis in December 1891, while working for the CSR in Yalalevu, Ba. By then, Montoorni had completed her first *girmit* and was in Nausori where, on 26 November, 1888, she gave birth to a girl who died of diarrhoea on 10 January, 1889. Her son Sookai returned alone to India on the *Hereford* in July 1894. His mother's brother Bootun and his wife had already left for India on the *Moy* on 14 May, 1889, before completing their full term for a free return passage.

In the early years, the *gimitiyas* were severely affected by the depressed economic conditions in Fiji of the 1880s, though by then many were staying on. By the beginning of 1900, it was clear that just as *girmitiyas* in other colonies were establishing new homes as permanent settlers, they were doing the same in Fiji. The building of mosques (in Navua in 1900; Labasa, 1902; Toorak, Suva, 1919), seeking places for obligatory congregational prayers, and requesting burial grounds for Muslims, all signalled permanent residence in Fiji.

Critical to the continuity of the religious culture and identity of immigrants is the institution of marriage. That institution, perhaps more than any other, was under daily threat and repeated assault in the *girmit* lines and plantations. That it survived owes nothing to European overseers and most Indian *sirdars*; its success testifies to the courage and tenacity in the religious values of the female *girmitiyas*. Religious marriages for those under *girmit* were not recognised, de facto relationships were the accepted norm and, in many cases, these proved enduring and stable partnerships. Those who came from India married and who were husbands and wives of identical faith would normally have been married according to religious rites. *Girmit* led to several partnership-marriages across the religious divide. This fascinating field still awaits detailed research and analysis.

Of those Muslims who came with families, Professor Brij Lal informs us that there were 406 husband and wife types, 68 two-parent families with children, 73 single mothers, four single fathers and 26 groupings of some other kind.[2] This is helpful in enabling us to conclude that there were sufficiently large numbers of Muslim families likely to have children who would perpetuate settlements begun by their parents for consolidating the Muslim *ummah* in Fiji. Some returned to India, others remained, some finding land to continue farming, others doing labouring jobs in towns emerging near plantations, sugar mills and administrative centres during the 1879-1919 *girmit* period. Some who came alone took partners for life and began families from which many of us are descended.

Let me share my analysis of two ships, both out of Calcutta. Of the 66 Muslims who arrived on the *Ganges* in 1899, there were six married couples. Of four subsequent marriages involving partners from the same ship, in three instances Muslims married Muslims, in the fourth, a Muslim woman married a Hindu/Thakur from the Korociriciri plantation, where both were indentured. There were also 13 marriages with people who came on other ships; there were four Muslim-Muslim marriages and nine Muslim-Hindu marriages. Turning to the *Virawa* (1902), of the 17 Muslim women from it who married in Fiji, only seven took Muslim husbands. The urgency for a single woman was to find a male protector. Many women, including Muslim women, preferred the security of a partnership with a male of another religion to the risks of physical and moral violence, endemic in the *girmit* lines, and frequently the unpleasant fate of unattached women. My maternal grandmother, who was born in Fiji about 1900, when *girmit* was in full sway, frequently told me of the great fear of fathers for their young daughters and the haste to find them husbands to care for them, hence the early marriages of girls.

The strength of their faith and the fortitude of Muslim *girmitiyas* in Fiji are borne by their resistance to suicide. Fiji's indenture plantations had the highest suicide rates of the Empire's plantations. Again, using Professor Brij Lal's data, only 16 Muslims succumbed to it, out of a total of 212; the lowest rate compared with those of specific Hindu castes. For Muslims, suicide defies Divine Law, and is forbidden.[3]

Muslims and others resisted the depredations of *girmit* and protested against its iniquities when the opportunity arose or circumstances dictated. The British were wary of Muslims as a category, though in 1908, the Agent General of Immigration expressed sympathy for their concerns and contemplated assistance for the community. In the 1886 strife with their labourers, some employers feared a massacre during *Mohurram* celebrations, when they considered religious fervour would escalate – shades of India, 1857, a British mind-set not entirely absent in Fiji. In 1903, after a riot in the Fiji Depot in Calcutta, six *girmitiyas* arriving on the *Mersey* were repatriated on the same ship, five of them Muslims. In 1913, the Fiji authorities had difficulties: five Pathans, who had registered in Madras, claimed to have been misled about the nature of work on their recruitment in India. The group was broken up and the five reassigned to different estates.

The most noteworthy strike occurred in April 1907 in Labasa, involving mostly Pathans and a few Punjabis. Of the five leaders, Khan Zaman, Zerdad, Mahi and Budha were Muslim and Ganda Singh was a Punjabi. They claimed that they had been told in India they would not do manual labour but be employed by the Government or as domestic servants. They complained that their rations were insufficient and the food was unsuitable and poor in quality, while their wages were inadequate and their working hours long and accompanied by ill-treatment. There was unruliness and the risk of rioting and the 60 strikers were shifted to Suva, disbanded and distributed to different plantations. According to CSR overseer Leslie Pring of Labasa, the removal of Pathans and Muslim Punjabis from Labasa to Suva was for the best, but it was 'quite unnecessary to have sent the Hindu Punjabis'. He added: 'We always have difficulty in working Mussalmans but none in working Hindus.'[4] The Government and CSR also wanted no further recruiting of Pathans and Punjabis. Nevertheless, considerably more Pathans came as indentured labourers than designations on the indenture passes of Muslims suggest. *Girmit* could not curb the Pathans' will for independence.

Despite the risks, dangers and assaults on its integrity, the institution of marriage survived, without religious rites but as a genuine bond of lasting attachment and durable companionship, often across religious lines. Women willingly brought up their children in their husband's faith, even when this was different from their own, and simultaneously, albeit tacitly, retained their own. The role of these broad-minded and faithful wives was critical, indeed indispensable, in preserving the cherished past of Hindus and Muslims. They were the communicators of the cultures of their husbands to their children, their first teachers, the primary agents of essential socialising processes. They were many, honest and devoted, not the stereotypes painted by prejudiced missionaries, officials and planters, who sought to diminish the iniquities of a brutal system by denigrating its victims. It is to these women, who had learnt their faith and cultural ways from their mothers and families, that we owe the preservation of our religious and cultural values; they bequeathed to us an enviable legacy of tolerance and cross-cultural understanding, which we have not always acknowledged adequately and have sometimes betrayed, to our own disadvantage.

Besides keeping rituals and celebrating festivals, Muslims organised community projects to preserve unity and identity. These became evident in the creation of formal organisations for fund-raising and realising community objectives. Anjuman Hidayat Islam was formed in 1915 in Nausori, Anjuman Ishait El Islam in Lautoka in 1916 and Anjuman-e-Islam in 1919 in Suva, which was the basis for the nation-wide Fiji Muslim League, founded in Suva in 1926, and to this day the voice of most Sunni Muslims. The driving forces of these organisations were former *girmitiyas* and their sons and daughters.

Recognition also needs to be accorded to two Muslim interpreters and clerks who came from India to work for the Government and who contributed immensely to the upliftment of Muslims in Fiji. They were Abdul Aziz Khan and Mirza Salim Buksh. Khan became a successful businessman and the first president of the Fiji Muslim League at its inauguration in Suva in 1926. Mirza Salim Buksh retired from government service and later became the president of the Fiji Muslim League and was nominated to the Legislative Council as a Muslim representative by the Governor in the 1940s.

There were others as, throughout *girmit*, men emerged as leaders in matters of religion and community and cultural advancement. Pride in their faith and identity lay deep in their soul, crafted by the processes of a history in which struggle and success were inseparable twins, and despair distant and rare. Mulla Mirza Khan, Nasrullah Shah, Tawhir Khan (Lautoka) and Amir (Navua) are a few of them. The excellent contributions of very many Muslim *girmitiyas*, men and women, are memories, not consigned to written records, but always remembered by their friends, families and descendants. Whenever we commemorate their arrival, we recall their names and work, and their interaction with the country to which they had come to seek a secure livelihood.

Muslims adhered to their faith because, as some *girmityas* related, it was their faith that rescued them from the traumas of *girmit*, which Indians had reason to view as *narak* (hell). Hell, while a physical condition in *girmit's* brutal and violent system, was also a spiritual/moral state in which solace was found in faith — though Islam contends it is somewhat late to seek God when one is already assigned to perdition. But *girmit's narak* was man-made and the Divine could remove it and provide release for the sufferer caught unwittingly in its pernicious guiles, as many *girmityas* belatedly claimed. The *girmityas* used the comforting cloak of their traditional beliefs and values, and perceived in their retention the means of survival in situations where despair was always uncomfortably close. The symbiotic relationship between a Muslim and Islam in the pit of *girmit's narak* is perhaps best conveyed in the words of poet-philosopher Alama Mohammed Iqbal: 'At critical moments in their history it is Islam that has saved Muslims and not vice versa.'

At the end of *girmit*, Islam had anchored itself firmly in Pacific soil. Islam's survival guaranteed, Muslims strove to constitute a community which, in a colonial multicultural context, would ensure the security of livelihood and the fulfilment of aspirations of its members, individually and collectively. In 1920, the future was one of hope, and challenges.

NOTES

[1] Mujeeb, M. 1967. *The Indian Muslims*. London. p. 561.
[2] Lal, Brij V. 1983. *Girmityas. The Origins of Fiji Indians*. Canberra. p. 125.
[3] Lal, Brij V. 2000. 'Veil of Dishonour.' In Brij V. Lal, *Chalo Jahaji: A Journey through indenture in Fiji*. Canberra. pp. 215-38. This is the only detailed study of suicide among indentured labourers in Fiji.
[4] Colonial Secretary's Office File (CSO): No 2161 of 1907.

A family planting cane, Vunimoli, Labasa.
Cane farming is generally a family affair.

CHAPTER FIVE

Parlay Poems for the Indentured

Mohit Prasad

I.

In cold rasping of file on steel
Shredding steel each morning
at the same one hour of ritual
to mark onset of field tasking
taking the mark of raw sickle
pressing into warm salty hide
branding furrows on that soil
width by width scooped wave
breaking into crests for ratoon
seeking to break free of roots
the search for the mood moon
to answer why a hacked child
was part of the need for blood.

II.

Pidgin words fell as webs from rafters
A raft for red creased corrugated roof
A child left alone in the Line worded
fields in the mix of screamed tongues
with other children growing too fast
in the island erased differences whip
over steady whip floated easy sounds
of vowels pitter-pattered as wooden toys
whittled from stray wood until all spoke.

III.

On the plantation there was one song
And plenty musician jump starting legs
and arms in the warm swish of switches
when sun swilled down over bungalows
and crickets click clacked on verandahs
goat hide stretched tight on cored wood
burnt at edges for thudding of the rhythm
that washed up a jungle and dried ravine
into embers punkah awoken in a corner
where three men from four places
drank slowly kava and sang sadly
loss of liberty, homeland and women.

IV.

Smudges of red veiled threat to soiled morning
Haphazard the cold cut of a siren yelling clock
Hammered into foreheads with a pass number
The familiarity of the body with hour minutes
Stretching to pause beneath grey wire netting
Tying up of a stretch of dun unbleached linen
Holding up cores and limbs and eggs in place
Breath upon warm breath stealing of a woman
Alternate dawn and dusk tasking among men
Divine muttering flushed by water from chalice
Placed among idols on brown oil polished shelf.

V.

Handrails etched into Syrian hands
Warm from much gleeful rubbing
Of anticipated early morn landfall
After too many sea kept mornings
Fell foul of claw hook-rigged reef
snagged firm barnacled green keel
Among gay electric blue swift fish
Much shouting of shrill lead voices
Broke the flat sea glass faced death
Arms fell cold in chilled killer swell
Landlubbers sank in sifted black sand
Soles dragging across raw coral cuts
The island bows stiff cupped welcome.

VI.

For Tarscissus

Shared words spiced the mash of root crops.
Spread across plantain leaves on Saturday
Evening much welcomed for some respite
Slow clapping of palms chaffed on sandy
Husks gripped and ripped for white core
Pressed into oil and soap-scented package
An alms shank of pork boils in its lard
Intricate inlaid pearl shells in split canoes
Quaffed in smoke a distant lost memory
in ornamentation of weapons and spoons
For men from Ugi and San Christobal
After the *Emerald* punished the slaying
Of *Sandfly* coming from Sydney all way
To sermon cheering of Melanesian Mission
And labour traders chewed more tobacco
At the desk where agreements were signed
And men cargoed into the night to Fiji.

VII.

Harrowed this line from blue books of history
Danced its way into blown copper pot mystery
Master of a cabinet sculled a ship fitted in iron
Manacles wrought deep in thickets of tree trunks
Armed with the bite of gunpowder in tin cases
And glittering trinket cast-offs from glass blowers
Waste sewn and threaded by lascars between
Ships and shifts as fly ridden port Madagascar
Bow scraped against by a shark in love with snake
In the western port removed of wandering tribes
Gunshot to dreamtime of iron wrought edgings
And blow down shutters on wooden verandahs
Dots and circles on a rock face wept for clouds.

A suburb of the sugar city of Lautoka where Kanti Jinna worked for many years at the Western Regional Library.

CHAPTER SIX

Dada: *Bhaga to Dillon*

Kanti Jinna

BHAGA (SHORT FOR BHAGWAN), was 33 when he ventured out with two relatives, Makan and Manchu, on a boat trip to Fiji from Calcutta via Auckland. On reaching Suva and going through the usual quarantine rituals at Nukulau Island, he did some casual work with a barbershop in Cumming Street before deciding to work for himself. His open-air shop was at the Renwick Road end of the Morris Hedstrom columnar verandah along Nabukalou Creek. His tools, drapery and chair were deposited each night at Bhulabhai's tailoring shop at 7pm after a day's work which began at six in the morning. A room shared with two others above the current Wahley's Butchery in Cumming Street was where, as the eldest, Dada took charge of the cooking. Having tasted his cooking in later years, I can say that his room-mates were lucky.

Some 22 years later, when we shared accommodation at Desai Book Depot, where I was working to pay school fees and for school uniforms while at Marist Brothers High School, I asked Dada why he had come to Fiji. Before, whenever my brothers and I went to stay with him in Morristar (MH Compound), Lautoka, his one answer, which I believe was a shared vision of the day among many Gujaratis and surely a primary mission of most itinerant workers everywhere, was *paysa kamawa* — to earn money. The money was needed to sustain the family in India, to pay debts and to sponsor immediate relatives to Fiji. Bhaga Dada died in Vesma in 1962 on his second trip back to India, having fulfilled his obligations.

Youngest of the three sons of Parag, Bhaga was born in the village of Vesma, in the District of Surat, Gujarat, in 1896. His elder brothers, Madhu and Karson, had already started their traditional profession as barbers under the direction of their grandfather, Lakhu, going from house to house to earn their keep. Most of their payment was in grain, other food products and clothing, with the occasional cash payment, and there was a bit of land, too, on which they grew their subsistence crops. There was a bit more to be earned when they shaved a dead buffalo (for the skinners and leather-makers), although this task was usually given to women, and as *khandias* (pall-bearers) the young *nayees* (barbers) carried the dead to the cremation grounds. This was a job the young ones liked to do because there were a few bottles of toddy (fermented palm wine) and/or *desi daru* (country liquor) provided as a bonus when they reached the cremation grounds. But the job my grandfather enjoyed most was playing *dhol* (two drums beaten with sticks) as an accompaniment to the *shehnai* (wind instrument like a clarinet) when he was invited to weddings to provide music at strategic moments during the ceremony.

Bhaga, like all the young men in the village, was betrothed at the ripe young age of eight to be married off to Ramiben from the village of Sonwadi. The marriage was consummated when Rami was 14. Their first-born, my aunt, was called Lakhmi, and she was born in Sonwadi at my grandmother's. There were two boys, Jinna (the closest spelling to the correct name in Gujarati meaning younger one) and Nanu (meaning smaller one), and two more girls, Mangi (born on Tuesday) and Bhikhi (one who was born after many penances were performed to have another child, hopefully another boy). I have no record of my *dada* (grandfather) ever having gone to school.

Bhaga Dada's love for music and moving around from village to village, sleeping at railway stations, drinking toddy in clay pots at the local drinking huts, and smoking *bidis* (hand-wrapped tobacco leaves) would have given him an adventurous and individualistic character, which would have inspired him to look for *pardes* (another country), but this was to happen only after he had fulfilled his family obligations. None of my grandfather's siblings ever ventured overseas.

It was during his travels that two significant things happened in my grandfather's life. He met and heard about people from the villages of Surat and Navsari who had made boat trips to foreign lands where they could earn lots of money and free themselves from the awful debt they had inherited from previous generations. It was the custom that debts were carried and honoured by subsequent generations, to be paid in most cases by the eldest male child or by the one who had the means to pay it off. A family's *izzat* (honour) depended on their progeny, as did their ability to remove the yoke of eternal.

The second significant event in my grandfather's life was that he met my maternal grandfather at a drink-fest after a wedding, where he had gone to a 'gig'. He wanted to polish off a few clay pots of toddy and get away to the railway station, sleep on the platform and rest until it was time to catch the train home. It was essential that you took your *bistar*, bed-roll, with you when travelling. But his plans went askew when he was invited to a small meal at Chhana Jeram's house and was asked to stay the night there. They were of the same *jat*, caste. To their mutual joy, it was discovered that both my grandmothers were pregnant and, because they had struck up a friendship, what better way to seal a relationship than to promise a betrothal if the issues were of separate sexes. Bhaga Parag and Rami's son Jinna was born in Vesma and Chhana Jeram and Dhanki's daughter Ganga was born in Narod (two miles from Maroli, where the wedding and the railway station was).

In 1933, Dada brought his 16-year-old son, my father, to
Fiji. My father was married, but had to leave his wife behind,
which led to bitter conflicts between him, my grandfather and
my father's cousins. But my father was not alone in this
predicament. Like him, there were many young men who lived as
'married bachelors' in Fiji (colonial immigration laws did not
permit wives to join their husbands in the colonies). Alone,
isolated and with plenty of time on their hands, the men devised
ways of entertaining themselves. *Natak* (theatrical) groups were
formed in towns such as Suva and Ba where there was a
concentration of Gujaratis. The first play in Suva was *Bharthari*,
which had created a history of its own on the Gujarati stage in
India. The sacred name of Yogiraj, later Raja Bharthari, portrays
the quality of asceticism, penance and sacrifice. After many of
life's disillusionments, he disassociates himself from all the joys
(including his queen Rani Pingla) and sorrows of life and attains
Shiva Tatva and many of the virtues of Buddhism, including the
role of mendicant. So big was the emotional impact of this play
that many men gave up the worldly family life and sought *sanyas*
(renunciation). My father was given the part of Raja Bharthari
and he did not escape this impact and decided to take *sanyas*,
much to the annoyance of Dada and my uncles. He was literally
manhandled and forced to get my mother across to Fiji as soon as
it was legally possible. Ganga Ben arrived in Suva in early 1938.

With the arrival of Ba (Mother), life began stabilising
between my parents and the immediate family, consisting of
grandfather, uncles and cousins. A barbershop for sale in Jhandighar
(Flagstaff) was bought with money from savings and loans based on
jabaan (promise). Soon a little room was rented across the road
behind the current Bhura and Jokhan Service Station. Not much
later, at the end of January 1939, their first-born, Kanti, arrived,
with the talk of war in the air and more hard times to come. The
spirit of adventure and the lust for gold and riches in the distant
towns of Tavua and Vatukoula took my parents out of Suva for

a couple of years, but wealth was just as elusive there and they returned with their second son, Raman, this time to live in Samabula, in Sukhu Mahajan's building on Kings Road.

Samabula became home for the Jinna family for 45 years. The first 15 years were spent in our two-room house next to Ning Soong 'Chaina', Ram Roop Tailor, Shiw Kumar 'Nau' and his talkative and charismatic son Chandra Bhan Pande, and Malitch Baba (Kewal Doho — 'old man' — who had gone on the Salt March to Dandi with Mahatma Gandhi), with immediate neighbours Rama & Sons. In the next storey above Ning Soong stayed Eroni Vuli, his wife Setaita, their daughter Emma, who kept writing love poems to me, and their son Setariki. I still treasure Emma's autograph ('Some love one, some love two, but I love one, and that is you'). One neighbour, Tomasi Vakatora, later became a distinguished public figure in Fiji as a co-architect of Fiji's multiracial 1997 constitution. Retired Sargeant Ram Jag and his two wives had a greengrocers' shop across the road in Ramessar Building; Chooti ('ant') had his tailoring shop next to him. Upstairs in the building stayed my schoolmate Henry Sokimi, who spoke Samoan and Rotuman. Some Sunday evenings, Henry's little brothers, sisters and cousins used to sing songs and perform *mekes* (Fijian action songs), wearing paper *salusalus* (garlands) around their necks and a string of leaves around their tiny waists, on our verandah to earn a penny each for their ice blocks. I still remember '*e tei na fakalele ma koya, e tuku mai kela ka uwe*'. Hari Prasad Pathak, who ran the dart-board stall next to the *jhuluwa*, a locally made ferris wheel, during the *Ram Lila* to raise money for the temple, was our Pitaji (father) and his wife Amma (mother) and their daughters, Jogmati and Benmati lived on the Main Kings Road further up, where my friend, nicknamed 'Pushtai', lived in a Pathak-owned two-storey building. One seldom called anyone by name. It was always respectfully *masterji, mausi, anna, tacina, jahaji* or *Khan Saheb* and we greeted everyone with a *Bula, Dasanam, Ram Ram, Salaam Veilokum* or *Sat Sri Akal* (cultural greetings).

Samabula was Suva's non-commercial hub of activity in
the 1940s. It was a microcosm of a truly multicultural community,
each proud of its own heritage and tradition, but not letting that
stand in the way of amicable interaction. We all felt an integral
part of the community. That kind of spirit and togetherness and
tolerance, of understanding and acceptance, is now gone, but not
the memories, and the experiences that enriched our lives.

The Shiu Mandir Bhavan lay behind us and the annual
Ram Lila was a grand affair attracting thousands. Rawan's army
never had a chance against the red army of Ram because there
was no one who wanted to wear black and be on the loser's side.
Many a time we donned the red shirt to be a monkey with
Hanuman, acted by Mahabir Swamy, who started the day's
episode by *aarti* and swallowing a cube of burning camphor.
Samabula was a Sanatan Dharam enclave. The Sikh Gurudwara
was a must-visit every Sunday at noon because at the end of the
readings of the *Guru Granth Saheb*, Hawaldar, or another member
of the Prabandhak Committee, would scoop up a huge handful of
halwa dripping with ghee and plonk it into our eagerly waiting
hands. Bhaiji Channan Singh 'Kanwal' and Hawaldar had a shop
a few doors up our end of the street and there was always a lolly or
two for *Jinneh di mundiya* (Jinna's children) whenever we went
across to purchase some groceries. The Muslim *masjid* was
another sacred edifice constructed by the Muslim League and
their land, like the property of the Hindus and Sikhs, was
provided by the Colonial Government after the various religious
groups made representations. Religious harmony prevailed in
the community. Our Muslim neighbours, M. T. Khan and his
brothers, Mohammed Taiyab Khan and Bob Khan, made sure
that a bowl of *sewai* was sent to Jhinna(h) Bhai at Eid, with the
occasional pound or two of goat meat if there was some to spare.

On the learned end of Samabula were the educationist
Arya Samajis, such as Pandit Ami Chand Vidyalankar, who
wrote the Hindi Primers we read at school — *Hindi ki Pahli Pothi,*

etc. We all loved the poem: *Dum dumma dum dum, Dhol bajaye hum, Nache kude hum, dum dumma dum dum.* My favourite, though, was *Do pahiye ki cycle, daur dikhati khel, dena parta hai nahi, is me pani tel.* Close to his home was Pandit Gopendra Narayan Pathik and further still several Arya Samaji homes that contributed pupils to the Arya Kanya Pathshala (AKP – girls' school). Many events took place at the school. Every Sunday there was the *havan*, where the orange-turbaned leaders of the Arya Samaj congregated. There you saw legendary leaders such as Vilayati Ram, J. P. Maharaj, Dr Ram Lakhan, Thakur Kundan Singh and, occasionally, Pandit Vishnu Deo.

AKP had two items of interest for me. I observed that older boys were attracted to girls, because they paraded in good numbers to participate in the Sunday *hawan*, *kirtan* and cultural items that followed. The second interest was in the kindergarten room, which was transformed into an *akhada* (training place) two times a week and in which some of Fiji's top wrestlers — Tiger Shankar, Roshan Singh, Nanka Singh and Kupp-Swami — trained to retain their various 'belts'. My brother Raman and I used to turn up each week at our father's behest to become fearless fighters. Our main task each week was to *dund pilo* — sit-ups and presses 50 times — and later massage the champion wrestlers. We knew when we switched to using pig fat (*suwar ke charbi*) instead of other scented oils that there was going to be a match against the arch enemies in Sabeto and Ba, the dreaded 'Khans'.

Then there was the 'Sangam', the cultural organisation of the southern Indians. At the Sangam Hall, one could hear the *shehnai, tasa, dhol* and other percussion instruments being played some evenings, with the climax coming once a year with the fire-walking ceremony. Father gave his annual five tons of firewood for the fire-walking ceremony, which earned him a seat near the rope that kept all the spectators at bay. Just when the fire-walkers were about to enter the fire pit, father would be a metre away from the burning hot coals with his hands joined in prayer and his eyes closed. For a few minutes, he was in another world, a devotee of Goddess Shakti Mata.

A hard-working committee member, organiser and devotee, Yangtesh Permal Reddy would assume a key role in all Sangam proceedings. On Saturdays, we saw him as a young entrepreneur bringing in produce and household items from Nausori early in the morning and vending them to eager purchasers in homes. During the week, he attended Samabula Government Boys' School, where 'Master Head' was the great educator and a member of the great Badri Maharaj lineage from Raki Raki, and later Marist Brothers High School. On Sunday nights, Y. P. and Chandrabhan would take me to the Hindi movies at Lilac Theatre. We were a party of six, joined by Babu Bhikha, Ram Adhar and Shiri Kisun. I always admired the ticket-seller, Mr Dalton, and the owner, John Grant, because they all wore suits and black ties. So impressed were we that on one of the picture nights, the six of us went to the photo studio across the road from the theatre, used the studio's ties and coats and had our photo taken.

Samabula had other charms. We had Jolly Brothers, the best soccer team in Fiji, with (Master) Nandlal Bachu, Ran Pal, Parshu and Bachu, who, together with the Sangam players, made up the bulk of the Suva Reps and a good portion of the Fiji team as well. And we had unforgettable characters, such as Kunj Bihari (*Chuttar Bhari* — Big Arse), Ram Din 'Langadwa', because he had a limp (and two wives, Barki and Chotki), and their son Surend 'mutera', who spoke through only one side of his mouth. And the scandal of the year when Parshu Bachu married Sakina, a Muslim girl! *E ka hoi gai* — what was the world coming to! That was the topic for a few nights when the Gujaratis met for their nightly *dairo* (drinks) to relax and exchange news of the events of the day, tell jokes and gossip on our front verandah. Jeraj Nagji, Popat Valji (father of two of the prettiest girls in town and husband of the local version of film critic Babu Rao Patel of Film

India, the know-all of Hindi movies), and the cock-eyed Chaggan Bediya. Everyone had an opinion on just about everything, especially after their nip(s) of whisky or gin, forbidden to 'Sonars'. The whisky or gin was bought by father through his licence to purchase each month one bottle of liquor and a dozen bottles of beer.

Everyone was quiet, however, twice a week for 15 or 30 minutes depending on the day, when the ZJV radio came on and Niranjan Singh was on the air. '*Chupona, chupona, o pyari sajaniya, humse chupona chupona*' (Don't shy away from me, my beloved) was the signal to listen to the only radio in the neighbourhood. Bappa had a 'Bush', which was quite large with an enormous battery to power it. The audience would increase gradually and, when the Fijian program came on, and our Fijian neighbours gathered in our front room, where my parents and my sisters slept on two large beds, our house would be chockers. The night I will never forget was 30 January, 1947, when Kewal Doho and a room full of Indian men sat listening, some crying openly, to the news of the assassination of Mahatma Gandhi, immortalised in Mohammed Rafi's haunting song, *Suno suno e duniya walo, Bapu ki yeh amar kahani* (Listen, o people of the world, to Bapuji's everlasting story).

But all good things must come to an end. We grew up. I had by now had two years at Marist Brothers High School, with classmates such as Bramha Nand Sharma, Manek Vithal, Clive Amputch, James Ah Koy and Dron Rishikesh Prasad, the only one with a watch so he got to ring the school bell. By then, I had had eight years at St Columbus, the non-European section of the Catholic School. St Felix was for the part and full Europeans. James Ah Koy was classified as a Chinese pupil in those days, although he now sits in parliament as a Fijian. In class two, Brother Cormack, the head teacher, allowed my father to distribute *jalebi* and *gulab jamun* (Indian sweets) to the whole school, bought from Musadilal Halwai's shop in Waimanu Road, because I had my *mundan* (head-shaving ceremony) at the age of five. My parents had taken a vow that hair from my first haircut would be sent to Unai Hot Springs in Gujarat. Before I had my head shaved, I had a *churki* and Mother used to plait my hair every day.

In Form Four, at the age of 14, just before I was to sit for the Junior Cambridge Examinations, I took courage and went to my father's barbershop, now called Jinna Bros, in Cumming Street, and asked to talk to him. I asked him if I could become a Catholic. He asked me why. I told him that for the past 10 years we had prayers five times a day at school and I went to the cathedral at times and the school chapel often. He asked me how much I knew about our faith. I told him that I joined him in daily prayers, lit the *diya* each morning and sat with him at the Satya Narayan *kathas* whenever they were held at home. He asked me how much I knew about 'our religion' and I said not much. My father and I made a pact that day. He asked me to study 'our religion' and, when I knew enough, compare it with the Catholic faith and then, if I still wanted to change my religion, he would have no objection. We did not talk about Hinduism or Christianity again, but to this day, my quest continues to find anything that would make me change my faith.

Brothers Placid, Moore, Anthony and Cassian saw some promise in my organising ability. I was made captain of the Marist C Soccer Team in the Suva Soccer League, was put in charge of certain library duties, was part of the school choir, a member of the school debating team, secretary of the school Lambert (then Tasman) House and in charge of stamp collections and accounting for sales and auctions of books, stamps, etc. I believe I had an early introduction to working as a part of a team and accepting responsibility. I consider myself fortunate to have attended Marist from 1952 to 1955 with some of the best students, sportsmen and athletes of Fiji.

My first job was as telephone boy for Viti Taxis, owned and operated by C. P. Bidesi, businessman, politician and social worker extraordinaire. I felt quite empowered, because of my English-speaking ability, to send Yengtaiya or Shiu to jobs that had come from important European customers. My pay, if any, went directly to my father. I worked as a car guard for Burns Philp at the Suva Wharf for 11 shillings and four pence a week, but walked off the job after a month when a co-worker called me a black bastard. I lost a job, he lost a tooth and some blood. The accounts job at the Suva Aerated Water Factory was boring and not as good as my next one as tea boy and messenger for Sir Henry Scott during the school holidays of 1952. I worked for three weeks at five shillings a week and got a bonus of five shillings for having done an excellent job. I always credit the tip to the help I gave to Maurice Scott, his son, in boarding up his home at Laucala Bay during the terrible cyclone of that year. I was given nice cups of tea and food for my services while my father was wandering all over Suva looking for me during the storm.

My father taught me to be proud of who we were and of myself and to always treat everyone as an equal and never to feel inferior. The hairdressing clan has been classed at the verge of the *Vaishyas* and *Sudras varna* in the Hindu caste system. Bappa felt that the *nau* had a very important role to play in the community and it was quite interdependent of all the other occupations. He was an important leader in the Gujarati hairdressing fraternity and often chaired meetings to keep them together, to raise funds to help people in difficulty, and cooperate with each other, especially when it came to setting up charges for various services they performed in the barbershops. He had much more success in making his compatriots feel that they were Maisuria Rajputs (also known as Bhatias). *Hajjam* is a very common term used for barbers in India, but my father and many of his contemporaries postulated a theory, supported by some of my own research, that our forefathers came from an area on the border of Jammu and Himachal Pradesh in India, where they had

a common *kul devi* (family deity) known as Jwalamukhi Mata and
the Gotra shared between Kashyap and Vashist. Maisurias believe
that between 400 and 500 years ago, in a dispute among the
Rajputs, a whole colony of *kshatriyas* fled the land and ended up
in Gujarat, some 500 kilometres away. Not having land and
wanting to settle in a new country, they took to hairdressing.

In 1957, old Mrs Jugnu Singh of Samabula made one of
those noble offerings to a *nau* when she offered her house on 60
perches of Crown land to my father for £500 payable whenever
he had money. My family occupied the home for 30 years. It was
the greatest day in my father's life when he acquired a house of
his own. My parents and their seven children had a roof over
their heads and a patch of land they could call their own after
24 years of toil. For the first time, any intention of returning to
India was for ever banished from my parents' minds. Fiji was their
home ... for good.

I went to study at St Peters College and later Auckland
University College. Y. P. joined me during the first year. We had a
wonderful time together. Auckland was beginning to boom and
the Harbour Bridge had just opened. I had three years there, saw
Billy Graham and 52,000 people at his rally, the numbers
paralleled only by the All Blacks vs British Lions and All Blacks
vs Springboks rugby union matches. Don 'the Boot' was in his
prime. Fiji did not attract such a large crowd, but I did see Paula
Nayacakalou crunch his head on the goal post, score the try and
then faint. After studying for my medical intermediate and many
enjoyable adventures, I returned home in 1959.

S. B. Desai was the first to persuade father to get me to
manage the Lautoka Branch of the Desai Book Depot, with
promises of greater things to come. Father was persuaded by his
peers that joining the Fiji Police directly into the inspectoral
ranks was not a job meant for Gujaratis. There was a similar
argument when I wanted to join Air India as Lautoka Manager,
and again when I was approached by Qantas and CSR. The

message finally sank in in 1964, a month after I was married, that the only way to change my career was to not tell father about it. I was offered a job by Bob Pearce (with Radike Qereqeretabua) in the newly established Library Service in Fiji. Bob and Radike are the two most wonderful individuals I have ever had the pleasure of meeting.

The next 25 years were what Maslow would have described as my having achieved the first step in the hierarchical order. I was earning enough for *roti* (food) and *kapra* (clothes), but not quite the *makaan* (house). With my earliest (and existing) friends in Lautoka, Amrat Morarji, Narayan Narsaiya, Hari Punja, Amratlal Captain and Y. P., we combined with many willing individuals to make our contribution to a changing community through the Jaycees (establishing the Sugar Festival), the Lautoka Hospital Week Committee, the establishment of the Lautoka Gujarati Sports Association, the commencement of the first inter-secondary schools quiz competitions, and, with Surendra Prasad, the Diwali Festival. I also learnt to play tennis and cricket and continued my interest in soccer, as a player and administrator.

The year 1964 was an exciting one. Fiji noted an unprecedented growth in its economy. I was married in March, became a public servant in May, three Ministers of State were appointed to experiment with self-government, universal franchise was introduced and my daughter, Meenakshi, was born in December. Having resisted marriage for 24 years, I was surprised one Sunday afternoon after a cricket match in Nadi to see my parents at the pitch. Looking at me now, one would question my sporting prowess, but many stones ago I kept wicket at various times for the United, Exodus and Sports Cricket Clubs, Lautoka Gujaratis and even made a cameo appearance for the Lautoka XI in the Crompton Cup Competition in Suva one Easter. When did you get in was my question? They answered they had arrived midday to see Maganbhai's daughter, and told me that my engagement had been finalised. They advised me to make my own arrangements to see Jyoti. The wedding date was not finalised, but it would be at the same time as my sister's, sometime early in 1964. The good Lord has been kind to me. Jyoti has been a partner and friend for almost 40 years.

I could be credited with starting World War II when I was born, but that was nothing compared with the actions of James Anthony, my senior at Marist and son of *bara malik* Toma, an old friend of my father, who combined with my customer Apisai Mohammed Tora to lead Fiji's first multiracial strike against an expatriate oil company. There was turmoil everywhere, especially in Suva and Lautoka, and lots of rumblings in Ba and Nadi. In my opinion, the first and symbolically the most important revolution in Fiji came with the riots in Suva. The riots shook the colonial establishment to its core. Without the upheaval that followed, and the ensuing commissions of inquiry and some soul searching by the Colonial Government, there would have been no university for Fiji (and no Library Service of Fiji, I might add), and no real changes in the education and health systems.

My work with the Library Service of Fiji with Radike Qereqeretabua, Bob Pearce, Dennis Edwards and, later, as chief librarian, gave me a variety of experiences in management and administration. Keeping a balance of genders, race, age and progressing the concept of written rather than oral literature and traditions was a challenge I had to share with the University Library, developing and promulgating future plans and convincing the bureaucracy of the importance of and necessity for libraries to provide information and education in a growing Fiji. The mobile libraries, book-box schemes, departmental and branch libraries, took me to various parts of Fiji and overseas and it is heartening to see that some of these institutions established in the early days continue to function so well.

I left Fiji in 1984, when I was able to exercise my option at the age of 45 to take early retirement from the Fiji Public Service.

Localisation had introduced competition, not always merit-based, for senior positions and reduced opportunities for upward mobility or lateral movement for many public servants. Salaries and the taxation system prohibited single-income families from sending their children to tertiary institutions, forcing many Fiji citizens to migrate. I entered the third phase of my life in Canberra 20 years ago this year.

My tryst with Australia started in 1962 when I attented the Jaycees Multinational Conference in Melbourne and met the Thompson family, George, Pat, Wayne, Anne and Christopher, and then travelled to Canberra to meet with the Hughes, Ron, Sheila, Glynnis, Gary and David. Our friendships have continued these four decades and Pat, now a widow, still travels to Canberra to see the rest of her extended family. *Dadi* Pat brings stories of her childhood travels to Rhodesia, her love for her pilot husband, who served in India during the war, and the joys that her growing grandchildren bring her. Uncle Ron and Aunty Sheila share their rich heritage from the Counties of Ireland and the melodies of Carnarvon and Wales. I remember in 1962, Ron took me to a lookout in Canberra and showed me where a lake, 13km long and 35km in circumference, was going to be built. I thought to myself, Canberra being the same size as Suva in population (32,000), that he could really spin a yarn like they did back home in Fiji. When I returned in 1966, sure enough, Lake Burley Griffin was there, full to the brim, and Canberra now had a population of more than 60,000. The population of Canberra has now increased to 320,000. Australia willingly shares its political, social and economic progress with migrants from all over the world. A good educational and social base inculcated by the quality of life and cultural mores in Fiji has helped many a person to settle so well within the multicultural society of Australia.

But it would take a bitter person to say that their love for Fiji has diminished. And it hurts. It really hurts when we hear of coups, bloody or not. It hurts when we hear of a slower than expected progress in the reform of the education and health systems. And it hurts in a different way when the Fiji Sevens lose. It hurts when devastating floods and cyclones hit the islands causing damage and taking lives, and when the needy cannot be helped. It hurts when age-old problems associated with land remain unresolved. I will always miss Fiji; the mixed smell of heat, soil and moisture after a passing shower, the cacophony of barks and howls of dogs taking turns to provide a continuous orchestrated noise throughout the night, the laughter and yells of young boys and girls starting in low volume, increasing as they get closer and subsiding as they walk past your home, a series of single followed by a triple clapping of hands and the shouting of *maca* in unison as a *yaqona* session proceeds, and, in the football season, *Ba, Ba Ba, Kaila* as a load of supporters using the side of the bus for musical accompaniment drives past celebrating yet another victory for boys in black and white. Yes, I do miss Fiji, but I am also very fond of Canberra, where I live, and Australia, my adopted country. I feel quite at ease being Australian and Fijian.

Our children, Meena and Rohit, have married and settled in a country where they have spent more than half their life. Both have lived a life very different from what Bhaga Parag or Rami could ever have imagined. Their Dada Jinna died two years after Rohit was born. Both his grandchildren were a source of pride and love for him. What he could not continue, Dadi Ganga did until 10 years ago when she died in Canberra at the age of 77. I remember telling my mother that man had been to the Moon and showed her a piece of rock that was being displayed by the United States Information Service in the Western Regional Library in 1969. *Chanda Mama* (the moon) could never be violated by human kind, she insisted She was so adamant that it took me many years and a lot of proving to get her to accept this fact. But the wheels keep turning and with them comes change.

What of the future? Will my grandchildren ever enjoy playing 'Sit here' on a *paakad ke ped*, banyan tree, away from the concrete jungle? Seventy-four years ago Bhaga left Vesma for Fiji and was later joined by his two sons and a daughter. Today, only the widow of his grandson Amrat, his daughter Mangi and her son Dilip and family remain in Fiji. Every other blood child is either in India, Canada, England, America or Australia. Kanti and Jyoti advised and assisted Rohit in selecting his wife Yoshika, but will they ever consider selecting a spouse for their daughters, Kanishka and Prishika, or their son Dillon? When Meena and William's children are born, will they ever talk about the origins of the Maisurias and the Bhatias? And what will India and Fiji mean to the generation born in Australia?

One can feel only a certain sadness that a part of my heritage will end with me, but that is the essence of life: change.

*Nadi market, mixed and multiracial — a commercial centre as
well as a meeting place. Similar to Nausori, home to Dilkusha.*

CHAPTER SEVEN

Dilkusha

Vijay Mishra

Dilkusha, you is a bitch.
Tomato (after V. S. Naipaul)

To be a Dilkusha boy is to be someone apart.
Puri and Bill Shakespeare

ON MY WAY back from Dunedin in late October I spent an evening with my brother in Sydney. It was a Friday and, unknown to me, he had organised a party: the invitees were primarily Indian friends with whom he had developed some intimacy these past 15 or so years. They came with their harmonium and tablas for a characteristically Indian evening with lots of film songs. In Perth, I had grown accustomed to such evenings and knew the pattern well. As people began to arrive in their Chirag Din (of Bombay) shirts and Satya Paul (of Delhi) designer saris, I noticed two men not quite in sync with the rest: they wore different-coloured shirts, a lot more subdued, more grey and beige and green than pink and blue; their belts sat across their navels without much evidence of a paunch; they walked with a different swagger and spoke with an unmistakable Pacific lilt; their Hindi was embarrassingly ungrammatical. Their looks, too, placed them apart from the general monotony of fair, rounded Punjabi faces; they were darker, muscular, sinewy, working class to the core.

I looked at them closely and recognised them. They were two of Ram Jati Singh's sons: Narendra and Upendra. I hadn't seen Narendra since 1958, and Upendra (or Uppi) since 1961, although this is not altogether correct as Upendra and I met briefly at the University of Tasmania in 2002. Regardless, for dramatic effect, let us say that for a long period of my life I had lost touch with Uppi. Both brothers had a fascinating history, which is part of Fiji's seafaring lore. Once, their boat stalled and was shipwrecked on their way from Bua to Point Ellington, Raki Raki. They spent three harrowing days and nights afloat on beds tied together to make rafts before being picked up by a fishing trawler. When Uppi came to Dilkusha Boys' in 1955 and shared a desk with me, his skin had broken into sores and had a yellowish, sickly look to it. He took a full year to recover. I spoke to him for a few minutes and then Narendra introduced himself with the customary, 'Remember me?' As if to establish a point of reference around which a conversation may revolve, he added, 'Do you remember Dilkusha?'

'Yes, Dilkusha,' I sighed, 'a happy heart indeed.' 'Wasn't it Nawab Bahadur's locality close to Chandrapore in E. M. Forster's *A Passage to India?*' I sounded terribly pompous (a show-off as they say in Fiji or a smarty-pants in Australia) and was glad that the many nouns in the sentence didn't quite connect as Narendra simply asked, 'What did you say?' 'Nothing,' I remarked, but something had happened, my imagination (never particularly good) seemed to be on the move and then I recalled my brother's first words at the airport a few hours earlier. He had embraced me as I emerged from customs and said, 'Just a few moments before I was thinking about meeting you at the airport. Did you know I've been doing this for nearly 40 years, ever since that December day at Nausori-Luvluv Airport when you came back home to

Dilkusha from Wellington for a short break in 1964?' I was touched by the remark. 'Yes,' I said, 'it has been a long time and, as we said all those years ago, after the first journey there is no other.' So, really I never came back to Dilkusha after 1964.

My brother stayed on a little longer, but even his Dilkusha was to come to an end when he left in late 1968. 'Yes, Dilkusha,' I had said to Narendra. Yes, Dilkusha indeed, and its story has to be told not in its entirety but in parts; and certainly not by me because I am too bookish, I have no sense of metaphor, my voice will get in the way of the narrative and I'll miss the wood for the trees (see, no sense of metaphor, I told you so). I think I'll let my brother speak. He can say things about me; he can place Dilkusha in a more personal context and, at any rate, he was the charmer, the more personable person, and he is bonded to Dilkusha in ways in which I never was. He smelt it, he felt it, he danced with it, he knew Dilkusha as a body, I knew it only as an idea. That's the big difference, and all those years ago I sometimes envied his capacity to grasp the heart of Dilkusha, to feel it within himself, disappear into it and, when it was gone, to feel its loss. After he left Dilkusha, the place was never the same. So I'll let him speak, only silently editing his voice to provide a prop here and there, to correct matters of fact without tampering with his interpretation, create a third-person detachment where necessary. I think you will like his voice: gentle, soft, comforting. I seem to have lost the capacity to soothe: it profits no man ... Reverend Deoki used to say without completing the sentence from one of the gospels. Sadly, I forget which. *Koi lauta de mere beete hue din* ... (Give me back those days of yester years, days not meant to return ...). As Narendra, Upendra and I listened, my brother told the story of Dilkusha, not as a capacious narrative, but selectively.

Harry K. came to Dilkusha from Nakelo on 27 August, 1947. I know this because this is what Harry K., my father, better known as Buka (which is what we called him instead of dad, or father or *Pitaji*, or Dada or Mama or whatever one picked up in an extended family), wrote in red on the bathroom wall with a huge paint brush. The wall was never repainted and so the date remained, staring at us whenever we stood under the shower. We were — father, myself, my older brother — from Nakelo. My mother was from Suva Point and because she was the daughter of Hankar Singh, the horse-trainer and polo player, we were born there. That's the way births took place; mothers went to wherever they felt comfortable to be delivered of their child. But we never said that we were from Suva, although our birth certificates declared as much. Yes, to the traditional Fijian opening remark for a *talanoa* (being Nakelo people, we spoke Fijian), 'Where are you from?' — 'O *vaka tikotiko mai vei*' — we always said, 'Nakelo'. Yes, wretched, swampy, sickly, festering, backward Nakelo, that's where we were from.

My father was born there, came to Dilkusha Boys' School to do his School Leaving Certificate, swam across flooded rivers to sit for his exams, missed one or two and then, I believe, at the third try, the weather being fantastic, he arrived on time and passed. He was selected to go to Natabua Teachers' College, the thought of which sent him into a depression from which he was saved by Ram Padarath, headmaster of Dilkusha Boys' and a rising star in the Dilkusha Christian community. He had converted, called himself Benjamin and, with his chatty wife Charlotte, virtually ran the school. 'Harry K., why are you so glum, you've got a place at Natabua, Lautoka, the premier government teachers' college, and you're not even appreciative?' At this, Harry K. turned totally maudlin and incoherent. He mumbled something about his poverty-stricken life, a single shirt on his back, something about a punctured tyre on his rusty Hercules bicycle, and threw in a *chaupai* from the *Manas*: 'Ka *barkha jab krisi sukhaane*' ('Why does it rain when the crops are dead?'). 'Get to the point, I have little time,' said Ram Padarath. 'Do you need help of some kind?' Harry K. mumbled, 'Davuilevu,' the name of the adjoining Methodist Teachers' College and said that he'd rather go there than Natabua, although it wasn't government-run, and he loved his mum, our grandmother, fondly known in Nakelo as Adi Kelera, very much.

Ram Padarath was a fair, lanky man; his wife, charitable and god-fearing. She said, 'Ben, I do think that for a Nakelo boy, Natabua is on the other side of the island, perhaps Davuilevu is best for him.' At which Ram Padarath smiled and Harry K. not only went to Davuilevu next-door, but, on completing his teacher training, he ended up teaching Class One at his old school. For the first seven years, he commuted from Nakelo and then, on August 27, 1947, wife and two children in tow (me eight months old, my brother about two) and two wooden suitcases in hand, he got on the *Tui Tebara* bus to Nausori and from there walked across the bridge, past the bamboo groves, up the winding road to one of the Dilkusha Boys' School teachers' quarters recently vacated by Silas's father, or so Silas said. It wasn't much of a quarters, wooden with an open verandah in front, in the centre three rooms of variable use, depending on the size of the family, and a kitchen and bathroom at the back. The space between the kitchen and the living area had been haphazardly covered over so that the house had lost its symmetry. Curiously, the pit latrine (plantation culture's contribution to hygiene, and non-existent in village India), was in front of the house, but covered by the foliage of a 'sun sun' vine. The house was flattened in the 1952 cyclone, but we survived thanks to the half-brick walls of the bathroom, to which we had finally retreated as the cyclone gained strength, and which remained standing. The cyclone destroyed the house, but it was swiftly rebuilt (we spent a full week at Ram Padarath's house sleeping in a long row on the verandah, with Rohini at one end and Adishwar at the other). As it was made of wood and Lysaght iron, the new house held together remarkably well in the great earthquake of 1953.

School quarters did little to change Harry K.'s teaching or learning. He continued to teach Class One (and, later, Class

Four) and read the Hindi newspapers, *Shanti Dut*, *Fiji Samachar* and *Jagriti*, and one novel, *The Vicar of Wakefield*. When asked why he stopped reading fiction, he would reply, 'I eat hearty without Greek', which I think he thought was not a language but a local variety of fish with a fanciful English name. I must add that when my brother did well at Lelean, my father was overheard saying to Badlu outside Wing Zoing Wah, 'My son reads large books.' He was referring to the geography textbook by L. Dudley Stamp on loan from school. Nor did he do the other fashionable thing, converting to Christianity, although he liked to be called 'Harry' against the godly 'Hari'. Many others did and alliterative Christian names were not uncommon: Michael Manik or Michael Mathura or Michael Mahesh or Nancy Nisha or Maureen Maya. To keep a semblance of Hinduism in the family (after all, he maintained that 'Mishra' was a perfectly pukka caste name, and Gautam *gotra* to boot), he turned to one 'Bum Bum', a priest from Sawani, erratic to the core and with a marble or two missing, who would turn up periodically, and often unannounced, to undertake a *pooja* or even a *katha* behind closed wooden shutters. Those were the days when holy offerings of *roth* and *halva* were eaten in rooms full of smoke (there is no Hindu ritual without fire), followed by constipation.

Once Reverend Deoki happened to walk past and smelt the incense (clarified butter and sugar poured on fire) reeking from gaps in the wooden house. That Sunday during morning sermon, he abruptly announced from the pulpit, 'Stand up all those who believe in Isa Masih, our Lord Christ!' There were many of us in the congregation. I stood up, my brother did, too (we were very young then); Master Hari Prasad, the brutal Class Three teacher who slapped 'Bottle' so hard and for so long that for many years he woke up shivering and screaming at night, stood up, as did all the Dilkusha boarders. Aloysius Biju Prasad stood up, and Michael Manik, Michael Mahesh and Michael Mathura did, too, but then they were Christians. But Master Shiu

Prasad (clearly Dilkusha's most intelligent man, who, given the chance, would have been equal to the legendary Brahma Nand Singh) did not; and nor did Harry K. People whispered afterwards and Miss Smith, the matriarch of Dilkusha (who retired to live in Colo-i-Suva many years later at the age of 80, but who left for Australia, sadly, after the cruel murder of Miss Furnivall), never forgave them, although her attitude changed magically when, in recompense or self-indulgent ingratiation, I told Miss Smith that I wanted to be a padre. She enthused about it to Harry K. and I got a beating.

Harry K.'s passions were few: the Hindi language (which he knew very well indeed and which he taught at Senior Cambridge level at Lelean); the *Ramacharitamanas* of Tulsi Das, the aforementioned newspapers and *The Vicar of Wakefield* and, if we are to believe Charlotte, the art of conversing with women. When I think about it, I am surprised that he didn't fall for the fashion of going to the cinema when Ibu Bhai built the new Empire Theatre in Nausori in 1950, something that Dilkusha people took up with great regularity. There was one other passion though. Harry K.'s dream was to go back to cane farming, his father's profession. To that end, he gradually saved enough money to buy a cane farm, but when he did, in 1959, the CSR closed the mill. So he had to be content with Dilkusha, where he lived in mission quarters for some 12 years, and then in his own house nearby until he died. He had left Nakelo to come to Dilkusha. He moved nowhere else; he was never inquisitive about the rest of Fiji, let alone the world outside. For him, Dilkusha was the world. He made few 'establishment' friends, although later in life Reverend Deoki would be a regular visitor to our house and Memsahib, his wife, struck up a friendship with my mother. Instead, his friends were the hostel cook, Kuppuswami, who spoke Hindi with a decidedly Tamil intonation and knew none of the politer forms of Hindi verbs, the grass-cutter, Banwari, and the hopelessly inept, Badlu, who held no profession. Sick and world-weary after Rabuka's coup of 1987, Harry K. was persuaded by me to come to Sydney for treatment, which he did, only to leave abruptly, still sick and unwell, to return to his centre of the world, Dilkusha. He died soon afterwards, but at least in Dilkusha. 'If I were to die, it must be in Dilkusha,' he had said.

Yes, Dilkusha, to which people came to live and die. What was its allure, why do my eyes soften, my eyelids flicker whenever I utter the name? What was Dilkusha? I recall, slowly, quietly, gathering around me information to construct a history or shall we say a geography, for Dilkusha lives in my memory as a space rather than as history, although there is no story without history. Speaking of history — and here I have in mind history as a discipline — I must say that Dilkusha people were damn good at it: Vimal Vincent Robert Padre Shakespeare-Stratford-upon-Avon, as he was known to sign his name, passed History I at Auckland University; Titus Prabhakar Deoki and Ian Surendra Deoki did the same, as did David Robert (no middle name I suspect here), Vimal's father, before them; and Reverend Ramsey Ramnarayan Deoki even earlier had read not only history but theology. John Ram Sharan, of course, had done one better: he read history, English and education at Auckland University College. Dilkusha requires no history, its people were saturated with historical knowledge. Let that pass. I pause to recollect something else. A father's memory is always so haunting; talking about him and, indeed, internalising his knowledge as one's own (he alone knew all the secrets of Dilkusha) unsettles the mind, plays tricks with memory. And the pen, too (the technology of writing through which my story gets to people beyond my immediate audience), has a mind of its own, and likes to create patterns, as facts are transformed into art. The pen declares a freedom that is beyond will; it has a heart of its own; its truths peculiar to its own logic, sometimes compassionate, often defiant, invariably idiosyncratic, and not necessarily sincere to the oral version.

From my father, I heard about Reverend Blackett and Reverend Loy and Reverend T. C. Carne, latter-day Methodist missionaries to Dilkusha. In the works of historians such as Brij Lal and Ken Gillion, I have read about one Reverend Burton with whom the *girmitiya*, Totaram Sanadhya, discoursed on religion. Burton was a Methodist missionary who had some success converting 'bound coolies' in Nausori, but I can't be too sure. The Nausori mill was the first sugar mill built in Fiji and it makes sense that the Australian Methodist Mission Society would have sent an evangelist to save the souls of these lost *girmitiyas*. Dilkusha, it seems, was the Indian wing of the mission's more comprehensive Fijian activities in Davuilevu, the bigger diocese. Large, with an impressive church — built in memory of Rev Thomas Baker, who was eaten by Fijians (Baker was god-fearing no doubt, but impossibly imperious) — it was the nerve centre of missionary activity in that part of the island. The church or Baker Hall, as it was called, doubled as classrooms as well as a chapel, and Lelean Memorial School effectively began there. It was a landmark structure, its presence diminished somewhat only after the Nausori reservoir was built on the hill in adjoining Waila.

Baker's death became part of the Dilkusha-Davuilevu imagery and his ghost was said to haunt the dormitories of students who came to Lelean. Fijian students in particular shook their heads whenever Thomas Baker's name was mentioned. There was a curse, they said, and for this their pagan gods, who had led them astray in the first place, were to blame. One god in particular, the Nakelo deity Bati Dua ('He of the One Tooth', a passionate drinker of kava), so my father thought, had a lot to answer for. But there is hope that Baker's soul has been finally laid to rest. As I narrate my brother's narrative, I (this is the author-as-amanuensis speaking) notice a headline in the *Australian* of Friday November 14, 2003: 'Apology casts out a cannibal curse.' The accompanying photographs show villagers performing an ancient dance of ritualistic cleansing and the tearful village chief, Ratu Nawawabalavu, direct descendant of the chief who condemned Baker to death and who, they say, relished eating his tongue and fingers because Baker had showed disrespect towards chiefly protocol (Baker had touched the chief's hair), embracing one of Baker's Australian descendants. History comes full circle and here I am in Sydney (my brother's voice continues) narrating this story. Believe, don't believe, as Salman Rushdie's narrators are fond of saying. I guess I feel that way about my tale of Dilkusha: believe, don't believe, but this is the truth. If it reads like fiction, then that's not my fault: Dilkusha was always a dream to all of us (or, at any rate, to those who remember her glorious years), before sluttish time got her, before she became available to everybody, before she became just another courtesan like Chappanchuri, Nanki, Ulfat, Char Ana or Magalesi. This last phase, which also marked the end of the myth of Dilkusha, mercifully, came after my time.

As a geographical space, Dilkusha is a kind of appendage to Davuilevu, separated from it by a stream. From the banks of the Rewa River looking south, two streams mark off the boundaries of Dilkusha — to the left is Davuilevu, to the right Waila. The area is probably no more than two kilometres wide and two kilometres deep. Yet within it there are hills and valleys, paddocks and playing fields, guava patches, mango groves and schools, teachers' quarters, a church, an orphanage, the reverend's house on top of the hill, a catechist's lodging, a large boys' hostel and much else besides. During school term there could be as many as 400 people living in Dilkusha. In my days, the church had not been unceremoniously dumped across King's Road near Tomato's house. Houses across the road or beyond the western stream were not really part of Dilkusha because these were built on freehold blocks. But, for us, they were and we always felt that Dilkusha in our imagination extended beyond the western (right) stream as far as Hancock Road, next to Rupai's corner shop.

If you walked under the bridge from Tomato's house, past the landing from which Santokhi rowed his punt, took the path alongside the river bank and walked westward, you would have come across Chintamani's coconut palm-filled backyard (Chintamani was the mother of 'Frisco' Bunyan, who took a Qantas flight and disappeared, and a woman we associated with the tale of Bilwamangal, the man who swam across treacherous waters to be with his Chintamani, or someone like her); headmaster Padarath's architecturally challenged house (with the row of jamun trees, and an incomplete 'Gothic' wing from which for many years screams and cries were heard if you happened to walk past it); Phuli Mausi's house (she was the daughter of a Bengali for, her father was educated and a real Bengali, too, who went mad because, in Dilkusha alone, children's passion led to a father's madness); Safar's house (where women from Fijian villages came and left with young babies); before reaching David Robert's. It was at Robert's that I struck up a close friendship with Kamal Clarence Robert ('Bill Shakespeare'), David's second son, the only man I know who believed in nothing because he had no notion of truth. We had an intense friendship, which came to an end when I left Dilkusha in 1968. He died, distraught and lonely, in Sydney and, although I knew he was there for many years, I never renewed contact. Like Dilkusha, he, too, was something (somebody) to which you never returned because to renew contact with someone from Dilkusha meant reconnecting with a loss; it was never an occasion for a reverie or a simple retrospect: *aye dost mujhe ab yaad na kar* (O my friend of the ancient of days, do not remember me now). Which is why I have never returned to Dilkusha, nor made a point of seeking out Dilkusha friends. But then in life someone always comes along and says, 'Yes, Dilkusha, where people loved to distraction and went mad for passion, a place that sent more people to St Giles than any other I know. Yes, Dilkusha indeed.' And, for one moment, I am elsewhere, crossing time to relish, as a *rasa*, the mesmeric power of the place.

Across the road from the Robert household you would see
Cecil's house on the right (yes, Cecil Gulab Singh, Silas's older
brother, who started the trend of Dilkusha boys running off with
orphanage girls: *bhagaya lai ge*), to which, for some unknown
reason, Saizad Ali, master of Bollywood cinema, came regularly
and at odd hours. Next to Cecil's house stood Master Charles
Williams' and then the catechist Munshiji's. Charles (or Chapla,
after Chaplin, as we called him) requires a longer, more
imaginative gloss and I will return to him shortly: he is necessary
for my narrative to move forward. Munshiji I can dispense with
in a few words. Two or three people from Dilkusha ended up on
Makogai (the island where lepers were taken in those days) and
Munshiji (or so they say) was one of them. That must have
happened long before he became a catechist, for I remember him
as a jovial fellow masquerading as Father Christmas on *Bara Din*
(Fiji Hindi for Christmas), who finally had to leave the church
because his daughter married outside the faith to a Muslim man.
And Muslim households remained mysteries to us. Who lived
in them, what happened to them, was quite beyond our
understanding. So the pink house stood with no other sign of life
beyond Munshiji's other daughter Aida occasionally pruning the
hibiscus. There was another Muslim house, though unrelated
to Dilkusha, further down past the reservoir, next to Pampi's
rice mill, the Bakridi house, where it was said some 50
people, including Saizad and his parents, lived in one house,
intermarrying and interbreeding.

Anyone's tale could stand in for Dilkusha, metonymically,
so to speak. I could weave stories around Cecil or David Swami or
Kishori or Silas or even Johnny (Silas and Cecil's brother).
I could even build one around the transient visitors, the *musafirs*,
who came to Dilkusha Hostel as boarders: Robert Surendra,
Samuel Sidal Ramaiya (whose love for Lalita, unrequited, led to
poetry), the runner 'Koro', even Kashyap, Laleshwar, Chatu Nair,
Dharmesh, Raymond and others. Or perhaps around John

Bharat, not a transient but a fixture, who regularly cried on Father's Day and who sent a *farmaish* to the Fiji Broadcasting Commission on behalf of Master Shiu Prasad, our shy but brilliant primary school teacher. The *farmaish* or request was for the song from *Shree 420*: *mudh mudh ke na dekh* (Don't look this way my beloved). John Bharat, it was also said, sent the fictitious notice to Radio Fiji in 1959 that Reverend Deoki had died. Or even around Adishwar 'Spike' Padarath, a man of immense wit and great compassion. There will be time enough for their tales, or the writing of the story of Dilkusha through their eyes, and for each narrative the centre would be different. And, even as I speak, even as I gather my thoughts together, I cannot let go of Dilkusha Hostel easily for it was the place where heroes of our time made their mark and it was the place where everyone converged.

To the hostel came boarders who went to Dilkusha Boys' and Lelean Memorial, primary and secondary schools. Narendra, too, came to it as a primary school student in 1953, the year of the earthquake. The hostel was a solid structure made of concrete (a rare architectural feat in a sea of wooden houses), large enough to accommodate some 80 students in its three dormitories and a refuge to everyone when the floods began to hit the plains of Nausori after the mill closed and the river was no longer dredged to carry punts and tugboats such as the *Ratu Popi*. It had unusually wide corridors all around the three dormitories with long desks for homework and dining. The warden, his deputies and a few others, including John Bharat and Silas, were housed in rooms at the front. A large kitchen was at the side and a row of latrines at the back separated by a small playing field. A steep, narrow road connected it to the Waila Road below. The Rewa River and Nausori town were readily visible. Facing the river, to the left of the hostel, was Dilkusha Boys'; to its right, beyond the paddocks and the guava patch, was Dilkusha Girls'. Reverend Deoki's bungalow was on the hill slightly to the north-east and our house was just across the valley in front. In fact, we were so clearly visible to the hostel boys that we had very little privacy. But the house was not as exposed as our friend Ashish's (Boogi's). His house, well really Master Shiu Prasad's as Boogi was one of his seven children, was barely yards down the steep road from Dilkusha Hostel next to the imposing tamarind tree. Boogi's Mum was the gentlest of women in Dilkusha and would call us in for a feed whenever we walked past her house during meal times.

There were other houses, but I have cluttered this part of my story with enough detail. The point that I want to make, however, is that my story can find its centre here, and, in some ways, it already has. To make it explicit though I would have had to say more about Silas, amazing, indomitable Silas, struck by polio when barely 16, but a survivor, and a man of magnetic attraction and charm. To his room, located at the far end of the front part of the hostel, people came with their dreams, their gossip, their problems. His is a story that my brother can tell because he knows him much better. It was with him (and with Saizad Ali and Johnny Bakridi) that he learnt to love Bollywood films, and perhaps even literature (*Lolita* and *Lady Chatterley's Lover* were in Silas's library). At any rate, Silas was one of the first to leave Dilkusha, in 1962, just when I began to understand the place.

So my Dilkusha is best rendered, its intricacies understood, not through Silas or anyone else, but through Chapla, he of the fantastic imagination and youthful looks, he whose house was across the road from Kamal Robert's and he who finally disappeared in Canada leaving no trace of himself. Chapla taught me in Class Six, introduced me to *Phantom* comics (his favourite expression, 'Dunderheads, idiots and fools', was straight out of an early *Phantom* comic), and his style affected me in more ways than one.

To Dilkusha and its environs (as far as Rupai's corner store, as I said), came many permanent or transient people and, ever since Reverend Deoki's arrival in 1953, they invariably arrived with many daughters. So, when the Health Inspector came, Dilkusha swooned at the sight of his daughters; when Phuli Mausi returned, Dilkusha swooned yet again; but when Chapla came, Dilkusha boys were in a frenzy because Chapla had not one, not two, but six daughters! Somehow Christianity or the mixing of religions produced grand specimens of women; even the Health Inspector's wife was a Muslim who made him convert first to Christianity ('David'), then to Islam ('Habibullah'). Phuli Mausi's husband, too, was a Muslim-Christian, although I suspect that, like all Hindu converts, deep inside him nothing ever changed. But it is with Chapla that I want to carry forward the story of Dilkusha. Chapla came in 1956, lived here and there and then built his house across the road from David Robert's. He was part of a long-established Fiji Christian family with roots in Levuka and Lautoka; he had done his rounds in various Methodist schools and then appeared more or less unannounced to teach Class Six after David Prasad, son of the well-known Fiji educator, Gaya Prasad, suddenly left. Dilkusha teachers were all alike in temperament, largely because they were all products of Ram Padarath's patrician world. Chapla stood out: he was worldly in a sea of Methodist puritans, and mildly iconoclastic in a world where, Europeans apart (and there were a few who ran the orphanage and Dilkusha Girls' School), power was centred on the all-powerful Reverend Deoki and his headmaster Ram Padarath.

In the early years, I can't say that I got to know him — after all, I was only 10 when he taught me in Class Six. But when I look back, thinking about Dilkusha, his image keeps flitting past me. because in some ways, like me, he tasted Dilkusha rather differently. The Methodist puritans were aghast when some said that the young missionary women running Dilkusha Girls' School found him attractive or when Pippy's cousin, it was said, took a fancy to him. I can't say if there was any truth in these rumours (well, I know the truth, but his memory is too sacred for me to divulge secrets). And once, when Henry Nath was caught embracing one of his daughters (who was supposedly sick and hadn't gone to school), Chapla pretended that he had merely come home to collect his office keys. But I recall him best as the centre of the event that marked my brother's departure on a Fiji Government scholarship to Wellington. There was much excitement in the months before he left. Chatu Nair, a boarder at the hostel, felt that we should have a party just before Christmas to bid him farewell and he drew up a list of names.

There were many on the list of some 40 people whose names I have since forgotten, but those I remember were: Arvind, Raveen, Vijay, Aruna, Lorraine, Maureen, Lalita, Finau, Louisa, Raymond, Ashish, Chatu, Hari Bilas, John McDowell, Byron Buick-Constable, Tomato, Kamal Clarence, Girlie, Veena, Rosaline, Pearl, Prem. We needed Reverend Deoki's permission for a Saturday party (to finish before midnight or else we would be into the Sabbath) in one of the dormitories of the hostel. He agreed (my brother was seen as a successful Dilkusha boy and deserving of a farewell), on condition that we found a suitable person to supervise us. We approached a few Dilkusha Boys' teachers, who politely declined. Then I thought of Chapla, not the Reverend's favourite, but at least we knew he would accept the responsibility. We were surprised when Reverend Deoki said it was fine and, under Chapla's supervision, we could have a farewell party. That Saturday morning my brother and Chatu went to the Empire Café in High Street, Toorak, to get boxes of cup cakes glazed with icing (the Bow Sang variety in downtown Nausori was clearly not good enough), while Kamal Clarence and I organised the soft drinks and decorated the empty dormitory which now, without its line of string beds and mosquito nets, looked like a hall. Tomato provided us with music: Elvis, the Shadows, Buddy Holly and the Crickets, Ritchie Valens and the ever-present 45" vinyl records, 'gore gore o ba ke chore' and 'kisi mai o kisi yani'. That evening we put on our pencil-thin ties, 55/45 terylene/worsted wool Island Tailors hipster slacks and doused our shirt collars with cheap bottled fragrance kept in a gunny-sack for Bum Bum's use after a *pooja* (it was used as holy water to bless the devotees). Chapla came dressed in black; the girls in styles reminiscent of Ava Gardner in *Mogambo*.

It was the kind of night that only Dilkusha could offer, but the hall itself, which we had so carefully cleaned and decorated with crepe paper, was largely empty that evening. The mango groves and guava patches resounded with giggles and laughter; time was forgotten and gradually the clock crept towards midnight. At some point, I looked at the largely empty hall and saw Bilas trying to perform the twist with someone and Byron attempting an impossible hula-hoop routine with Rosaline. Then, suddenly, I heard people rushing back into the hall. Minutes after, there came a deep voice. 'STOP IT!' Reverend Deoki stood behind me. 'This is a Christian community, and it is past midnight. Observe the Sabbath and depart immediately.' And then, as an afterthought, he asked, 'But where is Master Charles Williams?' Chapla was nowhere to be seen. We said we didn't know. The Reverend's voice reached the heights of a most difficult hymn as he bellowed, 'Go and find him!' Tomato, son of god-fearing Alexander Thakur, disappeared. Chatu Nair, in need of a good reference for his career from the padre, disappeared. My brother was nowhere to be seen (I suspect he was with the Health Inspector's daughter), as I said softly to the Reverend, 'I'll find him.' That night I ran all over Dilkusha, but there was no trace of Chapla.

By the time I returned, the Reverend, torch in hand and daughters in line, had walked up the steps towards his house. John, Byron and the rest of the Suva crowd had taken taxis back home, but without Finau and Louisa, who, together with Arvind and Raveen, were unaccounted for. As Kamal Robert and I cleared the place, I saw Chapla coming towards me. 'I hope you had a splendid party. Has everybody left?' I said, 'Yes, but where

have you been?' 'I went out for a smoke,' he said. I nodded.
Beyond, I could see a light in one of the rooms of the teachers'
quarters at the girls' school going out. Chapla also saw it; he
smiled and moved on. 'Puri,' he said, 'you're a fine boy, drop by
for a coconut drink one of these days.' So began my closer
intimacy with Chapla. Not that we met or spoke on a regular
basis (I was barely 17 that Saturday night in December 1963), but
I felt that we understood each other.

When I returned to Dilkusha three years after my own first
foray overseas (by that time my brother had been out of Dilkusha
for eight years), Chapla's daughters had left, and Chapla himself,
they said, had disappeared (to Canada, it was whispered, where
he died in a freak accident in Vancouver); the Health Inspector's
daughter had left us all heart-broken by running off with a
Polynesian; the Reverend's family had left; most of the Padarath
family had left (headmaster Padarath had died some years before,
shattered and saddened by life); Phuli Mausi's family had left for
England, her daughter Nancy had married another ex-Lelean and
Dilkusha boy, and, many years later, died in an accident in
Canada. David Robert had died, his LLB still incomplete and his
family gone; Cecil had finally left after failing to sell his Cecil's
Pest Control business; Saizad had also disappeared, once again in
Canada, the refuge of many Dilkusha men and women; and
Tomato had turned recluse.

Of course, many years before, the journey begun by
Bunyan had been followed by Silas, who had also taken a Qantas
flight to Hawaii. Dilkusha, for me, had become empty; the people
who made it had left and I felt cheated. There were new faces in
old houses, but they were meaningless faces. The houses
themselves lost their familiarity, the grand jackfruit tree at the
entrance of Dilkusha Boys' looked forlorn and the silence outside
the row of houses before Rupai's corner store was unnerving. My
spirit had already left Dilkusha and years later my body did, too –
for Australia. And, in 1989, Harry K. died. But, for me, Dilkusha

had disappeared long before then, for I have no story to tell about Dilkusha after 1968, the year of my own first departure. I sometimes feel that, for me, when Dilkusha died (with the many departures), an old Fiji also died. I have never returned to Fiji, except to attend my father's funeral, because with the end of Dilkusha there was nothing to return to, for, like my father, the world was Dilkusha.

My brother's narrative ended. I turned to Upendra and Narendra. They remembered many of the names but not their stories. But then Harry K. alone knew Dilkusha's secrets and it was from him that we got to know them. The evening had turned dark and outdoor lights were switched on. The other Indians looked fidgety, some sulked as this had been a private narrative shared by only four of us. It was meaningless to them even if they had picked up snippets here and there. We felt like a select group; no, not select, more like an elect apart, who just happened to know Dilkusha. For to know Dilkusha was to know a certain kind of transgression unavailable to Indian boys and girls elsewhere in Fiji; it was to know what bodies smelt like, it was to crush frangipani in coconut oil and smell wild jasmine in the glorious moonlit sky on one's way to Endeavour meetings or Reverend Deoki's sermons ('*yadi mai manushiyon aur svarga dutoon ki boliyaan boloon aur prem na rakhoon ...*' [Though I speak with the tongues of men and of angels, and have not charity ...]); it was to learn how to cry while still young, to understand loss and know how to yearn and desire; finally, it was to sing 'If days were doves I would have caged them'. It was Silas, who also knew Dilkusha's secrets (but not as well as Harry K.) and who functioned very much like a magnet drawing people towards him, who had told us, 'When you sense Pippy or Theodora or Girlie some yards behind you, drop a six-pence coin and pretend that you're looking for it: *bas chavanni giraye ke khoje lagna*.' In the end, believe, don't believe; Dilkusha can be rendered only as fiction and, thankfully, because it can be rendered only in this manner, it has a permanence that only art can give. Tomato had said, 'Dilkusha, you is a bitch' after reading V. S. Naipaul's *The Suffrage of Elvira*; we liked her even more because she was so elusive, so deliciously ambiguous, and so free. But then we lost her, too, and that's the pain that hurts whenever memory takes us back to Dilkusha.

The Indians at the party now began to talk, about cricket, about wealth, about cars, about riches, about flats, houses, children's education: to be a doctor is a blessing but to be a dentist divine, they said. But Dilkusha was not something you bought like real estate; it was a different order of happiness, a fragile happiness ('but thereof come in the end despondency and madness'); it was lived experience and these were things that only Dilkusha people knew. As my brother's narrative, mellowed and smoked with a dash of Lagavulin, slowly reverberated around us, I sensed that Dilkusha was possible because of a radically new form of socialisation that post-indenture culture created for a people illiterate in origin, but with a passion for life and an irreligious attitude towards it. At my brother's party, sitting amid another group of Indians, ethnically alike and with the same gods to worship, we nevertheless sensed our alterity, our difference. 'Yes Dilkusha,' I sighed and looked at the empty sky. There was no smell of jasmine.

*Squatter settlement, Wairabetia, Lautoka. An increasingly
common scene on the fringes of urban centres.*

CHAPTER EIGHT

Upahār Gaon

Susanna Trnka

IN LATE MAY 2000, my neighbour and I stood by the fence that separated our homes a few kilometres outside Nausori town, discussing the latest news. In the months leading up to the May 19th coup, our exchanges had consisted of the latest gossip about weddings, births, deaths and upcoming *pujas* (religious ceremonies), frequently accompanied by a plate of food passed over the top of the fence. But, in the midst of the turmoil that followed George Speight's attempted coup, the news had been of looting, school closures and attacks. On this particular day, my husband and I had heard on the radio that a two-day curfew had just been announced. It was set to start at 6pm and was announced at 5.45pm, with the solemn warning that everyone had just 15 minutes to get into their homes. We immediately went outside to discuss this latest development with our neighbours.

When Sangita and I met up at the fence, she seemed really dispirited. Her face looked haggard and tired and she appeared deeply worried. We talked about the worsening political crisis and her concern about the future for her three teenage children. I then asked her about the implications of the curfew order. Does this mean that we can't leave our houses at all, not even to buy some milk or a newspaper at the corner store? Sangita shook her head in surprise. 'We can go there!' she cried defiantly, her voice tinged with anger. 'This,' and she gestured up and down the street, 'is our home. It is *our* settlement.'

I did not get a chance to test Sangita's assertion as the 48-hour curfew was called off. It turned out to be just one of many confusing announcements that had us and our neighbours reeling from day to day, from one moment to another. Much has been said about how Fiji came to be plunged into curfews and gun battles. But we could also trace the history of this moment from another direction, asking not about the events that led George Speight to storm into Parliament, but looking at what led to Sangita's claim that the surrounding houses and street were all part of 'our home, our settlement'. What made this a territory to which she claimed certain rights, regardless of what the Government might be doing to curtail them?

A popular image of the Indo-Fijian community in tourist brochures, in histories of Fiji, and in anthropological accounts, is that rural Indo-Fijians live in 'settlements'. The Indo-Fijian settlement is described as dispersed, far-flung houses, initially deceptive in its lack of formal centralisation. It is often compared with the indigenous Fijian village or *koro*. The *koro* occupies a bounded geographic space, while settlements have no distinct boundaries between them. The *koro* has a clearly delineated political structure, while the settlement lacks formal political leadership. The *koro* is frequently noted as an important organising principle in rural Fijians' lives, while the settlement is sometimes described as if it was merely a backdrop of houses and farms in which rural Indians happened to live.

The comparison is also made with other village societies. Anthropologist Adrian Mayer, writing in the 1950s, distinguished Indo-Fijian 'settlements' from the 'villages' he had previously researched in India — in order to highlight the 'looseness' of Indo-Fijian settlements in contrast with the more rigid social organisation of villages in India.[1] In his *Peasants in the Pacific*, Mayer described the dispersed layout of three Indo-Fijian settlements in Viti Levu and Vanua Levu, concluding that even the settlement that was 'most nearly a village' was not quite so. 'The houses stretched for about a mile, and there was no street, no square [*maidaan*] or temple which provided a central meeting place,' he wrote.[2] He then, however, went on to vividly describe the many political, religious and economic activities that created a sense of group belonging among the settlement's members.

As a social anthropologist, I am interested in understanding how people in different parts of the world organise and give meaning to their social relations. At university, I decided to study social anthropology because I was curious about the diverse forms of human social organisation and systems of belief. I was drawn to questions such as: why do some cultures promote arranged marriages while others expect individuals to find their own spouses? How is it that some people think that prayer can heal illness while others find this idea ludicrous? Because my parents were immigrants to the US from Eastern Europe, I was particularly interested in how the cultures of migrant people were adapted to new surroundings. Long discussions about Fiji with an Indo-Fijian colleague in California channelled these interests into a decision to study the social situation of Indians in Fiji.

I went to Fiji decades after Mayer, but reached similar impressions of the bonds that hold rural and semi-rural Indo-Fijian residents together. I arrived from the US early in 1999 and spent 10 months living in Suva with my husband and two-year-old daughter. In many ways, social life in Suva reminded me of life in cities I had lived in and near throughout the world —Washington, D.C., San Francisco, Prague, New York — all places where I rarely met the people living next-door to me and where I considered myself lucky if I even knew my neighbours' names. On our street in Flagstaff, the residents didn't seem to know one another well or to have much social connection. There were no obligations between neighbours and, from what I could observe, very little interaction between them. There was no central, organised space of

community life. I made a few friends at the University of the South
Pacific and at the local *mandir* (temple), but none of them knew
each other. When I attended *pujas* at the *mandir*, I saw dozens of
families and individuals assemble for the prayer and then disperse
at the end of the evening, each going his or her own way.

After 10 months in Suva, we moved to a residential area
on the outskirts of Nausori town. Initially, I saw little difference
between life here and in Suva, and I thought of the neighbourhood as an extension of the capital, with houses arranged up and
down the streets with little thought as to who might live in them.
By my count, almost three-quarters of the adult and adolescent
residents travelled to Suva for work or for schooling. The rest
worked either in the vicinity of Nausori town or ran small-scale
businesses from their own homes. Local businesses included
farming, raising commercial crops, car repair, plumbing, house
painting and tailoring.

The area had been settled only comparatively recently.
Despite the nearby sugar plantations and the CSR's
establishment of a cane-crushing plant in Nausori in 1880, this
part of Nausori had remained sparsely populated until a few
Indian families settled there in the 1940s. This was followed by a
growing influx of Indian residents in the late 1950s. Fijian
residents began to move in in the 1980s and the area has been
multicultural and multi-religious from then on, though the
Indian population remains predominant.

From the perspective of a newcomer, the settlement
seemed haphazard, with the neighbourhood composed of scattered
Fijian (all of them Christian) and Indian (predominantly Hindu,
but also Christian and Muslim) households. There were no
distinct village boundaries. There was no sense of a central
political authority, no *turaga ni koro* (head of village) whom
I could approach for permission to move into the place.

But my assumption that dispersed houses meant dispersed
neighbours was soon corrected. The day I moved in, residents

who knew I was there to 'learn about Indian culture' invited me to the nearby *mandir* in a school down the road. They started regularly sending us food over the fence. And, when a local elderly man died a few weeks later, a neighbour told me I should attend his funeral. At first, I protested that since I had not known the man or his family, it would be rude for me to attend. But you live in this neighbourhood, my neighbour told me, so you should go 'out of respect'. I followed her advice and found that attending the funeral afforded me an important insight into some of the social relations that linked members of the community together.

The funeral ceremony took place in the front courtyard of the dead man's house. The hastily constructed wooden benches overflowed with people who had come to pay their last respects. Besides the deceased person's extended family, some of whom had travelled from overseas, there were members of the *mandali* the family prayed with. Many women from the local *kirtan* or devotional singing group were also present, as were Hindu neighbours from the street. I was later told that at least one member of each household should attend such events to 'represent' their family's presence. A group of Fijian women from a neighbouring house also came, bearing plates of food for the bereaved family. There was nothing notable about this assortment of people except that it was one of so many occasions on which they all came together to honour the dead and support the living.

I attended many funerals (and weddings) during my stay in this neighbourhood, some in order to meet people, some because I wanted to understand the ritual structure of these events, but many simply 'out of respect'. Perhaps one of the most important moments in my understanding of what brought all these people together occurred after a Gita reading during my first week in the neighbourhood. After the pandit's recitation, all of the men retired behind the house. An elderly Hindu woman urged me to follow them into a courtyard where about 25 men were assembled, some of them around a bowl of grog, others singing *bhajans* (devotional songs). 'Those are village people [*gaonwalla*] who are singing,' she whispered. From which village are they, I asked? She repeated that they were village people. From which village, I asked again? A bit exasperated by this continued lack of understanding, the woman cried out, 'From *this* village.'

When I asked other residents, they agreed that the neighbourhood was indeed a *gaon* or village. It's because of the close feelings between neighbours, one explained. In a village like this, there should never be any enmity between people, another said. The more time I spent with residents, the more I came to know about the ethics of generosity and respect that its residents believed should govern their relations. Many expressed these as an extension of their religious convictions. While residents were not always successful in practising what they preached, there was a clearly shared sentiment that as *gaonwallas*, they *should* attend another family's weddings and funerals, take care of a neighbour who was sick or elderly, and exchange food and sometimes labour on a casual, everyday basis. These principles of community life were strikingly different from what I had experienced in Flagstaff.

I later asked a Suva resident who knew the area well what he thought of calling it a *gaon*. He agreed with the neighbourhood being a village, because some of its residents kept cows there. He was joking, but was also alluding to a familiar characterisation of rural spaces as being more 'traditional' than urban ones, in terms of differences in modern and traditional economic livelihoods rather than different forms of community bonds. To him, Nausori was a more 'backward' place because some of its residents relied on agriculture to make a living.

The people I met in Nausori agreed with this distinction of Nausori as more rural than Suva, but without the disparaging connotations. They did not aspire to the cosmopolitanism that was seen to characterise Suva. Living so close to the capital (it is only a 20-minute drive from Nausori town to Suva), they could have emphasised the continuities between these two areas, continuities that were the first things I noticed when I moved there. Instead, they insisted that Suva and Nausori were distinctly different due to what they called the lack of 'friendliness' between city-dwellers versus their own participation in the moral obligations and duties of villagers. As the majority of Indian residents called the neighbourhood a *gaon*, with Sangita's statement one of the few that I recorded that used the term *settlement*, I have followed their example. In my writings, I refer to the neighbourhood with the pseudonym *Upahār Gaon* or Gift Village to acknowledge this sentiment as well as the ethics of generosity and respect that residents consider underlie village relations.

A name goes far in creating a sense of unity, but why are some places attributed the sentiments of 'villages' and not others? How is a sense of community cultivated? How is a row of houses turned into 'our home'? Indian anthropologist Arjun Appadurai has written extensively about the processes involved in creating a sense of community or what he calls 'locality', and he defines it as 'a structure of feeling that is produced by particular forms of intentional activity'.[3] One of the points that I draw from Appadurai is that while places have histories — such as a significant battle or an important public ceremony that took place there — through which people attach meaning to them, there are also continuing, everyday acts that invest sites with meaning. So there are two sides to constructing a community, its history as well as its everyday relations. Looking at this neighbourhood, we can ask what are the historical bases as well as the continuing activities that turn these rows of individual, fenced properties into a place associated with a sense of community?

Living in Upahār Gaon, I discovered some of the historical relationships and ordinary everyday acts through which these community bonds were cultivated. First, I noticed that the settlement was not as haphazard as I had originally imagined. Many of the Indo-Fijian families were related and had come from similar parts of the country, mostly the interior of Viti Levu. By conducting household surveys and tracing ties of blood and marriage between village residents, I could delineate numerous histories of how the first member of a family moved into the village and, over the course of years or decades, assisted his or her extended family in joining him or her there. One example is 45-year-old Priya, who came to Upahār Gaon from Muaniweni after her marriage at the age of 18. Her husband had also grown up in the interior, but on their wedding he bought his first house in the village. Soon his younger brother, with his wife and children, joined them in a house on the other side of the village. Then Priya's maternal cousin bought a house across the street. About 25 years after Priya moved there, her brother and his family moved into Upahār Gaon. During the 2000 coup, there was talk of Priya's mother, who still lived in the interior, joining them. While I was unable to conduct similar residential histories in Suva, it seems likely that given the number of relatives living close to one another, residential patterns in Upahār Gaon are influenced by kin relations more than they are in the city.

While the webs of kinship are strong, the majority of the residents are not related by blood or marriage, but they cultivate different kinds of links, religion being one of the most powerful. As an outsider who moved into the neighbourhood expressing a desire to be included in any kinds of social events that were being held, I found myself much more frequently being invited to Hindu religious festivals and prayer services than to south Indian cultural festivals or school ceremonies, though I went to those as well.

Feelings of solidarity among Sanatan Hindus are forged through their almost daily interactions to pray, plan religious functions, take part in family events (weddings, birthdays, etc.), gossip or exchange food. There are three *mandali* organisations, each of which has its own community of followers. There is some friendly jockeying between these groups so that when devotees from one *mandali* returned from a *Ram Naumi* celebration near Suva Point, the young boys among them laughed and jeered at the other *mandali's* devotees who had yet to head out to the celebrations. But there is also a palpable sense of solidarity among Hindus who celebrate various religious festivals, such as *Holi, Ram Naumi* and *Diwali* by visibly taking over public spaces and adorning their homes, temples and their bodies. In Upahār Gaon, Hindus outnumber followers of other faiths, but there are Christian congregations that meet in the neighbourhood with other Christians attending churches based outside the village. A Muslim family also holds community prayer services in their home.

But religion is just one way of imagining one's place in the world. Social bonds in Upahār Gaon also consist of relations created through cultural commonalities, class solidarities and exchanges of labour and material goods.[4] Aside from their different religious affiliations, Indo-Fijian residents in Upahār Gaon stress similarities between themselves based on language, dress and, to some extent, food, as well as the shared historical legacy of being the descendants of *girmitiyas*, an issue to which I will return later. Other links include professional bonds between neighbours in similar occupations, who regularly share car rides into the city or exchange news of their work. During the 2000 coup, there was the shared bond of fear as residents exchanged information and advice for protection. Many Indian and Fijian neighbours found themselves exchanging news of the latest violence over the fences between their homes. A security patrol made up of Indian and Fijian men walked the streets at night to keep an eye out for the possibility of violence. In other words, people can and do create bonds between themselves in many different ways.

If we consider community as something that is *created* through everyday acts, then we can see some of these acts as not only a response to bonds already in place, but as the creation and re-creation of these bonds. The act of attending a funeral, for example, is a moment that not only expresses community sentiment, but creates it. People come together out of respect for the deceased and his or her family because they already consider themselves as part of a *gaon*, but by doing so they also reaffirm themselves as *gaonwallas*. Such moments form the basis of a community that is organised through the perception of shared moral rights and obligations.

Much has been said of Indo-Fijian men's activities in sustaining such community sensibilities. Mayer's account of community relations focused predominantly on men's roles as organisers of religious rites, as participants in economic production and exchange, and as members of local political factions. More recently, anthropologist Donald Brenneis has analysed men's roles in managing community-wide conflict, looking, for example, at how certain forms of social goodwill are cultivated by men only.[5]

Less has been written about women's roles in such activities. But, as a woman anthropologist, I found it not only easier to focus on women's contributions, but impossible not to do so. Even though I tried to devote time to interacting with women and men, a place was more often made for me in the kitchen rather than around a basin of grog or at *mandali* committee meetings.

Spending most of my time around married and widowed women, I found there was very little time for sitting down and chatting, asking anthropological questions and jotting down their responses in my notebooks. Rather I spent a lot of time peeling pumpkins and rolling out *roti* (leavened bread) — though I never came close to the perfectly circular ones made by village women, but always ended up with something a bit ragged, like the coastline of Viti Levu. Our conversations took place while washing plates and looking after young children. Like many local women, I soon learned to look forward to lengthy religious festivals as providing spaces for women to gossip before and after the prayers.

But I also discovered the long and often tedious physical labour it takes to put on such events. In addition to their formal paid labour and their household duties, Hindu women are expected as members of the *mandali* to contribute to the labour necessary for religious activities. In this neighbourhood, a women's *kirtan* club functions in part as a labour unit for the various village *mandalis*, its members undertaking the majority of the shopping, cooking and cleaning necessary for prayer ceremonies, which, during major festivals, can involve up to 100 people. Women pick flowers, string *māliyā* or flower garlands, prepare the *prasād* (holy food offerings) and meals for all of the devotees at major festivals. Women also assist one another with the labour necessary for family-sponsoring religious functions, such as funerals, weddings or household *Ramayana* readings. These events require cooking huge amounts of food. Funeral feasts usually involve up to 30 different vegetarian dishes, and women commonly stay up the night before to complete their cooking. It was not unusual to see some of the older women of the household drifting off to sleep during the funeral feast due to the late night before. There are also the overall preparations such as house cleaning and purchasing and preparing the objects necessary for prayer ceremonies.

Women are aware of their considerable contribution, but are often reluctant to talk about it for fear that it might make them appear boastful or proud. One common way they speak about their labour is to note its deleterious effects on their bodies. In a local medical clinic, I watched as dozens of women came in complaining of generalised body pain such as sore backs, arms and legs. When women were given the opportunity to explain why they thought they felt this way, they frequently said that the pain was caused by hard physical labour. As one woman simply put it, 'Sometimes after I work, my head hurts.' Many different kinds of work could provoke such pain. It might have been housework, crouching over piles of laundry that needed hand-washing. It might have been farm labour. It might have been the work of preparing large-scale religious events. Or it might have been physically intensive blue-collar work such as hunching over a sewing machine in a garment factory. Or, more likely, it was a combination of a number of these.

Much of this work is spoken of as women's contributions to cultivating peace (*shānti*) and happiness (*khushī*) among not only their family members but the larger religious community they belong to. For example, women's participation in significant religious practices, such as hosting a *Ramayana* reading, taking part in *pujas*, or singing devotional songs, is considered to spread *khushī* and *shānti* throughout the community. As one woman explained to me, it is important when hosting a *Ramayana* reading to make everyone who comes to your home *khush* or happy. There should therefore be no 'bad words' spoken in the house, the food you cook should be particularly pleasing to your guests, and the atmosphere should be generally conducive to promoting happiness, she said. There is thus at times a very explicit awareness that it is a woman's moral duty to contribute to the well-being of others.

My intention here is not to privilege women's labour over men's, but to suggest that men and women worked to produce the sensibility of community, sometimes in similar and sometimes in different ways. Occasionally, people are self-conscious about the social effects of their efforts, as when women discuss the need to work to keep harmony and peace in their families. But usually actions such as the passing of a plate of food over a fence or attending a funeral out of respect are done without much thought being given to how they help establish community bonds. Yet these actions do not need to be undertaken. Residents could live as their counterparts in parts of Suva do. But, consciously and unconsciously, they choose to honour their relationships to one another as *gaonwallas* and cultivate the bonds between them.

There was, however, a marked increase in the self-consciousness of some of their actions during the 2000 coup. With the abridgement of Indo-Fijians' political rights, as well as outright calls for increased Indo-Fijian emigration, the political implications of Indo-Fijians' involvement in any kind of community life in Fiji was subject to question. This is not to say that activities that had previously been non-political suddenly became politicised. At any time, the construction and maintenance of local communities takes place in the larger context of national politics. But activities such as food exchange or even an exchange of greetings between Indian and Fijian neighbours, which might not usually be given a second thought, become even more politically significant in times of violence.

One of the interesting turns in community talk that happened in Upahār Gaon during the coup was the importance attributed to the topic of physical labour. Previously discussed primarily in terms of contributions to one's family, religious community or *gaon*, work was increasingly talked about as a contribution to the nation in order to justify and defend Indians' place in the nation. Moreover, it was the labour of the present as well as the legacy of indentured labour that were increasingly referred to by Indian residents to assert their right to stay in Fiji.

One of the many occasions on which this sentiment was expressed to me occurred when my husband and I joined an impromptu discussion of the local history of the village. Caught by a heavy rain shower at the corner store one afternoon, John joined a group of Indian men around a basin of grog while I settled on the shop steps with the woman who was minding the counter. The men around the basin were reflecting on how the area had previously been 'wild' and uncultivated. 'Indians are the ones who developed this country,' one man declared. 'They did the hard work.'

Upahār Gaon's residents were not the only ones making such statements. In public forums, many Indo-Fijians made a point of discussing how indentured labour was not only a matter of self or familial survival, but how it contributed to building up the nation of Fiji. A Fiji Girmit Council representative was, for example, quoted in the *Fiji Times* as stating that it is 'sad that Indians have been questioned about their loyalty to Fiji after toiling and sweating for the last 130 years'. The article ran under the headline 'Slaves of the Economy' and much of it was devoted to depicting how strenuously Indians labour and 'sweat like buffaloes' for the development of the national economy.[6]

Many of these images of the Indian labourer conjure up the classic colonial characterisation of Fiji as a 'three-legged stool'. In this metaphor, which has been widely attributed to Ratu Sir Lala Sukuna, each of Fiji's three ethnic groups constitute a leg without whose support the stool would topple over. Europeans were thought to supply the capital and organisation necessary to drive the economy of Fiji, indigenous Fijians gave the land, and Indians contributed the labour. The metaphor is too simple to describe either colonial times or the decades since independence. Not only does the image of an ethnic-based three-legged stool ignore the power imbalance between these three groups, it pays no attention to how relationships to labour and economic production Many of these images of the Indian labourer conjure up the classic colonial characterisation of Fiji as a 'three-legged stool'. In this metaphor, which has been widely attributed to Ratu Sir Lala Sukuna, each of Fiji's three ethnic groups constitute a leg without whose support the stool would topple over. Europeans were thought to supply the capital and organisation necessary to drive the economy of Fiji, indigenous Fijians gave the land, and Indians contributed the labour. The metaphor is too simple to describe either colonial times or the decades since independence. Not only does the image of an ethnic-based three-legged stool ignore the power imbalance between these three groups, it pays no attention to how relationships to labour and economic production are determined largely by class. Not all Indo-Fijians are in the same position, but, depending on their economic status, they are more or less in control of their own labour and the labour of others.

In local narratives, however, many Indo-Fijians followed the national discourse by describing their relationship to Fiji in terms of their ethnic group's participation in indentured and contemporary labour. The fact that the majority of Indo-Fijians are the descendants of the girmitiyas was spoken of as more than their shared heritage, but as the basis of their right to continue labouring in Fiji.

It was this history as well as the continuing bonds between neighbours to which Sangita referred when she called the street 'our home, our settlement' and when other residents called each other gaonwalla. To name this neighbourhood a gaon or to call it 'our home', was to assert that it was more than a string of houses and that by making it something more, its residents had certain inalienable rights over this space. Clearly, her statement also expressed a political stand. *Let the Government do what it wants with a curfew, here we can go wherever we want!* Sangita proclaimed, powerfully portraying her local community as in defiance of the Government's prerogatives over power. This is not to suggest that Sangita was ready to break Upahār Gaon away from the Republic of the Fiji Islands. Throughout the coup, Sangita and other villagers hoped for an amicable and cooperative relationship with the Government of Fiji, which they expressed through their evocations of the legacy of Indian labour. In fact, both of these assertions were asking for the same thing: recognition of the contributions and rights of the descendants of indentured labourers, who were actively creating and maintaining new ties to sustain a place for themselves in Fiji.

It was in times of such political turmoil and in those of relative political peacefulness that Upahār Gaon's residents undertook the work necessary to create a sense of community and interconnectedness in the lives of residents. I came away from my experience of having lived among them with the understanding that the gaon in Fiji is a product not so much of its place in the geography of Fiji (or whether or not its residents keep cows), but of the work its members undertake to make it so. These activities are undertaken, sometimes self-consciously, in relation to the legacies of the Colonial State as well as to the current political status of Indo-Fijians in Fiji. Within this space, the sensibility of taking part in a community is cultivated through the everyday work of women and men, who act to transform scattered houses into the meaningful sites of everyday life.

NOTES

[1]   Mayer, Adrian. 1973. 2nd ed. *Peasants in the Pacific: A study of Fiji Indian rural society*. Berkeley. p. xiii.

[2]   Ibid., p. 19.

[3]   Appadurai, Arjun. 1997. *Modernity at Large: Cultural Dimensions of Globalization*. Minneapolis. p. 182.

[4]   Another possible factor that might distinguish residents' relationships in Upahār Gaon from areas in Suva is length of residence. It is likely that the urban population is more transient, making the creation of relationships with neighbours more difficult to attain. But again, comparative data on residential patterns in neighbourhoods in Suva and in Nausori is necessary before making this conclusion.

[5]   Brenneis, Donald. 1984. 'Grog and Gossip in Bhatgaon: Style and Substance in Fiji Indian Conversation.' *American Ethnologist*. Vol. 11, No. 3. pp. 487–506.

[6]   Sharma, Seema. 2000. 'Slaves of the Economy.' *Fiji Times*, 4 June, 2000. p. 12.

Cane farm, Namata, Sigatoka. The thatched hut is a rarity now but — when Annie Sutton was growing up in Viti Levu — this was the only building on the farm.

CHAPTER NINE

Sa I Levuka Ga

Annie Sutton

I FIRST SET foot on Ovalau on 26 January, 1980, tired, excited and apprehensive. At first glance, Levuka, the only town on the island, seemed like the abandoned set of a western movie (the kind in which Mel Brooks could have had a lot of fun), not dilapidated, just deserted. Only the horses and drunken cowpokes were missing. That first impression was formed as I was driven slowly through the town. I was on my way to St John's College, a co-educational Catholic day and boarding school run by the Marist Fathers and Marist Sisters. Cawaci, the locality in which St John's is situated, is six kilometres north of Levuka. I was most excited about finally arriving there, as I had looked forward to going to boarding school for a whole year. It had been a long wait.

After a whole day's travelling, I was finally there. I had left home in Monasavu early that morning, after a huge, noisy and excited breakfast with Mum and my four brothers. My three elder brothers had attended Xavier College in Ba (Vincent from 1974–77, Victor from 1976–79 and Ricky from 1979–82), so they were old hands at the boarding game. Vernon, four years younger than me, complained bitterly that he was the one missing out on all the fun. Vincent drove me to the airport, where I caught a Fiji Air flight to Nausori. From there, I caught the afternoon flight into Bureta airport, which serviced Ovalau, with a dozen other St John's students.

Levuka was the capital of Fiji from 10 October, 1874, until 1881, when Suva became the new and permanent capital. Today, Levuka is quite a picturesque little town, squashed as it is between the mountain and the Koro Sea. It is a charming and beautiful remnant of the colonial era; a living museum. Apart from a handful of newly renovated buildings, very little has changed in the past 100 or so years. The Ovalau Club, Masonic Lodge, Marist Convent Primary School, Catholic Church and the Royal Hotel are some of the oldest buildings in Levuka. Sadly, the Masonic Lodge was burnt down in the aftermath of the 2000 coup.

The main street, Beach Street, is wide enough, just, to be called a two-way street. The larger vehicles have to pull over to allow smaller ones to pass. There used to be a bus service that started in town and went in either direction — as far as Tokou Village in the south and Cawaci in the north. There were two services in the morning, which brought day students (and some staff) from all over Ovalau to St John's, and two in the afternoon, which returned them home. In the late 1980s, the family who owned the buses migrated to New Zealand. Since then carrier trucks and taxis ferry people around the island.

The part-government-owned PAFCO cannery, the largest employer on the island, and the movie theatre are bookends to this clean and quaint little town, which exudes 19th century elegance. Glitz? Glamour? No, there is none of that. But there is an abundance of charm and character, and the local denizens are the friendliest, kindest, most generous and most honest you'll meet anywhere in Fiji.

In the aftermath of the coups of 1987, there was no trouble on the entire island. The Tui Levuka famously turned away a boatload of soldiers from Suva, advising the authorities in Suva that Ovalau was not going to go the way of the rest of the country. During the troubles of 2000, there was only one incident on the entire island: the unfortunate arson attack on the Masonic Lodge. Even now, however, there is disagreement among the people of Levuka about whether it was a deliberate attack or not.

During my three years there, and on many subsequent visits, I did not encounter any racial problems on the island. Not even at college. I do not know whether that is because in a small community, where everyone is struggling to make ends meet, and where everyone knows everyone else's business, people are drawn to each other more than in larger, more competitive communities. There were inter-racial marriages and people did not just *seem* to get on, they *did* get on. And very well at that. Even the shopkeepers were on friendly terms with the people. However, that may have had something to do with the fact that the shopkeepers had a habit of sticking bounced cheques on their windows!

One of the things that struck me as I arrived in Levuka was the whiff of Levuka's own Chanel No. 5 — the stench of rotting fish from the cannery. No one else seemed bothered by it, but I never got used to it. The town though, was perfect. I had spent a fair bit of my life in Nadi town. But the small and quiet town I now found myself in, together with the familiarity of the people of Levuka, was a great contrast to the sprawl, noise, dirt, concrete and impersonal bustle of Nadi.

In his 1845 account of Fiji, Commodore Wilkes wrote, 'Each island has its own peculiar beauty, but the eye as well as mind felt more satisfaction in resting upon Ovalau.' And St John's College, tucked away in Cawaci, several miles north of Levuka town, seemed to me the most beautiful part of Ovalau. The main school buildings, the church of St John the Baptist, the presbytery and boys' dormitories and dining room sat on lush, green flat ground. Behind that was farm land (owned and cultivated by the school) and, rising majestically behind that, was a volcanic mountain range. Mt Tomuna was the tallest part of that range. And the view of the school from the top of Mt Tomuna was breathtakingly spectacular. There were bridges built over creeks flowing on either side of the main campus. These creeks were fed by waterfalls and rivers that started somewhere near Mt Tomuna. On either side of the creeks were staff quarters. Beyond the second bridge lay the girls' hostel. That bridge formed a very important boundary: after school hours the girls were not allowed to cross the bridge over the creek to school and the boys were not allowed to come into the girls' side of the property. As far as I know, this rule was never broken. It was said that if you wanted to cross the bridge after hours and without permission, it was best if you packed your bags first. I don't know whether time spent packing your bags meant you had time to re-think your proposed actions, or whether it was meant to save the Sisters a whole lot of hassle.

The striking thing about St John's was that there were people there from every part of Fiji and Rotuma. We had students from the most isolated villages and islands, and from all towns. Even the staff came from all over Fiji: there were Chinese, Fijians, Indians and Rotumans. Some were from Australia and Canada, several were Peace Corps volunteers. The Fathers were New Zealanders and the Sisters were from Ireland, Northern Ireland, New Zealand, France and Fiji. We had our own mini United Nations. In those three wonderful and fun-filled years, I got to know most of the students and staff. It was interesting to hear about where they came from, what sort of lives they had led, about the customs and traditions of the different parts of Fiji, and wherever else they came from.

The first half of my first term there was a lot of fun. Everything — the rules, the people, the classes, the food — was a wonderful novelty. It was not everything that the *Just William* series and Enid Blyton's books had promised, but it was great fun to be sleeping in a large dormitory with other girls, and to have so many people to chat and muck around with during free time.

There was always a guitar about and singing along with it was a favourite activity, along with telling ghost stories by torchlight and boogieing to 1970s disco music on Sunday evenings. Towards the middle of term, however, I began to miss my home and family.

At the end of 1979, home had moved from Nadi to Monasavu, in the centre of Viti Levu. Mum had sold our restaurant (but kept its name, Curry Kona) when she won a lucrative three-year contract to operate the staff canteen at Monasavu. Her business now was to feed the Fiji Electricity Authority senior staff working on the hydro-electric dam project.

Dad was a Gujarati Hindu and Mum a Malayali Catholic. They had five children, an average of two years apart. I was the fourth child, and only daughter. Dad always told me I was supposed to be the last child, as he finally had the daughter he had always wanted. I reckon I would have been thoroughly spoilt (which is worse than being just spoilt!) if I had been the only daughter *and* last child.

In the mid-1970s, my parents separated and then divorced. Mum moved us to Nadi town from Votualevu. We continued attending Mt St Mary's Primary School in Martintar. Vincent and Victor were already at Xavier. Despite the move, nothing really changed. We had the same Votualevu and school friends and made new ones in town; we had the same teachers, the same parents and we talked the same. We were a bit of a novelty for a while because we were the only kids with divorced parents. But we still saw Dad. He visited us in town regularly, and sometimes arrived in a drunken state to harass Mum in the restaurant. It must have been embarrassing for her. Worse, Dad would ring her the next morning to ask her if she was all right, because he'd heard that some drunk had been causing trouble for her, and that she'd had to call the police. I don't think she ever told him that *he* was the drunk who had caused her all that trouble. I don't think she thought it would change anything. But it gave us something else to laugh about. Joking about such things was the best way we knew of coping with the situation.

Although I missed home, much to my surprise, I realised during the first-term holidays that St John's was a haven for me. I realised I needed structure, but also supportive people around me. Mum, with a business to concentrate on and five of us to worry about, did not have the time. And, if she did find some time, she simply did not have the energy. At St John's, I was safe, and everything I needed was there. Provided I obeyed the rules, studied when I was meant to study, played sport when I was meant to, and was always in the right place, I was fine. But it wasn't all fun and games: we had jobs to do as well. We had specific chores, which were changed half-way through each term, so that we got to do almost every job that was going by the time we left Cawaci. The chores included cleaning the dining room, dormitories, toilets, classrooms, laboratories, offices and staffrooms. Our regular routine had us out of bed at 5:45am, Mass at 6:30am, weeding or chores after Mass, breakfast and then a quick walk to school. The girl boarders returned to the hostel for lunch. After school we had more chores, sports training, free time, study and then dinner. After dinner we had more free time, night prayers, yet more study and then bed.

The routine changed on Saturday: after Mass and breakfast, we did our chores until late-morning: 131 girls descended on the hostel and school buildings with buckets, brooms, mops and cloths and scrubbed everything from top to bottom. The Sisters helped and supervised, and we couldn't return to the hostel until they were satisfied with the results. Sometimes I had the rather easy task of cleaning the main staffroom. This was great because I got to read all the notices pinned on the staff noticeboard, and therefore had advance warning of proposed changes. Naturally, I did the right thing and passed on some of the plans to the girls! Sister Mary Frances always came into the staffroom to check my work before she let me go. And every time it was the same routine. She dramatically ran one finger along a shelf, examined the finger and announced, 'Miss Lal, I can grow *dalo* on this shelf.' And I'd think: you obviously have no idea how or where to grow *dalo*. Then we'd laugh, and I would pack all my cleaning gear and go 'home'. Sister Mary Frances always called the girls' hostel home. It was nothing like my home.

For starters, my home was normally filled with boys. Here, I was surrounded by women and girls. No matter how hard I tried, there was just no getting away from them! I liked having people around me, but not for every single minute of every day. At home, I had the freedom and space to disappear with a book for a bit of quiet time, or get on my bicycle and pedal off to visit friends and acquaintances in settlements and villages around Nadi. Or have music blaring on the stereo. At Cawaci, I was constantly hemmed in by people and rules. I finally found a place on the beach that was my own — in an old dead tree with branches sticking out here and there, so that it resembled an over-sized echidna. Some of the branches intertwined to make a seat, and it was there that I could sit, albeit slightly uncomfortably, with a book and disappear into my own world. I deliberately picked that tree because it stood on its own — there was just enough room for me.

Unlike home, I did not have the freedom to read any old book. Strict apartheid was practised in the library. Seniors (Forms Five and Six) had their own section, which included some interesting books. For my first two years, I was restricted to the Juniors (Forms Three and Four) section — these books I thought were either beneath me or were things I had already read. And, shockingly, there were no newspapers about. At home, we fought over who got to read which newspaper first! Father Fitz, who taught me for each of the three years I was there, and who knew I loved nothing better than to read a good book, solved that problem by leaving books (usually on modern European or world history) from the Fathers' library on my desk. (I can credit him for my love of history.) I still did not have access to daily newspapers, but this problem was partially solved when I was given chores in the convent. There, I read the daily newspapers to my heart's content because the other girls always warned me when the Sisters were approaching! I was bell-ringer in my final year, and that was a bonus because I always knew in advance who was going to be where!

Another thing that made St John's different from home was that when I was there, I did not have to work in Curry Kona, which Mum opened in 1974. She couldn't afford to pay the staff much so, at the end of the school day, the staff went home. Our jobs included taking orders, serving the customers, making *rotis* and preparing the meat, seafood and vegetables so that they were ready for Mum to cook. We also washed the dishes and cleaned the kitchen and dining area. We did these chores in between doing our homework. My favourite job was that of cashier. One time a large group of tourists came in. Just before they settled their bill, Mum told me they were French, and that when they paid, I was to say '*Merci beaucoup*'. Thank you. I did, and they were so touched that they pooled all their Fijian currency and gave it to me as a tip: $78. I learnt quickly. Suddenly, there were Japanese and French phrase books under the till! I did not miss the restaurant work so much as meeting different people every day. One Australian tourist once helped me with my homework — it was only after he and his wife had left that Mum told me he was the Premier of NSW, Neville Wran.

On Saturday evenings after prayers and tired after our chores, sports and a bit of study, all the girls marched down to the school hall to watch a movie. The Fathers and Sisters supervised us at the movies – the boys sat on one side and the girls on the other. There wasn't much of an aisle separating us, and sometimes a few 'couples' managed to get close to each other. We usually watched a western, sometimes comedies such as Peter

Sellers' *The Party*. *The Party* was hugely popular and, for weeks afterwards, we all wandered about with faux Indian accents, saying '*Birdie num, num*' to anyone and everyone.

Sunday mornings, after Saturday night's movie, we were allowed a sleep-in. We got up at 6:15 instead of 5:45. Luxury! After Mass and breakfast, we attended 'conferences'. Sister Miriama took the junior girls for talks and Sister Mary Frances did the same with the seniors. Mostly, the talks were of a religious bent, but sometimes it was 'girl talk'; things about growing up, how to behave in different social settings and the like. I did not care for this. I found it irrelevant, but it did not occur to me that others may have found the talks interesting or informative. And, speaking of irrelevant things, I remember the first thing we were taught on arrival at college was how to make our beds. I was astounded to learn that we needed to be taught how to put sheets on beds and it took me several months to realise that there were only a few among us who slept on beds and mattresses at home. The majority of girls were from villages and would have slept on mats on the floor.

On the second Sunday of the month we were allowed to visit friends and relatives in Levuka, or go into town for a bit of shopping. The friendliness of the Levuka people caught me by surprise, and I was invited to visit people I did not know. They were mostly friends of my relatives and friends, and they sent messages to school with their children asking me to pay them a visit on 'Free Sunday'. Not only did they entertain me and provide a lovely home-cooked meal, but they waved me off with several containers of food. From second term in my first year, I usually visited relatives of my best friends. On normal Sundays, we had free time from lunch-time until 5pm. This was when we all trooped off to the Point. The Point marked the boundary between school property and the village of Nauouo. The Point included a rocky outcrop that jutted about 50 metres out to sea. This is where we swam among bright tropical fish, and where many of us learnt to dive. We always had a lot of fun there. Sometimes we would spot a shark. This was when I discovered that the actors in the *Jaws* movies had nothing on us. The blood-curdling screams and noisy splashing back to the beach of about 50 girls was a sight to behold. I reckon many sharks died of laughter at that Point! By the next Sunday, though, the shark sighting was long forgotten and we were back at the Point.

Apart from study, friends, the gardens and other chores, there were other things to keep us fully occupied. The college had beehives and goats. In my third year, I joined the bee-keepers and goat-herders. This was a lot of fun and, apart from breaking the regular monotony, it was the only way of working with boys outside the classroom. Father McGuire, the college bursar and my favourite mathematics teacher (because he did not terrorise me), was the head bee man and goat-herd. He introduced goats to the college farm as a way of earning much needed cash for the day-to-day costs of running the college. There were many Indians on the island and, for Indians, a celebration is never complete without goat curry — so they were our customers. I was not much interested in the bees and my contribution there was minimal — I just wandered about aimlessly with the smoker while everyone else did some real work. Goats were different — you could cuddle them even if they did reek a bit! And they had a tendency to head-butt if they did not approve of being caught and having their feet inspected. I enjoyed mucking around with the goats. For me, it was also a chance to get away from the constant supervision of the Sisters, which I found suffocating. The friendly banter with the boys provided a connection to my life at home.

Father McGuire also organised our bushwalks to Mt Tomuna. All girls had the option of going on these organised tramps. A handful of senior boys always volunteered to help with stragglers and to man the ropes at the top of Mt Tomuna, which we needed to haul ourselves over rocks and on to the peak. In my second year, Father McGuire managed to take us on a second tramp — up the 99 Steps in Levuka. On the way back down, there was a swimming pool, which was fed by a waterfall. The swims there and in the 'pool' at the end of the Mt Tomuna treks were always the highlight of the day. The next year, Father McGuire decided that a yearly hike to Mt Tomuna was not enough, and he took us on a more adventurous tramp. For this, we were bussed from the college to Lovoni village. After seeking permission from the Tui Lovoni, we tramped back from Lovoni across the middle of the island to the village of Draiba, just to the south of Levuka. The bus collected us from there and returned us to the hostel, exhausted but happy. It was astounding how we could chat away no matter how tired we were. These tramps were a lot of fun, but also difficult if you were not fit.

We were mostly fit. First term was taken up with athletics. Running around and chucking things was not my idea of a good time. I preferred being a noisy member of the cheer squad. The second year I was there I tried to get out of the athletics trials, which were compulsory for every student. I had a whinge to our principal, Father Fitz, about my crook knees and he clucked sympathetically. The very next day, however, I discovered with a shudder that he had volunteered me for five events — the maximum. Two of my good friends, Makereta Tuitoga and Lusia Qera, felt sorry for me and ran with me, all the while telling jokes! Needless to say, I came last in every event.

I lived for second term, which was hockey season. I did not like netball because, when I had played it in primary school in Nadi, my team was always thrashed by the Namaka Public School team, by at least 50 points. The only other option was hockey. I knew nothing about hockey, but I wanted to play a sport, so I put my name down for it. Later, I found out that when Sister Miriama and Sister Mary Frances worked out which positions the girls would be placed in, they had one name left: mine. They decided that since I wore glasses and was pretty skinny, I would be safest as goalkeeper. In my first year, I was in

D Team with the rest of the third formers. The next year I made it to C Team!

Within days of working out how to put on the monster protective leg pads, I discovered I loved the game. Every recess and lunch break of every school day in term two, I would trot out with a couple of hockey sticks and balls and get my friends, Frances Bingwor, Rosie Anthony and Margaret Kotoisuva, to hit the balls to me. In the first two years the four of us were in the same hockey teams. In fifth form, in 1982, I was overjoyed at being chosen in the A Team, which won the annual Westmere Tournament, which was the secondary school girls' competition.

As I say, my best friends were Frances, Rosie and Margaret. Although they were all from Suva, none of them knew each other before we met at St John's. The three of them just drifted toward each other about a week after we all met. It took me a long while to settle down with a particular group. I had many friends at my primary school and we all hung around together in a very large and noisy group. Things were different at St John's, where everyone got along, but they all seemed to have one or two special friends. I was happy to be friends with anyone and everyone.

I don't recall having any problems with any students related to my ethnicity, or theirs. It simply was not an issue. Whether this was because I was also Catholic (the majority of students and staff were Catholic), I can't say. I did not feel any different to the other students. For me, the race issue never surfaced, except once briefly during the radio broadcast of the results of the 1982 general elections. Every time a seat won by the Alliance Party was announced, a raucous cheer rang out from the girls. I was aware that the majority was ignorant of politics, and therefore treated the election as nothing more than a game. For them, it was like a rugby match: when your team scored, you cheered. I did not feel threatened at all, just profoundly sad at their ignorance and the way they, like almost everyone else, reduced politics to a competition along racial lines.

At the beginning of 1982, Mum and two of my four brothers moved to Sydney. Another brother and I were to follow at the end of 1982. This suited me just fine. By this time, Frances and I had known each other for two years. We visited each other's families during the holidays. We were inseparable at college and during the holidays. It was a pretty good arrangement and not only did we get to know each other's families very well, we became quite good at visiting other college friends and their families during the holidays. There were quite a lot of us from Nadi at St John's and we got up to some pretty harmless mischief away from the supervision of the Sisters.

Once, when I was staying with Frances's family during the school holidays, I went with them to a traditional Fijian ceremony on the chiefly island of Bau. The ceremony was called *Mata ni Gone*. Translated directly, it means 'face of the child/ren'. One of Frances's relatives was from Bau, and he was taking his children to his village, on the island, for the first time. He was introducing his children to the people of his village. It is an important event because it forms an important link between the child and his or her relatives from the village. As well, the ceremony formalises the obligations that fall on the people of the village toward the child, and vice versa. I had never heard of this ceremony before, and I felt privileged to take part and witness the event.

With Frances and her family, I was lucky to attend numerous other traditional Fijian ceremonies associated with births, deaths and marriages. These gave me an insight into the importance of culture, tradition and family life in Fijian communities, of which I otherwise would have remained ignorant. These were special and treasured moments which I would not have had the opportunity to experience firsthand if I had not met Frances at St John's.

My Indian heritage was important, too. For four years, I learnt classical Indian dancing, and we were regularly exposed to Indian culture at soirees that Mum organised at our home in Nadi town with musicians and artists from the Indian Cultural Centre in Suva. She also often organised for people from Nadi and surrounding areas to gather at our home for poetry readings and singing. These evenings normally ended with those present asking her to sing *Mere Veena*, a love song. I also joined a group of Gujarati girls who performed dances — sacred and popular — at Gujarati weddings. However, most of the dances we performed were *dandhia* — with sticks. For these, I wore one of Mum's best saris, to the knees only, and a huge, horrible wig to hide the fact that I had very short hair.

In 1982, my final year at Cawaci, the truck the Sisters used for shopping and transport broke down for the last time. They organised for the shopping to be delivered by the shop owner, but someone had to do the daily mail run as we could not survive without the daily mail call at tea time. Sister Mary Frances asked me to go into town every afternoon on the first bus to collect the mail from the post office, and the newspaper from one of the shops. I was under strict instructions to return on the second (and last!) bus. Soon enough, the boys discovered I was on the mail run and, almost immediately, they had an assignment for me: they gave me money to buy cigarettes, which I was to chuck out of the bus window as it approached the bridge just before the school property. We did not encounter any problems until two months into the operation when the Chinese shopkeeper developed a conscience. She rang Sister Mary Frances and told her what I was doing. I was not punished because I never admitted being the culprit. Sister Mary Frances knew it was me, of course, but after she publicly announced that she knew what was happening, the requests from the boys stopped. Sister Mary Frances, however, continued to trust me with the mail run. I found ways of repaying that trust — I had to. That was the way things were done at St John's; you were given chances to redeem yourself.

I had a lot of fun at St John's, and I engaged in a bit of study from time to time. I made many friends among the staff and students, who taught me quite a lot about friendship, tolerance, sacrifice and life in general, but mostly about myself. They continue to influence me to this day. I was exposed to people, cultures, traditions and ways of living that I would not otherwise have been exposed to. The friendships I made there have endured and strengthened even though most of us are now spread over several countries. And we still get together around the *tanoa* in Sydney and in various parts of Fiji to reminisce about old times and old friends, and to make new memories. A little bit of Levuka is in all of us who attended St John's. And, when we get together, we always sing the old love song that takes us back to where it all began, *Sa I Levuka Ga*.

Fijian and Indo-Fijian children at play, Rahimtullah Memorial School, Maro, Sigatoka. Soccer is the most common game in played in schools in the cane belt.

CHAPTER TEN

Soccer

Mohit Prasad

For My Father
Hari Prasad aka 'Harry Cop'
Captain, Nadroga Soccer Team 1960–64

Old Man of Sixty

I am an old man of sixty
Backward I do not walk
Because I play soccer
And exercise daily without much talk

Young men are defeated by me
I make clear straight scores
Amazed spectators exclaim
'Well done, Budha!
Thou know the tricks of the game'

Thrilled with happiness
One day, I came home
And sat to have a meal
Thus spake to my wife
'Mother of Munna

I have to go to Ba to see soccer
Ask Munna to run out
And have the bus stopped.'

Hearing this, the mother of Munna
Pulled out a fire-wood from the hearth
Her arguments led to stick-fighting
'Sons harvest cane in the field
They do not go to Suva even
You are ready to go to Ba
Are you not ashamed of this?'
Quietly in my mind I thought
Quietly I should slip away now
If a woman beats her husband
Curse on that stock of man.

— *Prem Yogi 'Maam'*
(Translated from Hindi by J. S. Kanwal)[1]

Soccer, more than any other sport, has been an integral part of the Indo-Fijian historical experience. It has provided an outlet for the expression of a popular culture with its own set of icons, values and a continuum that has contributed more to an Indo-Fijian sense of identity and belonging, to their sense of time and place, than is usually acknowledged. Despite the chaos and convulsions of recent times, soccer continues to inspire attachment and affection and a sense of solidarity among a people for whom there have been few occasions for celebration in recent years. I discuss here how a simple game with a round ball, moved by the feet, head and body — but not by the hand — towards and into two opposing sets of almost anything to delineate an upright, usually rectangular space, has come to occupy a central part in Indo-Fijian social life.

Organised soccer in Fiji existed through local and district club competitions from the turn of the 20th century. It was then a predominantly European sport and formed an integral part of the social activities of the colonial officials, planters and settlers, traders, army officials and missionaries. Clubhouses emerged in suitable locations to provide the food, drinks and entertainment associated with the sport. The clubs remained the exclusive domain of the *sahibs*. French missionaries are credited with introducing soccer to Levuka in the latter part of the 19th century. Soccer was an important Saturday social activity with Fijian teams competing for the prestigious Ricarnie Cup on a provincial basis. Among the teams were Shamrock (Suva), Kadavu (Suva), Lomaiviti (Suva), Bau (Suva) and Ovalau (Levuka).[2] Games were played regularly by barefoot players of great speed, stamina and ball control. In western Viti Levu, interest in soccer among Fijians emerged in the 1920s and 1930s, with Lautoka as the centre of the sport. Many clubs competed under the leadership of Ratu Meli Qoro, who had a long playing career with the Namoli Native Soccer Club. Ratu Meli was also one of the earliest Fijian referees and a regular official at most of the inter-district tournaments held in the 1940s by the Fiji Indian Football Association. J. K. Gopal, a contemporary of Qoro and other Fijian players in the '30s and '40s, recounted that soccer provided one of the strongest common grounds for the intermixing among Indians and Fijians.[3]

Mission schools spread soccer to Fijians in the early part of the 20th century, accounting for the rise of competitive and communally organised soccer feasts or *magitis*, which provided a fierce dose of physicality and rivalry to their games. The Reverend Brother Mark, a Marist missionary from New Zealand, is believed to have been the first person to introduce soccer to Suva, especially to Indians. Brother Mark's commitment to introducing organised soccer began at Marist Brothers Indian School at Toorak in Suva. His presence led to the popularity of the game, especially around the central Suva area, with Toorak as the base for social games on weekends. Following the natural progression innate in sports, teams sprung up from these informal games and gradually developed into clubs. The role of the Catholic Brothers in the introduction and development of soccer continued well into the 1960s and beyond. Brother Bertrand, another well-known Marist priest and teacher, was the coach of the first Fiji national side in 1951.

By 1920, some of the first generation of Indo-Fijians had their first taste of soccer as students in Christian mission schools. But there was a gap of almost 18 years before a national body to administer the sport was formed. A part of the reason for this was the fact that Indo-Fijian society was evolving slowly and discovering social and sporting activities after 40 years of indenture. The one serious attempt at forming a soccer association in Fiji was by the Indian Reform League, established in 1926. The league was a quasi-political-social body formed to promote the welfare of the Indo-Fijians while working cooperatively with the colonial administration and Christian missionary groups. Most of the members of the league were businessmen or educated urban Indo-Fijian white-collar workers and professionals.

A large part of the league's energy was spent organising various sports competitions for the Indo-Fijians, among them cricket, hockey, lawn tennis and soccer. In 1928, the league formed a localised rather than a national body to organise soccer in and around Suva. This was only logical since the league was largely Suva-based. Continuing the tradition of the Sunshine (Suva) and Sitare Hind (Rewa) soccer clubs from 1922, other clubs had sprung up in the area and organised friendly matches among themselves. The teams from Suva played at the Marist Brothers Indian school grounds in Toorak, while the Rewa teams played at the Dilkusha grounds. In December 1927, the league had organised a very successful schools soccer competition at Albert Park.

Encouraged by their success in organising school soccer, the league decided to arrange a football competition for the adult teams in Suva in 1928. Dr I. Hamilton Beattie, the editor of the *Vriddhi*, a monthly Hindi and English magazine, donated a trophy named after his magazine for the competition. At the annual general meeting of the league at the Imperial Picture Theatre on Sunday 22 January, 1928, a special association football league committee was also chosen, with S. V. Singh as the first secretary. The league members came to hold influential posts when the Fiji Indian Football Association was formed a decade later. Among these future administrative figures with the Fiji Indian FA were J. F. Grant, I. Ramjan, A. Raymond, A. G. Sahu Khan, C. S. Narain, G. Suchit and D. Dudley.[4]

Many of the names, representing the continuation of a family tradition, surfaced later in competitions run by the Fiji Indian FA. The Grant, Sahu Khan, Dudley, Narain and Ramjan families were formidable names in Indo-Fijian popular culture in various sports and entertainment circles. Among others who made notable contributions were those from the Koi, Sukhu, Mahabir, A. G. Prasad (Indian Reform), Ganpat, Swann, Dass, Columbus, Gurwaiya, James (Toorak), Prasad, Munshi, Thomas, Swamy, Rasul (Union), Ram, Rama, Lochan, Wilson, Phillip, Suruju (Dilkusha) and Nath, Amputch, Bilas, Harakh, Phulwari and Ram Deo (Rewa) families. In many ways, these players and administrators formalised the soccer tradition from the pre-1920 period among Indo-Fijians by playing in an organised competition. Their participation in the Vriddhi Cup from 1928 onwards set a benchmark for other districts to organise soccer competitions under a local controlling body.

The first game between the Indian Reform and Toorak sides was played on 14 May, 1928, the 49th anniversary of the arrival of Indian indentured labourers to Fiji. This first season was followed closely by people in the Suva and Rewa areas and was viewed with some envy by the north-western districts, forming the basis of the rivalry that has long existed between southern and western teams in Fiji soccer. The league saw teams attracting their own legion of fans based largely on geographical closeness to the base of the team or familial ties. The family formed an important part of the early tradition of club soccer and some of the older clubs in Suva, Rewa and Lautoka can trace their origins to a particular family. The large and extended nature of Indo-Fijian families made it possible for a club to be formed from just one or two families. In many ways, this was responsible for the sectarian nature of clubs.

The soccer pitch became the ground of the sporting religion for the newly freed Indo-Fijian communities after the abolition of indenture in 1920. Village soccer teams stamped a visible mark of identity for Indo-Fijian communities. Education, of prime concern for Indo-Fijians, brought sport with it. For the rural and urban committee-run 'Indian' schools, soccer was the main sport. The soccer pitch was an important part of the school infrastructure. The additional land for the inevitable playing field, designed for soccer, was never questioned. The village school also provided the village recreation grounds, devoted primarily to soccer, but also used for an extensive range of cultural and religious activities requiring a communal space, such as *Ram Lila*.[5] This is why you can come across school soccer pitches perched precariously on the ridge of a hill or cliff, on the banks of a river, or carved out of the middle of hills in Fiji.

Workers, farmers and schoolboys made up teams in weekend knock-out competitions. The prospect of a soccer game at the end of a hard week of labour was a welcome tonic for their jaded limbs and minds. Side bets added spice to the sporting activity. Played on village grounds or playing fields developed by the CSR, these weekly matches were the precursor to organised clubs. According to anecdotal reports, the games were community-based events with teams usually made up of players from a particular area. Faiz Mohammed, one of the earliest figures of Fiji soccer, has recalled teams such as Morning Star, Nausori Central, Vuci, Sitare Hind and Wainibokasi being family-based forerunners from Rewa of the club sides that proliferated in the 1920s.[6]

The matches provided the opportunity for much social interaction and intermingling among the people, helped no doubt by the ready presence of *yaqona*, which had become an integral part of the Indo-Fijian social fabric. The consumption of *yaqona* formed an integral part of the development of an identity that distinguishes Indo-Fijians from their origins. Bazaar soccer and *yaqona* went hand-in-hand as one of the most important means of social interaction and the creation of an Indo-Fijian identity. The emphasis on fund-raising activities and competition for trophies and prizes remained a secondary matter. In time, the school soccer pitch replaced, or became an addition to, the village or company grounds and was the centre of bazaar soccer. The grog or *yaqona* stall, to which the Indians were partial, was usually to be found at the entrance to the bazaar as it is now to be found in the sprawl of the municipal markets.

The youth wing members of village committees usually organised soccer competitions. Schoolteachers were an integral part of the organisation of such games as referees, players or tournament coordinators. Prominent locals, usually the village shopkeeper or other businessmen, were invited to patronise the tournament. The rough and ready nature of the play was due in a large part to the excess of enthusiasm of the players rather than any concern for skills or teamwork. Team practice, if any, consisted largely of a game in the afternoons on any available fallow land for a few days prior to competition. Unlike their urban cousins, who had organised training geared for league competitions, village soccer was a largely social event in the early days.

Fans of the game, however, such as the late Ram Sunder Bansraj, a former Fiji Indian FA treasurer (1958–68), recall village teams often taking part in town competitions by the 1950s. These urban teams were better organised with regular training and the emphasis on skills and teamwork:

*These boys lived on soccer ... they organised their whole lives on
the football ... there was much status in playing soccer and the
initiative had to come from the players ... if you slacked off ...
there would be any number of youngsters ready to take over.*[7]

Bazaar soccer enjoyed its heyday in the '50s and '60s.
Although bazaar soccer is still played in some places, it has lost
much of its colour. Full 11-a-side soccer is rarely played in such
competitions as it has been replaced by the abbreviated code of
seven-a-side soccer for logistical reasons. The growth of club
league competitions in the districts and easier transportation
enabled many village teams to participate on a regular basis in
the urban areas.

The Inter District Championship (IDC) tournament in
many ways jump-started the organisation and administration of
soccer, which developed into the governing body that is now
known as the Fiji Football Association. The foundation
members, Suva, Rewa, Ba, Levuka and Lautoka, participated in
the first IDC held on 9 and 10 October, 1938, for the Lloyd-
Farebrother trophy, donated by Lloyd and Company of Sydney
and A. S. Farebrother. Sir Harry Luke, the Governor of Fiji and
first patron of the Fiji Indian FA, opened the tournament. The
Fiji Indian FA was formalised on 8 October, 1938, in the offices
of A. S. Farebrother and Company in Suva. It's formation met
the need for a governing body to organise and control soccer
centrally. The immediate purpose behind the formation of the
Fiji Indian FA was to organise and conduct the inaugural IDC.
The constitution and structural framework for the body was
adopted six months later, on 22 April, 1939, in Lautoka.

Its formation was heralded as a landmark event. The *Fiji
Times* of 8 October, 1938, noted:

*This evening the most important event in Fiji's soccer history
will take place when the visiting delegates together with those of
Suva, meet to form the controlling soccer football council for all*

of Fiji. This same council will make the draws for the fixtures under question. Notice of the draw will appear in the window of the hub by 8.30pm. The meeting will be held at the offices of Messrs A. S. Farebrother and Co. at 8pm. Mr B. M. Janniff is the secretary pro-tem.

The formal beginning of a 'soccer football council' wasthe administrative base, which led to the growth of soccer in Fiji. The importance of A. S. Farebrother has not gone unrecognised. His initial tenure as the foundation president of the Fiji Indian FA laid the groundwork for a group of largely volunteer individuals to dedicate their time and energy to the promotion of soccer. The debt owed to the founding president and his contribution to the development of organised soccer is most fittingly commemorated by the IDC trophy, which bears his name. The irony that an Englishman was the first president of an ostensibly Indian association did not hinder an appreciation of his pioneering efforts. Justice Sir Moti Tikaram, a former president of Fiji Indian FA (1959–60), recalled that:

I did not know Mr Farebrother personally, as I was only 13 or 14 years of age then. But I do recall vividly his strong personality. He had a determined look on his roundish face, which he carried on a tall and largish frame. He was always seen in a white double-breasted suit and a felt hat. Notwithstanding his apparently hard exterior and a reputation for growling, he was a kind person and reputed to be generous to a fault. Fiji soccer owes a heavy debt of gratitude to this pioneering personality.[8]

This picture of a loquacious English gentleman as a pivotal figure behind the formation of the Fiji Indian FA speaks strongly of the power of soccer to break down cultural, historical and racial divides. Farebrother can be added to the list of pioneering European influences and patrons who helped Indo-Fijians in areas as diverse as education, civil rights, literacy, welfare organisation and sport.

The framing of the first Fiji Indian FA constitution was preceded by a conference on soccer held on 22 April, 1939, at the Narsey Hall in Lautoka. The main brief of the conference, according to the *Fiji Times* of 26 April, 1939, was 'to draw up a constitution governing Indian soccer throughout the colony. Present were Anrud Singh (Rewa), Hari Charan (Rewa), Edward Grant (Nadi), Charles Wilson (Sigatoka), B. R. Dutta (Suva) and B. Janniff (Levuka). The conference was presided over by A. S. Farebrother.'[9] The conference was instrumental in reinforcing the founding tenets of the Fiji Indian FA. The interests of the mainly Indian soccer players and fans of the association were protected by the clause which excluded those of 'non-Asiatic origins' from playing in competitions or for districts affiliated with Fiji Indian FA. Abdul Lateef, the president at the time of the change from Fiji Indian FA to Fiji Football Association (FFA) in 1961, contends that 'the overwhelming interest and participation of Indian players made the decision only natural and there was no politics involved'.[10]

Under the presidency of Tulsi Ram Sharma, Fiji soccer grew through the war years. Sharma, the first Fiji-born Indian to qualify as a lawyer, served two other terms as president (1948–50 and 1954). He set a precedent for lawyers heading soccer in Fiji. To date, seven lawyers have served as president. Parallels with lawyers and the political leadership of Indo-Fijian society over the years are easily drawn. The structure and organisation of the Fiji Indian FA and the FFA mirrors the larger political scenario under the largely communal political realities of Indo-Fijians. This is mainly in terms of organisation and structure and, in its own way, shadows closely the sectarian divides that haunt the Indo-Fijian community. Independent and sometimes fiercely and jealously guarded as an Indo-Fijian cultural institution, the Fiji Indian FA provided the springboard for the establishment of soccer as one of the main forms of popular culture for Indo-Fijians. Even operating out of cardboard boxes from the trunks of the Vauxhalls and Holdens of the time, the Fiji Indian FA was always strong on organisation, accountability and a sense of obligation to ensure the development of soccer, although expectations and results did not always match intentions.

The establishment of Allied military bases in Fiji during World War II added to the existing infrastructure, especially in the area of transport and communication. Road, air and sea transport reduced the travelling time between urban centres on the main islands. Increasingly, sports were dominated by Indians or Fijians, especially team sports with mass appeal such as rugby, football, netball, hockey and cricket. United competitions were organised in sports such as hockey and cricket by the 1950s due to lack of numbers among the Europeans. Private sports and social clubs, especially those that were a product of the early colonial rule or were established for patronage by the expatriate staff of the CSR, continued to cater for the establishment but were slowly being opened up, more by necessity for membership and revenue than goodwill, for the growing Indo-Fijian and Fijian middle class.

The rapid growth of urban centres provided a new professional class of workers in various fields. Teaching was one of them. Primary and secondary teachers helped establish the forerunner of youth development programs by establishing district and national level inter-primary and inter-secondary soccer competitions. The increasing role of the media in presenting detailed coverage of local and overseas soccer, through the *Fiji Times* and *Shanti Dut*, also had a positive impact on the development of soccer. The *Fiji Times* has an impressive record of covering soccer and other sports from the very beginning. The IDC received extended coverage, starting from team selection to build-up and match reports. The coverage of district and club games added to the pride one felt in playing soccer. The exploits of soccer players graced the pages of the *Fiji Times* and this was an immense status symbol.

In 1951, the Fiji Indian FA donated a trophy for a competition to be organised by the Fiji Secondary Schools Soccer Association, which had been established in 1950. Natabua High School was the inaugural champion. In time, the secondary school championship finals were held on the same stage as the IDC. The Fiji Teachers' Union (FTU) initiated school soccer competitions as early as 1939. The Rewa branch of the FTU had organised a senior boys' school soccer competition on 2 August, 1939. This early involvement in sports by the FTU characterised an important aspect of teacher involvement in the development of youth soccer. The FTU branches are still active in the organisation of inter-school competitions at the primary school level in a zonal competition, despite the formation of the Fiji Primary Schools Soccer Association in 1975.

Soccer was and remains an important Indo-Fijian sports especially at this level, in terms of participation and support. Farouk Janeman, Fiji FA Youth Development Coordinator and a former star player from the '70s, said that there was almost equal participation between the two main ethnic groups at the youth level. He added that at the district and national age group levels this parity was maintained. At the senior levels, according to Janeman, there are more Fijian players, for a variety of reasons including a greater commitment to the game, while Indo-Fijians' commitments to education and employment prevent serious engagement with a largely amateur sport which presents little possibility of a long-term career.

The number of lawyers, bureaucrats and other professionals in the district and national associations demonstrates the high regard for the game in the Indo-Fijian community. Over the years, soccer has remained quite separate from politics in Fiji. This policy was in place in 1938 and attests to the shrewdness of the association's administrators in deciding that the divisive forces in politics should not be allowed on the soccer field. With their non-alignment policies, the FFA was to attract the support of a broad

spectrum of political parties and governments, which were aware
of the need to make a good impression on the large crowds that
the game has drawn from all communities, especially since the
'60s. And, an invitations to open and close FFA-organised
tournaments, are happily accepted by politicians. A list of chief
guests at the IDC would read like a who's who of Fiji and has
included all governors, governors-general, prime ministers and
presidents.

In political terms, the 1950s were a watershed era in
defining identities based on culture and ethnicity. Some Indo-
Fijians wanted the game to remain identifiably Indian. One of
the delegates to the 1944 annual general meeting of the
association in Rakiraki demanded that 'Hindi, as their mother
tongue, should be rightfully used to conduct the meetings of the
Fiji Indian FA'. Then president, Tulsi Ram Sharma, summarily
dismissed the motion. By the 1950s, such exclusionary
viewpoints had subsided, and new initiatives were being taken to
open the game up on a national scale to all races. A succession of
liberal, inclusive and like-minded presidents — Moti Tikaram
(1959) and Abdul Lateef (1960–62) — led the way. Lateef, a
gregarious lawyer and aficionado of Rewa soccer, has been one of
the true characters of Fiji soccer. He insisted that the change of
soccer into a multiracial sport was part of its natural progression:

> *People were ready for it, and so was the sport. The time was*
> *ripe for soccer to become a truly multiracial and national sport.*
> *Most sports were played along racial lines, and this was a*
> *reflection of the nature of society in which we lived. Sports and*
> *its divisions [were] an everyday example of the divide-and-rule*
> *system of colonialism in which the various races were complicit*
> *partners as well as being victims of a process and system at play.*
> *But we were also getting ready by the 1960s for a more*
> *interactive society and soccer followed the trend of the times and*
> *opened up for good.*[11]

Soccer in Fiji is also played along sectarian lines in tournaments organised by various groups. The Easter weekend is unofficially set aside by the FFA for these tournaments. All major sectarian groups, including Muslims, Gujaratis, south Indians-Sangam, north Indians-Sanatan, Arya Samaji and Sikhs, have soccer competitions usually held in tandem with their annual conventions and meetings. Social and cultural activities, including traditional dances and musical performances, take place. Soccer takes centre-stage with district sides in recent years being joined by representative teams from the second-shift diaspora in Australia, New Zealand, Canada and the US. Other sports have been added to soccer, with women's netball the most prominent among volleyball, tennis, cricket and golf. These annual sectarian conventions and soccer tournaments reinforce the particular origins and sense of identity of the various groups that make up the Indo-Fijian diaspora.

Sectarian soccer in Fiji traces its origins in parallel lines to the formation of the Fiji Indian FA. However, the violence or tension that usually comes with such a division has been largely absent because of the common origins of most of the groups and the lack of an extremist fringe among them. The much more heterogeneous nature of the origins of clubs, district and school soccer and the smaller geographical space allowed much more interaction among players. The growth of a common soccer culture, with its emphasis on district loyalty, created a deep sense of fellowship among players and fans that transcended these sectarian schisms. Violence or ethnic tensions between Indo-Fijians and Fijians who play together at all levels are almost non-existent. One of the features of soccer in Fiji is the language code-switching among players from the two major groups and one-on-one social and cultural interaction evident among players and fans.

The idea of a common Fiji soccer culture beyond sectarian and ethnic divides is also brought out in the status and position accorded to soccer players. J. K. Gopal, M. T. Ali and Noor

Mohammed, some of the few remaining players from the inaugural days of the Fiji Indian FA, point out that soccer accorded them status and power that cut across all groups in society. Their incentive to perform they attributed in part to individual pride and the elevated status that they were accorded as soccer players. 'We came before the film stars and singers, and we were idolised by many of our fans,' remarked Ali. He remembers that their status was such that:

> Among the earliest photographs that were collected and placed on the wall in houses were of local soccer players and from other sports. These used to be copies from newspapers later, but in the early days they were copies of photographs taken at the studios which were prominently displayed and [which were] a major selling point. I remember walking down with some of my playing friends around Nausori, when we were invited into one of the Fijian bures … on the riverbank. I felt embarrassed to see one of my studio photographs stuck on the wall. My host did not know that it was my picture, as we looked quite different in our everyday clothes [compared with when we had] our soccer gear on. He was lost for words when one of my friends pointed out that I was the person in the photograph. Only then did I realise the important status in which I was regarded and it gave me more cause to do even better while playing.[12]

Ali's account also demonstrates the feeling of district pride and the following of the fortunes of the soccer sides by the Fijian community in this early period.

One of the features of these early teams was the attention they paid to uniforms and playing equipment for the players. Photographs from as early as 1930 show that particular attention was paid to presenting the right image for the game. Players wearing boots and socks of uniform types and set out in a uniform way characterise the group photo of the Dilkusha Excelsior team from Rewa in 1930. Their proud poise is evident in their erect posture and the serious expressions on their faces. The photo documenting their lives and their association with soccer becomes an important marker of an evolving identity. A similar picture emerges from the group photograph of the participating teams during the Indian Association Football League in 1928.[13] Slicked-back hair and proud arms folded across their chests, the players of the Sunshine Football Team of 1922 display their obvious pride and their idea of a team. The players stand erect in military precision around the leading figure of their captain, S. S. Deoki, who has his hands on the soccer ball, as the centre of the universe in this photograph. The picture in composition is one of unified and uniform precision of a complete being. In the picture, the pre-eminence of the captain is seen through his neatly folded socks and a pair of boots, with the other team members barefoot.

Clubs followed a structured hierarchy of administration with a patron at the head. Prominent local citizens, usually Indian businessmen or CSR or colonial officials, were preferred for this position. More intimately involved members then contested the other important positions of president, vice-presidents, secretary, treasurer/auditor, captain and related assistant positions. Some of these positions, especially those of the vice-presidents were created to salve the egos of unsuccessful contestants for the position of president. For example, the *Fiji Times* of 2 June, 1939, reported, 'In Ba the General Meeting of the All Blacks was held at the Krishna Theatre on Sunday, May 21st, 1939.' The details of the report bear out the highly structured nature of club organisation and the prominence accorded to the meeting by the relatively expensive nature of the venue for the meeting. True to form, the patron was C. V. Caldwell, District Commissioner.

The social and community spirit of soccer was demonstrated by the many social and benefit matches organised to raise funds to meet community needs and to provide entertainment for the sick or infirm. In July 1939, the Bhartiya Sports Club played at the leper colony on Makogai Island to provide 'entertainment and

hope' to the patients there. Sister Mary Stella, in her moving
account of the leper colony in *Makogai — Image of Hope*, points
out that on the island 'soccer and cricket were favourite games'.[14]
During the war years, many soccer charity matches were organised
and money was donated to the Soldiers' Fund. The social
responsibility taken by the mainly Indo-Fijian soccer fraternity
during World War II gives a balanced insight into Indo-Fijian
attitudes and their contribution to the war effort in Fiji. This
provides some counterweight to the stereotyped notion of the lack
of Indo-Fijian initiatives during the war.

Soccer also provided its own language (kick and chase —
maaro-bhaago-daage-toso/carpet soccer), icons (Pele, Charlton,
Faiz Mohammed 'Skipper', Dhir Singh 'Maina', Augustine
Thoman 'Auggie'), iconography (Suva-Black Cat as Mascot, Ba-
All Blacks, Rewa-Reds, Lautoka-Blues), myths and legends
(Augustine Thoman dive-heading the winning IDC goal in
1962). Among the soccer circles, talk was of the burgeoning local
clubs, village bazaar soccer and district soccer scenes. Fierce
loyalty to village, club and district would become hallmarks of
Fiji soccer fans in these early days. In the largely religious and
mythological realms of most of early Indo-Fijian poetry and folk
song compositions, soccer was elevated to the pantheons. Pandit
Pratap Chandra Sharma, a well-known Indo-Fijian poet and folk
song lyricist from Rewa, wrote the following poem in Hindi
(translated by J. S. Kanwal):

> *Of all the ball games*
> *Soccer is the most beautiful*
> *Each limb is rejuvenated in action*
> *At play fascinating are the skilful*
>
> *'There will be a game of soccer'*
> *This news creates sensation around*
> *Filling excitement in their hearts*
> *People crowd together in the ground*

Mutual differences are forgotten in the ground
Sentiments of universal friendship watched rightly
Related as human beings, opening arms
All hug one another tightly

Some of fight are presented by those
Who use swords and fists with their hands
But game of soccer shows us all
Clean fight with feet in the sports-lands

The swordsman could win laurels
After cutting and killing people
But soccer men get prize-cups
And receive them from the hands of the Governor

Soccer is game, it is fun too
Soccer is exercise, it is struggle too
Players displaying spirit of sportsmanship
Win name and fame in this world[15]

The poem found currency in written form as a published work and became the subject of oral performance as it was turned into a folk song. There is a clear emphasis on the idea of universal brotherhood (soccer being male and patriarchal) and commonality of purpose from 'soccer men' who 'get prize-cups' from the 'hands of the Governor'. The notion of receiving the 'prize-cup' from the Governor relates directly to the usual practice of the colonial British Governor usually being the patron of Fiji soccer and chief guest at the prize-giving. The links between soccer as the 'most beautiful' and notions of physical beauty and exercise are maintained alongside the idea of a 'clean fight with feet' and the spiritual dimension of creative play that transcends all barriers as 'Mutual differences are forgotten' at the news that 'There will be a game of soccer'.

The idea of geographical identity with a sense of belonging in Fiji, especially for Indo-Fijians, had not been clearly defined during indenture. Indenture was a period of contracts with clear delineation of work areas. Contracts of labour, land and capital aimed at ensuring the economic viability of the colony, and any sense of identity or of belonging was secondary to that principal concern. The growth of soccer, among other things, provided a sense of identity to the growing population of Fiji-born Indians and Indo-Fijians. Soccer and identification with the village or district was a tangible sense of identity. District loyalty through soccer helped define a sense of belonging and pride to a geographical area. Success and failure on the soccer pitch would help plot the seismograph of emotions and morale within the community of Indo-Fijians as an important part of the cultural palette that was evolving in Fiji. Indo-Fijian historian and writer Brij V. Lal noted in an interview that 'The local village [soccer] sides were a source of village pride and the stature and success of an area were sometimes closely aligned to the fortunes and misfortunes on the soccer field'.[16] This continues in Fiji despite the upheavals of coups and the reinvigoration of extremist nationalism.

NOTES

1 Kanwal, J. S. 1980. *A Hundred Years of Hindi in Fiji*. Suva.
2 *Fiji Times*, 18 September, 1924. p. 8.
3 Gopal, J. K. Interview, 8 September, 1997.
4 *Fiji Times*, 25 January, 1928. p. 11.
5 Dramatisation of the *Ramayana*, usually as large-scale productions combining various local Hindu religious groups. After indenture and for much of the mid- to late 1900s, this was an important cultural event that has, in recent years, declined, with fewer and fewer stagings of the dramatisation. A recent *Ram Lila* in Sydney, organised by the Fiji Indian Social and Cultural Association, featured the use of Fiji-Hindi for some of the comic scenes to mixed reception.
6 Kanwal, J. S. *A Hundred Years of Hindi in Fiji*. p. 40.
7 Prasad, Mohit. *Sixty Years of Soccer in Fiji*. Suva. p. 29.
8 *Fiji Soccer Tribune*. 1991. Suva. p. 47.
9 *Fiji Times*, 26 April, 1939. p. 4.
10 Lateef, Abdul. Interview, 15 September, 1997.
11 Prasad, Mohit. *Sixty Years of Soccer in Fiji*. p. 52.
12 Ali, M.T. Interview, 17 September, 1997.
13 Prasad, 36.
14 Sister Mary Stella, *Makogai-Image of Hope*. (Christchurch: Leper's Trust Board New Zealand, 1978) 79.
15 Kanwal 42.
16 Brij V. Lal, Interview, 9 September. 2003.

Wairuku Indian School, Ra. A typical classroom in many rural schools.
This was the first 'Indian' school in Fiji, started by Pandit Badri Maharaj.

CHAPTER ELEVEN

The Qawa 'Epidemic'

Jacqueline Leckie

'MASS HYSTERIA AT Qawa Primary School.' This was the initial diagnosis given on 13 November, 1968, by Labasa doctor G. R. Randall, concerning 18 girls, aged eight to 14 years, afflicted with a 'mysterious illness' originating at Qawa Indian Primary School, Vunivau, near Labasa. The symptoms included hyperventilation and twitching of the hands and arms.[1] Randall embellished this in an article published the next year in the *Fiji School of Medicine Journal*. 'Of 13 of the girls affected, all of them behav[ed] in almost exactly the same manner. They were all over-breathing, taking deep inspirations and exhaling with a musical wheeze, at a rate of about 50 respirations per minute. Some were standing, some sitting, some tended to faint and quickly recover.'[2]

This epidemic of hysteria apparently required greater Western medical expertise so Dr Sell, who was a psychiatrist and the Medical Superintendent of St Giles, flew to Labasa on 15 November, 1968. St Giles was a public psychiatric hospital originally established in 1884 as Suva's Public Lunatic Asylum. This was one of the few colonial mental health facilities in the Pacific Islands. It was an institution of containment, care and cure mostly for severely mentally disordered people of all ethnicities, men and women, the very young and the elderly. Although colonial concern

about the care and control of a few very disorderly mentally ill
girmitiyas may have been one reason for establishing a mental
asylum, admissions until about 1914 comprised relatively similar
proportions of ethnic Fijians and Indo-Fijians.

Then, quite sharply, the number of Indian patients
increased, especially after 1919, when most indentures had ceased.
The rate of Indo-Fijian admissions continued to be higher than
ethnic Fijians until the 1960s. From the 1970s, we have greater
parity between these two major ethnic categories. In contrast, the
medical officers in charge were always Europeans, until the
appointment of Dr Isaac Karim in 1961 and when Dr Ram
Narayan became the first Indo-Fijian Medical Superintendent at
St Giles in 1974. Samoan and ethnic Fijian warders or attendants
did most of the hands-on caring during the colonial period.
Although in 1940 Fiji's Council of Chiefs asked the Government
to employ more Fijians and Indians as warders, it was not until
1966 that an Indo-Fijian orderly (Ashok Kumari) was appointed.

Dr Sell worked in Fiji with limited contact with Indo-
Fijian professionals. Instead, his experience, like most doctors
dealing with the hospitalised mentally ill, was mostly with Indo-
Fijians suffering from psychoses and major depression, congenital
neurological disorders and severe epilepsy. I have ascertained this
from examining about 3,000 medical admission records between
1884 and 1964. A few rare cases during these years were
diagnosed with hysteria and were mostly Indo-Fijian women.
Following Western medical wisdom of the period, expatriate
medical experts and the local doctors they trained at the Fiji
School of Medicine regarded hysteria as a female condition:
'as the most dramatic and infamous of "women's diseases" …
Throughout much of medical history, hysteria has represented,
quite literally, an embodiment of female nature in the eyes and
minds of male observers.'[3]

Despite Western medical fascination with the hysterical
condition, it tended to be relegated to the 'neuroses'. Such

conditions were not usually serious or disruptive enough to require certification of the patient as mentally insane and admission to a psychiatric facility. So, as with many other mental disorders, treatments were often sought initially from experts within local communities, who might be religious experts or medical healers. It seems that when this did not 'cure' the bizarre and worrying manifestations of mental disturbance, Indo-Fijian families would seek solutions from biomedically trained experts. In most instances, this was a doctor in a divisional hospital. A few affluent Indo-Fijians privately consulted expatriate experts, such as Dr Sell, concerning psychiatric, psychological and social problems.

Dr Sell did not base his investigations within the localised spatial and cultural context of the hysteria, but instead requested the girls report to Labasa Hospital. Only 12-year-old Rukshmi (not her real name) turned up. Sell's medical interview with her was typical of those between Indo-Fijian patients and European doctors. He relied on an interpreter (here the Chief Education Officer). Stereotypes concerning not only her culture but her gender and age would not have been questioned. Sell had served in East Africa, which informed his pre-existing conceptions concerning mass hysteria in 'exotic' countries. Randall referred to this as 'the problem of hysteria in unsophisticated communities'.

Unlike colonial officials, parents did not always search for causes. They looked for solutions so that their daughters could be returned to 'normality'. Their daughters were two weeks away from end-of-year exams, and we have no reason to assume that this was not a stressful period. Medical experts did highlight that some of these girls were transitioning through puberty, menarche and adolescence, although it is questionable if this applied to an eight-year-old in 1968. The correlation of young women's hormonal and reproductive changes with 'hysteria' (hysteria was considered a fake mental illness) serves only to pathologise and medicalise women's bodies, and erroneously link women's minds with reproduction.

Former Northern Division District Commissioner Aubrey Parke has provided a more sensitive discussion of the specific cultural and spatial context that may have precipitated the Qawa 'hysteria'. From contemporary and later fieldwork with informants, he focuses on Davuiyaliyali, one of the sacred pools of the local *yavusa*, Qawa-i-ra. This is a shallow depression in a rock formation on Qawa hill-top, known as the *tanoa* (kava bowl), where the spirits manifested as tiny prawns. The site commanded respect and fear with tales of the ghosts of a white horse and a man. As Parke emphasises, this 'was and still is a place of considerable supernatural significance to both Fijian and Indian communities'. But, in 1963, this was disturbed when the hill-top was levelled to prepare land for the construction of the Qawa school. Parke recounts that local Fijians and Indo-Fijians urged the contractor, Munsami Sirdar, to avoid the pool and rock at Davuiyaliyali, so as to not disturb the spirits. He persisted in bulldozing this, which resulted in the sacred pool being filled with loose stones. The story continues two years later when, after cutting grass on the school's playground, Munsami became ill the next day and had died by 1968. Parke recalled that local people attributed this to Munsami's attempt to bulldoze the rock and his effrontery to the spirits. Soon after, the girls began to be affected by the 'affliction', while some staff were afraid to work at the school.

Another story was that some schoolboys had thrown stones at an Indian grave near the school's playground, after which the ghost of a man appeared. Stones thrown at a mango tree near the school may also have disturbed spirits because leaves from this tree were used in Hindu religious ceremonies. Parke discusses these different narratives to locate hysteria within the context of spirit possession, whereby once normally benign spirits were disturbed by humans, the spirits then possessed human bodies.

Like many medical experts of their time, Dr Randall and Dr Sell subscribed to the theory of hysteria as contagion. Randall observed that after the initial outbreak at Qawa, the 'rumours of mysterious epidemics were rife'. The situation looked as if it would become more serious with 'more girls and maybe more schools being affected'. This was overlaid with preconceptions of 'primitive mass suggestibility', which were transferred from Sell's experience as a colonial psychiatrist in Africa to Fiji. He had temporarily closed two schools three or four years earlier after witnessing such hysteria among pupils and teachers in East Africa. A similar solution was applied to Qawa, where Sell ordered the school be closed for a week. He instructed firmly that the 'hysterical' girls remain with their families and be separated from one another. The isolation of hysterical individuals and avoidance of any public 'exorcism' was a favoured practice during epidemics of hysteria in European history. Sell made the following comments on mass hysteria among school children in Fiji:

> Because of the 'contagious' nature of the hysterical symptoms, and their dependence on the 'Zeitgeist' it probably occurs more often in children attending schools in primitive countries or in developing countries.

Medical historian Mark Micale has documented how in Western histories over the centuries hysteria has been a medical and diagnostic category as well as a descriptive term used in lay discourse. It has been a medical category with wide-ranging, shifting and nebulous meanings. But, 'in lay parlance, the word has traditionally denoted a common form of emotionally excessive behaviour'.[4] Nineteenth-century discourses embraced nervousness, neurasthenia and nerve prostration, and hysterical insanity, which were interpreted as a form of degeneration and 'out and out madness'. Doctors invoked the label hysteria to refer to any nervous malady with spastic or convulsive complications. When doctors saw twitching movements among the schoolgirls at Qawa, they also came up with a diagnosis of hysteria. Another textbook pattern of hysteria was that it was considered to be a condition that could simulate or imitate other disorders. So, when the schoolgirls were over-breathing for no physical or organic cause, hysteria appeared to be the appropriate category in which to assign such behaviour.

Micale has also explored how hysteria has been a metaphor for feminine stereotypes throughout modern Western history. Hysteria has long been a so-called women's disease. The ancient Greek physician, Hippocrates, attributed this to the movement of the uterus (*hystera*) from its usual position to other parts of the body, such as the throat (therefore neck constrictions were considered a typical female 'hysterical' symptom). Although by the 20th century this theory was discounted, the linking of hysteria with the reproductive aspects of women's corporeality and the apparently associated excesses of emotionality and femininity remained entrenched in popular and medical Western discourse. Dr Sell affirmed the correlation of hysteria with gender. He had never 'come across this in boys' and, like many doctors, he believed that 'the menarchal girl exposed to emotional tension is particularly at risk'. Sell did consider wider social tensions, although he linked this with gender. He urged the 'need to manipulate the precipitating factor in the environment — usually one of mounting emotional tension'.

This is one of the puzzles when we revisit the attribution of causation in the hysteria at Qawa. The doctors conflated both preconceptions about hysteria and gender with their assumptions about the superiority of Western biomedicine over Indian 'superstition'. They emphasised the collective hysteria of young women and considered that the parents were facilitating this through 'superstitious beliefs and practices' and resorting to 'witchdoctors'. I do not doubt that these doctors had humane intentions, but their records indicate the limitations of understanding about gender (especially young women) and ethnicity in Fiji within a medical and community context. None of the written accounts offer any insight into what the schoolgirls at Qawa thought was the cause of their unease and strange behaviour. It seems appropriate here to digress from the Qawa epidemic to consider two possibly relevant issues from the past: first, education and, secondly, mental illness and diagnosis and young Indo-Fijian women.

The Qawa incident reminds us of the chequered and vulnerable history of formal education for Indo-Fijian females. Clearly, the parents of the students at Qawa valued their daughters being educated. But, for many years, Indo-Fijian women had less access to formal education than Indo-Fijian males and indigenous women. A study published a quarter of a century after the Qawa 'epidemic' revealed that in a sample of market vendors in Suva, 44 per cent of Indo-Fijian women had no education compared with only 2 per cent of indigenous women. Reasons for such gendered ethnic disparities in education are complex. Indo-Fijian communities generally preferred to educate male children, but this must be considered against family labour and economic constraints. Indo-Fijian women tended to marry at younger ages than other ethnic groups in Fiji. In 1936, Fiji's Director of Education noted that Indo-Fijian women were 'usually withdrawn' from school before 11 years of age to prepare for marriage and to provide household labour.

Even in the 1990s, anthropologist Sue Carswell was reminded of dominant attitudes among Indo-Fijian farming families near Labasa: 'The girls should be only educated up to class eight [age 13], then keep two or three years home, stay home, just get some education in cooking food and how to put their houses [in order] and then 17, 18 they marry.'[5] Hassan Khan, Director of Fiji's Council of Social Services, confirmed this view in 1997, observing that investment in education still favoured boys rather than girls. Economic pressures have demarcated choices in allocating money and time for education for boys and girls. Another persistent influence on early marriage (and limited education) has been Hindu and Muslim ideologies surrounding female modesty. Despite these cultural and economic restrictions, it should be emphasised that the parents in Qawa in 1968 were part of a growing trend, even within relatively poor communities, that would see Indo-Fijian women attain formal education. Indo-Fijian women's educational opportunities also need to be set against colonial intransigence to educate Indian immigrants before World War II. The impact of these wider social and cultural issues on the girls at Qawa is impossible to pinpoint, but some may have experienced tension from the expectations of attaining educational success, current domestic responsibilities and the growing awareness of their future role as a bride.

Although the young women suffering from 'epidemic hysteria' at Qawa in 1968 were not mad, the fact that the Government's consultant psychiatrist was urgently brought in and ostensibly took control, that psychotropic medications were administered to at least one student, that other psychiatric arsenal were suggested, and that the few written records surrounding this resonate with 1960s Western psychiatric discourse, cannot be ignored. Dr Sell's presence in the Macuata region may have been a mystery to many parents at Qawa, but some and certainly most health professionals would have immediately associated him with St Giles, the final site of incarceration for the truly and legally 'mad'. This digression aims to take the emphasis on Indo-Fijians and mental distress into a wider discussion than published literature, which, quite rightly highlighted the appallingly high suicide rates among male girmitiyas[6] and the subsequent higher rates of suicide among Indo-Fijians compared with other ethnic groups in Fiji.[7]

Until about 1955, women comprised only about 25 per cent of admissions to St Giles, but thereafter admissions assumed a gendered balance. Moreover, Indo-Fijian females had a higher proportional increase than Fijian females. This probably did not reflect higher rates of mental illness within any specific ethnic group but, as Dr Randall indicated, the greater willingness by Indo-Fijians to access medical doctors and hospitals. We are still trying to understand the reasons for this increase in female admissions to St Giles during the post World War II period, but of equal concern was patients being admitted at much younger ages. I found that between 1947 and 1962, at least 25 people aged 16 and under were admitted to St Giles. The youngest was an Indo-Fijian girl, diagnosed with post-encephalic dementia. She was aged seven and spent six months there in 1961, and was readmitted during the next year. Most of these very young patients were female Indo-Fijians. The average age was 13 years, with diagnoses ranging from paranoia to schizophrenia to idiot and even hysteria. The explanations for this are unclear. It may reflect how some Indo-Fijian families, in response to economic pressures, residence in smaller families, but also with greater faith in modern Western medicine, were accessing health and State institutions during these years.

Solutions: The power of Western biomedicine

Western expertise attempted to examine 'commonsense' causes and scientific/medical explanations (and ultimately solutions). Because Rukshmi was the only 'subject' Sell had access to, he applied what to him was a rational and accurate test: Eysenck's Sway Test. 'In order to confirm, or exclude the original diagnosis of hysteria, the Education Officer was asked to suggest to the girl that she would start to fall backward if she placed her feet together and closed her eyes. This she proceeded to do almost at once and she was told to open her eyes and sit down on a bench. Eysenck's Sway Test is generally accepted as having a strong positive correlation with hysteria. The Girl stated she felt dizzy and strange and began to over-breathe and twitch her hands and arms. This was sufficient confirmation of the original diagnosis and she was told to stop what she was doing. She stopped immediately, and on being asked to leave the room, got up and left in a normal manner.' We learn little from this account about what Rukshmi had recently experienced at school, home or in the community. The reliance on observation and tests was indicative of how, after World War II, the globally increased faith in and use of testing in medicine and education was being applied to Fiji. Testing became the norm for diagnosis, but this also represented the application of scientific measurement to determine the normal/abnormal body, mind and social behaviour and assessments of delinquency or deviancy.

But in Labasa in 1968, Western biomedicine did not stop with tests. Although Sell's initial examination at Labasa hospital declared Rukhshmi 'normal', she was prescribed the strong antipsychotic drug Largactil (chlorpromazine) 'before she calmed down'. By the 1960s, this drug was used throughout Fiji in the control and treatment of patients with a wide variety of mental 'abnormalities', from, as in the Qawa case, hysteria, to elsewhere, schizophrenia, mania (today considered part of a bipolar mental disorder and other conditions) to epilepsy. Largactil was introduced to Fiji in 1955, only two years after its adoption in Western Europe and the US. Very large doses were often prescribed to sedate patients, including young people.

Unfortunately, Largactil could have profound side effects. Medical discourse labelled these with terms such as antichorinergic, extrapyramidal, Parkinsonism syndromes and tardive dyskinesia. The effects on the patient could range from a dry mouth to blurred vision, constipation, urinary hesitance, falls, bizarre muscle contractions, sedation, emotional blunting, withdrawal, apathy, shuffling gait, akathisia (motor restlessness), involuntary bizarre grimacing, lip smacking and tongue protrusion. The effects depended on the severity and length of medication and whether or not counteractive medication was prescribed. The main point is that heavily sedative and highly interventive medication could be prescribed when mentally disturbed patients such as Rukhsmi presented within a medical setting. Her feelings of being 'dizzy and strange' are not surprising given the medication used and the probing interest in her case. Isolation from her peers would have also heightened her unease. Rukhsmi never returned to school, but her hysterical classmates (who collectively underwent spiritual intervention) did. The difference between Rukshmi's outcome and the other girls was that her behaviour was individually pathologised, and seemingly verified by her medical history of unstable emotional behaviour during the previous three years. These were noted as 'black outs' and over-breathing episodes.

This conforms to the individual case method of Western biomedicine. 'So it seemed here we had the "trigger" girl, whom all the other girls were copying, and the whole epidemic could be traced to her, with the impending exams, and the impending menarche, tipping the "hysterically inclined" girls in the class into hysteria. The only girl who really needed any treatment was the "trigger" girl herself.' She was the only girl who came for treatment to the hospital. Sell had also suggested a form of electroconvulsive treatment (ECT) for hysteria. We 'must stop hyperventilation quickly — causes alkalinity of the blood which leads to impairment of consciousness which leads rapidly to dissociation and a rapid reinforcement of hysterical behaviour … If "global hystericus" present and one is near a physiotherapy department a couple of electrodes placed on either side of the throat and a quick burst of current, faradic or galvanic, will immediately cure — may need two or three treatments.'

Such technology does not appear to have been applied at Labasa, but, at St Giles in Suva during those years, ECT was widely administered to patients, especially those who were acute admissions. Sell further recommended anticonvulsant drugs, such as Diphenylhydantoin (Dilantin) to treat hysteria 'to inhibit mass cortical discharge'. This drug was usually prescribed for epilepsy. This was in keeping with Sell's biomedical explanation of mass hysteria: 'Mass hysteria appears to start as an anxiety-hysteria in response to "free-floating" fear and changes into conversion-hysteria when specific factors in the "anxiety-making" background are pinpointed … process of reinforcement of the deinhibition of the limbic system is set up … need for prompt and firm treatment.'

Solutions: Local Indo-Fijian cures

Parents were reluctant for their daughters to consult with Dr Sell. Dr Randall found this 'interesting, as normally the Indian population make more than full use of the Hospital, but on this occasion they had clearly decided that the whole affair was beyond the powers of Western medicine, and only their local "witch doctors" could get to the bottom of it'. Randall's terminology would be considered offensive today, but it was common within modern Western medical discourse during those years. Instead of depending on Western medical expertise, parents unsuccessfully consulted various Hindu healers before eventually taking their daughters for treatment to Amina, an Indian healer at Bulileka. It did not seem to matter that the girls were Hindu and the healer was Muslim. The girls stayed in her compound. Parke relates that Amina 'had acquired Fijian powers of healing while living on the island of Taveuni, renowned for its Fijian healers and witchdoctors'. She rubbed coconut oil on the girls' throats, prayed and calmed them, but when they left the compound the 'hysteria' returned. Sell suggested that Amina might have been applying Ayurvedic sympathetic treatment or Tantric therapy.

Amina had never been to the sacred pool, but she had knowledge that the spirits there were angry and so had afflicted the girls. She visualised figures like tiny children around the pool. She suggested that members of the school committee should ask the Fijian landowners to appease the spirits of the pool by presenting *yaqona* (kava) to them. Although Poe, the chief of the

Qawa-i-ra landowners, did this and asked forgiveness from the spirits, the girls continued to be affected. The next remedy the parents tried was to enlist the support of Mara Sirdar, the main *pujari* (prayer man) of the Vunivau Hindu fire-walking *mandir*. Parke provides us with details of the elaborate *puja* that Mara Sirdar offered at the school. This was primarily to cleanse the school of *shaitan* (evil spirits), reduce the young women's anxiety, and seek forgiveness for offences that the spirits of the pool might have suffered. He called on the support of Ganesh, the elephant god, to help protect the school and heal the girls. Mara Sirdar offered Hindu and Fijian propitiations. Around the perimeter of the pool he burned camphor and poured *yaqona* (kava) and he also poured milk into the pool.

Although this *puja* appeared to calm the girls' distress, a week later an even bigger Om Shanti *puja* was held with a *pandit* (priest) praying to nine major Hindu gods to exorcise the *shaitan*. Again, Parke has described the extensive preparation the parents made for this, including that for a *havan* (sacred fire) of dried mango twigs and cooking *prasad* (sacred food). The affected girls, with the exception of Rukshmi, actively participated in the *puja*. They faced the sun as this was the auspicious planet for the day and poured ghee on to the *hawar*. After the distribution of the *prasad*, the remains of the *puja* were placed under the sacred mango tree. Mara Sirdar also prepared talismans for each girl to wear around her neck as protection from evil spirits. They were instructed to treasure these copper cylinders, which had been filled with *bhabut* and *nim* leaves.

Sell was totally dismissive of this public ceremony. One 'should never highlight or dramatise the symptoms of hysteria or treat on communal or group lines. The grand Hindu ceremony of exorcising held last Sunday in Labasa was a perfect example of what not to do.' The ceremony not only displayed 'superstition', but was contrary to the medical wisdom of isolating hysterical and other troublesome patients.

It may appear initially that Western biomedicine and traditional healing/religion were polarised in method and rationale. Western experts, with their confident ethnocentric discourse and 'expert knowledge' that dismissed local healers, appeared to confirm this. Randall saw his explanations as 'perfectly logical and rational' in contrast with the parents, who were 'ignorant and superstitious'. Yet, although the European doctors were dismissive of local knowledge, they recognised that the parents had 'quite a different explanation'. Indeed, after Randall had reflected on the efficacy of the religious 'cure', he concluded his journal article with a curious reference to the possibility of the supernatural and acknowledged: 'There is much in their [Indo-Fijian] culture that defies logical explanation.' Equally, with hindsight, we can ask questions about the rationale behind medical analysis and suggested treatments for the 'Qawa epidemic'.

This points to the ambivalent relationship that health practitioners trained in Western biomedicine had with indigenous medicine and belief systems. As in 1968, indigenous healers have continued to be valued within Indo-Fijian and Fijian communities. These healers have called on an array of interventions from spiritual to community negotiations and the use of herbs, medicines, massage and diet to treat the mentally unwell. As Parke has carefully recounted, examples such as that at Qawa in 1968 are indicative of an intermingling of Hindu, Muslim and Fijian healing and spirituality. I would stress that such dynamics produced uniquely localised beliefs and practices in Fiji, which sometimes complemented Western and colonial modernity, and at other times disrupted this.

Although some doctors have been prepared to acknowledge alternative healing, most medical practitioners in Fiji, including Indo-Fijian professionals, retained their faith in the progress of biomedicine and were highly sceptical about traditional practices. Often these became subsumed under the derogatory term 'witchcraft'. 'Despite being illegal,' Dr Sell observed, 'witchcraft continues to be practised, though perhaps to a lesser extent than formerly. The witch doctor is generally quite competent to deal with these mental disorders which are open to suggestion but can do much harm when attempting to treat the psychoses; such attempts are not only useless but serve to delay the admission to hospital of patients who, if brought early to hospital, would respond rapidly to modern psychiatric treatment.'

In 1974, the Medical Superintendent of St Giles, Dr Ram Narayan, stated: 'The causes of physical and mental illnesses began to be understood in the Western medicine within the past 300 years and within the past 30 years have come an array of potent medical remedies such as antibiotics, and drugs used in the treatment of mental illness. These potent drugs have proved far more effective than the traditional suggestion and conviction of the healers.' But Dr Narayan recognised that indigenous healing might assist a patient and identified some psychological similarities with Western medical practice: 'Many of these [indigenous] healings are based on design to cluster the morale of the patient and his family and the effectiveness depends on the authority and conviction imparted to the patient and his family. The element of suggestion plays a large part as it does in Western medicine; and an intelligent doctor recognises this and uses it to make his treatment more effective.'

At Qawa School in 1968, a group of schoolgirls repeatedly exhibited bizarre behaviour, which, to most of the local community, was a sign of spirit possession. A few people were sceptical of this common understanding and, like the medical doctors, focused on individual and collective abnormal emotionality. This was framed in gendered terms and fitted into the old medical category of hysteria, considered indicative of the female condition. Modernists such as the doctors and a few local sceptics also regarded hysteria as a product of ignorance and primitive superstition.

NOTES

[1] This paper forms part of a broader project on the history of insanity in Fiji. For that reason, I have not attempted a thorough documentation of the evidence on which it is based. Where quotations are not cited, it should be assumed that they are from the archival record I have used. An especially helpful account for my own research was Parke, Aubrey. 1995. 'The Qawa Incident in 1968 and Other Cases of Spirit Possession: Religious Syncretism in Fiji.' *Journal of Pacific History*, 30:2. pp. 210–26.

[2] Randall, G. R. 1969. 'Epidemic Hysteria.' *Fiji School of Medicine Journal*, 4 (12). pp. 4–5.

[3] Micale, M. S. 1995. *Approaching Hysteria: Disease and its Interpretations*. Princeton, NJ. p. 68.

[4] Ibid., pp. 108–11.

[5] Personal communication.

[6] Lal, Brij V. 1985. 'Veil of Dishonour: Sexual Jealousy and Suicide on Fiji Plantations.' *Journal of Pacific History*, 20: 3. pp. 135–55.

[7] Haynes, R. H. 1987. 'Suicide and Social Response in Fiji: a historical survey.' *British Journal of Psychiatry*, 151. pp. 21–6.

*Bullock-drawn plough, a common sight in rural Fiji, preparing
the field for cane planting. Tractors are becoming more popular.*

CHAPTER TWELVE

Marriage

Brij V. Lal

BHOLA AND HIS wife Sukhraji were resting on the verandah of their lean-to house one hot afternoon when Nanka, their neighbour, dropped by. *'Ram Ram bhai,'* he said to Bhola — greetings brother — as he parked himself on a wooden crate. Sukhraji dashed to the kitchen to make tea as Bhola and Nanka engaged in small talk about village affairs. When Sukhraji returned with three enamel cups of black tea, Nanka turned towards her and asked, 'Can I say something *Bhauji?*' 'Yes, *Babu.*' Sukhraji never called village men by their name, she always called them *Babu* or *Badkau*, husband's younger and older brother, respectively. That was the village way. 'Dewa is ready for marriage,' Nanka said, adding mischievously, 'And you are not getting any younger either. Bhola *bhai*, you listen as well.' Bhola listened, but didn't say anything. 'You need someone besides Bhola *bhai* to look after you.' Nanka was what people in the village called a *muh-chutta*, a loudmouth, a harmless joker, an impotent flirt, not to be taken seriously.

'What are you people for?' Sukhraji replied instantaneously. 'He is your son, too.' This was village talk. 'Why don't you people do something about it instead of putting all the responsibility on just the two of us?' 'Was waiting for the word, *Bhauji,*' Nanka replied. 'All go now. But remember one thing, I will be the first to embrace the Samadhin [the bride's mother].' *Samdhin se chaati sab se pahile hum milaib.* 'You can do whatever you want with her,' Sukhraji replied smiling. 'Just find us a good homely girl for our boy.'

Dewa's future had been on Bhola's mind for some time, too, but he had not said anything to anyone. He had been married at 17, and Dewa was now nearly 20. 'You don't want to be a grandfather to your own children,' Bhola remembered old-timers saying. An unmarried man at that age caused comment, and Bhola had several younger children to think of. Besides, who knew when the passion of youth might lead him astray? Bhola thought of Asharfi's son Jhikka, who had made Dhanessar's daughter pregnant. The poor girl was sent away to another village, presumably to lose the child, but her brothers took their revenge. One night, as Jhikka was returning from a *Ramayan* recital, they ambushed him, beat him unconscious and threw him into the roadside ditch. No one said a word. No one volunteered information about the culprits to the police or the *panchayat*, the village council, and no one was ever apprehended. That was village justice. Rough and brutal and effective. Jhikka survived, but only as a chastened nervous wreck. Dewa was a good boy and Bhola wanted things to remain that way.

That night after dinner, Bhola and Sukhraji talked about Dewa. 'What Nanka Babu said is true,' Sukhraji said. 'I am getting on. We need another helping hand in the house.' 'Don't believe that flatterer,' Bhola replied, edging closer to his wife. 'He says that to everyone to make himself feel younger. You have at least another two sons in you.' '*Chup*. Hush. What if the children hear such talk?' The 'children', teenagers, were sleeping in the adjacent room in the huge thatched house. 'I want a break from all this routine. I want to visit relatives I haven't seen for years. Before it is too late. And grandchildren would be nice, too.' Everyone else their age in the village was already a grandparent.

Grandchildren! How fast time had flown, Bhola thought. It did not seem that long ago that he himself had been married.

They had suffered so much together: the death of two infant children, the disintegration of the joint household, the betrayal of family and friends, the poverty. But through all that the family had remained intact. His family was all that he had. He was immensely proud of that, and of his wife, who had been by his side faithfully all these years. 'Remember when we got married and you came here as a *dulhain* [young bride] for the first time?' Bhola asked Sukhraji. 'Do I remember? I remember everything as if it happened yesterday ...'

Sukhraji's parents lived across the Laqere River at the edge of the cane settlement by the sea. They had moved there a few years after the '*Badi Beemari*', the influenza epidemic of 1918. No one knew much about them, because they were not cane-growers. Her father, Chiriya, was a *girmitiya*. He had been a train driver for the CSR on the Tua Tua line, but that was all that was known about him. How he became a train driver, when he came to Fiji, and from which part of India, were all lost, like so much of the history of his people. (Her mother died when Sukhraji was still an infant.) After her father's death some time in the 1930s, she was raised by various distant relatives. They were good to her, but she knew her place in the family. She cooked, cleaned and worked on the farm to make herself useful and kept out of people's way.

If Bhola was worried about Dewa, parents of girls faced a much bigger problem. No fate was worse for a family than to have a girl who dishonoured its name. *Izzat*, or honour, is big among village people. Girls were married off soon after puberty. It was so in Sukhraji's case. One day, her aunt said, '*Ladki badi hoi gai hai.*' The girl is ready for marriage. 'Ready' meant the beginning of menstruation. Ganga, the village leader, was approached. Feelers went out and Bhola was identified as a good prospect. The family had a good name: no thieves or scoundrels or jailbirds in the family closet, and their caste status was compatible; one was a Kurmi, the other Ahir, both 'clean' cultivators. Family elders met and the marriage pact was sealed with an exchange of gifts. Sukhraji was betrothed at 13, and married two years later. Sukhraji came into a family of complete strangers, married to a man, a boy really, she had never seen before. She carried on her innocent shoulders the hopes of her entire family, knowing in her heart that she could never return to them no matter what her fate in the new home. No one would have her back. The gift of a girl-child, *kanya daan*, once given can never be returned. The break was final.

At first, things didn't go well for Sukhraji. She was dark, though with fine features, whereas Bhola was fair, like his mother. They called her *karikki*, the dark one, derisively. Her mother-in-law, whom she called '*Budhia*' ('old woman'), was a real terror, a real *kantaain*, Sukhraji remembered. What went through Budhia's mind no one knew. Perhaps in old age, uprooted and displaced, she was trying to recreate the remembered world of village India where mothers-in-law reigned supreme. 'Have you forgotten how you used to beat me so mercilessly as if I were a mere animal?' Sukhraji asked Bhola with a trace of bitterness. 'Cleaning and sweeping after everyone had already gone to bed. And getting up at four in the morning every day. Food had to be cooked just the way she wanted it, to perfection. One mistake and the terrible names she called me: *chinnar, kutia, haramin*.' Sukhraji turned directly towards Bhola, 'You never stood up for me, not once, even when I was innocent. You always took her side. Always the dutiful son. Remember how they taunted me when I did not become pregnant for three years? Barren woman, they said. Remember the day she gave me a piece of rope to hang myself so that you could marry another woman and have children. You stood there and said nothing.'

Bhola listened to this sudden, unexpected flood of memories with an aching heart. There was no reply to Sukhraji's bitterness and anger. She had spoken the truth. Yes, he was a dutiful son. He never stood up to his parents, especially his mother. He was her only son. Nothing, no abuse was worse for a man than to be called a henpecked husband. Keeping one's wife in line, even if it meant thrashing her occasionally, was one way of showing that he was the master of the house, the man in charge, retaining his position in his mother's eyes. Bhola reached for Sukhraji's bangled wrists. 'Times were different, then. But all that is in the past now. We have built up our life together from nothing. This house, our children, our farm, our good name: all this we have done together. All this is just as much yours as it is mine. God willing, we will be together for a long, long time.'

Sukhraji was calmer now. The words had drained her. This was the first time, now that she was about to become a mother-in-law, that she had spoken so candidly about her traumatic past. This moment of release of the truth of their relationship somehow made her feel stronger, freer. She was not bitter. Somewhere in her heart, she had forgiven her husband for his violent ways. Bhola had been a good husband and father. In any case, he was all she had.

A week later, Bhola's older half-brother, Ram Bihari, came to visit him. Ram Bihari lived in Wailevu, about seven miles away, but, as the eldest, he was still the family leader. The entire extended family all over Labasa never took a major decision without his consent or involvement. He was there whenever he was needed; the family's public face and spokesman. After the customary cup of black tea, Bhola said, 'Bhaiya, time has come to get Dewa married. He is ready for a new life. If you know of any family ...' Before he had finished, Ram Bihari interjected. 'I know, I know. That is why I have come here today. Nanka told me about this in the market the other day.' Bhola was relieved. 'November might be a good time,' he said. 'By then, the rice will have been harvested and the cane cut with enough money for the expenses. And we will have about six months to make all the necessary arrangements.'

'I don't know anyone in Boca or Bucaisau,' Ram Bihari continued. 'There may be a few families in between I have

missed, but they can't be very important if I haven't heard of
them. You know me.' Bhola did. Ram Bihari was well known
throughout Labasa; he knew everyone who mattered. He was
president of his village *Ramayan Mandali*, member of the District
Advisory Committee, patron of the Wailevu Primary School. He
will find someone suitable for us, Bhola thought to himself and
was relieved.

'We are not looking for anyone special,' Sukhraji said from
the back room, her head respectfully covered with a light shawl.
Women always did that in the presence of strangers or family
elders as a mark of respect and modesty. 'Education is not
important. What will we do with an educated daughter-in-law in
a home like ours? And money is not important either. Girls from
rich homes expect too much and cause trouble.' What Sukhraji
wanted was someone from a respectable family, who would be a
home-builder, who knew about *ghar grhasthi*. And then she
thought of something else. 'As long as she is not *langdi-looli*
[deformed], we will be happy. Someone wholesome like Guddu's
wife.' Guddu was Ram Bihari's eldest son.

Ram Bihari said, after finishing his cup of tea, 'I have heard
of someone in Dreketi.' Neither Bhola nor Sukhraji knew much
about the place or anyone there. There was no sugar cane there,
and people lived a subsistence lifestyle. '*Ek dam Chamar tola* [a real
backwater],' Bhola laughed. 'Don't laugh, Bhola,' Ram Bihari
chided his younger brother in his characteristic big-brotherly way.
'I know the place, I know people there.' Bhola had forgotten. Ram
Bihari's oldest daughter was married in Seaqaqa, half-way between
Tabia and Dreketi. 'It is just a matter of time before Dreketi goes
places. Tabia will be nothing then. I have heard about sugar cane
farms opening there in a few years' time. Then the Chamars will
become Brahmins!' '*Na bhaiya, khali khelwaar men bol diya* [I was
just joking],' Bhola said, slightly embarrassed.

Ram Bihari, of course, had his own agenda. Another
family connection in Dreketi would be good for him, more *daru-*

murga (alcohol-meat) parties. The people there had a legendary reputation for hospitality, happily hosting visitors for weeks on end. If there was a 'Friendly North', it had to be Dreketi. And his daughter would have another family close by to visit. Ram Bihari had Kallu's family in mind. He knew them well. He went there whenever he visited his daughter in Seaqaqa. Kallu had five daughters, only the eldest of whom was married. Ram Bihari was smitten with Kallu's wife, Dhania. She was appropriately named after the spicy coriander plant, quick, witty, seductive and flirtatious. Openly so. She bantered, teased and tempted with suggestive conversation. Dhania made men dance to the click of her fingers. Given a chance, I might be in luck, Ram Bihari thought to himself.

One day, Ram Bihari pointed to the unploughed field next to Kallu's house. 'These fields haven't been ploughed for a while it seems. You could get a good crop of maize and lentils before the rainy season starts.' Dhania smiled without batting an eyelid. 'That's true. But what can I do? We have useless men here. They don't seem to have strong ploughs in the village any more. Maybe you could stay a few days and plough the fields.' The sensual innuendo was rustic and direct. Ram Bihari smiled at the thought. On another occasion, Ram Bihari remarked about the number of milch cows in the village. 'It's such a waste,' Dhania replied. 'Men here don't know how to drink milk.' Definitely good prospects here!

Once Kallu asked Ram Bihari about marriageable boys for his daughters. It was then that Ram Bihari had thought of Dewa. 'My daughters are my sons,' Kallu said proudly. They worked the fields, even ploughed the land, and cooked and cleaned at home. 'They know everything about home-making.' What he didn't say was that his daughters were also headstrong, independent and sensual free spirits. They were their mother's daughters. It was because of this reputation that people were reluctant to marry into the family. Ram Bihari overlooked this. 'I will do everything for you *bhai*. I feel like we are *rishtedaar*,' he said. Like relatives already.

'You should meet the family yourself, Bhola,' Ram Bihari told his younger brother. 'We will all go,' Bhola replied. Two weeks later they hired Mallu's car and drove to Dreketi; Bhola, Ram Bihari, Nanka and Chillar, a village friend. Sukhraji wanted to go as well, but Ram Bihari objected. Bhola said nothing. 'Arranging a marriage is men's business,' Ram Bihari said with the authority of a family elder. 'Besides, it is a long trip.' Neither was Dewa invited, which was not unusual on the first visit. 'This is just the first visit, *beta*,' Ram Bihari told Dewa. 'Of course, you will meet the girl when things get firmer.'

The party received a great welcome. Kallu spared no expense to see that his guests received the very best. A goat was slaughtered. Kava and rum were in plentiful supply. Dhania maintained a discreet distance after greeting the guests, but smiling glances and seductive winks were exchanged with Ram Bihari. Munni, the girl to be married, brought in tea and savouries. 'This is the girl,' Kallu said. No one looked up. It was not the thing to do. Besides, there was little to see. Munni's face was covered with a white shawl. 'God willing, she will be our daughter soon, too,' Ram Bihari replied. As the *agua*, he did all the talking. He was in his element. Bhola, always a reserved man, hardly said a word. Things turned out exactly as Ram Bihari had hoped. A return visit was arranged 'to see the boy'.

Only when the marriage arrangements were almost finalised did Dewa get to see his future bride. Kallu, Dhania and Munni travelled to Nasea on the pretext of seeing their relatives. There was a remote, very remote, chance that Dewa might decline. For a girl to be rejected at that stage would be disastrous for the family. Questions would be asked and reasons for the failure speculated on endlessly. Kallu did not want to do anything that might jeopardise the chances of his other daughters. Dressed for the occasion in new tight, green terylene pants, red shirt and black shoes, Dewa was nervous. Over buttered bread and tea in Long Hip's café, he cast furtive glaces at Munni. She smiled shyly, showing her fine features. Wheat-brown skin, full lips, perfectly proportioned nose and properly covered but ample bosoms. Dewa liked what he saw; he was hooked. Sukhraji, too, was pleased. Munni, shy and dutiful-looking, would make the ideal daughter-in-law. The marriage pact was sealed. *Maarit Pukka.*

'Big wedding for the big boy,' Nanka said when Ram Bihari came to see Bhola a week later. 'The biggest the village has seen,' Ram Bihari promised. 'Big *dhoom dhadaka* (celebrations). I will bring the whole of Wailevu down for the wedding. Then they will see what our family is made of.' Showing off the extended family was all a part of a wedding. A display of family strength and solidarity. And it would do Ram Bihari's reputation no harm either. Bhola was anxious. He was not tight, but he was not ostentatious either. Friends and neighbours in the village and extended family members was all that he had in mind for the occasion. A three-day affair, not a week-long celebration. He considered extravagant marriages a waste of time and money. He would have to borrow money to cover the expenses. And he had to think of his other school-age children. Yet Dewa was his oldest son, and this was the first marriage in the family. Besides, who was he to question his elder brother's decision?

The wedding was a big affair all right. Hundreds of people came. Three buses were hired to take the bridal party to Dreketi, with two taxis for the immediate family. For his part, Kallu spared no expense. The best dancers and *qauwwali* singers were hired. *Yaqona* was in ample supply, and the food was plentiful and delicious: kadhi, puri, jeera dhall, kaddu, tamarind and tomato chutney. The guests were impressed, even seasoned wedding attenders. 'So when's the next wedding, Bhola *bhai?*' one asked. 'You have struck gold. Everyone deserves a *rishtedaar* [relation] like this.'

Sukhraji was emotional all week; a little sad at the thought of 'losing' her son to another woman. But she was composed when the bridal party returned. Munni looked so pretty, she thought, dolled up in a red sari, her hands and feet decorated with *mehdi*, the parting in her hair covered with *sindoor*. Momentarily, her mind drifted to her own wedding all those years ago. Women and young girls and boys peeked at the bride. Village women gave small gifts to see the bride's face. They would later comment on her complexion, her clothes and jewellery, the amount of bridal gifts she had received: the stuff of village gossip.

Sukhraji was proud finally to be a *saas*, a mother-in-law. She helped Munni cook *kichadi*, a simple traditional dish of rice and dhall. This is normally the first dish that a bride cooks. It is more a ritual than a test of cooking, to show the villagers and relatives that the daughter-in-law can cook and will be a good householder. In the evening, a goat was slaughtered and beer flowed for all those who had helped with the wedding preparations.

Over the next few days, as guests and relatives departed, the tin shed was dismantled and large cooking pots returned to the neighbours. Life began to return to normal in the Bhola household. Remembering her own ordeal, Sukhraji was gentle with her daughter-in-law. Like a patient teacher, she introduced Munni to the way things were done in the house. The way Bhola liked his food cooked. The amount of ghee on his roti, salt in the curry, sugar in the tea. She introduced Munni to the neighbours, took her along to weddings and birthdays in the village. She was, in effect, training her successor as the next 'mother' of the household.

Then things began to change. In small, petty acts of defiance, Munni began to assert her independence. Munni washed her own and Dewa's clothes only. She ate her dinner alone in her separate house, without waiting for the menfolk to finish theirs. She hid away choice portions of meat for just the two of them. She refused to get up early to prepare breakfast for the family. Headaches and other mysterious ailments became

increasingly common. Sukhraji noticed these things but was not
worried. This was not how she had imagined things would work
out, but times were different and these were early days.

One day when Sukhraji asked Munni to massage her sore
shoulder, Munni exploded. 'What's the matter with you? Ever
since I have come here, you have been developing one sickness
after another. Always expecting me to be at your beck and call.
Ask your husband to massage your arse. I am not your *naukarin*
[servant].' With that, she huffed away into her house. Sukhraji
was devastated, and began to cry. The complete unexpectedness
of it all. The language, the temper, and the rudeness. Munni
would have been skinned alive in days gone by. 'Maybe she is
upset about something,' Bhola said to Sukhraji. 'I will speak to
Dewa.' When Bhola spoke to Dewa the next day, Munni had
already told Dewa of the previous day's altercation. Dewa knew
that Munni's complaints over work were exaggerated. He knew
that his father always fetched water, and the boys chopped
firewood. His mother washed her own clothes and that of his
younger siblings. They all pitched in more than in most other
households in Tabia. But, out of a sense of solidarity with his wife,
he said nothing.

Dewa had something else on his mind. Tota, the next
eldest, was in the first year of secondary school. Dewa resented
that. He wanted Tota on the farm to do some of the work, so that
Dewa could have free time of his own. 'Look at Tota,' Dewa said
to Bhola. 'He is all suit-boot, and here I am busting my arse
working for nothing. For whom? For what? What use would *his*
education be for me? It will be good for all of us if he left school
and worked on the farm.'

This hurt Bhola. He was speechless. He hadn't heard Dewa
talk like this before. 'All this will be yours one day, Dewa,' Bhola
said. 'You know this farm cannot support all of you. Educating the
boys is not easy, I know. It is hard for all of us, especially you. But,
God willing, and with a bit of education, the boys will stand on

their own feet. How can I can look in their eyes and stop them from going to school when we know there is no future for them here? God will not forgive us.' 'But what about me and my future?' Dewa asked. He was deeply embittered that he had been forced to leave school, although he was a bright student, and was made to work on the farm. 'You didn't allow me to complete my schooling,' he said accusingly. 'I would have made something of myself, instead of being a miserable menial.'

'I know, Dewa. But those days were different. Your mother and I wanted the world for you. But we were an extended family then. We couldn't decide things for ourselves on our own. Everything had to be considered properly. When they all decided that you should leave school, there was little I could do but go along.' He continued, 'I know you have been working hard recently. Why don't you and *badki* take a break. Go and visit Dreketi. Spend some time there. We will manage.' When Dewa mentioned this to Munni that night, she was ecstatic. 'The sooner the better,' she said, 'before they change their mind, or something happens to your good-for-nothing brothers.'

Three days later, Dewa and Munni went to Dreketi. Dhania grilled Munni on all the gossip, from beginning to end, *poora jad pullai*. Munni was unhappy. Something had to be done. Soon. Kallu and Dhania came up with a plan. They had more land then was of use to them. Much of it was lying fallow anyway. They could transfer some of the wooded land, perhaps 10 acres across the road, jointly to Dewa and Munni. Dewa would provide a helping hand, there would be another male in the house, and they could all keep an eye on things.

Kallu mentioned the proposal to Dewa and Munni the next morning. Munni could not believe her ears. Her own piece of land. Her very own house. She would be her own boss. 'This is a godsend,' she said to herself. But Dewa remained subdued. His lack of enthusiasm surprised everyone. 'What do you think, *beta*?' Dhania asked. 'This is good for all of us. You will have your own piece of land, your own peace of mind. And we will have a son we have always wanted.'

'This is wonderful,' Dewa replied, betraying no emotion. 'It is a complete surprise. Let me think about it.' 'Take your time, *beta*,' Dhania said. 'There is no hurry.' Then she asked if Munni could remain in Dreketi a couple of weeks more. 'We haven't seen each other for a very long time. Look at the poor thing. She desperately needs a break.' Dewa agreed.

Dewa knew from the very beginning that Dreketi was not for him. Hard work was never his suit. Clearing virgin land for crops would be no picnic. Getting by with as little physical exertion as possible was his motto. But lazy though he was, Dewa was also a proud man. In Dreketi, he would be a *ghar damaad*, dependent son-in-law. His pride would be dented and his freedom curtailed. He no longer would be a 'man' in his own right. And Dewa had his mind set on something else. To escape farm work altogether, he was taking driving lessons in Mallu's car to realise his ambition of becoming a bus driver. Easy work and the prospect of illegal income from shortchanging illiterate passengers attracted him. Dreketi was a dead-end for a driver.

Dewa mentioned the offer of land to his parents. They said little, hoping Dewa would remain in Tabia and eventually take over the running of the household. Besides, a *ghar damaad* was a lowly, despised figure in the community, much like a henpecked husband. But Ram Bihari encouraged Dewa to go. 'Times are changing, Bhola,' he said. 'Extended family under one roof with a common kitchen is a thing of the past. How long can you expect Dewa to remain with you? He will move one day, like my own sons. And he may not have an offer like this then.' But Dewa's mind was already made up.

In Dreketi, Kallu and Dhania were doing their own scheming. They began to work on Munni, not that she needed extra persuasion. Tabia would always be a trap for her, they told her. Dewa's siblings were still of school age and she would have to look after them, and her own children when they came, for a very long time, perhaps for the best years of her life. And for what? When Munni mentioned the possibility of a separate household, Dhania countered, 'But where will you live? On a miserly plot of land, which won't be big enough even to grow baigan.' She continued, 'Yes, Dewa might one day inherit the land, but not while Bhola is still alive. He is 50-something now. Another 20 years. Another 20 years of hell for you. And there is no guarantee that the other boys will not want their share as well.' Dhania pressed on. 'Think, girl. How many times have you been to the town, to the cinema? When was the last time you bought clothes for yourself? How many times have you come to visit us since you have been married?'

Listening to her mother, Munni remembered why the family had been keen for her to get married in Tabia in the first place. She had been sent there on a mission to look for suitable husbands for her sisters. Teachers, clerks, policemen and men like that, in cash employment. That would be easier from Tabia than Dreketi. And she had dreams of regular visits to the town, to the shops full of fancy goods, movies, visits to relatives in other parts of the island. But all she had in Tabia was the deadening routine of daily household chores: cooking, cleaning and looking after everyone else.

'Leave him,' Dhania implored Munni. Her sisters chorused support. Kallu said nothing. 'We will go to Social Welfare. I know a *babu* there. I will explain things to them. You will get a good monthly allowance. If they can't pay that — and you know they can't — you will have Dewa living with you here. At last you will be your own boss.' All this made sense to Munni. She could not lose either way. When Dewa returned a fortnight later to fetch Munni, the old proposal came up again. Dewa could not tell the real reason why he could never live in Dreketi. He talked half-heartedly about the difficulty of having to start from nothing. The bullocks and farm implements he would have to buy and the building material for the new house.

'They are our concern, *beta*,' Dhania said. 'That is our responsibility.' Still sensing his reluctance, Dhania continued, 'It is noble of you to think about your brothers and sisters. But what about you and Munni, about your children and family?' Like a gushing tap, Dhania continued, while Munni sat with her eyes glued to the ground. 'You are giving your life, and Munni's life, for people who won't be there for you when you will need them. There is no future for you there, *beta*.' 'Some day,' Dewa said politely, hoping to diffuse the palpably mounting tension. 'By then, it might be too late,' Dhania replied. It was clear that Dewa was stalling, his mind made up. Dreketi would have to wait. 'Get ready, let's go,' Dewa said to Munni. 'The bus will arrive shortly.'

'No, Dewa, you go,' Dhania said to her son-in-law, using his name to his face for the first time. 'Go back to where you belong. Munni will stay where she properly belongs.' Dewa looked toward Munni, who kept her face averted. Dhania had spoken for her. Dewa left, thinking all this was a minor hiccup. They will eventually come to their senses. They didn't. A month later, a letter arrived from Shankar and Company. Munni had filed for divorce.

An approximate — not literal — version of this in Fiji Hindi is in 'Maarit', page 389

Morning prayer, Wairuku Indian School, Ra.

CHAPTER THIRTEEN

All Saints' Primary, Labasa

Christine Weir

IN THE MIDDLE of 1958, All Saints' Anglican School in Labasa welcomed a series of visitors, all of whom recorded their impressions in the school's logbook.[1] Bruce McCall, secretary of the Australian (Anglican) Board of Missions (the school's sponsors), described the school as 'very impressive'; Mr G. William of the Colonial Office commented on the 'opportunities for lively and creative activity'; and the Indian High Commissioner thought 'the discipline excellent and the girls and boys neatly dressed and well behaved ... they looked intelligent'. At the end of the year, 18 boys were accepted from Class Eight into secondary schools and the headmaster, Reverend K. Appasamy, could reflect on a highly successful year.

And, indeed, the All Saints' school logbooks of the 1950s and 1960s, now filmed by the Pacific Manuscripts Bureau in Canberra and available to researchers, show a thriving school. With a constant enrolment of about 400 students in Classes One to Eight, All Saints' was one of the largest schools in the district. It had a boarding hostel for about 20 boys, but most of the students were from the town and immediate surrounds — the children of shopkeepers, tradesmen and civil servants. With fees of 30 shillings a term,[2] it was beyond the financial reach of most small agriculturalists. This was acknowledged by the governing

board, but there was felt to be little alternative if the school was
to stay afloat financially. Rev Appasamy commented in 1956:
'What we lose in quantity may be balanced in quality.' He noted
with approval that in July 1957, 75 per cent of the boys were
wearing shoes, clearly a marker of affluence. While it had a
majority of Indo-Fijian students, All Saints' School offered the
relatively rare experience of a multiracial education, with about
50–60 Fijian and part-European students, according to the few
figures available of the racial composition of the school. Hindi
and Fijian were taught alongside English. The school was
coeducational in the first three years, the girls (or at least those
whose parents allowed them to continue, a proportion which
grew over the period) then going mostly to St Mary's Anglican
School, two miles away.

It was a lively school. The school's scout troop went on
regular hikes and camps: in 1952, they climbed the peak of
Bukalevu in March, and went on a 'tramping and island camp' in
June. In 1958, and in later years, the school troop won the local
proficiency challenge. There was a Brownie pack for the young
girls. The school regularly displayed produce at the Young
Farmers' Club Shows, sometimes winning prizes. The grounds
were planted with shrubs and trees, for beauty as well as an
agricultural exercise. In 1957, the boys planted 500 sticks of
cassava, 100 pineapple plants and a row of banana trees, and
constructed a pergola with creepers to camouflage the septic
tank, while the next year, under Augustine Sitaram's guidance,
senior boys planted a row of trees for Arbor Day. Soccer and
athletics were popular activities, All Saints' soccer team proving
particularly successful in the early 1950s, when one of their
teachers, Mohammed Yasim Khan, also played for the Labasa
soccer team. The students were regularly reminded of the empire
and their loyalties to it. Empire Day school gatherings were
addressed by the District Officer. Students attended films entitled
The Funeral of George VI, Royal Destiny and *A Queen is Crowned.*

Year groups went on end-of-year picnics to Malau, Batiri or the Three Sisters. Nurses and doctors visited the school to inspect teeth — finding in the process a distressing number of dental caries — and to inoculate children against tuberculosis and typhoid, and, by the mid-1960s, against the scourge of polio. All in all, this was a thriving and successful school.

And it was a Christian school, following a long tradition of mission involvement in the education of children. When the Methodists, the first Christian missionaries in Fiji, started village education, it was primarily to make their converts literate and able to read the Bible. Alongside this was the aim of 'civilising' Fijians and introducing 'British values'. Christianity and literacy had been readily adopted by Fijians and the small schools started by the Methodists soon became part of the village scene. Most were taken over by village committees during the 1930s, while the Methodist missions maintained responsibility for teacher training at Davuilevu, and at some secondary and higher elementary schools, including Lelean Memorial School for boys, Ballantine Memorial School for girls, Lautoka Boys' School and Jasper Williams School for girls.

In relation to the Indo-Fijians, the situation was different. Until 1901, the Methodist Church paid little attention to the *girmitiyas*, the indentured Indians. Although the Indian catechist, John Williams, arrived in 1892, the Mission Board in Sydney saw evangelising *girmitiyas* as low on their list of priorities.[3] What concerned missionaries was the effect of Indians on their Fijian converts, who had accepted Christianity at the hands of the Methodists, but who were as yet 'babes in the faith', had not reached Christian maturity and could be easily subverted by 'evil'. The proprietorial attitude of Methodist missions towards 'their' Fijian converts is clear in the 1910 comment of a Methodist visitor to Fiji, Mr Morley: 'If we do not Christianise these Indians, they will Paganise our Fijians.' While those who worked with Indians — particularly Hannah Dudley, John

Burton and Richard Piper — saw their conversion as an end in itself, the view that it was merely a means to the end of preserving the faith of Fijian Christians was prevalent among Methodists.

Education among Indo-Fijians was initially, as among Fijians, an aid to conversion and to enable the reading of the scriptures. But few conversions took place and Indians showed little interest in Christianity. Evangelism proved fruitless and frustrating; indeed, so frustrating that in 1919 the Methodists handed over their Indian work on Vanua Levu to the Anglicans and concentrated their efforts on Viti Levu. This explains why the non-Catholic Christian schools for Indo-Fijians in Labasa were run by the Anglicans; All Saints' School was started in 1924 by Miss Irene Cobb, an Australian lay missionary. The *girmityas*, however, while resisting attempts to convert them to Christianity, showed great interest in the education missions were offering. This remained true throughout the 20th century. Although the *girmityas* recognised early that education was their best means of economic advancement, indeed, even of survival, the Colonial Government was not much interested in providing such education.

Until the 1918 establishment of the (government-run) Natabua Indian School, mission education was the only education available to Indians and it remained important, especially at the higher grades. In 1944, 63 per cent of those Indian children who were in education attended committee schools, 7 per cent government schools and 30 per cent Christian mission schools.[4] While the absolute number of Indo-Fijian children in school was higher in the 1950s, the proportions in the various types of school remained fairly constant. Some writers have suggested that Indians resisted mission education; it seems rather that, though they might have preferred it to be run by groups other than Christian missions, they welcomed any high-quality education. As the Anglican priest, C. W. Whonsbon-Aston, put it: 'The Indian of today in Fiji … is healthy and eager for education and filled with the growing pains of emancipation.'[5]

Clearly, Indians worked hard to establish their committee schools in the 1920s and 1930s, they welcomed the Arya Samaj and Sanatan schools, and advocated the establishment of more government schools. Indian opinion welcomed the Stevens Report (1944), which suggested gradually abolishing the 'voluntary system' (whereby the Colonial Government gave grants-in-aid to mission and committee schools rather than establishing their own schools). This would have secularised education and, Stevens envisaged, would have encouraged multiracial schools.[6] But when the Government rejected most of Stevens' recommendations, since it calculated the voluntary system was cheaper, there was little Indians could do about it. In practice, any high-quality education was accepted, and most mission education was academically good. The Christian schools, such as Marist Brothers High School, Suva, and other Catholic schools, the Methodist schools in Lautoka and Suva, and the Anglican schools on Vanua Levu, were always over-subscribed.

From the point of view of the missions — Methodist, Catholic and Anglican — church schools had a twofold purpose: they were a way to expose students to Christianity in the hope that they might convert, and they were in themselves a service to the community. The hope of conversion was always present, but the very low success rate meant that arguments were developed in justification of Christian schools which acknowledged that most students were — and remained — non-Christian. These centred on the 'moral uplift' Christian education offered to all who were exposed to it. Few in Fiji expressed the issue as succinctly as the Education Committee of the World Missionary Conference (held in Edinburgh in 1910) when discussing Christian education in India, where the issues were similar. In India and Ceylon, Christian mission schools and colleges were maintained not just for the education of converts, indeed, it was a matter of concern that few Christian children were in school. Rather, there was a perceived need to change general attitudes in India — what was called the 'leavening' or diffusion principle. The report writers put it this way:

> So far as the ideals of 'the new India' are Christian or semi-Christian; so far as the conceptions of Divine Fatherhood and human brotherhood, and Christian moral ideals, have come to prevail; so far as caste distinctions have weakened and the true position of women recognised; so far as prejudice against Christ and Christianity has been broken down, it is to the education given in mission schools and colleges that a great part of this good result is attributed.[7]

It was acknowledged that most pupils in Christian schools and colleges were not Christian, but missionaries hoped that increased 'spiritual influence' might lead to a greater moral awareness and concern for other people, which would lead to a better society.

The same ideas can be seen at All Saints'. In 1939, the headmaster of All Saints', Rev R. L. Crampton, wrote in the logbook:

> As a teacher one is aware of the great responsibility involved in preparing young Indians to take their places in the community of this Colony. Firmly believing that our Lord's teaching is the best foundation in life, we endeavour to hand on this teaching.

Or, as Canon W. G. Thomas, in a general article on Fiji for an Australian audience, wrote:

> In [the Labasa Anglican schools] many hundreds of young men and women have been helped to become good and useful citizens and the influence and example of dedicated mission teachers have helped to shape their characters.[8]

But the argument for church schools could be developed beyond the 'leavening principle'. During the 1920s, influenced in part by the principles behind the Covenant of the League of Nations, Christian scholars began to argue that for moral and humanitarian reasons they should prepare 'less-developed peoples' for self-government and the end of colonialism, primarily through education. In other words, assisting the secular education of Pacific Island peoples could be seen as a Christian duty. In Fiji, there were two aspects of education in which the missions believed they possessed unique insights rooted in Christian ideals: in running multiracial institutions and in the education of girls. Most mission schools, on principle, at least attempted to attract students from varying ethnic backgrounds, though language difficulties could make this difficult at the primary level. Christian missions had long regarded the respectful treatment and advancement of women — in theory, at least — to be a marker of Western Christian culture. Methodists and Catholics emphasised the importance of girls' education; the Methodists prided themselves on the success of Dudley House School, Suva, and Jasper Williams School, Lautoka, in attracting and educating Indian girls.

The Anglican mission felt it important that All Saints' remain a multiracial school, even with a large Indo-Fijian majority, and made considerable efforts to have one Fijian teacher on the staff, teaching the Fijian language, even though the turn-over in such a position was high. While it was predominantly a boys' school, the acceptance of girls in All Saints' junior classes was an attempt to encourage girls' education, for it was believed that parents would be more likely to let their girls go to school if they could accompany their brothers while small. The Anglican mission took as much care and effort over staffing and equipping St Mary's Girls' School as it did for All Saints'. Indeed, missionary teachers were employed at St Mary's for considerably longer than at All Saints'.

It was, however, debatable just how effective schools were as evangelistic institutions. In the 1940s, the Methodists considered just this issue. A questionnaire was sent out from the Methodist office in Sydney to all involved in the Indian mission, attempting to ascertain why there were so few conversions among Indo-Fijians. Reasons suggested by missionaries for the lack of interest in Christianity included the growth of Indian nationalism, the arrogance of European missionaries, resulting in perceived discrimination against Indians, the growth of the Arya Samaj, and disunity and bickering among Indian Christians. Questions were also asked about the effectiveness in evangelism of the schools. Stanley Andrews, suggested that 'the influence of Christian teaching and example is remarkable ... no one leaves hostile to Christianity'.[9] Ivy Lapthorne commented on 'the educated, happy children in the schools' and especially noted the number of girls undertaking nursing courses after Christian education. Norman Wright saw schools as having 'the advantage of systematic Christian teaching and the opportunity to show the poverty and inadequacy of the old thought'. But he also noted how rare conversions were: between 1922 and 1944, 1,021 boys had passed through Lautoka Boys' School, but only 24 were baptised as a result of their Christian education there.

In general, the missionaries advocated more direct evangelism — more use of public preaching, home visiting and systematic Biblical study. Ramsay Deoki pointed out that most Indian Christians, certainly 'the most satisfactory and staunchest supporters of our work', had converted after direct evangelism rather than through schools. In general, direct evangelism was increased by the Methodists in the 1940s and 1950s. No new Indian schools were opened, though existing ones developed their secondary classes, and two of the existing schools were handed over to committee control in the 1950s. Established schools seem to have accepted that while conversions were unlikely, in the words of A. Harold Wood, 'the schools were respected in the community for their integrity of purpose and the quality of their teaching'.[10] While the Methodists may have come to this conclusion by the 1950s, the Anglicans, later in the field, were still struggling to assess the effectiveness of church schools; in many ways, the story of the 1950s and 1960s at All Saints' is the story of the Anglicans coming to terms with the limitations of schools as evangelistic institutions.

The tension between church schools as tools for evangelism and as preparation for secular citizenship showed itself over two practical issues: Christian staff recruitment and religious holidays. Until 1960, the head teacher of All Saints' was a missionary, usually a European priest, though from 1953 to 1955 a New Zealand woman missionary, Margaret Young, was in charge, and, from 1956 to 1959, the head was Indian-born, US-educated Rev K. Appasamy. He was a Fellow of the Royal Geographic Society with degrees from Hartford and Boston, and it is not clear why he was in Labasa; the Indian High Commissioner certainly thought he was wasting his time in a provincial primary school. Head teachers aimed to have Christian staff, but scarcity made this difficult. In most years, only three or four members of staff were Christian, though others, such as R. Chellappa Gouden, were married to Christians.[11] As Rev Wallace commented in 1952, 'The only way to get a Christian staff is to have our own Christian boys stay on as recognised teachers [i.e., as unqualified teachers].' He readily took on 'Jairam, who has recently been baptised' and who had just left Class Eight. There was competition between Christian schools for the few qualified Christian teachers. Jagdish Ram Sahay, a new teacher at All Saints' in 1961, left after two years to gain wider experience with the Methodists and became head teacher of Dudley High School in the late 1970s.

Since most students and staff were non-Christians, their desire to celebrate their own religious holidays became a contentious issue. A pragmatic man, Wallace closed the school in 1952 for the *Holi* festival and for *Ram Lila*. When Muslim teachers and students asked for leave for Eid, they were told that 'they were free to join in the worship of the festival and should count that their duty instead of coming to school, but that those who did not attend the festival should go to school'. Miss Young found herself in conflict with her staff when she tried to enforce only Christian holidays. She disapproved of teachers taking a day off for *Holi*, and when they requested leave for *Diwali* she refused, telling them it was not a school holiday. Three members of staff took absence regardless and were reported to the Education Officer. Appasamy was more pragmatic; faced with the choice of making *Diwali* or All Saints' Day (1 November) a school holiday, he chose *Diwali* because, he wrote, if he chose All Saints' Day most of the school would be absent on *Diwali* anyway and more time would be wasted.

In 1960, the first local, Jwala Prasad Singh, was appointed as headmaster. A Christian, he was married to Ethel, daughter of Methodist minister Ishwari Prasad, and they had both taught at All Saints' since 1947. In 1953, Jwala Singh was sponsored by the Anglicans to go to Auckland University for a year's study at undergraduate level and, on return, he gained promotion to Grade One teacher. As headmaster from 1960 to 1962, he appears to have run a successful school. The government inspectors praised his administration, and visiting teacher Moti Lal wrote, 'A very good start has been made by the present Head Master. Discipline has vastly improved.' Secondary Entrance results improved from eight passes in 1960 to 13 in 1961 and 20 in 1962. In practice, places at the less prestigious secondary schools were available to some children who had completed Class Eight but who had failed to pass all subjects in the Entrance Examination, so the numbers continuing on to secondary schools were somewhat higher. No fewer than four visiting clerics wrote glowing reports of the school in the logbook between September and December 1962. Singh ran his school with moderation and pragmatism; there were few disputes over religious matters. Indeed, the school was conforming to the Government's expectations of providing good education through grants to voluntary groups. Missions and school committees acted as suppliers of education to, and in close association with, the Colonial Government, with regular visits from government inspectors, agricultural advisors and health workers.

Jwala Prasad Singh's successor, Rev Peter Thirlwell, aimed to change the focus of the school, apparently reacting against Singh's academic and secular emphasis. Thirlwell wrote in the logbook in January 1963, 'It is the hope of the mission staff that All Saints' will once again become an effective instrument in the evangelisation [underlined] of this island.' The school day was extended to allow for 15 minutes of divinity for all students daily, though this soon proved problematic since there were only three Christian teachers on staff. When students and teachers were absent for *Holi*, they were reprimanded with the comment that 'this school observes Christian holy days'. May Day was 'observed in the Christian tradition as a day of Our Lady', with a sermon from the vicar and a hymn singing competition, and Ascension Day was similarly marked. All Saints' Day became the school holiday of choice and, when Hindu teachers requested leave for *Diwali*, they were refused. Half the students were absent anyway and the Hindu teachers complained to the Education Officer (Northern) – who was not inclined to become involved. The new regime did not last. Thirlwell left after less than a year, and his term can be seen as a last evangelical fling before the school settled down to being an academic school, without undue emphasis on religion.

For, during the 1950s and early 1960s, the Anglicans, like the Methodists, changed their policy to place more emphasis on the direct evangelism of the Indo-Fijian community, rather than relying on the indirect influence of schools. Mr Jivaratnam, who had been the woodwork and Hindi teacher at All Saints', left teaching to become a full-time evangelist with the Anglican Mission in 1955 and, by 1958, a woman evangelist was being sought from India.[12] It was now recognised that concentrating on the children was not enough; adult evangelism, bible study, home worship and village meetings were critical.[13] These years saw other Anglican initiatives with the development of the Bailey Clinic in Suva, and Sister Betty Slader's evangelism and medical work around the Rewa Delta from 1960. These projects, rather than the schools, were seen as the future of Anglican evangelism to the Indo-Fijians. The acceptance at St John's College, Suva, of Edward Armogam, the first Indo-Fijian Anglican ordination student, was a matter for great rejoicing.[14]

Back in Labasa, R. Kalyan Chandra, another Indian Christian, was appointed headmaster at the beginning of 1964. He ran a regime much like Jwala Singh's. Visitors again commented on the high standards of academic and agricultural work, comments which suggest such standards may have slipped under the previous regime. Nonetheless, Chandra's administration satisfied the religious authorities. Bishop John Vockler, visiting in late 1964, noted: 'I have been very impressed with the appearance of the grounds and the School, which I believe to be the outward appearance of a good spirit.' After only nine passes in the Secondary Entrance Examination in 1963 under Thirlwell, results steadily improved again; 16 out of 17 students passed in 1964 and all 28 candidates were successful in 1966. The new South Pacific Commission Tate reading scheme was introduced. All Saints' students won essay and other national competitions. In short, by the mid-1960s, the Anglican mission seems to have accepted the inevitability of very limited evangelical success, and concentrated on academic excellence and the extension of the school to secondary level in the mid-1970s. Its main task was now seen as the preparation of its charges to be good citizens of the new, independent Fiji.

NOTES

1 The All Saints' School logbooks for 1924–39 and 1952–70 have been filmed by the Pacific Manuscripts Bureau, ANU, and are to be found at PMB 430. The information in this chapter, unless otherwise indicated, comes from these logbooks.

2 This was the figure in 1956. Boarding fees were then £10 a term, or £7 plus 60 lb of rice.

3 For details of the Methodist catechists, teachers and missionaries to the Indo-Fijians, see Sidal, Morven. 1997. *Hannah Dudley, Hamari Maa: Honoured Mother, Educator and Missioner to the Indentured Indians of Fiji, 1864–1931.* Suva. Wood, A. Harold. 1978. *Overseas Missions of the Australian Methodist Church, vol. 2 — Fiji-Indian and Rotuma.* Melbourne. Thornley, Andrew. 1974. 'The Methodist Mission and Fiji's Indians: 1879–1920.' *New Zealand Journal of History,* 8:2. pp. 137–53.

4 Stephens, F. B. 1944. *Report on Education in Fiji.* Fiji Legislative Council Papers, Cmd 18. p. 12. For further discussion of Indo-Fijian educational demands and provision, see Lal, Brij V. 1992. *Broken Waves: A history of the Fiji Islands in the twentieth century.* Honolulu. pp. 83–6; 102–7; 158–63.

5 *ABM Review* (the monthly journal of the Australian Board of Missions, Sydney), October 1953. p. 151.

6 Stephens, F. B. *Report on Education.* pp. 58–60. The Stephens report is also discussed in Whitehead, Clive. 1978. *Education in Fiji: policy, problems and progress in primary and secondary education, 1939–1973.* Canberra. Chapters 4 and 5.

7 World Missionary Conference, Report of Commission III — *Education in Relation to the Christianisation of National Life,* 1910, Edinburgh. p. 11.

8 *ABM Review,* September 1954. p. 140.

9 The questionnaire and the responses to it are in file 238, Methodist Overseas Mission archives, Mitchell Library, Sydney.

10 Wood, A. Harold. *Overseas Missions,* vol. 2. p 52.

11 *ABM Review,* May 1956. p. 76.

12 *Ibid.,* June 1958.

13 *Ibid.,* August 1958. p. 104.

14 *Ibid.,* June 1960. p. 74.

*Cane farm, Nadhari Hill, Varavu, typical of the cane belt
in western Viti Levu. In many places, leases are not
being renewed, and productive farms are turning to bush.*

CHAPTER FOURTEEN

Primary Texts

Brij V. Lal

'MR JOE BUILDS a house.' That is the first sentence from the *Caribbean Readers Introductory Book One*. It is also the first sentence in English that I ever read or, rather, recited in chorus in grade one at age seven in Tabia Sanatan Dharam School. Mr Joe, a black farmer in neat white shirt and long pants and a light hat, had gathered on his farm an unforgettable array of characters: Miss Tibs the Cat, Mr Dan the Dog, Mr Grumps the Goat, Master Willy the Pig, Mrs Cuddy the Cow, Miss Peg the Donkey, Mother Hen and Percy the Chick. Fun-loving and loveable, they colluded and connived and spoke a language we all knew well. Mr Grumps, big-horned, was averse to work: 'What! Me! Work! No.' From a farming background ourselves, where house and farm work were a dreaded part of our daily routine, we understood him perfectly. Master Willy, with a perpetually puzzled look, endeared himself to everyone by finding Mr Joe's lost shoes. Miss Tibs, sniffy, did not like Master Willy. 'No. He must go. We do not like him,' she tells her friends haughtily. Mr Joe intervenes. 'Let me look at him,' he says. 'Yes. I like him. Let him stay here now and work.' Work? Master Willy, expecting to have a good time, expresses surprise, 'Oh!' And so things rolled along on Mr Joe's Caribbean farm. We, of course, had no idea what or where the Caribbean was, but that did not matter. First experiences often etch indelible imprints on our memories, and Mr Joe's family has remained with me, like yesterday's songs.

In the years after, we left our Caribbean friends behind and switched to the *Oxford English Readers for Africa* and the University of London series, *Reading for Meaning*. There we met John and Jane at a big railway station in London. John is leaving for a school in Oxford and Jane wants to cry but she cannot cry in a railway station 'in front of all the people'. That seemed strange to me, not to cry when something sad happened, such as farewelling your own brother. I learnt about the English stiff upper lip much later. We also met our African friends Luka and Rota, about our age, neat in their crisp new clothes, having a fun-filled holiday near Lake Victoria somewhere in Africa, learning to row, sail and fish. They loved travelling, they said, 'because we see so many new things when we travel'.

How we envied them. We never went anywhere because we couldn't afford to. Besides, there was nowhere exciting to go anyway. We dreaded school holidays because they meant hard field work, planting a paddy or hoeing cane, often on our own farm, but sometimes as hired hands on our neighbours'. Holidays cut us off completely from the world. We could not talk about the wonderful new world we were exploring, a world of words and books and pictures beyond even the imagined horizon of our parents. But it was still magical to think about the happy and carefree life of Luka and Rota and John and Jane, and to hope that someday we could be like them, too. That thought, the remote possibility of one day leaving the deadening routine of village life for something more interesting in some place far away, alleviated our anxieties.

We learnt about the history and geography of strange places: Oxford, Bournemouth, Yorkshire, Southampton, Dundee, Constantinople and Cairo, the Great Arctic Waste, the Lake of Galilee (a 'sheet of water shaped like a harp'). What was a harp? We had no idea. And Italy, where the 'march of the seasons is a constant pageantry of beauty and colour'. Pageantry of colour:

that confounded us. The only colours we knew in our tropical world were brown (earth) and green (grass) and blue (sea). Reference to life during an English winter left us completely bewildered, as did the piece on the power of Babylon under the great Nebuchadnezzar, the son of Nabopolassar, and Herodotus's stories about the 'enormous extent of the royal city and the massiveness of its walls', its remaining bits and pieces 'eloquent of its magnificence'. Big words sent us scurrying to the school's single well-thumbed dictionary.

We learnt the names of strange trees: oak, aspen, poplar, pear, sycamore, willow, fir, beech, when the only ones we knew were coconut, mango and tamarind. Flowers: daffodils, crocuses and tulips, when all we had around us was hibiscus, frangipani and marigold. We learnt about various forms of landscape: lakeland, savanna, steppe, desert and delta; about monsoon rains on the Tsana Plateau (wherever that was); about historical figures and events: Napoleon Bonaparte, the 'emperor of the French [who] was a strange man', but who was also 'one of the cleverest soldiers the world has seen'; Isaac Newton, who was 'often so deep in his thoughts that he would forget to eat his own dinner unless reminded to do so'; Oliver Goldsmith, 'the writer of delightful essays and stories'; about the *Armada*: 'Night sank upon the dusky beach, and on the purple sea/ Such night in England ne'er had been, nor e'er again shall be'; about the East India Company, which built 'goodly ships of such burthen as never were formerly used in merchandise'.

In later years, we read about the origins of writing ('Writing is a kind of drawing, for each letter is made up of straight lines or curves just as a picture is drawn by putting straight and curved lines in different positions'); about the importance of farming (reinforced by a piece of Chinese wisdom: 'The happiness of a nation is like a tree. Farming is its root, manufacture and commerce are its branches and leaves. If the root is harmed, the branches break off, the leaves fall and the tree dies.'). As children of farmers, we found these words reassuring. Some things, though, escaped us, such as the advice on 'How to Repair China': 'Put the white of an egg (after slightly beating it) on the edges of the broken pieces of china, using a fine paint-brush. Immediately dust one edge of the china with the powered lime, and put the two broken pieces together instantly.' We had no idea what china was. Nor, I suspect, did our teachers. But that somehow did not really matter. It was the pleasure of encountering the exotic that engaged us.

Then there were enchanting stories which taught us to be self-reliant, cautious, wary of strangers bearing gifts, to have your wits about you. Stories such as 'The Monkey and the Shark'. This was my favourite; it was everyone's favourite. The monkey and the shark were good friends. One day, the shark tells his friend that his family wants to meet him. The monkey, flattered, jumps on to the shark's back as he swims out to sea. Far away from land, the shark tells the monkey the real purpose of the invitation. 'I did not explain why I wanted you to come with me,' he says slyly. 'I did not ask you to come with me because I want you to see our home. I asked because our king is ill and the doctor says he will only get better if he eats the heart of a monkey. So I am taking you to him.' The monkey, his eyes bulging with fear, remained cool. He tells the shark that he left his heart in the tree. 'You see, we monkeys are not like other animals. We don't always carry our hearts with us. I left mine up in the tree. It isn't here, but if you take me back, I will get it.' The shark, trusting, turns back. Once safely up in the tree, the monkey says he is not coming down, he won't be fooled again. 'Do you think I am like the washerman's donkey?' 'The washerman's donkey?' the shark asks. 'I have never heard about her.' Monkey: 'What do you mean?' 'Please tell me about her.' 'I'll explain,' says the monkey. And so we move to the next story, and the next about 'Kintu and his Cow', 'The Hare and the Tortoise', 'The Blind Men and the Elephant'. Well-written, amply illustrated stories with a strong moral underpinning.

Our parents, themselves illiterate, asked us to read the stories to them as we sat cross-legged around the dim light of the kerosene lamp in our crowded, dung-plastered thatched hut after dinner: the radio had not yet arrived, television came decades later. We, in turn, listened to stories our *girmitiya* grandparents had told our parents, stories from the *Panchatantra* and *Baitaal Pachisi* about ghosts and goblins and frightening goings-on in the underworld, which terrified us in the unlit stillness of the night.

My favourites were the exchanges between Emperor Akbar and his quick-witted prime minister Birbal. There was no question that Birbal could not answer, no embarrassing situation from which he could not extricate himself. One star-lit night, Akbar and Birbal were sitting on the lawn outside the palace. Looking up at the sky, Akbar thought of a question which he thought Birbal would never be able to answer. 'Birbal, tell me how many stars are there in the sky?' the Emperor asked. '*Huzur* [Your Majesty],' replied Birbal, 'I will answer that question if you can tell me how much water there is in the ocean.' Akbar knew at once what a foolish question he had asked. Once Akbar thought of a prank to embarrass Birbal. The two were eating dates and throwing the seeds under their chairs. When Birbal left the room momentarily, Akbar pushed his heap of seeds under Birbal's chair. When Birbal returned, Akbar said loudly, 'Birbal, I did not know you were so greedy, eating so many dates.' Birbal noticed the large heap of seeds under his chair, but nothing under Akbar's. He immediately knew Akbar's trick. Unflustered, Birbal replied, '*Huzur*, I admit I am greedy. But I ate only the fruit and threw the seeds away. You have eaten the fruit as well as the seeds.' As usual, Birbal had the last laugh.

Stories such as these kept us engrossed, connected us to the world beyond the village, beyond the immediate, unremarkable experience of our daily life. The characters were unique in their own way; they sometimes had strange names (such as Sokoloko Bengosay!), and spoke a language we were just beginning to learn. But, for all the difference of time and place and history and culture, they were accessible. We understood their predicaments; they were universal.

There was the story about some children from a poor home somewhere in Africa pleading with the headmaster to admit them to his school. 'Please, sir,' the children say, 'we have come from a village very far away. We have often heard about your school. We have no school in our village. So we have never been to school before. We have never read any books. We have never written with pens. We have never even written on slates. We have not learned any English yet. Please, sir, we have never learned any lessons before, but we do want to learn now. We want to come to your school. We have washed our clothes very carefully. We have just bathed in the river. We have made our bodies nice and clean.'

We probably used different words, but the spirit of supplication was instantly recognisable. For us, growing up in post-war Fiji, education was not necessarily a birthright, but an act of goodwill, a gift from a neighbour or a kind-hearted relative: books had to be purchased, school fees paid, school uniform sewn, and cash was always in short supply. What was given could also be taken away. That fear haunted us. We were taught to be grateful for the small mercies that came our way. Picking up crumbs from the table was no shame for children from poor homes. One step at a time: that was the motto of my generation.

Our primary school was started by our parents to give us the education they themselves had missed. We were taught in Hindi and English. English took over in time, but Hindi remained one of the subjects we studied, alongside arithmetic and general knowledge. The English texts alerted us to the magical lives of children in other parts of the world, the Hindi texts enriched our understanding of our own culture. These texts, used in primary schools in the post-war years, were written by Pandit Ami Chandra, an India-born educationalist who had migrated to Fiji. His short books, 'pothis', as they were called, did for Hindi what the Caribbean and Oxford readers did for English. We were introduced to the alphabets, to picture stories and poems and then to complex subjects.

Each *pothi* began with a Hindu prayer, which we recited every morning before classes began, palms joined, heads bowed, eyes closed: '*Dono kar jod nava kar sheesh, Vinay hum karte hain Jagdish, Dijiye hum to vidyadaan, Karen jisse hum sab ka kalyan ...*' 'Our palms joined in prayer, we beg, O Lord, for Your blessing so that we can work for the betterment of humanity.' Muslim students prayed at the mosque across the road. In the Hindi books, we also learned about flowers, plants, fruits and animals (but those which were familiar to us), about the importance of being honest, respectful of parents and teachers and village elders, the value of good hygiene and sports and good husbandry. Here, too, we encountered Columbus, Magellan, Captain Cook, and great historical events such as the rounding of the Cape of Good Hope, the coronation of Queen Elizabeth and the arrival of Charles Kingsford Smith and the *Southern Cross* in Suva (which terrified Fijians, who scattered hurriedly shouting '*Sobo, Sobo*', 'Oh God, Oh God').

These books, too, had their morality tales. Such as the story about the goat and the fox. Once, a fox fell into a well. A goat walked up to the well and asked what the fox was doing inside. 'Sister,' the fox replied, 'I am having a cool, fresh drink.' 'I'm thirsty, too,' the goat said. 'Join me,' the fox replied. After a while, the fox told the goat that she wanted to get out. Could she stand on the goat's shoulder to get out of the well? 'Yes, sister,' said the goat. When the fox was safely outside, the goat asked her to help her get out, too. 'You should have thought about that before you jumped in. Goodbye.' The lesson: look before you leap.

The *pothis* had bits and pieces about Fiji. We came across Tailevu and the Yasawas, the wreck of the *Syria* in 1884, the arrival of Indian indentured labourers. But that was about it. The

Fiji stories bored us, they lacked romance and adventure. The stories that did catch our imagination were from Indian history: Moghul emperors (Jahangir and Akbar and Aurengzeb), the Taj Mahal and Ganga, the Nobel Laureate, Rabindranath Tagore, with his brooding eyes and white flowing beard, the fiercely anti-British Queen of Jhansi resplendent in white sari, riding a white horse and carrying a sword in her right hand, and Mahatma Gandhi, the slight, sparsely clad, toothless 'Uncrowned King of India'.

We read stories from the *Mahabharta* about the epic battle between the Kauravs and the Pandavas, and we recited them to our parents. We felt proud of our cultural heritage, proud to proclaim our cultural identity untainted by other, lesser influences. We were 'true' Indians, we liked to think, unlike those in the towns who had drifted away from their roots. Our main cultural reference point was India. We celebrated festivals and performed ritual ceremonies that our grandparents had brought from India. The stories, which we shared with our parents and others in the evenings, kept the memories of the ancestral land alive. We didn't know it then, but we children preserved a vital link between our past and our present.

A knowledge of Hindi enabled us to read aloud to our parents and other villagers weeklies such as *Jagriti* (The New Age), *Fiji Samachar* (The News of Fiji) and *Shanti Dut* (The Messenger of Peace). Radio was slowly making inroads into the more well-to-do households, but the newspapers were the real window on the convulsing outside world. We heard vague talk about our becoming independent from Great Britain someday, and news reports about a new party being formed to protect 'our' interests and our moral duty to support it. Still, for all the commotion, national politics were for most of us a distant, abstract proposition. The future of the sugar industry, caught in a devastating strike in 1960, was different. It was our lifeline. We had no sugar left at home; the crop was flowering in the fields, the cane-cutters were idle, and cash was in short supply. Everyone was trying to influence us one way or the other. We were told not to trust the radio news. We didn't. We relied on the Hindi newspapers, especially *Jagriti*. Father listened intently to every word. For him, sugar cane was his lifeblood.

We could read the *Ramayana*, the basic text for us orthodox (*Sanatani*) Hindus. Written in accessible language, it told the story of a virtuous prince, Rama, forced into exile for 14 years for no fault of his own. Wandering the forests, he encountered personal tragedies (his chaste wife Sita was abducted by the evil king, Ravana), conquered evil and eventually returned triumphant to his kingdom of Ayodhya. Good had conquered evil. In that story, our parents saw a rendition of their own predicament. They, too, had suffered much through no fault of their own. They, too, hoped that one day their poverty and petty humiliations in life would end. Reading the *Ramayana* to the accompaniment of dholak, dandtaal, majira and harmonium lightened our otherwise dreary evenings and bonded the scattered and fractured community and nourished its collective soul. In some way, the story also soothed the pain of poverty. It is easy enough now to criticise our people for shoring up fragments of their ancestral culture, but that was all they had. Without it, they would have been nothing, allowed to become nothing. The Hindi films, the Hindi music, the religious texts, the ceremonies and the rituals we performed with mundane regularity, kept us intact as a community.

Hindi has remained with me all these years. Some of the fluency has gone with the passage of time and long stretches spent away from home, but I am grateful for what remains, especially when I think of the sadness that the absence of the language has caused our Indo-Caribbean cousins. Their sense of loss, of rootlessness and alienation, is deep and painful. Hindi is the language of my emotion and prayer. I use it to connect with my past and my people, my cultural roots, my inner self. English is the language of my work. Acquiring it has not been easy, and many gaps remain. I am completely ignorant of its complex history and only passingly familiar with its deeper signs, metaphors and allusions. It took a long time to understand what 'Crossing the Rubicon' meant, or a 'Pandora's Box' or 'Achilles' Heel'.

The metaphors of our own culture and allusions to our past had no place in this new learning. I regret that now, but it did not seem to matter then. We were taught to learn, not question, the values of colonial education. Still, for all their cultural biases, the books opened new imaginative horizons for us, levelled hierarchy based on economic wealth and social status, connected us to other worlds and pasts, awakened our imagination, emphasised our common humanity across boundaries of culture and race, and sowed the seeds of future possibilities.

Word, the power of the written word, word as the carrier of information and the vehicle of knowledge, word as the tool of thought and creativity: those, for me, are the enduring legacies of the texts. For me still, knowledge comes from reading. Words I read in primary school about the importance of books have remained with me. Books were a 'very wonderful thing'. Some kinds of books were worth more than gold and silver because they brought to us knowledge 'which was gained by clever men who died long ago'. 'A person who owns some good books can see more and travel farther than the richest man in the world, for the rich man who just travels about may forget much that he sees, but the person who has the books need never forget. His books will be with him all his life.' We were told to treat books with great respect. 'When we have read a book, we should keep it carefully, for our memory of what is in it may fail, and then we may want to read it again. Books are the storehouses of all the knowledge in the world.' These words lodged deep in my consciousness. The printed word still retains its magic. A well-crafted sentence or paragraph, unexpected imagery or vivid metaphor, cause admiration and pleasure. The unique smell of a new book, its crisp, untouched pages promising adventure and discovery of unknown, unexplored worlds, still captivates me. Reading for me is synonymous with living. Come to think of it, it is life itself.

First published in the Canberra literary journal, Conversations, *Volume 4, Number 1, Winter, 2003.*

'Mr Tulsi's Store' in 1999. In its earlier days,
it was the social nerve centre of Tabia.

CHAPTER FIFTEEN

Masterji

Brij V. Lal

SIX O'CLOCK IN the evening is a special time in every Indo-Fijian home. The clattering noise of cooking from the kitchen and the shrieking and laughter of children at play cease abruptly as the entire family gathers around the radio set. The bell announcing the death notice rings three times. Then the voice intones sombrely: '*Dukh ke Saath Suchit Kiya Jaata Hai Ki …*' It is with regret that we announce the death of … The notice, the last of the day, is often long. When it ends, the volume is turned down and normal conversation resumes. Children scatter, and women return to their kitchen duties.

In Tabia, without electricity, running water or paved roads, where nothing interesting ever seems to happen, people are puzzled about the strange names of places they have never heard of before. Dabota, Tavua: what kind of place is that? Or Moto or Mangruru or Field 40? People wonder about the kind of Hindi spoken there, the clothes people wear, the crops they plant, the food they eat. Simla and Benares cause confusion: how did Indian place names travel to Fiji? Since no one in the family, possibly the entire village, has ever left Labasa, strange places remain strange, imbued with mystery, tantalising at the edge of comprehension.

If the dead person is vaguely known, there will be endless talk about family history. Connections will be made to distant relatives living in remote parts of the island. Invariably, at the end, someone will know someone related to the deceased. The connecting game provides relief from the chores of daily routine, reduces the sense of isolation and remoteness. The death of a relative, close or far, is another matter. Work will be rescheduled and preparations made to go to the funeral. People are particular about death; saying the last goodbye in person is a habit that has persisted. It is still the right thing to do.

We were sitting on the verandah of Mr Tulsi's Store early one evening, drinking kava and talking about the impending *Ram Lila* festival, when the death notice came over the radio. '*Dukh Ke Saath ...*' One of the names mentioned was that of Mr Ramsay Sita Ram. His address was given as Bureta Street, Samabula, a lower middle-class Indo-Fijian suburb of Suva. Listeners were asked to convey the news to close family members whose names accompanied the notice. '*Kripeya is khabar ko ...*' Judging by the silence that accompanied the announcement, Mr Sita Ram might as well have been a resident of Tabia. Mr Sita Ram was an early teacher at the Tabia Sanatan Dharam School. After a few years, he transferred to Wainikoro, or was it All Saints'? He returned to Tabia in the mid-1960s to end his teaching career just as I was completing my own primary education at the school. After all these years, he was still a respected household name in the village.

I had Mr Sita Ram in the penultimate year of primary school. He was one of my more memorable, not to say eccentric, teachers. He was short, five foot nothing, fair, bald with an eagle nose, and an incessant smoker. We mischievously called him '*Chandula Munda*' ('Baldie, Baldie'), because a bald man was a curious oddity in a settlement of men with full heads of hair. Mr Sita Ram did not live in one of the wooden tin-roofed teachers' quarters at the back of the school, but in Wailevu, about five miles away. He arrived at school about 8.30 in the morning and left in his bottle-green Morris Minor soon after the last school bell rang.

Mr Sita Ram was in his sixties when he taught us. To us, he appeared very ancient, a relic of another time and place. Other teachers seemed to treat him with the mild affection reserved for a genial older uncle, past his prime, no threat to anyone's career, harmless but full of wisdom and with an unrivalled knowledge of local history. To place children whose names he had difficulty remembering — Sukh Deo, Sambhu and Shankar Lal were all the same to him — he would ask us our fathers' or even grandfathers' names to establish our genealogy. His memory for this sort of detail was awesome (and awful) and frequently embarrassing. He would say, 'Useless — *bekaar* — like your father and his father before him', if someone got their sums wrong or could not spell a simple word or did not know who the Prime Minister of Bechuanland was. He knew all our secrets, our ancient family feuds, the disputes in the village.

When the mood seized him, he forgot whatever lesson he was teaching and, with the distant look of old men, focused on something high at the end of the room, and talked about the past. We did not seem to exist. He was talking to himself, reliving his part of the vanishing past. Abruptly, he would walk out of the classroom, light up a Craven A, stand on the verandah with his back to us and take a long, lingering puff that seemed to restore his peace of mind. He would then return and resume teaching. Effortlessly. I remembered this about Mr Sita Ram when I heard the news of his death.

'A very good man,' Jack — Jag Narayan — said after a long silence. Jack, now a farmer, was the village historian, whom people nicknamed Magellan because of his insatiable curiosity about world events. He was also one of the earliest pupils at Tabia Sanatan when Mr Sita Ram first taught there. 'They don't have teachers like that anymore.' Moti, another old-timer now a driver with the Public Works Department, agreed. 'Do you see any books in their houses now? Have you ever seen a teacher read for knowledge and pleasure?' Moti asked. The ensuing silence

distressed me because books had helped me escape the village,
connected me to other worlds and pasts. Without them, I would
have been nothing.

'Can't blame them, can you, bro?' Jack said. 'How can you,
with the way things are? Poverty, political troubles, the land
question. Everyone trying to migrate. Another *girmit* here, if you
ask me.' That word *girmit*, the memory of indenture and years of
struggle and degradation that accompanied it, had been on
people's lips quite a lot recently, reminding them of the glass
ceiling in the public service, the blocked promotions, the
imminent expiry of leases, and the end of promise. '"Child Our
Hope" they write on the blackboard,' Moti said cynically. 'What
Hope? Hope is Joke.'

The talk of decline depressed me. It was the same wherever
you looked. The quest for excellence, the passion for learning and
adventure and exploration, the burning of the midnight lamp,
had vanished. The insidious virus of mediocrity was quietly
corrupting the nation's soul. I tried to steer the conversation back
to Mr Sita Ram. 'A name like Ramsay: how did that happen?'
I asked. 'What was a Christian doing in a Hindu school? You
couldn't possibly have that now, could you?'

'Mix another bowl,' Moti said, scratching his leathery,
kava-cracked skin as he took a long puff on his *suluka*, rough
home-grown tobacco wrapped in newspaper. 'Master will pay,' he
said. I nodded yes. 'His father was Ram Sahai, so he changed his
name to Ramsay to sound like an English name. All so that he
could get admission to All Saints',' Jack informed me. I was
intrigued. This was news to me. 'You had to change your name to
go to a European school?'

'The old days were different,' Jack responded. 'It was
British raj. There were just a few schools. One in Wainikoro,
another in Bulileka, a few here and there. Children attended
these schools for a few years, enough to read and write. That was
it. But if you wanted to go on, you had to attend one of the

Christian schools.' I was missing something. 'So what did people expect from the schools?'

'Our parents were illiterate, but not stupid, Master,' Jack said. 'They knew that without education we would be nothing but a bunch of coolies, good-for-nothings. Education opened doors to a good marriage. We could read the newspapers. We were frogs in a pond: how could we know about the world except through reading? Our parents could get us to read and write letters.'

Jack was beginning to hit full stride, when Moti interjected, 'Don't forget about the *mahajans*, bro.' That reference puzzled me. He continued, 'In those days, Master, our people did not know how to read and write. When people went to the shop, they let the *Mahajan* write the price of goods we bought in a book. We did not have cash. People bought things on credit. They settled the account at the end of the month, in some cases at the end of the cane-cutting season. Then, when the time came to pay, they got this huge docket — for things they had never bought. You complained, but it was your word against the written record. The police could do nothing. That's the way it was. Why do you think our people remained poor after all that back-breaking work in the fields?'

Blaming others for your own misfortune is always comforting, I thought, and the oppressed are very good at playing victims. There were other reasons for poverty as well: the small plots of land people had, the restrictions the CSR placed on what they could or could not plant on them, the absence of cash employment, our own nonchalant attitude to work. I realised, possibly for the first time, that our quest for education was driven by this grim reality, to escape the rapacity of our own kind rather than by some grand vision for cultural enrichment and intellectual exploration.

How could someone like Mr Sita Ram, from this kind of background, growing up in the middle of nowhere, in the shadow of indenture, on the edge of everything, become a teacher in the late 1930s? It was an extraordinary achievement, when you think about it. It was just about the highest job you could aspire to. Teachers were the pillars of the community, respected for their learning and for their role as moral exemplars. Parents voluntarily handed over to them the responsibility for disciplining the pupils under their care.

Mr Sahai, Mr Sita Ram's father, was the reason for his son's success. He had been a *sirdar* in the Tuatua sector. There were some dark secrets in his past, Moti hinted, but it was hard to know what or whom to believe. Some said he was on the 'the other side', meaning with the CSR. But he wouldn't have been the only one, playing the two sides to his advantage. *Sirdars* were chosen to extract the maximum amount of work from those under their charge, providing what someone has called 'lackey leadership'. When his indenture ended, Mr Sahai came to Tabia. He was one of the village's first residents. He knew the District Officer (a former employee of the CSR), and so was able to buy a large block of freehold land across the river by Shiu Charan's store.

In a short time, Mr Sahai built up a big cane farm and employed people. Everyone called him 'Babuji'. Babuji could read and write. He wrote letters for the *girmitiyas*, and read them, for a little something, when they arrived. He arranged things for people, made connections with officialdom. He was the village *agua*, leader. From the farm and the gifts people gave him came the shop.

'You know how these people do business, Master,' Jack said. I didn't. 'Have you heard the story of the monkey and the cats?' No I hadn't. As I listened and reflected, I realised that I had assumed much about this place, but actually knew so little of its secret past.

'Once there were two cats,' Jack continued. 'One day they found a piece of roti. They decided to share it equally, but they couldn't trust each other to be fair. So they approached a monkey and asked him to divide the roti exactly in half. The monkey knew the trick. He deliberately split the roti into uneven sizes. Oh, this side is slightly bigger, he would say, so he would take a bite and kept on biting and adjusting until the roti was gone.'

'That, Master,' Jack concluded, 'was how our *Mahajans* and *Babus* got ahead and moved about.'

'Don't forget Dozen and One,' Moti reminded him. 'Yes, Mr Sahai here was Dozen and One, too, along with Nanka Boss in Laqere and Sukh Lal in Soisoi,' Jack continued. 'Well, Master, in those days, our people were not allowed to drink alcohol without a Government Permit. You had to be a man of good character, well connected and with money to get a permit. The permit allowed you to buy one bottle of spirit and a dozen bottles of beer a month. Mr Sahai himself was a teetotaller, but he sold the liquor to people in the village. At twice the price. That is how he made his money. That is how they all made their money.' It was probably an exaggeration, but we had our share of rogues and swindlers, more than we cared to concede. 'Behind every success story is a secret story, Master,' Moti summed up with a laugh.

'Babuji was not keen to start this school,' Jack said. 'Why?' I asked. It seemed such an obvious thing to do. 'Where will the teachers come from? Who will pay for the books? Where will you get land to build a school? Babuji asked these questions whenever people talked about education,' Jack continued. 'You can't feed and clothe your own families. How will the people pay school fees and the building fund? We all want education for our children, but this is not the time. Plant more maize, rice, cane and vegetables. Have a few cows and goats and chicken. Poverty is our biggest enemy. This is our main problem. Schools can come later.'

People disagreed. They needed schools and educated children precisely to break the hold of people like Mr Ram Sahai and the unending cycle of poverty and hopelessness. A small start was made at the local *kuti*, the community-cum-rest house, and a rudimentary primary school was started in 1945. From that came Tabia Sanatan.

Mr Sahai had other ideas for his own son. He enrolled him at All Saints' Primary boarding school for boys in Nasea town. Mr Sita Ram clearly remembered his father's words. 'Learn English good and proper, boy,' he had said. 'Learn the Sahibs' ways. See how white people rule the world. Learn their secrets. Open your eyes, boy. Look. Farm work is coolie work. Make yourself a man. Keep our name high. Ram Sahai. Remember that.' Mr Sita Ram had laughed when he finished recalling his father's words to me. The way the old man had pronounced it, Mr Sita Ram said, it sounded like 'Ram So High'.

But All Saints' accepted only Christian pupils or at least those who did not object to Christian teaching. No problems for Babuji, even though he was a regular speaker at *pujas*, marriages and funerals, and knew the appropriate verses from the scriptures, too, telling people that they must do everything to preserve their culture and identity. 'Without your religion, you are a rolling stone,' he would say, *bina pendi ke lotā*. In his own family, though, he was a different person. 'Religion doesn't put food on the table, boy,' he used to tell his young son.

And, so, Ramsay Sita Ram, at his father's behest, embraced the new faith, though with no particular enthusiasm. He finished his grade eight at All Saints', passed the Entrance Exam and joined the Nasinu Training College to prepare for a career as a primary school teacher. His first posting was to Wainikoro Government Primary. After a few years, he came to Tabia.

Jack remembered Mr Sita Ram vividly. 'He taught everything: Hindi, English, arithmetic, the whole lot. As a matter of fact, he was the only qualified teacher in the school.' 'Very keen on Indian history,' Moti volunteered. 'In those two or three years, we learnt by heart stories about Akbar and Birbal, about Jhansi ki Rani, about Shivaji, Tilak, Nehru, Gandhiji, Subhash Chandra Bose, the 1857 Mutiny.'

The list was impressive — and revolutionary. 'But weren't those books banned?' I asked, remembering how strictly the

Government controlled the flow of information, especially that which incited hatred of the British. The loyalty of the Indians was already suspect, and teaching about Bose and Gandhi would surely have been considered seditious.

'Mr Sita Ram got the stories from *Amrit Bazār Patrika*, *Azād*, and *Ghadr*,' Jack answered. His memory for names surprised me. It was for good reason that he was nicknamed Magellan! The parcel would be opened at the post office and its intended recipients put under surveillance, if not actually prosecuted and fined. I was perplexed how a teacher like Mr Sita Ram could get these papers, especially with a war on.

'From Chandu Bhai Patel, in Nasea town,' Jack said. 'He got the papers smuggled in somehow.' In crates carrying pots and pans and spices and clothes. And a little *baksheesh* to the customs officials didn't go astray either. Say what you want about these Gujaratis, I thought, but they helped us keep our heritage alive at a time when we were down and out, at the edge, ridiculed and reviled, beasts of burden, nothing more. Without the Hindi movies, the newspapers, the music and the religious texts they imported, we would have become nothing, like the proverbial washerman's donkey, belonging neither here nor there. *Na ghar ke na ghāt ke.*

Moti recalled another aspect of Mr Sita Ram's teaching. 'What did he say? All work and no play makes John a bad boy?' 'A dull boy,' I said. 'Something like that,' he continued. 'He taught us hockey, kabbaddi, rounders and soccer. Once or twice, we even took part in inter-school competition. Remember that, Jack?' 'How can I forget!' Jack replied. 'Once Mr Sita Ram took our soccer team to Vunimoli. That was our first outing. Boy, they were rough.' 'Nothing has changed,' Moti laughed.

'One big fellow, full-back, he kicked me so hard in the shin that I thought I had broken my right leg. Swollen like a big football. When father saw my injury, he thrashed me with a *chapki*. I ended up having a sore leg as well as a sore arse!' he laughed. But his father did not stop there. Jack continued, 'Father put on his singlet and went straight to the school. "Masterji, I send my boy to school to learn not to get his leg broken. I don't have money to mend his broken leg. Who will look after him? You? Stop this nonsense before someone gets seriously hurt." That was the end of my soccer playing days.'

Mr Sita Ram also insisted that students in higher grades should learn the basics and practicalities of good husbandry. Hands-on experience, planting radish, carrots, tomatoes, baigan, cabbage and lettuce. So he started a Young Farmers' Club. A special part of the school compound, by the creek, was set aside for gardening. Each student or a group of students were allotted a patch, which they prepared and planted and nurtured, watering it morning and evening, erecting scarecrows to keep birds away.

'That wasn't popular in the beginning,' Moti recalled. 'Some parents were actually angry at this "waste time" activity.' He remembered Mr Ramdhan coming to school one day telling Mr Sita Ram, 'I don't send my boy to school to learn how to plant beans. I can teach him that myself better than all of you put together. We have been farmers since before you were born.' 'Mr Sita Ram did not say much. He smiled gently, put his hands around Mr Ramdhan's shoulder and said, "Come *Kaka* [Uncle], let's have a cup of tea." I don't know what he said, but Mr Ramdhan calmed down, and walked away quietly.'

Some people thought that students would get to take home the vegetables they had planted. When they didn't, rumours spread that the teachers were keeping the vegetables for themselves. That was not true. Mr Sita Ram had other ideas. He used the money from the sale of the produce to buy books, pencils, writing pads for children from very poor homes, even uniforms. I could understand better now why his early pupils remembered Mr Sita Ram so fondly.

'So no one objected to a Christian teaching Hindu kids?' I returned to an earlier topic. 'Well, he wasn't really a Christian,'

Jack said. 'He may have been,' Moti interjected, 'but it didn't really matter. He was a good man, a good teacher. As the old-timers used to say, "It does not matter whether the cat is black or white, as long as it catches the mice."' How things had changed. It would be difficult now to find a Muslim who is a principal of a Hindu school. And vice versa.

'This religious *jhanjhat* [trouble] is a recent thing,' Jack said. 'In those days, we were all one, like one big family. We ate together, played together, went to school together. We were all one.' He remembered the names of the different head teachers of Tabia Sanatan in its early days: Mr Munshi, Mr Ashik Hussein, Mr Mitha Singh, Mr Simon Nagaiya. 'Look at all this religious *katchkatch* [bickering] now. You call this progress, Master?' His voice betrayed regret and sadness at the way things had turned out. 'It is the price of progress, bro,' I answered feebly.

During my remaining days in Labasa, I struggled with my own memories of Mr Sita Ram. I knew him when he was in his declining years, unconcerned about other people's approval or about the school's success rate in external exams, by which its public worth was measured. My memory of that period is dim. 'History matters, boy,' I recall him telling me one day after class. 'Memory is such a precious thing.' Our people's lack of curiosity about themselves, their past, the world around them, their non-interest in anything creative or imaginative, their penchant for petty, back-biting politics and myopic self-interest, distressed him immensely. 'Every home should have a dictionary, the Bible, Koran and the *Ramayana*,' he once told the class. Even in old age, his passion for discovery and exploration had not deserted him.

Nor had his mischievous sense of humour. One day, Mr Sita Ram asked the class, 'Which is the greatest empire in history?' 'The British Empire,' I answered. 'Correct.' 'Why does the sun never set on the British Empire?' Remembering all the red spots on the *Clarion Atlas*, I remarked about its global reach. 'No, boy. The sun never sets on the British Empire because God does not trust an Englishman in the dark,' he said with a huge chuckle that shook his jelly-like stomach. We were all puzzled. I remember Shiu, sitting next to me, asking in a whisper, 'Is that true? Why doesn't God trust an Englishman?' I had no idea, although Liaquat volunteered that the reason might be that English people reportedly used paper, not water, when they 'did their business'.

On another occasion, Mr Sita Ram was talking about the great monuments of world history: the Empire State Building, the Tower of London and Big Ben, the Leaning Tower of Pisa, the Golden Gate Bridge, the Pyramids of Egypt. Then he pointed to the grainy, black and white picture of the Taj Mahal in our textbook. That, he said, is the greatest Indian erection!

Mr Sita Ram also took our singing lessons. We were taught songs that we were expected to memorise and sing in class every month. We all had to take turns. It was awful, the entirely tuneless and screechy rendition of beautiful words. Most of the time we could hardly stop laughing hysterically at some poor fellow making a mess of things. The standard song of last resort was 'Raja Kekda Re, Tu To Pani Men Ke Raja ...' King Crab, you are the king of the sea ... For the truly vocally and musically challenged — and there were more than you might think — there was Baa Baa Black Sheep, Humpty Dumpty and Jack and Jill. Mr Sita Ram himself had a deep, rich voice. We beseeched him to sing during every singing lesson. He obliged with songs by C. H. Atma, Manna Dey and especially Mohammed Rafi. His favourite — our favourite — was 'Chal Chal Re Musafir Chal, Tu Us Dunia Men Chal ...' Go Traveller, Go To That Other World ...

Mr Sita Ram was tolerant of potentially expellable misdemeanours. We all knew that Sada Nand and Veer Mati were sweet on each other. In class, they exchanged coy glances and little handwritten notes hidden in books: 'Roses are red, violets are blue ...' That sort of thing. One day, someone reported this to Mr Sita Ram. Our hearts stopped. We knew that if he took this to the head teacher, Mr Subramani Goundan, Sada Nand would be severely caned (in front of the school assembly) and Veer Mati would be forced to leave school and would be married off soon afterwards. But Mr Sita Ram settled the matter himself. He took the two aside one day after school and talked to them in a fatherly tone about their future and the foolishness of what they were doing at their age. When Sada Nand and Veer Mati married a few years after leaving school, Mr Sita Ram was the guest of honour!

Because Mr Sita Ram himself came from a relatively wealthy background — the Morris Minor was an undoubted symbol of prosperity — you might think money did not matter much to him. On the contrary, he seemed acutely sensitive to the plight of others, especially bright children from poor backgrounds. He went out of his way to help them whenever he could.

One day, he talked about money and how our quest for it was so misplaced, leading us astray, away from the really important things in life, blinding us to its beauty. What he said remains with me. 'Money is not everything. Money can buy you books, but it can't buy you brain. Money can buy you the best food in the world, but it can't buy you appetite. Money can buy you the best cosmetics in the world, but it can't buy you beauty.' He went on like this for a long time, talking over our heads, talking to himself really. It was not until much later, after university, that I began to appreciate the profound truths of Mr Sita Ram's musings.

When we left the village for secondary school, and a few years later for university, we lost touch with our teachers and fellow students who had failed. But I ran into Mr Sita Ram in the Suva Market a couple of years ago. From a crowded distance, the bald, shrunken man sitting hunched on a wooden crate next to a vegetable stall looked vaguely familiar. Coming closer, I knew it had to be Mr Sita Ram. When I spoke his name tentatively, he looked up, took a puff, and recognised me instantly. He stood up, even shorter than I remembered him, hugged me, slapping me gently on the back. 'Good work, boy, good work,' he said with the broad smile of a proud teacher.

'Have a bowl,' Mr Sita Ram offered. When I smiled in abstinence, he replied, 'You can have one now!' He asked about my parents and seemed genuinely sorry to hear that both had died. 'Good people they were,' he said, as he looked into the distance, recalling the past. As for the other boys, I had lost touch a long time ago, and so had he.

Mr Sita Ram told me he had retired a long time ago, and joined his children in Suva. Sometime in the late 1970s, his two boys had migrated to Australia and his daughter was married in Canada. His wife had died a long time ago. Mr Sita Ram had been to Australia a couple of times, but did not like it. 'A poked beehive,' he said, 'not a place for me. Better at my age to be someone here than nobody there.' I understood what he meant.

I left Mr Sita Ram in the market, promising to keep in touch. But you know how it is: other commitments intervene and promises are forgotten. That was the last time I saw him. The news of Mr Sita Ram's death took me to a time and place I had nearly forgotten, reminded me of things that had quietly slipped into my subconsciousness, the kindness and generosity of people who paved our way into the world. People like Mr Sita Ram.

I went to Mr Sita Ram's basement flat in Bureta Street after I returned from Labasa. Why, I have no idea, but I felt it was the right thing to do. Perhaps it was the ancient urge to say the final goodbye in person. The landlord, Ram Gopal, invited me into the living room. After the customary cup of black tea, I asked about Mr Sita Ram's last days. Did he say anything? Were there any tell-tale signs of the impending end? Had he left any papers behind? 'Masterji seemed to be more reclusive in the last six months, more weighed down,' Gopal said. 'What really killed him, if you ask me,' he continued unasked, 'was the coup.' The committed multiracialist, Mr Sita Ram had joined the Alliance

Party after retirement. 'We all have to live together,' I remembered him saying all those years ago. 'Masterji read all the newspapers,' Gopal said, 'listened to the radio, he knew what was happening, what was coming. Another *girmit*, he had once said to me.'

Listening to Gopal, my mind wandered back to Tabia Sanatan and I remembered a patriotic poem that Mr Sita Ram had us memorise from one of Pandit Ami Chandra's Hindi *pothis*:

> *Fiji desh hamaara hai*
> *Praano se bhi pyara hai …*
> *The nation of Fiji is our homeland*
> *More beloved than life itself …*

These words helped me understand why Mr Sita Ram had lost his will to live, why the coup had broken his heart. As I was leaving, Gopal remembered a piece of paper on the bedside table on which Mr Sita Ram had written the first few lines of a haunting Rafi song:

> *Chal ud ja re panchi*
> *Ke ab ye desh hua begaana …*
> *Go, fly away little bird*
> *This place is not your home anymore …*

Preparing coconut chutney the traditional way,
grinding the flesh on a stone.

CHAPTER SIXTEEN

Shanta

Malcolm Tester

THE SLEEK BANTEIRANTE, commonly and unaffectionately known as the Bandit, climbed smoothly into the cloudless, early morning sky from Nausori Airport. My wife, Yvonne, sat quietly beside me on the narrow seat, visibly tense but relieved by the absence of storm clouds on the northern horizon. From this height, the varying shades of aquamarine, the intricate maze of coral reefs and the steep and leafy islands that thrust up through the Koro Sea looked harmless, though to an inexperienced mariner, it was full of menace. Flying conditions were smooth and, seemingly in no time, the rugged tropical coastline of Vanua Levu, with the small settlement of Savusavu, came into view. Our anxious eyes warmed to the absence of the turbulent black shrouds that so frequently torment the jagged mountain range along the southern coast of the island. Then the splendid spectacle of green hills, lush cool gullies, occasional stands of tall coconut palms and neat farm houses appeared along with a haphazard diorama of green cane fields, merging with recently harvested brown rectangles, edged by the dark sea, as we descended into Waiqele Airport.

Our taxi driver had an unfortunately persistent cough, which erupted every 10 seconds during the 10-kilometre trip into Labasa. But it failed to dent our fascination with the exotic appearance of this quintessentially Indian town whose long, straight main street seemed to be a continuum of small colourful shops offering Indian clothing, food, jewellery and a noisy celebration of Bollywood music. Only the sight of the Morris Hedstrom supermarket reminded us that we were, indeed, still in Fiji. The steady flow of toiling, smoky trucks and the frequent warning siren of the little red and yellow sugar train, heavily laden with cut cane, indicated that all roads in Labasa lead to the Fiji Sugar Corporation Mill on the far side of the river. A plume of syrupy black smoke indicated that the crushing season was in full swing. Even at this early hour, the footpaths were busy, with Indian faces clearly outnumbering their indigenous neighbours. Europeans were a rarity here. Our bronchitic driver dropped us off at the elderly yet still elegant Grand Eastern Hotel just beside the river and almost opposite the swarming bus depot from which emerged hundreds of eager young, mostly Indian boys and girls of all ages, ranging from tiny infants to graceful young women and tall, moustached youths, each in immaculate school uniforms, chatting cheerfully as they headed off towards their various schools and colleges.

As I sat contemplating the exotic spectacle during the drive from the airport, vivid images and recollections from a former time came flooding back and I realised that, in a sense, my journey to this remote island had begun 25 years earlier. That was when I had travelled to India as a member of a Rotary-sponsored medical team, which toured the northern province of the Punjab to perform cataract and minor eye operations. It was an exhilarating experience, at once bizarre yet appropriate, and many events from that trip remain with me.

The first was the hospitality of the Indian families who opened their homes and hearts to my colleague, Sam, and me, complete strangers from a far land, at times arriving unexpected and uninvited in the middle of the night. Some spoke no English, yet we were able to communicate in a universal code of goodwill and tolerance. Some gave up their own beds to provide us with a comfortable place to sleep, and all granted us an unconditional, albeit often unexpected, welcome. We were treated as honoured guests, fed specially prepared delicacies by the warm, maternal women of the household and we left each home with a treasured gift of friendship. This I will never forget.

Nor will the recollection of the patience and acceptance of the poor and unfortunate people we examined and treated ever fade from my consciousness. The multitude of bent, elderly men and women who attended our screening clinics each day, each one full of hope that this year they would be found sufficiently blind to be granted the longed-for cataract operation. The eye camp bus came to their town only once every two or three years. To be eligible for surgery, a lack of resources, human and mechanical, demanded that only those whose milky white pupils guaranteed total blindness could be accepted. Those who could see a few fingers held up two feet from their face had to come back next time. Though legally blind, their vision was still considered sufficiently good to make surgery unnecessary.

Years of neglect, inadequate diet, poor health, insufficient medical care and ignorance had taken its toll. Their patience, as they sat in endless queues waiting to be seen, was a mark of their conditioning and an acceptance of their fate. If they weren't seen one day, they simply returned to wait again the next in unspoken hope. I also recall their unflinching stoicism in accepting the wicked jab of the long needle as it penetrated their lower eyelid to deliver the sharp yet numbing dose of local anaesthetic to the space behind the eyeball, delivered pre-operatively by the tall turbaned gentleman, whose principal job was to drive the clinic bus.

My admiration for these proud people of rural India was made complete when I was called on to perform surgery on an eight-year-old boy with a large and uncosmetic turn in each eye. In Western countries, such surgery is properly performed on children under general anaesthesia, but in the abandoned schoolroom, which we had converted into an operating theatre that day, there were no facilities for general anaesthesia or sedatives and tranquillisers. So I had to operate with the child wide awake and inevitably fearful of what was happening. I imagined that he was as terrified as I was nervous as I approached him with a syringe and needle to inject the local anaesthetic directly into the sensitive tissues of both eyes. But I was overwhelmed by the tenderness of his father as he whispered encouragement and inspiration into the child's ear while I administered the anaesthetising injection. I can recall clearly every moment of that operation; the father speaking calmly and quietly to his son and the child lying motionless and uncomplaining during the hour-long procedure.

But the memory most indelibly imprinted on my mind is of my very last patient. The sun was lowering in a golden glow of dust and smoke as I packed up my meagre collection of instruments on the final day of the trip. It was my wife's birthday, the first time we had spent it apart. The frustration and stress from seeing so many blind and deformed patients was almost suffocating. Although we had performed several hundred operations, the numbers receiving surgery were only a tiny percentage of those who needed it and many others were incurably blind as a result of infection, injury or neglect. Although we were somewhat self-conscious and embarrassed at having to leave the two young trainee eye surgeons who had accompanied us, we were emotionally drained and anxious to return home. We were in a town called Batala and, as I prepared to walk out to the bus for the final time, the young Punjabi nurse who had been my assistant and interpreter throughout the trip called to me, 'Doctor, there is one more patient for you to see. He has just arrived!'

'Tell him I have finished. Tell him he is too late. Tell him to come back tomorrow to see one of the young clinic doctors.' I replied. 'But Doctor, he has walked for three days from Kashmir, just to see you, the doctor who has come from Australia.' The concept of a patient walking for three days to have his eyes examined was so confronting and so totally beyond my comprehension, that I had no option but to examine him. As I reluctantly unpacked my ophthalmoscope, I turned to see a youngish man, possibly in his late thirties, dressed only in a *dhoti*, with a blanket across his shoulder and worn sandals, holding a rough wooden staff. He was thin, dirty and unshaven and seemed to be exhausted by his long walk.

I found that he was blind, the retina in each eye having been destroyed by some catastrophic event, possibly an infection or diabetes. I asked my nurse to tell him, as gently as she could, that I was sorry but there was nothing anyone could do to help him. Without a word, he turned and silently felt his way from the room, shuffling out into the dry dusty road before turning back in the direction of Kashmir. I had failed the final test. I was overcome by a feeling of inadequacy and guilt, emotions that took days to subside and which were to return, painfully, years later in physically different, yet emotionally similar circumstances. In Fiji.

My initial involvement in voluntary service in Fiji had been to collect discarded medical equipment in Australia for health centres and hospitals lacking these items. It soon developed into informal clinics conducted in remote rural or island Fijian communities where I would examine and treat simple eye problems, distribute donated reading glasses to those who could no longer read the Bible or arrange for surgery in one of the mainland hospitals. Yvonne, a retired nurse, would be sought out by the village women for advice on their feminine problems or childhood illnesses as well as to check blood pressure and blood sugar levels in the diabetics. This was satisfying work, and was helpful to the over-worked local doctors. I soon became a regular visitor to two of the larger hospitals, where I consulted with my Fiji colleagues in their hospital clinics, helped with some surgery and joined them in larger outreach clinics to distant sub-divisional health centres.

As with most Australian visitors to Fiji, my initial contacts were almost exclusively with indigenous Fijians whose ready smiles, seemingly uncomplicated attitude to life and good humour have for years won the hearts of tourists from all around the world. Contact with Indo-Fijians was usually confined to taxi drivers who often drove badly and madly in their ancient wrecks, persistent duty free shopkeepers who seemed not to understand the meaning of 'No! I don't want to buy it' and the unsmiling clerks who manned the cash registers in tourist hotels and resorts.

It would probably be true to say that Indo-Fijians make up a large percentage of the wealthiest in Fiji, but it would be equally true that they also represent the poorest. As time went by and our circle of service and acquaintances expanded, we got to meet more of them and recognised the hardship they suffered. We came to admire their determination and the sacrifices they made to educate their children. How their children could emerge each morning from makeshift squatter dwellings of galvanised iron, or simple farmhouses, dressed in gleaming school uniforms with shined shoes and eager faces was a revelation.

While conventional ophthalmic overseas aid organisations direct their facilities and resources mostly to cataract surgery, as I did while in India, I became increasingly aware of and preoccupied with what I perceived to be a growing incidence of people, especially the poor and disadvantaged, living in outlying communities, who were suffering from diabetes-related eye problems. As in most Pacific Islands, Fiji has a very high incidence of diabetes, not only among indigenous Fijians but in people of Indian descent. Sadly, diabetes is one of the commonest causes of working-age blindness world-wide and I became alarmed at the numbers of blind diabetics I was seeing. I soon found out that the association between diabetes and blindness was not widely acknowledged or recognised in Fiji. There were no facilities for treating established diabetic retinopathy and the concept of regular eye screening and early laser surgery, the most effective measure in reducing the rate of blindness in the Western world, was unknown.

During a casual conversation with a Sydney colleague who specialised in diabetes medicine, I mentioned the apparent increasing frequency of diabetes in Fiji and my fear that many hundreds of Fijian diabetics appeared to be losing their sight. We debated whether it could be a widespread phenomenon or a series of chance encounters. We had serious suspicions, but no proof. Together, we formed a team comprising two nurses from the Sydney Diabetes Centre, myself and a doctor from the Lautoka Hospital.

In the course of one week, we conducted clinics in Sigatoka on the Coral Coast, where most of the patients were Fijian, then Nadi and Lautoka, before heading further north to the mostly Indian towns of Ba, Tavua and Rakiraki. By the end of the week, we had examined more than 500 patients, finally choosing 446 known diabetics for our study. This was hot, dry work necessitating many hours of travel in the cramped confines of a short-wheelbase Toyota Landcruiser. We experienced long, exhausting days, with the numbers of those identified with severely elevated blood sugar levels rising dramatically each day. Many were already blind, and we also encountered other serious complications of diabetes, including lower-limb amputation, incapacity from stroke, heart attack and renal insufficiency.

It was disappointing to discover that few patients were aware either of the risk diabetes posed to their vision or the need for regular eye screening. But, mostly, I was dismayed by the inadequacy of the medical facilities needed to provide accurate diagnosis, the intermittent availability of appropriate medication and a complete absence of public understanding of the disease process, its risk, and the importance of good management.

On the final day of our team's visit, we arose at six in the morning anticipating a long drive and a busy day. Our plans were upset badly when our transport was delayed, so we were two hours late arriving at the first clinic in the small town of Tavua. Expecting only a small crowd, we were surprised by the large number of people sitting chatting in the shade of the new health centre. An expectant hush fell over the assembled group as we filed quickly into the neat clinic room. We had planned to have an early lunch before moving on to Ba, where more than 100 people were expected, but 2.30pm found us still hard at work.

We slipped out one at a time to eat a hurried meal of curried chicken and taro, not wanting to close down the clinic out of respect for the patients, some of whom had been waiting since early morning. Many faced long bus trips home and the buses left early with drivers not prepared to wait for those who might be held up. Eventually, we finished and were quickly back on the road, arriving in Ba after 3pm to find a large group of patients waiting under an enormous mango tree outside the small room that was to house our clinic in the Ba Methodist Hospital.

It had been a long and tiring week for the medical team. We were all disturbed by the degree of visual loss detected on this northern leg of our trip, where the population was predominantly Indo-Fijian. There seemed to be no end to the number of patients suffering from the ravages of diabetic retinopathy. The heat and humidity were enervating and, by 4.30pm, we were physically wilting. We had all worked as quickly and as efficiently as possible, thanks to the untiring effort and initiative of two volunteer medical students whose job it was to administer the dilating eye drops well in advance to facilitate the eye examinations and to help Belinda and Fiona, the two nurses, in organising and collecting blood and urine samples.

Ba is essentially an Indian town with sugar farming and the mill the major source of local employment. The Indian cane farmers were descendants of *girmitiyas*. Most of the patients we examined in Ba were Indo-Fijians, third or fourth generation, who had mostly forgotten their common roots although many retained some of the characteristics of their forefathers.

Shanta was one such lady. She was sitting in the small, overcrowded room with six other people, patiently waiting her turn to be examined by the medical team that had come from Australia to help her. Like many of the other people who had been waiting quietly for most of the day, she had been suffering from visual problems for many years, probably never knowing it was the result of her diabetes. Shanta obviously had not allowed this defect to prevent her from raising her family and working with her husband in their garden and small field of cane. Years of hard manual work were reflected in her lined face, her dirt-engraved fingers and callused feet. She was in her forties, modestly dressed in a clean, brightly coloured sari and her hair was neatly groomed, pulled back into a tight bun. Although her shoes and handbag were clearly old and well-worn, she sat proudly and confidently waiting for me to examine her eyes.

Having revived my flagging body and spirits for the moment, I murmured a greeting before peering into Shanta's widely dilated pupils. I sighed despondently as I saw that her retina had been almost completely destroyed. Normal tissue had been replaced by white fibrous strands, which had torn and detached much of what was left of her retina. Laser photocoagulation might have saved her sight if it could have been applied many years before, but now none of the wonders of modern medicine could help restore Shanta's sight. Although this scene had been enacted too many times during the preceding week, it seemed that all the sadness, frustration and impotence that we were experiencing materialised in the form of this small, dignified Indo-Fijian lady.

Sadly, I placed my hand on Shanta's shoulder and said quietly, 'I am sorry, there is nothing I can do to help you.' The rest of the room went suddenly quiet and, as the entire team stopped what they were doing, she quietly bowed her head, put her arms around my waist and started to sob silently. Unable to contain her own anguish, one of the nurses fled the room with tears streaming down her face. My own eyes were moist and all I could do was stand there, trying to comfort Shanta with a protective arm around her shoulders, as she continued to cry against my chest.

My mind immediately returned to the small dusty room in Batala and the same overpowering mix of inadequacy and guilt flooded my mind as I stood there uselessly trying to comfort this small lady. What useful purpose was I serving for these unfortunate people? What was I doing here? Why wasn't I back where I belonged in my well-regulated routine in my modern, comfortable, air-conditioned surgery in Lismore, examining people who enjoy, but often do not appreciate, the benefits of a health service that is luxurious compared with what these people receive? Was I achieving anything or providing any benefit to these people by being here?

Like most of the 500 people we examined that week, Shanta had heard about the visit of the Australian eye doctor, advertised in the *Fiji Times*. Like most of them, she came with hope and expectations that I would be able to restore her sight. I felt I had let her, and all those like her, down. I had shattered her hopes. There was nothing I could do, nothing I could say. I was overcome not only by sadness for Shanta and all the other blind people we had seen, but by the fact that they lived in a seemingly developed country, just four hours from Australia with all its health services and modern facilities. The contrast was profound and shocking. As my thoughts cleared, I resolved that this situation could not be allowed to continue and I realised that I must seek the funds necessary to provide education and free laser treatment to every one of those unfortunate and sad Fijian people, faced needlessly with an unfulfilled life of shadows and dependence on family or neighbours.

The data from this survey was published in the February 1999 issue of *The Australian and New Zealand Journal of Ophthalmology*. It demonstrated that diabetic retinopathy was extremely common in

Fiji, that it was more common in Indo-Fijians than others and, when the results were compared with a similar cohort of Indo- and indigenous Fijians living in Sydney, it revealed that in Fiji, the disease appeared to develop earlier and more aggressively. Suggested reasons included late diagnosis of diabetes, poor blood sugar control and no access, for the poor, to laser surgery. This research was the catalyst for a project to address the needs of these mostly disadvantaged people whose existence contrasted so strongly with the popular tourist perception of how idyllic it must be to live in a tropical paradise. As soon as I returned to Australia, I set to work to create the program that would afford these people free laser treatment, that would offer the chance of regular eye screening for all diabetics and that would create better public awareness of diabetes and how best to reduce the risk of complications from stroke, heart attack, kidney failure and, especially, blindness.

The aim of my project, which I called the 'Beam of Hope', was simply to reduce the incidence of diabetes-induced blindness in Fiji. To achieve this ambitious aim, copious funds would be required to purchase two ophthalmic lasers, to train health professionals in all aspects of the disease, its recognition, management and techniques of laser surgery, and to establish a long-term program of public education. The project was ambitious and daunting, the budget was huge and we had no funds. But, within months of my Rotary Club being formed, and with no experience in fund-raising, I asked my fellow Rotarians of the Summerland Sunrise Club in Lismore to accept the challenge of raising more than $100,000 to realise my dream of eliminating unnecessary diabetic blindness in Fiji. With generous help from mostly pensioner patients, who would self-consciously slip me a five-dollar note 'For your work in Fiji', and service clubs in Lismore, augmented by a Rotary International Grant, we raised more than $300,000 during the next two frantic years.

On 9 May, 1999, the President of Fiji, Ratu Sir Kamisese Mara, officially opened the Rotary Ophthalmic Laser Unit in the

CWM Hospital in Suva. Fiji finally had a freely accessible laser clinic where the poor and the disadvantaged could receive the only treatment capable of arresting the invisible disease process insidiously destroying their vision. The principal thrust of this and all projects designed to improve public health, however, is public education and awareness campaigns. From the moment the laser clinic was established, we immediately began broadcasting information emphasising the need for improved diabetes awareness and at least half of our project funds have been reserved and spent on public awareness programs broadcast on each of the three major language radio stations, Hindi, Fijian and English. Our radio and television programs have continued to stress the value of good control of blood sugar, accompanied by regular eye examination as a means of reducing the rate of blindness by up to 90 per cent, while printed information is produced constantly in newspapers and Ministry of Health documents.

Since the Beam of Hope's implementation in 1999, increasingly well-attended eye screening clinics have become regular events throughout Viti Levu. In 2003, all diabetics in Fiji must surely have been aware of the association between high blood sugar levels and damage to the retina. Radio and TV continues to broadcast multilingual advice about the value of diet, exercise and regular eye examination. Control of diabetes is improving and blood sugar levels are slowly coming down. Each year, more and more diabetics attend for routine eye examination, which can diagnose the retinal disease causing blindness before permanent damage and loss of sight occurs, at the early stage of development when laser surgery is most effective. There is growing confidence that the project is beginning to produce significant benefits in Viti Levu, where 80 per cent of the population lives.

Vanua Levu is Fiji's second-largest island, with a population of about 160,000 people, mostly Indo-Fijian descendants of *girmitiyas*. Because their native leases are expiring, many of these farming families are being evicted from cane farms which their families have tilled for a century. There is little employment in Labasa, the island's main town, so poverty and confusion is growing within many of these families. No longer able to earn a living from cane, many are now growing vegetables which they sell in the riverside markets. These people are third- or fourth-generation Fijians. They no longer consider India their home. Most have never visited India and few have any desire to visit a country they know only through movies and vernacular radio. In times of social unrest and turmoil precipitated by mindless coups aimed at dislodging predominantly Indian, and legitimately elected, governments in Suva, they often find themselves targets of marauding youths interested only in violence and mayhem. They frequently feel isolated and insecure in their own country.

The numbers of patients with diabetes attending the grossly over-crowded medical outpatient clinic at Labasa Hospital are almost doubling every year. Dr Sandeep Nakhate is a young ophthalmic surgeon who trained at the prestigious Eye Institute in Bombay. Anxious to escape the crowded, competitive rat-race in that huge city, he brought his lovely wife Manisha and two small daughters to Fiji and quickly found himself in charge of the tiny eye clinic in Labasa Hospital. He is the only eye specialist on the island. He soon found himself inundated with diabetic patients. They had heard the message my project brought them on the radio so they came to have their eyes examined. Tragically, more than half were found to be in need of laser surgery, with the number growing daily, but only a tiny percentage of the impoverished group could afford the cost of flying to Suva for the several sessions of laser surgery required for effective treatment.

Aware of the Beam of Hope project, Sandeep invited me to visit Labasa and sought my assistance. If the information he had provided was accurate, he had a potential tragedy on his

hands. He was in urgent need of a retinal laser facility and it was
he who was on the phone to greet us as we began unpacking our
meagre belongings in the comfortable Labhasa hotel room. We
had much to discuss and many plans to make.

Instantly likeable, Sandeep was an impressive young man
and his intellect and dedication to the task became apparent
during our first meeting. We spent the afternoon examining
diabetic patients and found that more than half had severe
diabetic retinopathy. None could afford the airfare to Suva.
I found it impossible yet again not to be emotionally distressed by
the hopelessness of their situation. Once again, I was meeting
hard-working, dignified people whose sight was either lost or
severely compromised simply because they were poor and had
been born in a town where time seemed to have stood still as the
world passed them by. Seeing them sitting patiently for hours in
the over-crowded corridors of the hospital waiting area, squeezing
into the tiny eye clinic, which barely had room for the doctor,
nurse and two or three patients, I found it difficult once again to
rationalise the irony of Australia, with all its modern and
efficient medical facilities, lying just four hours away over the
western horizon, while for all the difference it made, these
deprived people could still be living in a remote village in India
where the eye camp bus visited once every two years.

As I examined the next patient, Chandra, my mind
wandered back once again to Shanta, whose unbridled despair
had provided the catalyst for the Beam of Hope project.
Chandra's slim frame gave lie to the popular concept that a
diabetic is inevitably obese, but her blood sugar level was much
too high. She had not been able to test it herself for four months.
Her prescription for medication had run out three weeks before,
but she had not been able to find transport to return to the
hospital to get more tablets. Like so many of her generation,
Chandra spoke no English but through Sandeep I learned that
her only recollection of her great-grandfather was that he came

to Fiji in the last years of the 19th century. If she had ever known his place of origin, she had certainly forgotten it.

Her ancient Hindi resonated with hints of the Telugu, which Sandeep instantly recognised. She was burnished a deep shade of mahogany from endless hours in the sun planting and weeding the lentils and vegetables which formed her staple diet. She wore a traditional sari, a deep shade of red with matching top, little jewellery but with the ubiquitous thongs on her feet. Her medical records indicated that just five years before she had enjoyed normal vision, but today she was effectively blind with end-stage, inoperable retinopathy in one eye and a tangle of sinister new blood vessels violating the inner sanctum of her second eye. Bleeding had already occurred. I wondered, for the hundredth time, what factors were at work to cause this devastating disease to develop so rapidly in these Indo-Fijian people. Major surgery and extensive laser photocoagulation was required urgently to preserve what little vision was left, but where could she obtain such intervention? If she lived in Australia, the treatment she required could be found in any major ophthalmic hospital. I repeated the hope-shattering words that now came so easily to my lips, though never without a deep sense of regret and impotence. 'I am sorry, but there is nothing we can do to restore your sight.'

Those who have worked in developing countries will know that privacy is a rare commodity in a crowded public clinic. That diagnoses, explanations and brutally frank verdicts are invariably pronounced in front of three or four other patients, seated together in the small rooms we use as clinics, is accepted as standard, though regrettable practice. Often these good people, usually strangers but occasionally neighbours, friends or relatives waiting their turn for judgment, will intervene in the conversations, offering their own version of events, how quickly a relative with similar problems had lost their sight and sometimes, hopefully, offering a comforting word. But there is no privacy.

They listen with interest as Sandeep translates my
inevitable question. Could she afford to go to Australia? They
nod their heads in accord with her response. While her family
had retained the lease on their small acreage, her husband was
sickly and unable to properly manage the farm and the price of
sugar was falling. Money was scarce. Like everyone I saw that day,
she could not afford the $140 it would cost to fly to Suva, let
alone travel to Australia or New Zealand. She was doomed. Her
vision would soon be totally extinguished and there was nothing
we could do for her. Unlike Shanta in Ba, Chandra didn't
weep or show any outward sign of distress. Maintaining an
extraordinary dignity in front of her fellow women, she sat
silently for a few moments as we articulated empty hopes that
perhaps there might be a faint chance that the disease process
would slow down if she could improve her blood sugar control,
then she thanked me quietly, made an appointment with the
nurse to return in three months and left the room with the help
of a relative who had been waiting at the door.

Each subsequent day was a repeat of the first and my story
could have described the Saras, Vishnus, Rams or Madhos, but the
ending would always have been the same. Long-suffering, hard-
working, dignified people, resigned to their sentence of life with
just shadows and shapes, fighting for their existence in a foreign
homeland. Of course, not all the *girmitiyas* or their descendants
became farmers. Many became merchants and shopkeepers, others
teachers and accountants and doctors and lawyers. Many of these
people had remained in Labasa, or had returned after studying
abroad and they now formed a solid nucleus of community leaders
in the town. We met them all during the ensuing days, which
provided the most dramatic and inspirational expression of
community support Yvonne and I have ever witnessed.

We can truthfully say that Labasa is home to the most
welcoming and hospitable people we have encountered in all our
travels in Fiji. We were embraced by well-wishers and supporters

representing the leading community service clubs, Rotary and Lions. When my plans to raise $100,000 towards the establishment of an ophthalmic laser unit and installation of new surgical equipment designed to improve the quality of eye services in Labasa were revealed, the power of total community involvement was dramatically demonstrated by a pledge that proceeds from the Annual Festival of the Friendly North would be donated to the fund. This was a touching demonstration of a community, united by a common background, anxious to contribute the entire earnings of a year's planning and organisation for the welfare of the least fortunate among them.

In a town and island community where poverty and hardship went hand-in-hand, I was amazed to learn that the week-long September Festival was expected to return a minimum of $20,000. I had already received an unexpected but very welcome grant of $40,000 from the Australian High Commission in Suva, a pledge of support from the Fijian Government and the promise of aid from the New Zealand High Commission. Without selling a single raffle ticket on the hot, humid streets of Lismore or Suva, our quest for funding was already well advanced. It is my fervent hope and wish that by the time these words are published the clinic will be in full operation and that early laser surgery will put an end to the sad stories we have encountered.

What is sorely required before our dreams can be realised, in addition to further funds, is a new air-conditioned clinic room where the delicate laser equipment can be housed and operated, and an additional doctor and many nurses to assist the inevitable increased flow of patients seeking treatment. The Director of Northern Health and the hospital CEO have promised to find a room and hopefully young graduate nurses can be recruited to work in the various clinics, health centres and subdivisional hospitals of the northern island, and to participate in the screening clinics, which will be an integral part of the exciting, new future of hope for diabetic patients.

No one will be happier than me if the Beam of Hope Project proves to be the decisive factor that ultimately removes the spectre of potential blindness from diabetes sufferers, whether they be Fijian or Indian. Rightly, none will contemplate or care how their good fortune came to be. Few of them will ever know the torment or handicap their mothers and fathers suffered in their sightless world before laser surgery and public awareness came to Fiji. None of them will ever know or care who initiated their release from this threat. But I can and will always remember the faces of Mere, the Fijian nurse from Sigatoka who lost her legs before she lost her sight; Semi, the young man from Lautoka, who also lost both legs and his sight in a single year; Madhu, who fought unsuccessfully to retain her vision; and Chandra, who progressed from normal vision to total blindness in the space of just five years. I will remember their anguish, their pain, the acceptance of their burden and their quiet dignity. Along with dozens like them, each played a decisive role in creating a better future for others.

Sadly, Shanta, the small, sad lady from Ba will never benefit from the miracle of laser technology and she will never know that it was she who inspired the creation and the successful implementation of the Beam of Hope Project. The thousands of people who have and will receive laser treatment will never know that she made it possible for them to live out their days retaining useful vision while she continues to endure a world of semi-darkness. They will never know her, but I will never forget Shanta.

A daughter of the soil in the field, the orhni *around*
her head offering protection against the fierce sun. Women in
rural areas often cover their heads in the presence of strangers or elders.

CHAPTER SEVENTEEN

Aisha

Padma Lal

AISHA HAD JUST returned from the field to meet with me. Her deeply creased forehead, callosed hands and well-worn old blue ankle-length *lahanga* (long skirt), a white blouse and tattered *orhni* (shawl) signalled that she was a struggling daughter of the soil. Aisha is a rarity in Fiji: she is an Indo-Fijian woman cutting cane. Until recently, cane-cutting was an all-male, all-Indo-Fijian occupation. But things have been changing in recent years. Now, many indigenous Fijians are working as 'substitute' cutters, often to raise money for community projects back home in the islands or on the mainland. For Indo-Fijian men, cutting cane now is an occupation of last resort. But an Indo-Fijian woman cutting cane? And a woman close to 70, at a time when people retire to savour their heard-earned sunset years enjoying grandchildren, dispensing advice to younger members of the family.

Aisha told me she took up cane-cutting after her husband died soon after the 1987 coup. The cane-cutting gang of which the family had been a member for several decades began to play up, exploiting her vulnerability. Sometimes, for no obvious reason, her crop would be the last to be cut. Sometimes, her cane would not be cut at all. So, out of sheer desperation and to ensure that her voice was represented in the cane-cutting gang, which made important decisions, she joined the gang and took up cane-cutting herself. Village life has its undoubted virtues, I realised as I listened to Aisha, but it can also be brutally cruel for people who are poor and vulnerable, particularly today in Fiji when people seem to have lost all sense of compassion and appear to have become more selfish, focused exclusively on their own narrow, self-serving interests.

I had gone to Aisha's house to attempt to capture a typical cane-farming scene and an atypical cane-cutter's story, scenes that belong to another era and are not likely to survive for much longer, despite all the talk of reforms in the sugar industry. Aisha sat down on the bench under the mango tree outside the *belo* — a traditional storage house for farm implements, fertiliser and weedicide used in the cane fields. She slowly undid the *orhni* wrapped around her head to provide some protection from the hot sun, and put it back over her shoulder. Rural Indo-Fijian women even today cover their heads as a gesture of respect in the presence of strangers or elders. She wiped her perspiring face with the *orhni* and then we began to talk.

'*Beta*, what can I tell you,' she said with a tinge of sadness and regret. 'I am happy working and living here. This is where I've lived since I married Somu's father.' Somu was her eldest son, who was still on the farm but who lived with his own family — a scene common in many cane families, usually following a son's marriage and the tension that develops with the daughter-in-law. Somu's father, as happened in many Indo-Fijian cane-farming families, had allowed his son to build a separate house on the farm. 'This is the only place I know. This has been our home for as long as I can remember. My late husband and all his 13 brothers and sisters were born on the cane farm.' Aisha and her 10 brothers and sisters grew up on a cane farm not far away. 'That was the only world we knew. But now,' she said, 'it is a *kabarsthaan* [graveyard] of memories. Some part of me dies every day.' After a short pause, she said, 'The past is all I have. There is no future for me here. My lease will expire next year. I don't know what will happen then. Where will we go if the lease is not renewed? There has been no word from the Native Land people.' She turned her head away from me and looked into the distance with tears in her eyes. My eyes, too, were moist.

Aisha was not alone in this predicament. Agricultural leases began expiring in large numbers after 1997, when the first of the leases automatically renewed some 20 years ago under the Agricultural and Landlord and Tenants Act (ALTA) expired. Since then, more than 5,500 native ALTA agricultural leases have expired. Of these, some 4,160 were cane leases and just more than 20 per cent of these cane leases have been renewed to sitting tenants or their children as either cane land (743)) or residential leases (105). The majority — more than 50 per cent — of the tenants, many of whom can trace their link to the expired lease for several generations, had to uproot their families to start all over again somewhere else, repeating the experience of their *girmitiya* forefathers a century earlier: unskilled, unwanted, uprooted, on the move.

'My children want me to go and live with them overseas,' Aisha said. Two of her sons were abroad, one in Sydney and one in Auckland. They are among some 80,000 Indo-Fijians who have left Fiji since the 1987 coups for greener pastures in Australia, New Zealand and North America. Her sons wanted to sponsor her, though at her age a successful emigration visa could not be guaranteed. Like so many people of her age, Aisha was apprehensive about making the move. 'What will I do there?' she asked. 'I have lived on this farm since I got married 50 years ago. Even though Somu's father is no longer on this Earth, his soul is still here. I cannot leave him.' These simple, heartfelt words captured the essence of village family relationships that seem now to belong to another era.

'*Maan maryada* [respect], *rasmo rivaz* [our own way of doing things] are important to people of my age, *beta*,' Aisha continued unprompted. She had met children born and raised overseas and didn't seem to like what she saw. She could not relate to them. 'They do not seem to have the same respect for the elders as we used to have in our time.' I know exactly what she means, having lived in Canberra for the past decade and seeing how the younger generation interacts with their parents and relatives. The clash of values between two competing traditions, Indian and Western, inevitably produces friction, which can rupture relationships. For young people, no subject is taboo and they express opinions in words and gestures that are at odds with values of deference and respect that we grew up with. From sex and sensuality, from individual rights to relationships — all get talked about in public, without embarrassment. It can be a very disconcerting experience for people from a more traditional background. 'Here I have my independence. I can go where I want to and when I want. I have people to talk to in my own language. What will I do overseas? *English baat jaanit nahi hai* (I don't know English), I will become totally dependent on my children.' Seeing what a feisty and proud woman Aisha was, I knew the overseas lifestyle was not for her. She would be a lost soul in the soulless surburbia of Auckland or Sydney. Listening to Aisha reminded me of my own father-in-law's experience. We had sponsored him to come to Australia to spend some time with us. We had hoped for an extended visit of several months, but soon after arriving in Australia, he began to miss his routine, his friends and relatives, even his animals. Being unlettered, he could not understand the new world around him, he could not communicate with his grandchildren in his own language. He missed his beloved Tabia desperately, and returned after just a few weeks.

'This cane farm is my soul,' Aisha said when we returned to the subject of cane farming, 'just as it was for my father and grandfather. I am a daughter of a *girmitiya*, grew up on a cane farm, married a cane farmer and had all my children on the cane farm.' Aisha had vague memories of stories old people told about the past. Like many in Fiji, she had no knowledge of where in

India her ancestors came from, when, or on what ship. That kind of knowledge was not valued then, and much of it is regrettably lost to history now. But she remembered that her family was always involved in farming, unlike some who had moved to the towns and ventured into other professions. '*Khoon pasina se hum log e jamin ke sawara banaya hai, beta.*' We have cared for this land with our blood and sweat. 'I never thought that after living a lifetime on this piece of land, I would have to ever contemplate having to find another abode.' In that struggle, too, Aisha was not alone.

Aisha's farm had seen better days, I realised as I looked around. It was not very lush nor properly weeded. It had an unkempt look about it. No new cane plant could be seen. I assume that the uncertainty of lease renewal led to a lack of investment of time and energy in the farm, and the use of little fertiliser. It is a common enough response throughout the country. As leases expire, families wait during the grace period pondering their future. The grace period is nothing more than an extension of their agony. Not knowing whether they will be there the next year, growers rely on ratoon crop. Today, less than 10 per cent of the farmers have planted any new cane in contrast with the almost 80 per cent planting before the coup of 1987. The evidence of decline and decay was visible everywhere.

'Who in their right mind would plant cane today?' Aisha said, reading my mind. 'Plant cane is too expensive. You have to hire tractors and additional labour to help in planting. This costs money. With ratoon all you need is to put in some *masala* [fertiliser] and *dawai* [weedicide] and you can still get some returns.' Having recently done a farm survey, I am aware that in times of uncertainty, farmers, particularly those whose leases are close to expiry, use small amounts of fertiliser, the bare minimum, far less than the recommended rate for ratoon crops. It is an understandable, if unfortunate, response for, in the end, productivity suffers.

'I should face reality,' Aisha said with sad resignation. 'After all, leased land is leased land. Leases will expire some day. It is just that I did not ever think that this day would come for me. We had no problems with renewals in the past. We did not even have to pay any goodwill nor did we have to run around to get our leases renewed. Before, our leaders had negotiated renewals on our behalf. Why is it that our *neta log* [elected leaders] today are unable to negotiate lease renewals on our behalf?' Before I could say anything, she continued unprompted. 'Everyone has to now pay goodwill. This time the *mataqali* has asked for $5,000 goodwill. We were lucky because we had to pay only $5,000 for a 10-acre block. Our neighbour had to pay $10,000 for his six acres. Hanif across the road paid $15,000 for his 10 acres.'

I knew Aisha was forgetting that most of them always paid goodwill or premium, as they called it, to the *mataqali* chief. What is different now is that goodwill is also demanded by the NLTB, which euphemistically calls it payment for New Lease Consideration (NLC). According to the NLTB, the NLC is supposed to 'reflect the value of improvements on the land at the date of expiry' and the 'landowners' goodwill to again give up their exclusive possession' of land. The tragic irony in this escapes the decision-makers. The very same people who made the improvements are now being asked to pay for the improvements they made or else risk non-renewal.

'I can afford to pay the extra goodwill because my farm is one of the more productive ones,' Aisha continued. Her land was Class I, which meant cane yield was more than 85 tonnes per hectare. From the Fiji Sugar Corporation records, I know that the annual cane output from her 10 acres (4.5 ha) of land has always been more than 500 tonnes. She is among less than 30 per cent of the growers in Fiji producing such large volumes of cane. Most growers in her sector and elsewhere produce less than 100 tonnes a year. 'I will be able to get a loan from the Sugar Fund and they know that I can pay off the goodwill from my cane income,' said Aisha. 'Many of my neighbours are in worse situations: *bahut kharaab haalat hai un ke.'* She mentioned the names of two families who had to relocate when their leases were not renewed and they could not pay the goodwill demanded by the *mataqali* and the NLTB. Munna had uprooted his wooden house, loaded it on a lorry, drove it to his daughter's home and rebuilt it in their backyard. Munif departed, leaving his concrete house behind. Nobody knew where he and his family went.

Aisha considered herself lucky despite all the gloom and doom around her. She accepted her fate, her *kismet*, with equanimity. 'My children live abroad. They are very successful. And all that because of the income from the cane.' She did not deny that the cane farm had been good for her and the family. Income from cane sustained the family all those years and continued to do so. Money from sugar cane made it possible for all the children to be educated, all but one having gone to university. Her house was made of concrete and her vegetable garden provided her daily requirements of beans, baigan, bhaji and mircha. She made her own coconut oil for cooking.

One grandson lived with Aisha. She worried about his future constantly. His parents died in a car accident, and she looked after him since he was a baby. He unfortunately did poorly at school, and failed the Fiji Junior. He could not get a job in town. The job market was glutted with graduates. 'Nowadays, everyone wants a diploma or a certificate to hire someone for even a clerk's or a salesman's job.' The grandson had three little children of his own. His prospects for migrating were low because one of his children was mentally handicapped. Besides, he had no marketable skills. The hope was that his children would be able to migrate. It is the hope of most Indo-Fijian families.

'I know I do not have long to live, but where will Ramu go?' Aisha asked forlornly. 'What will he do if the lease is not renewed?' But she was optimistic, as most desperate people can be, hoping against hope that her lease would be renewed, just as it was the last time. Her bigger worry was how her grandson would survive on the land. 'There are too many changes in the air,' she said. 'This restructure, that re-structure. I hear the company [FSC] wants to get rid of rail transport. The daily radio talk is so confusing to people like us. And they speak in a language that poor, illiterate people like me find hard to understand.' Last year Aisha, like many others, had to convert from rail to lorry to shift her cane because the FSC could not supply enough rail-trucks on time or, if supplied, the growers could not be sure their cane would reach the mill within 48 hours as required. In recent years, much of the cane reached the mill 48 hours after being harvested. With every day's delay, the recoverable sugar decreases as the cane deteriorates. 'For generations, our cane was transported via rail. This is the first time in a hundred years that this did not happen,' said Aisha. 'But we are happy that the council had arranged FSC to pay some compensation for the extra cost of transporting cane by lorry.'

It may not be the last time if the FSC has its way. FSC has deliberately neglected the rail system, and uses this as an argument to encourage farmers to use lorry transport even though they clog up the road traffic. This is ironical. Elsewhere in the world, rail systems have been strengthened since they are found to be a highly cost-effective mode of transporation when high-volume goods have to be moved. It seems the Government, which has a 71 per cent share in the FSC, has provided a perverse incentive to the FSC to deliberately not invest in the rail system. Currently, the FSC pays a small lorry conversion rate, a rate that increases with 'air distance' and not the distance travelled by road. The rebate or conversion rate is not anywhere near the true cost of lorry transport. Perhaps the FSC has been able to get the Government to surreptitiously reduce the sharing formula between the miller and the growers, as happened when the Government increased the export tax in 2003 from 3 per cent to

10 per cent. Everyone knows that the FSC had been arguing for a reduction in the growers' share stipulated under the Denning Arbitration and Kermode Award.

Aisha's thoughts wandered back to one of her real concerns. 'What will happen when I am no longer on this Earth? How will my grandson manage with cane farming, particularly harvesting? We are lucky because I cut my own cane with the help of Ramu. I can beat any young men of today in cutting cane. *Jawaan admin ke garda khawaye sakit hai,*' she said playfully with a chuckle. I know she is fortunate because she and her grandson both cut cane. They do not use hired cutters. This is not very common today. Before the 1987 coup, most families used to cut their own cane; today, less than one in two Indo-Fijian families do so. Others rely on substitute cutters. Because of a shortage of cutters — another indirect effect of mass migrations since the coups — it is the substitute cutters' market. Substitute cutters are demanding much higher rates for the cutting of cane than what has been agreed to by the gangs and lodged as part of the Memorandum of Gang Agreement (MOGA).

Under the MOGA, members agree among themselves before the start of the harvesting season about the schedule of farms to be cut in the first, second, third and, if necessary, fourth rounds, and the rates growers will pay for the harvest of their cane. Despite the agreement, substitute cutters can demand almost double the MOGA rate for cane-cutting as well as additional funds for buying things such as shoes, knives, billy-cans and food. One substitute in the Labasa district demanded $5 a day for green cane on top of the MOGA rate of $7/tonne for green cane and $6 a day for burnt cane, in addition to the $6/t provided for in the agreement. Such a pricing system encourages burning of the cane before harvest. Substitutes, who are assured of $12/t, often force growers to burn their cane, or burn the cane themselves, to lighten their work. This demand, together with regular mill breakdowns and a late start to the cane-crushing

season, puts added pressure on growers to burn their cane. It is
not surprising that today more than half the cane delivered to the
mills has been burnt, compared with 15 per cent before 1987.
Burning cane is not without risk; farmers may end up paying a
penalty if the cane is not delivered within 48 hours. Delays occur
with the frequently troubled lorry or rail delivery system. During
crushing season, cane trucks are found sitting in the sun for hours
past the passover points, with every hour of delay meaning lower
sugar content.

'I know the industry is not doing too well,' Aisha told me.
'Nothing like this used to happen during the CSR days. We used
to complain about the price of cane we got then, but at least our
cane was cut and delivered on time.' Memory was playing tricks
on her, for it was not just during the CSR days, but, before the
coups, under the FSC that cane was delivered within reasonable
time, when they could get cash advances as well as advice about
best farming practice from the FSC. Nothing of this sort happens
today. As a cost-cutting measure, the FSC stopped all extension
work a couple of years ago, and discontinued giving cash
advances. Now even the banks are reluctant to lend to cane
farmers because of the possibility of non-renewal of leases and
other uncertainties caused by the FSC arbitrarily declaring that it
would accept only a portion of the cane grown — 2.8 million
tonnes of an estimated 3.4 million tonnes. A shortage of funds
could perhaps be another reason why few farmers are planting
new cane, and are putting in the bare minimum of fertiliser.
Planting cane requires money, as does good husbandry. Very few
farmers have ready cash.

There is regular news of the mills breaking down,
worsening the situation with the approaching rainy season. This
caused deep concern to Aisha and many farmers like her. It is
perhaps out of desperation that some farmers burn their cane to
'jump the queue' and get their cane quickly to the mills. But this
does not help the farmers or the industry. While burning *per se* is

not the problem, delayed burnt cane means mills cannot produce grade-one sugar. And regular customers of Fijian sugar are growing wary of buying poor-quality sugar. Recently, even a trusted customer from Britain rejected our sugar.

'We all have known about these problems for years. No one seems to be doing anything,' Aisha said with subdued anger. 'Everyone is blaming everyone else. The company [FSC] says the problem lies with us, the growers, because we burn the cane. But we feel we are the victims. The company does not give us the quotas on time, the rail system is unreliable, the mills keep stopping and the cane is not moved quickly enough in the yard. Go to the mills and see it for yourself. There is always a backlog of rail and lorries in the mill yard. You can see the trucks and lorries queued up for hours, sometimes days. You may even find lorry drivers sleeping under their lorries and wherever they can find some protection from heat and dust and rain.' She was speaking the truth. I am aware that at times the queue is so long that lorry drivers have to stay in the mill yard for two to three nights, with their wives or sons bringing in food, relieving themselves in the nearby bushes or in between the snakes of rail trucks. There is only one toilet — at the mill gate — which is not functioning most of the time.

'On top of all this,' Aisha continued, 'we hear of outside threats of lower prices for our sugar. What have we done to deserve this? Why is the world against us?' These, I know, are not merely threats, but a likely eventuality after 2006, when the current Cotanou Agreement expires. Under this agreement, previously known as the Lome Convention, Fiji's export amount was guaranteed in perpetuity, but not the price. The European Union — our main trading partner under the World Trade Organisation (WTO) — is under considerable pressure to remove price support. Recently, major sugar suppliers— countries such as Australia, Brazil and Thailand — have taken the EU to the WTO tribunal to make them remove the price subsidies that

Fiji and other African, Caribbean and Pacific nations have enjoyed for some of their commodities. 'Tell me, what should we do?' I think to myself, very little, as Fiji is a price taker and the push for globalisation is like a tornado — there is very little that a small country such as Fiji can do. But surely domestic issues such as mill breakdowns, delays in quotas and land lease renewals can be tackled.

'Have you talked to political leaders about this?' I asked tentatively. This touched a raw nerve. Aisha was fed up with politicians. And she had a lot to say about them as well. 'They are feathering their own nests,' she said bitterly. '*Pet puja* [self interest]. They are all playing games, scoring points off each other. They want us to believe they are genuinely interested in the farmers' welfare when they do not give a damn what happens to us. If they did, wouldn't you expect the unions, the council [Sugar Cane Growers Council] and the politicians to work together to help farmers? No they would not. *Ek bole aam to dusara bole imli* (One says it's mango, another says it's tamarind). They cannot agree among themselves. If anything, you can always count on someone to stand up and contradict whatever is being said by someone else in the interest of the growers and the industry. Look what happened when the leases began expiring in 1997. Instead of working with the landowners to negotiate the renewal of leases, some politicians encouraged farmers to leave their farms – in some cases, even before their leases had actually expired. They were given all sorts of promises, promises of tickets to migrate, new aid money. After listening to them, some of the farmers from places like Wainikoro and Daku left their homes and their farms in 2000. Went to makeshift Valelawa camp, with faith in their leaders. Some whose leases had expired refused to be resettled at new sites in Naduri because our leaders promised them bigger things. They stayed in makeshift houses, without jobs or land, with nothing to support their families. Children could not go to school. After waiting for months, some families had to put their tail between their legs and go back to their own villages to start all over again. We all know that politicians' promises are like a sieve. Nothing stays.'

'But do our people ever learn?' Aisha continued, 'No, they do not. Even though people realise that for us Hindustanis to live peacefully in this country we have to work together with the Kai Vitis. Many people vote for the party that preaches racial policies rather than the party that represents cooperation and multiracialism. Look at what happened in recent by-elections. I wonder if Fiji has lost its chance of "being the way the world should be".'

Aisha's thoughts again returned to her own immediate family, to her grandson's future. I realised, as she spoke, that this was something that really haunted her. 'How will my grandson make a living?' His future on the farm was not bright. He will have to learn new things, focus on producing cane with high amounts of sugar. Otherwise, his income will decline because, under the new cane payment system, the price he will get will depend on the sugar content of his cane. He will have to be extra careful with his farm management practices so that he produces the best output of sugar. He will have to choose appropriate, sweeter varieties. He may have to think about getting contract harvesting because not many people in his sector might want to cut cane. Substitute cutters do not cut cane properly, often leaving large amounts of stump, the sweetest part of the cane, in the ground. He will have to learn new skills in bookkeeping. In short, he will have to reinvent himself.

But I know that even if he was to reinvent himself, the future of the sugar industry will remain uncertain unless the Government swallows some bittersweet pills and substantially reforms the industry as a whole. For one, the FSC has to be totally revamped. To do this, more than organisational restructuring is needed. Reorganising the FSC is like rearranging deck chairs on the *Titanic*. Reform is needed all along the production-harvest-transport and milling chain. In the milling sector, changes are needed all the way from the top management — the board, the senior management and the mill workers — to the field — the field officers, the locomotive drivers.

Management at all levels has been allowed to deteriorate. From my analysis of FSC's milling performance and reports from the ground, it seems a rot has set in at every part of the industry. The FSC has been running at a loss since 1999, even though the gross revenue has increased steadily. In 2002, the FSC made a record loss of $24 million, largely because of poor management decisions, including allowing the recovery of sugar already contained in the cane produced by growers to decrease from 90–94 per cent before 1989 to less than 85 per cent, and, in one mill area, even as low as 78 per cent, in recent years. There are also reports of corruption in the way quotas are allocated in the field. During my farm survey, I received many reports in all the mill areas that locomotive drivers delivered more trucks to certain areas than what was released from the depots, with the loco drivers 'selling' trucks for $2–3 each.

If this is true, it is no wonder that some growers have to wait for hours and days for their harvest quotas, when neighbouring gangs are able to finish their harvests well before the season is over. Every day of delay in quota and trucks means an increase in the cost of the cane harvest, because growers have to provide extra *yaqona*, tea, gulgulas and, in some cases, even meals, while the gang waits around for the quotas to be delivered by the field officers. Such delays could add extra costs of anywhere from $100–200 to farmers such as Aisha. While this may not be critical for Aisha, for small farmers producing less than 100 tonnes a year, it could mean an additional $2–3 a tonne in harvest costs. This, together with farmers not paying particular attention to farm husbandry, could mean that many farms may become financially unviable even under the current inflated prices of two-three times the world price which Fiji enjoys. What

will happen when the preferential EU prices end in 2006? I kept these thoughts to myself.

'As long as my grandson continues to work on the farm and rely on himself,' Aisha said with vague, fatalistic hope, 'and continues the good practices he learned from me and my husband, I think he will be all right.' The quiet dignity and inexhaustible patience of women such as Aisha — whom I began calling *chaachi* (aunty) half-way through our talk as a heartfelt gesture of affection and respect — touches you in ways that words cannot express. Innocent people caught in a tragedy not of their making, living in a world over which they have no control, living in vanishing hope and on the sufferance of others.

'*Khuda Hafiz, beta,*' Aisha said to me as I took my leave in the gathering darkness. 'I am glad I do not have long to live. *Bhaut din nahin bacha hai. Inshallah.*'

Sri Siva Subramaniya Swami Temple, Nadi,
an iconic landmark for Hindus, opened on 15 July, 1994.

CHAPTER EIGHTEEN

A Passage to Sydney

John Connell and Sushma Raj

QUITE WHEN THE first Indo-Fijian left Fiji to settle in Sydney will probably never be known, but it was well into the second half of the 20th century. Certainly, the migration of Indo-Fijians to Australia has been a very recent one, greatly influenced by the 1987 and 2000 coups. This account examines the emergence of a new Indo-Fijian diaspora, as Indo-Fijians leave Fiji for various destinations. It focuses on Australia, the most important of these destinations, and the substantial changes in the lives of Indo-Fijians there, especially with the rise of a second-generation with more tenuous ties to Fiji. Indeed, as numbers in Australia have increased, so links with Australia and with the old 'homeland' of India have tended to become more important in people's lives.

The story of the original Indian migration to Fiji is curiously better known and documented than the more recent emergence of an Indo-Fijian diaspora, the phenomenon of 'twice-migrants'[1] who, in a few generations, have experienced two great migration moves. The flight from Fiji, and the growth of overseas Indo-Fijian populations, especially in Australia, New Zealand and Canada, has created a distinct diaspora, and one that in Australia is now growing much faster than the Indo-Fijian population in Fiji itself.

In earlier post-war years, from about the 1960s onwards, there was substantial migration from Fiji. Early emigration peaked in 1968, when there were grave fears of independence, and the brain-drain had already become a concern.[2] In those years, migration was as much to North America, and especially Canada, as it was to Australasia, and population numbers grew in such west coast cities as Vancouver. By contrast, indigenous Fijians rarely migrated and, even at the end of the century, made up a small proportion of all emigrants.

In a settler colony such as Australia, from the earliest colonial years, there were always many migrants from distant lands. Though Chinese settlers gave a particular ethnic diversity to the 19th century, they were not the only Asian residents. A handful of Indians arrived in the early 19th century, such as one group of 40 Indians recruited as labourers in 1837: Hindus were preferred because they were said to be 'not addicted to opium, wine and spirits'.[3] Despite other Indian migrants in later years, migration from Fiji was slight until the 1980s, when it slowly began to increase.[4] After 1987, it accelerated dramatically after two military coups in Fiji that were motivated partly by opposition to Indians. A third quasi-coup in 2000 further accentuated that pattern of emigration, which again was dominated by relatively skilled groups who were more easily able to migrate. In 2001, there were some 44,261 Fiji-born people in Australia; most of these were Indo-Fijians, suggesting about 30,000 Indo-Fijian migrants in Australia, alongside numerous children born to those migrants in Australia.

Over time, the Indo-Fijian population of Australia has become increasingly concentrated in New South Wales, and in the Sydney metropolitan area. This pattern of concentration has paralleled that of other recent migrant groups, as Sydney has grown to become a world city, to some extent at the expense of the second-largest city, Melbourne, partly because of its being the principal centre of finance and IT industries in Australia.[5] Indo-Fijians, however, live in all Australian cities and some, such as a handful of doctors, have moved to small rural towns.

Chain migration has largely followed familiar patterns, as migrants join those kin who are already established and can help them with the provision of housing and employment.[6] Indo-Fijians are only slightly concentrated within Sydney (and elsewhere) and these concentrations are much less evident than those of rather earlier groups from China and Vietnam. The limited concentrations that exist are in the west and south of Sydney, especially around Liverpool and Blacktown, where there is relatively cheap housing that is reasonably accessible to new employment centres. Here, there are identifiable clusters of organisations and stores.

> *Niche businesses have grown in the west but also in Newtown's 'Little India'. Spice shops are numerous, [there are] more than 40 around Liverpool, Blacktown, Fairfield, Lakemba. The Fiji Bula Shop in Rooty Hill serves all Indian, Asian and Pacific Island communities in the west. ASPAC Groceries offers one-stop shopping for all — Fijian, Indian, Pakistani, Asian and Island food — grocery items, fresh vegetables, waka (kava root), lawena (powdered kava) and even jungli murga (wild rooster), plus the latest Indian CDs, music, videos, VCDs, DVDs. Beauty shops, sari shops and jewellers add to the distinctiveness of the store clusters.*

Nonetheless, at the start of the present millennium, and in some part because of the similarly rapid recent migration from south Asia, there were very visible groups of Indians, or seemingly Indian migrants, in Australia, and with them a growing number of institutions of various kinds, from specialty and general stores to restaurants and temples.

From the 1970s onwards, it became evident that Indo-Fijian migration was characterised by some selectivity of education and skills, a pattern that even more evidently characterised Indian migration to Australia.[7] Indo-Fijian migrants usually arrive as fluent English speakers, a situation that tends to privilege them relative to most other Asian migrant populations. Migration from Fiji has constituted a significant brain-drain from Fiji, most evident within the health profession, where it remains a source of major concern,[8] but it is also true of engineers, accountants, teachers[9] and other professional categories. Migration, as elsewhere, has tended to be somewhat selective in circumstances where skills are increasingly valuable in securing migration opportunities.

> *The scenario of elderly people from a farming background being left behind, and the younger Indo-Fijian generation migrating to other countries is now common in Fiji. The professional category, young people via marriage or as overseas students, or students who have completed their studies in Fiji are applying for residency elsewhere. Chain migration via family sponsorship is also on the rise. This mass exodus means that a lot of families have been split. This has led to many people feeling lonely, depressed and confused about a secure future anywhere. Almost all my Indo-Fijian workmates in Fiji (Labasa College, Laucala Bay Secondary School, All Saints' Secondary School, D.A.V. Boys') have migrated overseas, especially to Australia. They are all trying to re-establish a new life in a new setting in Australia, just like their ancestors had done 125 years ago in Fiji.*

Political factors may have dominated reasons for migration from Fiji, as it became more difficult for Indo-Fijians to live and participate in a normal life. People have, however, always migrated for other reasons, particularly to secure better skilled employment and to gain new opportunities for their children. Most Indo-Fijian health workers, for example, moved for a combination of political and other reasons, often to do with the education of their children and difficult working conditions within the Fiji health system. For almost all migrants, Sydney has been the obvious choice and other cities are perceived as being somewhat inferior substitutes.

I had already graduated from the University of the South Pacific
and was in my second year of teaching in Labasa College when
the 'Girmit Centenary' Celebration took place in Fiji in 1979. I
remember taking part in the celebrations with others in a
multiracial, prosperous, free and independent environment. We
all had a stable and bright future ahead of us in a country where
our ancestors, the girmitiyas and their descendants, had
contributed in so many different ways towards its development.
At that time, very few Indians had planned to leave Fiji for
ever. Why would they want to leave? After all, it was their
'home', or at least they regarded it as their 'home' ... and 25
years down the track, here we are in Australia, celebrating the
125th anniversary of the descendants of the girmitiyas.

From the first moments of settlement, and even before,
migration was intended to be permanent. Not one of 10 health
workers, for example, intended to return. Indo-Fijians are thus
very different from other Pacific Islander migrants. Though they
may stay overseas for decades, almost all other migrants at least
'intend' to return even if that intent is never tested. Indo-Fijians
intend to stay, and do stay. Return migration is quite rare.

Most Indo-Fijians, as skilled migrants, have been able to
retain the occupations they had in Fiji with limited need to
take up unskilled occupations or substantially retrain. Census
definitions prevent a detailed analysis of the employment and
occupational structure of those who have migrated, but it is
evident that many more are in professional jobs, especially
in businesses, than are other migrants from Pacific Islands.
Moreover, upward mobility is rapid.

As in Fiji, Indo-Fijians have prospered and become prominent
in many areas of the economic sphere. Professionals have
usually found similar white-collar jobs. There are many Indo-
Fijian teachers who teach at various levels, from primary
schools to university. Accounting jobs are also taken up by most

who were already in the field in Fiji. There are some doctors, dentists and solicitors. Many females are nurses, though at times this is a change of job from being a doctor in Fiji. Blue-collar jobs are mostly taken by those who had not worked in Fiji, or those whose qualifications have not been recognised in Australia (process workers, machinists, food industry, etc). For the latter group, it may be just a transition job while upgrading [their skills].

Not only Indo-Fijians, but Indians have come from different places, and for different reasons, they have lived in Sydney for more than one generation, have different languages, regional origins and religions. They have varied educational levels, jobs and recreational pursuits. They live in different parts of Sydney and beyond. They do not see themselves as one community, do not function as a community and only from the outside, where they are lumped in with Sri Lankans, Mauritians and others, does there seem to be one homogeneous group, but that homogeneity is based on simplistic and erroneous notions of ethnicity. And the community, such as it is, is in a constant state of flux as emigration and immigration continue.

To the outside world, 'Indo-Fijians' have been perceived as a homogeneous group with a common way of life. This ethnic 'labelling', however, is not justified since individuals and sub-cultural groups identify themselves differently in different contexts. The main bonding feature is that most Indo-Fijians are a derivative of the experience of the indenture system in India (coming mostly from areas around Calcutta depot: Bengal, Bihar and Uttar Pradesh; and Madras depot: Malabar, North Arcot, Vizakapatnam, Tanjore). Punjabis and Gujeratis, coming later as free settlers, shared rather different characteristics.

At the same time, there have been attempts to forge a singular identity in Australia. In 1995, an editorial in *India Link*, one of the many community newspapers in Sydney, raised the perennial question of 'Who is an Indian' and argued against the census classification by birthplace on the grounds that this discounted origin and ethnicity, and, specifically, that it excluded members of various diasporic Indian communities settled in Australia, such as those born in and originating from Fiji, Africa and many other parts of the world. It asserted that any distinction between Indians born inside or outside India was pointless since all people of Indian origin shared a common pool of culture.[10] While there may be something of a 'common pool of culture', there are very considerable differences within the Indian population of Australia. Indeed, *India Link* has produced an essentialisation of Indian culture as an ethnic phenomenon, and a homogeneous category independent of any notions of geography and time. Indo-Fijians are distinct from and share certain characteristics with 'once-migrants' from India.

Many migrants, because of the uncertainties of migration and their new contact with Indian Indians, have begun to examine their own histories, family trees and connections with India.

> *Tracing my ancestors back in India:*
>
> My father (pitaji), *Babu Lal Singh*. My grandfather (baba), *Bhagwan Singh*, met my grandmother (dadi, who was called Jamuna) on the ship on which they travelled from India to Fiji. 'She was from Agra,' related my mother in a phone call from Fiji, and 'might have been married before'. My grandfather's ancestors were from Jullundhar (Nanomajara) in Punjab. My grandfather had managed to keep in contact with his family in India and inherited four acres of land (char bigha jamin). He made a provision in his will for it to be transferred to my father after his death. Since there was no chance of my family moving back to India, my father agreed to transfer the land to the Guru Nanak Mission. That organisation still sends regular

newsletters and other correspondence to my eldest sister's address in Fiji, and gives us a feeling of belonging in the local community. Both my parents and two sisters have visited the place (and have photos taken with relatives). On my trip to India, I did not get a chance to go there. Next trip!

Though there are organisations that purport to represent all Indians, most associations in Sydney and in Australia represent regional and language groups. The Fiji Indian Social and Cultural Association of Australia loosely links all Indo-Fijians. A few communal events are aimed specifically at Indo-Fijians, such as the Bula Hibiscus festival, held in Autumn. Kava, a distinctive Fijian drink of medicinal and ceremonial importance, flows relatively freely (and *bula* is 'hello' in the Fijian language). Otherwise, many institutions have limited links to geography, but more to particular religions, sports or regions.

Indo-Fijians have tended to lose their Indian-language skills faster than those who have migrated from India, a result of there being fewer kin at 'home' in Fiji, absorption in English-language businesses, media and education — and a determination to stay in Australia. By contrast, they have tended to retain or revitalise religious attachments, notably to the Assemblies of God,[11] but also to Hindu temples. Caste systems, almost forgotten in Fiji, have lost any real relevance in Australia.

Over time, it seemed that the Hindi language was fading away among the young generation of Indo-Fijians in Sydney. Lately, however, it is being revived with classes springing up almost everywhere! In Sydney, Hindi is taught at Plumpton Primary and Crawford Public Schools with a nominal grant from the Government. Some organisations have also organised classes for everybody: the Australian Hindu Multicultural Association Inc. and the Sanatan Cultural Centre. The Australian Institute of Hindi Language Studies based at Rooty Hill High School provides another language school. Sanskrit classes are also held at some language centres. Some language schools include aspects of Hindu religion, culture, music, diwali celebrations, recitals, Hindi scriptures, and so on. Some Indo-Fijians also attend classes run by Indian Indians.

Attend one of the charity dinner nights, or religious gatherings or puja, or weddings, or parties, or festivals ... with musical concerts, songs , dances, food... and you can get a glimpse of Indo-Fijian unity and diversity in action.

Food preferences retain strong Indian orientations, with most Indo-Fijians regularly eating Indian food at home. Widely available commodities, such as tinned ghee, are imported from India, but information on the availability of less commonplace items can be a zealously guarded secret. Entrepreneurs have opened Indian restaurants, but this is exceptionally an Indo-Fijian phenomenon. Indo-Fijians themselves (or at least women) tend to feel they are not Fijian, nor are they Australian, but neither are they Indian, in the sense that they are 'less than willing to embrace all aspects of their "Indian" cultural heritage', but rather believe that central to their Indian-ness is a liking for Indian food, drink and Hindi films.[12] Once again, this is a remarkably essentialist and simplistic notion of what it means to be Indian, focused solely on patterns of consumption.

Ethnic food is in abundance and readily available today compared with 15 years ago. Curry, roti, rice and Indian savouries are still widely consumed. The dietary habits have changed to some extent, especially with the younger generation, who have resorted to other foods which are easier to consume while at school or work. Food from other cultures has found a place in the diets of Indo-Fijians, notably Chinese food and pizzas.

Such social trends may be cyclical and are always contextual. In the earliest years of migration, as one Indo-Fijian pointed out, it was hard to 'be Indian' since there was too small a community for it to be possible to start a religious group, wear Indian clothes or be a vegetarian.[13] Ironically, as the Indo-Fijian population has become larger, these opportunities are there in abundance for those who wish to retain and nurture aspects of Indian identity, rather than relinquish familiar practices.

At the same time, Indo-Fijians live not only within a broadly Australian environment, but more evidently within an Indian environment, where there is a vast range of institutions that are similar to those of Fiji and India. Once again, these range from stores to temples, from fortune-tellers to sports teams. These are supported by a wide range of newspapers, including the monthly *Fiji Times* (the same title as the main newspaper in Fiji), and regular radio programs (in Hindi and other Indian languages). Satellite dishes enable access to Indian TV channels, and give easy Australian access to Bollywood movies, which are highly popular in Fiji. In a subtle way, Indo-Fijians become a little closer to India.

Attending temple festivals is one of the few activities that draws together Hindu migrants from India and Fiji, as institutions create new connections. Otherwise, for most Indo-Fijians, their country of origin is more important than their ancestral home, and they are more likely to socialise with Muslims from Fiji rather than with other Hindus.[14] Language unites and divides; the Hindi of Indo-Fijians is now scarcely that of those from India.

Popular culture has emerged as a new context of unity. Bollywood and Indian popular music further link Indo-Fijians and others, while cricket, a passion in India but of slight importance in Fiji, has proved to be a new source of identity, as Indo-Fijian youth identify with Indian cricket.

Some deliberate attempts have been made to forge ties between Indo-Fijians in Australia and India. Thus the Uttar Pradesh State Government has sponsored a Discover Your Indian Roots project in association with the Indian Tourist Office. Efforts have also been made by various individuals, organisations and governments to keep the Indian diaspora heritage alive. India has officially set aside 9 January each year to celebrate the Pravasi Bharatiya Divas to rejuvenate its bond with the 'global Indian family' (in 1915 on this date, Mahatma Ghandi returned to India from South Africa).

> My sisters returned to briefly stay in our 'home' village in Jullundhar. Relatives suggested that they might stay permanently since there was land and a double-storey house that were under-used. They found the experience very interesting and emotional, but the idea of settling there was out of the question, despite all the warmth, hospitality and respect. My sister, Prem Kaur Singh, related her feelings: 'Though I felt very proud, I still did not feel a sense of belonging to the place. We are still foreigners there. Our lifestyle and ideas have changed over time. We are more used to the Western way of living, and our relatives and family are now in Fiji and Australia.'

Within Australia, the India Australia Fair (renamed from the India Fair) is organised by the United Indian Associations Inc. (UIA) and is usually held at Fairfield Showground in western Sydney close to Indian Independence Day (15 August). The diverse elements of the Indian community (including Indo-Fijians) get an opportunity to display the variety of food, Indian dresses, cultural events from different parts of India, business-related services and so on. Other organisations, such as the Federation of Australian Indian Associations, have taken initiatives to reunite the Indian diaspora by organising festivals such as the Spring Festival.

Numerous Indo-Fijians have gone as tourists to India and at least some, including those who have experienced racism in Australia and found migration a problematic experience, have gone beyond this so that they 'are now trying to re-establish their identities and many of them are looking towards India, the land of their ancestors, as source for their identity'.[15] While Ghosh has argued that 'For many Indo-Fijians until very recently India remained the repository of their identity and dreams of motherland',[16] this, too, is contextual and just as many have discovered that India is a perplexing and unfamiliar place that can offer no illusion of homecoming. At least as many see their future as wholly bound up in Australia.

Migrants are forever assessing and changing identities, even when they are least conscious of this. Whether in the effort to maintain a continuity of custom, or to modify it, and assimilate to a new nation or new diaspora, culture and identity inevitably change. Changes are always most apparent among second generations, usually those educated in multicultural contexts, where expectations of education are quite different from those overseas. Only now are there significant numbers of second-generation Indo-Fijian youth and few of their stories have yet been told.

Nevertheless, it is evident that second-generation youth have created at least one form of new popular culture, centred around the dance-party scene that is at once a part of the wider Sydney Indian dance-party scene and of a global club culture. It has its own web site, desi.com, which recognises the way in which youth have effectively crossed national boundaries to identify as *desi*, a colloquial term for anyone 'native' to south Asia, but one that now includes youth from other parts of the Indian diaspora.

The Indian dance-party scene is a major component of youth culture in Sydney, and a major location for the construction of social networks that are at once Indian and Australian. The music is a remixing of bhangra and Hindi film music, which may originate from various parts of the diaspora, including Britain and North America, and the dance crowd are almost entirely youth of Indian ethnicity, whether from south Asia or Fiji, in an utterly different social world from that of their parents.

Music and dance distinguish Indo-Fijian groups. The older generation enjoy mostly old, classical ghazals. Bhajan Kirtan Mela *and singing competitions are often organised.* Lok Geet *(folk songs) are sung mostly by women at weddings and special occasions. These are mostly very old songs carried through by oral tradition since the* girmit *times. At one stage, it was a dying art, but recently, there has been a great demand for this type of music. New tapes and CDs are also produced because of the high market demand. The younger generation are much more into remixes and hip-hop.*

In some ways, youth, many of whom are well educated, have created a kind of hybrid 'third space'[17] that is somewhere between notions of assimilation and 'ethnic authenticity', even though neither such polar position could be possible within the diaspora. The dance scene demonstrates a remarkable mix of 'coolness' and independence from older generations, but also nostalgia (for an India that may never have been seen, but is there in the music).

But not all second-generation Indo-Fijians inhabit the club scene, though all have changed in other ways. Accents and preferred foods have become Australian, sport has taken on new dimensions as rugby league (effectively unknown in Fiji) becomes popular. Penrith's triumph against Sydney City (Eastern Suburbs) in the 2003 Grand Final was seen as a triumph to many, a victory for the west of Sydney, where most live, and for the underdogs and battlers. The Indian and Australian cricket teams are enthusiastically supported. Soccer is still the winter sport of choice, with Fijian airline Air Pacific sponsoring an annual tournament in western Sydney with local Indo-Fijian teams representing 10 different Fijian districts.

Sydney, one of the great global and cosmopolitan cities in the world, has attracted a large proportion of Indo-Fijian migrants. With so many different cultures here, cultural change is inescapable: whether as 'Chutneyfication', a term used by Salman Rushdie, cultural assimilation, hybridity or racial intermixing, not only has Rudyard Kipling been proved wrong as the East has met the West, but the cultural mix has been vastly more complex, especially with the second generation. Though there may be resistance as far as intermarriages are concerned, it has increased, even among the first generation. Mingling of cultures is apparent in music, food, dance, dress, sport, the workplace and every daily activity of significance.

Having lived in a multicultural setting in Fiji for more than a century, Indo-Fijians are better prepared to 'negotiate' their space within the Australian community, and have had less difficulty feeling comfortable in their new setting. Isolated cases of discrimination, prejudice and racism have not been irreconcilable, though the transition has been most difficult for elderly parents and for women who have faced difficulties in asserting new expectations of gender roles.[18] Women in Sydney are more likely than those in Fiji to have jobs and seek support and respect from males that is not always forthcoming. Matrimonial advertisements are still common in the Indo-Fijian press and represent an arena where choice may still be highly constrained. Generational differences, some causing social conflict, have become a familiar feature of migrant life.

Among Indo-Fijians in Sydney, as among migrants anywhere else in the world, there is conservation and dissolution. Hybridity and change are tempered by family loyalties and locations, generational shifts, employment and education, class structure, housing and, ultimately, the diversity of personal preferences. Communities are always in a constant state of flux as migrants come and go and the wider society itself changes.

Any notion of a cohesive community is challenged by time and geography, within and outside Fiji, and does not correspond with ideas of identity and nationhood at the start of a new millennium. Indo-Fijians in Sydney constitute an ever-changing and heterogeneous group to which the term 'community' can readily be applied only from the outside.

In Sydney at least, it is easier than at any time in the past for migrants to retain their identities, though this has little to do with the formal structures of multiculturalism. Indeed, it may seem paradoxical that it is technological innovation and change, whether of transport and trade or of e-mail and telecommunications, that has permitted such continuity. Choices that were rarely possible in the past have enabled continuity as much as they have stimulated change: continuity with Fiji and change through new connections with India.

> By doing research on the girmitiyas, I realised that 'uprooting' your 'home' and already established networks and starting a completely new life in a completely new environment was much more difficult in the past compared with today. Things have changed over time. With transnational links, 'Indian' commodities are easier to obtain via businesspeople making trips to India (mostly Gujeratis and Punjabis). Many students have gone to study in India. Religious people, musicians, singers, dancers from India also made trips to Fiji, and make more to Australia. Through improvements in transnational links, alongside renewed Indian links, Westernisation now influences every aspect of education, music and every aspect of social life.

Ideas of home and identity are constantly being negotiated and are ever changing, shaped and reshaped by migration and transnationalism. As one Indo-Fijian told Devleena Ghosh: 'What is Indian about me is my religion and culture. But I suppose my home is still Fiji. My parents come for a visit here but they don't want to live here even after the coups. I think as long as I have family in Fiji it will be home in my head.' She later returned to Fiji, but not long afterwards returned again to Sydney, saying, 'Maybe I have three homes — India, Fiji and Australia. Or maybe I have no home at all.'[19] Ghosh concludes that Indo-

Fijian women in Sydney have created a 'borderland' — or perhaps a third space — which combines narratives, experiences and memories from India, Australia and Fiji.[20] For migrants from Fiji forced to rethink their relationships to what is often seen as the trilogy of 'India, the mythical and sacred homeland of the past, Fiji, the emotional homeland, and Australia, the new and secure homeland',[21] establishing identity and constructing community pose greater problems than for almost any other group of migrants.

> On the whole, Indo-Fijians have adjusted well to the new country, Australia. Family ties in Fiji keep them in touch, and they visit Fiji for weddings, funerals, etc. However, the majority feel Australia is now their 'home'. Fiji is a place of relatives and a destination for holiday trips, but it is only one declining fragment of home. Australia has become the effective home while the original country, India, still remains the spiritual home for most Indo-Fijians, even after so many years.

Attitudes to migration are ever in flux, shaped within Fiji and through the experiences of those who have long been in Australia. For the moment, migration remains eagerly sought after and the Indo-Fijian community continues to grow. As the political editor of the *Fiji Times* (Sydney) wrote in October 2003,

To a keen observer there will be at least one family member within an Indo-Fijian family who has already migrated overseas. These are not sugar cane farmers but educated Indo-Fijians — doctors, teachers, academics, computer programmers, accountants, engineers and mechanics. The hot topic round a typical Indo-Fijian gathering in Fiji is the annual American visa lottery and the endless search by parents for a suitable match for their single sons and daughters. In the past ten years the Indo-Fijian community has changed. No longer do they advocate large families, and the community as a whole has become ferociously overseas focused.[22]

The quest for migration opportunities has accelerated as the economics of sugar and the expiry of land leases have transformed rural Indo-Fijian life and livelihoods.

Sushma's mother writes from Labasa in December 2003:

Fiji ke halat bahut kharab ho gai hae
(The situation in Fiji is very bad now)
Hindustani par bahut museebat aah rahi hae
(Indians are facing a lot of problems)
Jameen le lete hain, ghar men se nikal dete hai
(Their land is taken away, they are forced to leave their homes)
Atyachar karte hain
(They commit atrocities [against us])
Girmit se kamti nahi hae ye time
(Today is no less than girmit*)*
Naojawan bhagte hai
(Young people are leaving)
Budhe log rahi jate hain, inhi ke gulami karte hai …
(Older people are left behind, slaving for them [Fijians])
Kuch samajh me nahi ata age kya bité gi
(Don't know what will happen in the future)
Sushma Devi bhul chuk sudhar le, bahut ache nahi likh pati hu
(Sushma, pardon any mistakes, can't write too well)
Meri aankh kharab hae
(My eyes are bad)
Bacho ko asirvadh, sabko namaste
(Blessing to the children and greetings to everyone)
Mai hu aap ki mataji

(From your mataji *[mother])*

In 2003, Indus Film produced the very first film on the migration of Indo-Fijians to Australia: *Flight from a Paradise* — 'a moving story of sacrifices to escape from a country which no longer feels like home'. This typical Bollywood movie tells the story of Karan, Pooja and their teenage son, Aman. Pooja divorces Karan and enters into a marriage of convenience to obtain Australian citizenship, but later, through a marriage bureau run by an Indo-Fijian migrant, she meets and falls in love with another man. Further plot complications follow, raising a series of twists that reflect on the challenges facing all migrants and the particular difficulties of leaving a place 'so enriched by their ancestors', which once was home and Paradise.

During the same time period, Australia, too, has changed; it is more evidently a country of Asian migration and settlement and Indians are now familiar components of that scene. Hundreds of Indian restaurants now exist; Bollywood movies, notably *Monsoon Wedding*, which also reflects on many of the issues discussed here, are slowly reaching a wider audience and such movies as *Bend It Like Beckham*, and the books of Arundhati Roy, Vikram Seth (and perhaps even Salman Rushdie) have enabled some Australians at least to have a greater understanding of a south Asian world which may still be largely unfamiliar, but is now closer to Australia than ever before.

Outside their own worlds, Indo-Fijians are indistinguishable to the wider world from Indian migrants from any other part of the world. Though they have retained substantial parts of their Fijian social lives, and regularly communicate with kin back 'home', the passage to Sydney has also been, in several ways, a passage to India.

---

* Italicised passages are Sushma's words.

NOTES

[1] Voigt-Graf, C. 2002. *The Construction of Transnational Spaces. Travelling Between India, Fiji and Australia.* Unpublished PhD thesis, University of Sydney.

[2] Buchignani, N. 1979. 'The effect of Canadian immigration on the political economy of Fiji.' In O. Mehmet (ed.), *Poverty and Social Change in Southeast Asia*, Ottawa. pp. 265–83.

[3] Bilimoria, P. and C. Voigt-Graf. 2001. 'Indians.' In J. Jupp (ed.), *The Australian People*, Cambridge. pp. 426–34.

[4] Connell, J. 1987. 'Population growth and emigration: maintaining a balance.' In M. J. Taylor (ed.), *Fiji: Future Imperfect*, Sydney. pp. 14–32.

[5] Connell, J. 2003. 'Neither Indian Nor Australian? Contemporary Indian Migration to Sydney.' In K. Singh (ed.), *India and Australasia: History, Culture and Society*, New Delhi.

[6] Raj, S. 1991. *Fiji Indian Migration to Sydney.* Unpublished MA thesis, University of Sydney.

[7] Connell, J. 'Neither Indian Nor Australian?'

[8] Connell, J. 2001. *The Migration of Skilled Health Personnel in the Pacific Region.* WHO Manila, mimeo.

[9] Voigt-Graf, C. 2003. 'Fijian teachers on the move: causes, implications and policies.' *Asia-Pacific Viewpoint*, 44. pp. 163–75.

[10] Lakha, S. and M. Stevenson. 2001. 'Indian Identity in Multicultural Melbourne. Some Preliminary Observations.' *Journal of Intercultural Studies*, 22. pp. 245–62.

[11] Lal, B. 2001. 'Fiji Indians.' In J. Jupp (ed.), *The Australian People*, Cambridge. pp. 438–9.

[12] Ghosh, D. 2000. 'Home Away From Home: The Indo-Fijian Community in Sydney.' In I. Ang, S. Chalmers, L. Law and M. Thomas (eds), *Alter/Asians. Asian-Australian Identities in Art, Media and Popular Culture*, Sydney. p. 77.

[13] Ibid., p.81.

[14] Bilimoria, P. and C. Voigt-Graf. 'Indians.' p. 432.

[15] Rai, S. 2002. 'Discover India.' *Hamara Focus*, 1 (1), September. p. 10.

[16] Ghosh, D. 'Home Away From Home.' p. 7.

[17] Bhabha, H. 1994. *The Location of Culture.* London.

[18] Chand, A. 2001. *Fiji Indians. Creating a Home Away From Home.* Sydney.

[19] Ghosh, D. 'Home Away From Home.' pp. 81–2.

[20] Connell, J. 'Neither Indian Nor Australian?'

[21] Voigt-Graf, C. *The Construction of Transnational Spaces.* p. 247.

[22] Ramesh, S. 2003. 'Indo-Fijians Looking Abroad for Brighter Future.' *Pacific Islands Report*, 22 October, 2003.

Natadola Beach, Sigatoka.

CHAPTER NINETEEN

Goodbye to Paradise

Vijendra Kumar

I LEFT FIJI in 1991 sad and disillusioned. Sad because the country of my birth, where our ancestors' bones lie interred, no longer made me feel welcome. Disillusioned because a nation once internationally hailed as a peaceful paradise and a showcase for democracy and multiracial harmony turned out, in the end, to be a purgatory for half its people. For beneath the thin veneer of a civilised and enlightened society lurked serious undercurrents of racial tension and hostility. These surfaced with devastating effect after an obscure army colonel and his cohorts ousted the new democratically elected Fiji Labour-National Federation Party Government of Dr Timoci Bavadra at gunpoint on 14 May, 1987. This treasonous act started Fiji's descent into chaos and lawlessness, which continue to plague the country and will continue to do so into the future.

As the first locally born and the only ethnic Indian to hold the editorial reins of the 134-year-old *Fiji Times*, the national daily newspaper, I was always conscious of the awesome responsibility that position imposed on me. It was always a hot seat, but after Sitiveni Rabuka's coup, the heat became almost unbearable. After suffering four years of harassment, intimidation and outright threats, I could no longer honestly and without fear discharge my professional duties. I applied to migrate to Australia.

Fortunately, we — my wife and three children — were accepted. Through the support of my employers, News Ltd, I was able to secure a job with the *Courier-Mail* in Brisbane, where I remained for 10 years until retirement at the end of 2001.

Since arriving in Australia, I have returned to Fiji only once, in 1995. This visit reinforced my belief that Fiji Indians face a bleak future in their own country, feeling marginalised and alienated, uprooted and unwanted. There was, of course, another coup, the third, in 2000, a more violent and bloody affair costing several lives. The country has since been on a mad roller-coaster ride and no one knows where or how it will end.

On the day of the May coup in 1987, I was driving towards Raki Raki via the Kings Road with my family for a weekend holiday at the Raki Raki Hotel. Luckily, I had the car radio on. Just as we had passed Korovou town in the verdant countryside of Tailevu, the announcer alerted listeners to an impending important broadcast. A few minutes later, Sitiveni Rabuka came on the air to announce that he had seized power and the army was now in total control of the country. We were stunned. When the enormity of his action dawned on me, I turned around to return home and then to my office.

When I was within range of radio telephone contact, I got in touch with my staff. My offsider, Mark Garrett, had already marshalled the reporters and photographers to cover the unfolding events. I was back in my office shortly after noon. I was later asked to attend a meeting in the Prime Minister's office, together with other editors and media executives. When we arrived there, I had my first look at the man who had turned the country upside-down. Rabuka was in full military regalia, occupying the Prime Minister's chair. He had a well-trimmed handle-bar moustache, looked athletic and surprisingly self-confident. He explained, in a well-modulated tone, his reasons for the coup and hoped the press would give him fair coverage. The main reason he acted, he said, was to pre-empt the violence and disorder he felt were escalating throughout the main urban areas.

He answered our questions politely and appeared to accept with good grace our warning that the press would be critical of his action. The meeting ended and we all returned to our offices to continue with the production of the next edition. We produced the next day's edition of the *Fiji Times* with a fairly extensive coverage of the event. Our front-page headline simply said 'COUP' in huge letters. It was shown all over the world when the story was picked up by the international media. That edition was the last one for that period because, soon after it hit the streets on Saturday morning, the army moved in, seized our printing plant and barred all staff from entering the premises. The same thing happened to the *Fiji Sun*. The army wanted to censor every edition. We refused, and so did the *Sun*. The radio stations had little choice other than to bend. It was nearly a month before we were able to resume publication.

With a virtual news blackout throughout the country, all sorts of wild rumours began circulating. Fear gripped the nation, exacerbated by army checkpoints, roadblocks and patrols by heavily armed soldiers. To strengthen his hold on power, Rabuka called in hundreds of reserves and asked civilians sympathetic to the coup to don army fatigues and help the armed forces. Many answered the call and some exploited this opportunity to settle personal scores.

With their leaders locked up in jail, the Indian people were apprehensive about their leaders' fate and their own lives. Hundreds of them began fleeing to other countries. Those who had visas were the first to go. Others were helped by relatives living in such countries as Canada, the US, New Zealand and Australia. Meanwhile, Rabuka was finding it difficult to cobble together a government. He had obviously hoped to seize power and transfer it to the defeated Alliance Party. Only after a great deal of persuasion and horse-trading was he able to get the ousted Prime Minister, Ratu Sir Kamisese Mara, to lead a semi-civilian government.

Ratu Mara was not entirely comfortable with this arrangement and agreed to negotiate with Dr Bavadra's group to try to form a more broad-based coalition government. After protracted talks lasting several weeks, the two parties achieved a breakthrough during a meeting at Pacific Harbour. What emerged was a power-sharing arrangement that would have allayed the fears of the Indian community and returned the country to a more stable and democratic state under a government of national unity. But before the ink had dried on the so-called Deuba Accord, Rabuka scuttled the agreement by staging his second coup on 27 September. This coup was far more vicious, with the army casting aside all pretense of civilised behaviour. It came down heavily (mostly) on non-Fijians. Anyone who showed even the slightest opposition or resistance was mercilessly harassed. Abuses of human rights were rampant.

About a dozen armed soldiers raided our offices shortly after midday. They came barging in through the front and back doors and ordered everyone out at gunpoint. They were hyped up and I am sure they would have reacted violently if any of us had resisted. Some of our reporters talking on the phone had the phones forcibly snatched from their hands and were told to get out. I remember one of our women staff telling me later that she felt these soldiers were not regulars but were from the *taukei* army reservists and other criminals who had been recruited to help Rabuka's cause.

Within 10 minutes, our premises were taken over by the troops and guards brandishing M16s, barring anyone from entering the building. Our presses fell silent for the second time and remained so for nearly seven weeks, resulting in a nation-wide news blackout. This period was like an endless night of terror for the people, especially Indians. Scores were arbitrarily arrested and locked up. Criminals had an open season and some of the most horrific crimes were committed during this dark period. With their activities curtailed and our newsroom barred to us, our reporters were unable to cover many of these events, but did manage to document as many of the abuses as possible, although we were not able to publish them.

Perhaps the worst incident was the attack on a family which had lived in peace and harmony with their Fijian neighbours near the Rewa Delta. A gang raided their home one night, raped the women and then looted and pillaged their house. The terrified family later fled, leaving everything behind. I understand a sympathetic foreign diplomatic mission arranged for them to move abroad. Likewise, a Vesari family had to abandon its home when villagers from a neighbouring *koro* drove them out and seized their property. Many similar tragic events happened all around the country, but most of the excesses were confined to the Suva and Nausori areas. Arson and looting of Indian-owned shops by lawless mobs were obviously orchestrated by radical elements within the pro-coup group. It was all part of a strategy to instil fear and uncertainty in the Indian community.

Several academics from the university were rounded up and locked up. One was abducted by soldiers, taken into the jungle and horrifically tortured. Luckily for him, he escaped when his lone guard fell asleep. Another was incarcerated for about two weeks and brutalised because he had written a critical review of Rabuka's ghost-written biography. The country was essentially under martial law. All government institutions and services were under the control of the army. Soldiers took over all air and sea ports and manned customs and immigration departments, with civilian officers being relegated to roles as mere powerless functionaries. It was here that some of the worst abuses occurred.

People travelling abroad were harassed and subjected to humiliating personal searches. Those trying to take out money had their cash impounded without receipts. Much of this money ended up in the pockets of those conducting the searches. Women had to surrender their jewellery if the officers felt they were taking out assets illegally. Bribery and corruption became a way of life.

Rabuka declared Fiji a republic, severing a 113-year-old link with the British Crown. He named himself Commander and Head of Government and also took charge of the Home Affairs and Public Service Commission portfolios. The Governor-General, Ratu Sir Penaia Ganilau, became the new republic's first president. This government came into power on 9 October, 1987. Of the 23 ministers, only two were Indians, Mrs Irene Jai Narayan (Indian Affairs) and Dr Ahmed Ali (without a portfolio). But the military administration lasted barely two months.

Behind the scenes, Rabuka was trying to woo back Ratu Mara and his team to take over a job that he was clearly finding difficult to do. Most of the electorally beaten old Alliance Party warhorses were soon back in government with Ratu Mara as prime minister in what was called an interim government formed in December, 1987. Mrs Narayan retained her post but Ali was dropped. Retaining the Home Affairs ministry, Rabuka was still the real power behind the throne because he had the guns to back him up. Mrs Narayan, a former National Federation Party leader, who had unsuccessfully — and surprisingly — contested the 1987 elections on an Alliance Party ticket, was criticised by her people for being opportunistic and maligned for colluding with a military-backed government. But I believe (as she herself claimed) that she made this choice to help her people. Because of her influence with Rabuka, she interceded successfully several times on behalf of families whose members had been arrested, abducted or harassed by the army.

Soon after our paper was shut down, we began trying through various avenues to resume publication. Many in Rabuka's team did not want to see the *Fiji Times* get a new life. With the backing of the Government, a new Fijian-owned daily, the *Post*, had been launched soon after the first coup. It was, of course, in the Government's interest to give succour to its own mouthpiece. Despite running up against opposition, we persisted in trying to get our presses rolling again.

I finally decided to make direct representations to Rabuka himself. Our chief executive, Rex Gardner, and I sought an appointment with him. Surprisingly, he agreed to see us. When we met him, he said he could not understand why we had not been allowed to resume publication. He felt this was perhaps a matter for his Minister for Information, however, he said he would consult his colleagues who were meeting in an adjoining room. He left us to talk to them and was back after a few minutes. 'They are not keen to see you back in action,' he said. 'But I have overruled them.' All he wanted was an assurance that we would not publish any material that might foment racial hatred. We were happy to give this undertaking as we would merely be complying with the law and our own policy of promoting racial harmony, not stirring up tension. So, after about six weeks, we were back on the newsstands.

But the new Minister for Information, Ratu Inoke Kubuabola, made our life difficult. He took malicious delight in summoning our new chief executive, Geoff Hussey, and me to his office at every opportunity to point out perceived and imagined infractions and to express his displeasure. It was humiliating to be treated like errant schoolboys. Any criticism or adverse report concerning the Government or its ministers would irk Ratu Inoke. If we published a report about a rape or an attack on a tourist, we were accused of scaring off tourists. In such an oppressive environment, it was not easy to function as a free and fearless press. However, we persisted in doing our best to cover all the news, constantly testing the waters. We continued to comment editorially on matters of national interest; sometimes we got away with it when touching on controversial issues and occasionally we were subjected to angry outbursts from officialdom. Other coup supporters kept up a barrage of criticism of some of our reports. One ridiculous incident that springs to mind is our innocuous reference to a Fijian university professor as 'Mr' and not 'Professor' at each reference, which upset a reader.

He accused us of not giving due recognition to Fijian academics! Such was the politically charged environment.

One night, after midnight, they came looking for me at my home at Caubati. About a dozen armed soldiers surrounded the house. Two of them came to the back door and began knocking heavily. We all woke up and, when I opened the door, one of the officers told me I was to accompany them to the military barracks. I dressed hastily and was escorted into the back seat of a military vehicle. On either side of me sat soldiers carrying M16s. I was taken into what I believed was an interrogation room at the Queen Elizabeth Barracks at Nabua, not too far from my home. I was told to sit on a chair while an armed guard was posted beside me.

As I waited for someone to question me, an officer, probably a captain, came in. He apparently knew me and ordered me to sit straight and look at the wall in front, not to move at all. The bastard was enjoying his moment of triumph at humiliating the editor of the national daily. He then barked certain orders to the guard in Fijian, telling him to ensure that I behaved. That poor bloke, perhaps a simple villager, was probably more nervous than I was. He did not even dare look at me. After about half an hour, another officer, wearing civilian clothes, came in with a pen and pad and began to question me about a report we had published. It was based on wire copy from Wellington in which Rabuka had given an interview to a New Zealand journalist. Rabuka claimed he had been misquoted and when I was able to convince my interrogator that whatever error, if any, had been made by the wire agency and not by us, I was safely escorted back home.

I was probably more fortunate than many others who were dragged up to the barracks on trumped-up charges. I was not ill-treated except for the rude behaviour of that arrogant captain. To the credit of the army, I must record that my interrogator apologised for the inconvenience caused to me. But the harassment and intimidation continued through other means. One day I received a call from a friend who had an inside line into the coup-makers' group. He warned me of a plan to attack me at night when I would be driving home after putting the paper to bed. He did not know when and where this would happen but had heard that some criminals would be hired to do the job.

This nexus between certain politicians and lawless elements was not surprising. My friend suggested I change my route. I accepted his advice and stopped driving to and from work along my usual route. Instead, I got our trusted company driver, Jo Koroi, to drive me home every night in different vehicles. I did this for about a week and then resumed my normal routine. I do not to this day know how reliable my friend's information was, but I saw no harm in taking precautions. The company also hired security guards to protect us at home. Anyway, the attack never happened. Another attempt to frighten me was the despatching of a live rifle bullet through the mail. It arrived one morning in an envelope with a warning 'Watch out'. I handed it over to the police. I later learnt that a few other people had received similar packages.

Certain images of the coup have left an indelible mark on my memory. I can still see a huge crowd of men, women and children singing and dancing in front of the Suva Town Hall. When Rabuka appeared on the balcony, he was greeted with a loud cheer. I was standing close to the scene on the periphery of Ratu Sukuna Park when Ratu Sir Penaia arrived in his official chauffeur-driven limousine. I was shocked and saddened when some in the crowd jeered and threw rotten oranges and banana skins at his car. Never had I seen a high chief being shown such disrespect.

Ratu Penaia, as Governor-General, had initially resisted the coup, largely at the urging of the Chief Justice, Sir Timoci Tuivaga, and his brother judges. The judges advised him to defend his office and not to bow to pressure from Rabuka to take up the position of president of his republic. It has since emerged that Ratu Mara also advised Ratu Penaia to stand fast until he had had a chance to seek an audience with the Queen. Unfortunately, Ratu Penaia caved in to Rabuka's overtures while Ratu Mara was still on his way to London. I understand Ratu Mara was furious when he arrived in London and learnt that Ratu Penaia had thrown in his lot with Rabuka. It is unclear what Ratu Mara had hoped to achieve in his meeting with the Queen, although as a Privy Councillor, he would have been granted an audience.

Perhaps the most shocking drama was the lighting of a lovo-type fire in the government buildings precinct, right in front of the statue of that great son of Fiji, Ratu Sir Lala Sukuna. A gang of young men wearing grass skirts, their faces smeared with black war paint, armed themselves with wooden spears and kept the fire going night and day. It was a barbaric action aimed at reminding, and frightening, people by evoking memories of Fiji's savage past. Ratu Sir Lala, the nation's great soldier, scholar and statesman, must surely have turned in his grave at such obscenity.

Ratu Sir Lala was ahead of his time. He was a true chief, a visionary and patriot. I did not know him personally, but I became a great admirer of his after reading his speeches and his biography. I did, however, get to know his widow, Lady Liku, quite well. After his death, she earned a living by managing a troupe of women dancers who performed for tourists at hotels and resorts. One day I received a call from her, asking if I could get her group photographed before they left on an overseas tour. I turned up with a photographer at the old Suva Bus Station, where she was waiting with her party. We struck up a conversation and she began talking about her late husband. She was fiercely proud of him and said he was a true chief. She had little time for most other chiefs because she felt they were selfish and had little interest in the welfare of their people. Ratu Sir Lala, she told me, had died a virtual pauper, having given everything to his people. He did not even leave a home. One of Rabuka's more decent gestures, after he had been in government for a while, was to bequeath to Lady Liku a government-owned house in the Domain area. She at last had a place she could call her own.

Another disturbing picture that many people will never forget is that of black-masked men who marched into Parliament House and drove Dr Bavadra's government members out at gunpoint. Some of them took up positions on the roof of the government buildings and around the perimeter. The appearance of these armed men, faces hidden beneath balaclavas, fuelled suspicions that some foreign terrorists or others might have had a hand in the coup. When questioned later, Rabuka said the men were an elite group of soldiers he had trained and selected for the action. The masks were to protect their identities, just in case the coup failed. The men would then have faced treason trials.

The coups brought out the best and the worst in people. Although Rabuka's actions were generally popular with many Fijians, not all of them by any means supported him. There were several who condemned the coups and some even offered help and protection to Indians who were being harassed. But there were others who settled personal scores in the climate of fear and suspicion engendered by the military take-over. Saddest of all, some journalists brought dishonour to their profession by becoming ardent supporters of the coups and betraying their colleagues. A senior Radio Fiji journalist found himself locked up in jail after a colleague apparently reported him to the army. A sympathetic senior Fijian police officer, who knew him personally, tried to get him released but could not sway the military brass. Still today, he does not know who fingered him or for what reason.

As time passed, Rabuka apparently began to realise that his coups had cost Fiji dearly. Fiji had become an international pariah and had been kicked out of the Commonwealth. The economy was in ruins, tourism was down and investment dollars had dried up. Rabuka began discussions with Jai Ram Reddy, the former Leader of the Opposition, now on the International

Criminal Court for Rwanda, on ways of returning the country to constitutional democracy and the rule of law. In the process, the two became good friends and tried to build bridges of mutual trust and respect between the two main communities. Their talks bore fruit and a new constitution was adopted that provided the framework for fresh elections on a fair and equitable basis.

The tragedy was that Rabuka and Reddy failed to lead their parties to victory in the 1999 general elections. The Fiji Labour Party, led by the mercurial Mahendra Chaudhry, swooped to a landslide victory and he became the first person of Indian descent to hold the Prime Minister's post. Regrettably, the genie that Rabuka had unleashed in 1987 was still a threat and it reappeared in the form of one George Speight, and Fiji was once again rocked by a violent upheaval. The Labour Party had barely been in power for a year when its life ended.

History shows that once a country goes through the trauma of a coup, it becomes difficult to restore democracy. Although coup-makers' corpses eventually end up rotting on the dung-heap of history, the countries experiencing such dislocation continue to wallow in a social, economic and political quagmire for a long time. The road to recovery is often treacherous and uncertain. If there isn't another Speight or Rabuka, there is always an ambitious young colonel waiting in the wings to strike out again. Such has been the fate of many an African and South American country. The question is: can Fiji go against the tide of history?

The coups have caused enormous damage to the fabric of family life. As many Indians have sought life in new lands, children have been separated from parents, brothers and sisters have gone different ways and, in some cases, wives have been parted from their husbands. The reputation of many a noble person has either been tarnished or destroyed because of their association with the coup plotters or because of their silence at crucial times. Perhaps the most tragic fall from grace is that of Ratu Mara.

As the father of modern Fiji and its long-serving Prime Minister, he became a towering figure on the international stage. His status and influence were far greater than one would expect of someone from such a small island nation. Because he failed to condemn the first coup and instead headed the post-coup regime, his international stature shattered and crumbled into dust. Here was a titan who surely could have gone on to greater things, but who fell victim to hubris. He was being mentioned as a possible candidate for the United Nations as well as for the Commonwealth Secretary-General's job. Ratu Mara should have been able to live out his sunset years as an elder statesman, enjoying universal love and respect from his people. But this was not to be. After Speight's coup, he suffered the ultimate humiliation when he was removed as the President of Fiji – by leaders of the Fiji military. Despite his failings, it is a sad reflection on the people of a country who have so dishonoured the father of the nation.

The first shipload of our ancestors arrived in this former British colonial outpost in 1879. Others followed until the indenture system was abolished in 1920 after its abuses were publicised in India. Through their blood, sweat and tears, our forefathers transformed this South Pacific backwater into the most prosperous and progressive nation in the region. But their sacrifices are not appreciated today. A steady exodus of betrayed Indians continues to seek new homes abroad. Those doomed to remain behind face a new form of serfdom. They are virtually landless and are being deprived of their political rights. They also suffer discrimination in education and job opportunities. Worse still, they are experiencing religious persecution, as evidenced by renewed calls by church leaders for Fiji to be made a Christian State and increasing incidents of arson and desecration of temples. In a strange twist of fate, they seem to be experiencing a new chapter in the *girmit* saga.

In Indian mythology, there is a belief that when Lord Krishna vanquished the huge *Kalia Naag*, the black serpent, it pleaded for its life. The merciful Krishna granted it sanctuary on a remote island paradise. Some believe Fiji was that blessed paradise. Strangely, Fijian folklore tells of a serpent supposedly residing in a cave in the Nakauvadra Hills near Tavua. But myths are just myths, just as the much-vaunted myth of Fiji being a paradise has proved to be a tragic illusion.

Indo-Fijian women at Nadi market on a Saturday morning —
colourful saris are a common sight in towns.

CHAPTER TWENTY

Immeasurable Distances

Shrishti Sharma

IN ANY JOURNEY one either likes to or is made to pause and reflect. Something goes wrong, or nothing extraordinary is happening and we begin to wonder why. Like the historical importance of a country, or the legacy of one's life, the location where one is born and bred is important, whether one considers it to be or not. In the present, however, the moment is of greater importance than what constitutes it or served as the backbone of its eventuation.

Sure, we have our forefathers — but does indenture really speak to us anymore? Has it ever? Does politics really concern us anymore? Perhaps in high school it did, when injustice was a trendy emotion. Where were the scholarships going? Where had our proud high school traditions been abandoned? But now? As much as one likes to believe in fortitude, those strings tied in teenage years are made to stretch long, long distances these days. From Ba, Nadi, Lautoka or Suva to Auckland, San Francisco, Sydney or London.

We are young, so it goes that many things we say or do may be remembered. Fondly or otherwise. But the thing is, what can we say or do that hasn't already been said or done? Besides treading cautiously on the barren footholds of a mega-pixel world, where enormity is often favoured above all things petite and precious, where the colliding of equally stubborn old and new generations of migrant families forms the drama of everyday life, escapism often seems the only attractive option. Where there *are* some of us who feebly attempt to salvage some version of the past, confusion as to what it is we are trying to rescue often mars any attempts made.

Are many of us really bothered to be unknown martyrs? Not really. We are just living. If we make an attempt to *understand* the process, what follows is a dialogue between trembling minds, and comfortably volatile lifestyles. The result? The surprised blueprint of an emotional bridge between Ba and Sydney, or Lautoka and Auckland, or perhaps ...

———

There were four of us. There had always been four of us. It was December and we were going home. It was a trip we had planned for quite a while, a break away from studies. Time to recuperate from the effects of change and time. And distance.

Fiji was and was not home to us now. While we were away, we never yearned for the benefits of our home, save for the solitude and quietness of the beaches. We were content without the petty family disputes and old-fashioned outlook on life we knew we would find at home. What we did miss was the feel of the place where we had grown up.

Vikash was the eldest of us by a few months. Tall, fair, dark-eyed and sombre, his looks belied a dispassionate maturity towards life that just did not exist as yet. His countenance always held the promise of something more. But when this would be achieved was a question left unasked or answered   .

He was the grandson of an ex-FSC worker, Mr Gurchand Singh Prasad. *Aaja loved the mill*, he'd always said. *And he hates what has become of it today. He will do something to fix it some day. He has vowed. And I am sure he will keep his word.* This was always said with a firm forward jerk of the head. Vikash was known for his idealism. He took as much pleasure in delivering his statements as he did in their content. To any beholder, the passion in his eyes suggested that nothing more was as keenly necessary as the act of deliverance itself.

It was no great mystery where he got his idealism from. The Prasads were a family of idealists, and Vikash's parents were no exception. The adorable Mrs Prasad always had nothing but praise for her three sons, the two eldest of whom were too well-acquainted with the sordid streets of Suva to be spoken of with the same pride as Vikash. And then there was Mr Prasad. *Had they all but been successfully settled in Australia,* he was known to tell us repeatedly, referring to his two older children, *then nothing would have gone wrong.* We never said anything to that.

For now, we were in the beaten-up red Toyota Corona, Vikash's pride and joy, waiting in the strong December heat outside Nadi Airport for two of our other friends to arrive. The car had been left in the car park for Vikki, courtesy of Prasad Uncle, after a recent trip to Parmal's Garage. It was too hot to speak, despite the newly installed air-conditioning. Vikki was fiddling with it, as if it was some foreign object that had invaded his dusty private buggy.

'Leave it yaar,' I protested. 'It's one of the good inventions of the modern world. Trust me.' I grinned at him widely, playing with the straps on my black top. He looked at me and didn't say a word. My skin was clamming up with the moisture in the air. The only sign of Vikki's discomfort was his slightly scrunched brow. We sat in an uncertain silence. One of the many we were to experience on this trip.

We both looked out our respective windows then and didn't speak while we waited for the others. Not much of an exchange had taken place between the two of us really, even on the plane ride, besides civil chit-chat and humorous recollections of the past. But that was enough. Time and distance had all but rid us of the magic of friendship. Had it not been for telephone calls, frequent or not, even casual conversation would have been an effort.

Vikki looked older but was otherwise unchanged. He had always been immaculately dressed and stylish in his gestures, his gait and general persona. I wondered if, in completing his engineering degree, he had fulfilled his life-plan: 'What Papa wants from me is not just an ideal. Not just an unrealistic expectation. It's a rightful desire of a father for his son to succeed. What could be more of an *ashirwaad*, a greater blessing, than that?' This was Vikki's answer to my desperate queries towards the end of Form Seven three years ago. Despite the passing of so much time, I was still wondering when he would be certain as to what *he* wanted from life. Much to my irritation, he lived on the premise that to hold such expectations was a father's *karam* (fate), and to satisfy them, a son's *dharam* (duty). We learnt later that as a 'Blessed Expectation', engineering was second best. Prasad Uncle's dearest wish, for his son to enter Medicine, had died when Vikki failed to receive a scholarship after the '99 coup. Ironically, I had declined my offer from FSM out of a long-held desire to study overseas. Now, with a partially completed genetics/psychology degree, and post-graduate medicine prospects, I had no regrets.

When we passed from phase one into phase two — passionate and angry childhood into nonchalant adulthood — I never quite realised. I remembered how we had celebrated the year Vikki and I had got reading glasses and were christened proud, high-school nerds. I didn't think any of that giggly, innocent self-centredness had left me, but then again, I did not know how I had changed, and Vikki chose not to comment.

With green leaves fluttering in the near distance and a few frangipanis nodding in the occasional breeze, long strings of cars, bright glinting steel and groups of families walking about in the car park, a definite alteration was noticeable around Nadi International Airport. The monument of departure and arrival that stood before us had changed. How, it was hard to pinpoint. Was it neater, more colourful, more up to date? Neither of us had been able to decide when walking past the ribbonned-off sections, unmistakably regarded as 'relatives only'.

I noticed the newly renovated cafeteria. The meals looked good. There were also more salesmen and women outside Tapoo's Duty Free, earnest in their blue-shirts, inviting passengers to take advantage of the Johnny Walker and Jim Bean specials of the day. 'Specials of every day,' Vikash had chuckled cynically.

Shree would have relished that change, I thought, smiling to myself. I was sure he had often convinced a few of his fellow passengers to be his partners in crime. 'Just *ek* bottle *bhaiyya*,' he'd have pleaded innocently. 'Just think, the night would be made more *shaandaar* (beautiful), with your help.' And that would be that. Many passengers would have been cajoled into his private export of liquor from his place of departure. His relatives would have often been regaled with embellished versions of his success — 'It was a struggle, but I thought of the Lord Krishna and was able to charm the customs officer on duty just by my word. After all, the Lord invented the game, albeit with *makkhan* and not whiskey.'

Vikash, Beena and I had heard these ramblings many times now, and were tired of the façade behind which Shree hid. But then again, any alteration in his character would have rid Shree of his and our sense of who he was. For, without the mischief, the deviousness and his disengagement from his own mortality, Shree would not be Shree.

As it so happened, Shree was next to arrive, bringing just one large suitcase, bulging with his prized bottled possessions. In cargoes, a bright-red hula shirt, Ray-bans and his pearly whites visible a mile away, Shree was unmistakable. 'BROTHER!' he screamed as he made his way towards us. Vikash and I couldn't resist laughing out loud. He arrived at the car and, as Vikki emerged from the driver's seat, Shree slapped him hard on the back. They hugged for a while, and then said something to each other that I wasn't meant to hear. They may have shed some tears as well, I'd never know. I looked over at the two men, completely different in character and appearance. Shree's dark-skinned, round-eyed, ever-smiling face, and Vikki's self-restrained, fair-skinned, controlled presence. Strangely enough Vikki, not Shree, was the one with the inch-long scar on the side of his left eyebrow.

'LADY!' Shree yelled out his pet name for me and came around to give me a hug while Vikki loaded his suitcase into the car. I was surprised to notice that he did not smell of whiskey or beer and gazed at him questioningly. He either didn't notice my inquiring glance or chose not to acknowledge it and hurriedly explained that Beena was just caught up in customs. 'Something to do with chutney and pickles … I don't know,' he drawled. 'Women's nonsense.'

The irony of the situation didn't escape any of us. Beena was a control freak, and we all laughed at her expense, wondering whether the foodstuff had been smuggled into her bag by one of her future in-laws. Because of Beena's character, none of us had been surprised by news of her impending marriage. In a time-honoured fashion, Beena's black and white outlook on life meant that she had travelled the traditional path that decades of Indian lifestyle had not changed, in this country or overseas. Through her early departure from high school and her migrant's life in Australia, she had proven her independence. Her naivety, however, remained an unmistakable product of upbringing by a pundit father, traditional (yet frustrated) mother and her large extended family of confused siblings. Today this had justly earned her a story-book wedding to a story-book *dulha* in story-book time — right after completing her three-year commerce degree.

As Vikki returned to the driver's seat, Shree finally pulled away from me and held me at arm's length. 'Long time, *na?*' he said lightly, smiling as usual. I could feel his body trembling slightly, perhaps with the avid, childlike anticipation of a new game to play, or a long-awaited concert to see. '*Mem-sahib*, the years have not rid you of that all-knowing look in your eyes.' He pulled away and started to turn around, only to flick his right index finger across the tip of my nose. 'Still a head-turner.'

———

As it happened, Beena was absent on our trip back to Vikki's home, where we were to spend most of our holiday. We had waited another half-hour for her arrival when Vikki's cell-phone rang. It was Beena, calling to tell us that, much to her irritation, her in-laws had arrived unexpectedly to pick her up instead. We stifled her apologies by extracting a firm promise that she would drop by that evening for dinner.

Our reception at Vikki's home was warm and jovial, as expected. Mrs Prasad pressed cookies and tea on us as soon as we entered. Dressed in a casual green cotton *mumu*, her hair in disarray, with fresh tears in her kohl-black eyes, and a welcoming smile on her exhausted face, she gave each of us a hug. Prasad Uncle was just as moved, and his tall, distinguished figure was stooped with the emotion of seeing his youngest son again. His serious bespectacled face and balding and greying appearance seemed to be a mask, weathered by decades of emotion, so much so that he seemed smaller in stature than Vikki when in fact he was half a foot taller

'You have the makings of a grand beard-holder, *beta*,' was his only comment after hugging his son. Vikki merely smiled in acceptance of the statement. 'I thought Vikki hated beards!' I whispered to Shree and he giggled softly. Father and son insisted on carrying our bags to our rooms. Shree and I sat in the living room, a metre away from the portable fan, and silently watched them go, talking in hushed tones.

No one else was home; a blessing as neither of us were quite ready to deal with doting grandmothers and inquisitive aunts and uncles, let alone feisty little cousins, nieces and nephews. Vikki's family was so large it had become a joke between the four of us that some of them had just snuck into the clan, relation or not. Vikki found this amusing as he enjoyed the company of his extended family, even if just to lose himself among them. He used to do this on many occasions. When clashes at home got too frustrating, Vikki could be found with any one of his clan members, yarning or laughing away, in a

corner of the tin shed Prasad Uncle had put up in his yard. As a
parent, Uncle spoke sparingly but imposed high expectations —
a damaging combination, I thought, angrily. Quickly, I turned my
attention back to the present, for the sake of enjoying the rest of
the holiday.

———————

'The boy does not eat!! Look at him!' Aunty complained
over sizzling samosas, her tiny frame fluttering between the
chopping board, the sink and the fridge, in quick, harmonious
movements. 'Become skin and bones, all of you.'

'I am sure he does, Aunty, it's just that you have not seen
him in a while. And being young. You know. We tend to be more
conscious of what and how much we eat,' I tried to assure her,
unsuccessfully.

'*Nai*, this just won't do. You are home, you eat.'

She need not have worried though. My taste buds were
already craving her generously spiced cooking. The next batch of
samosas emerged tanned and scorched into the serving dish.
The oil remaining on them bubbled and I savoured the aroma,
knowing I probably wouldn't see such home-made Indian
delicacies again for a while. I carried the dish into the lounge.

'The salwaar looks good on you still,' Aunty chuckled behind
me, and I laughed. It was a promise made between us long ago that I
would wear the traditional kurtha and pants she had made me at
least once every time I visited her. I liked the feel of the soft cotton
on my skin. As the weather had cooled for the evening, it was
pleasant to wear the costume. Somehow it felt right to wear it here.

The men had moved to the porch to watch the retreating
sun over bowls of *yaqona* and light wine. Fiji Bitter was being
passed around as well; Uncle and Shree seemed to be enjoying it
the most. Beena had arrived an hour ago and was sitting
demurely on the edge of the railings of the porch, quietly sipping
her wine. In a simple grey skirt and white cotton top, her short,

straight hair pulled back in a pony-tail — typical Beena style —
she was fitting in and catching up without fuss. Relaxation Fiji-
style, I thought contentedly, and watched my footing as I passed
the sliding glass doors. Leaving the hot, aroma-filled kitchen and
the unkempt lounge, the cool breeze of the outside air was very
welcoming, as was the glowing orange of the late-afternoon sky.

'Samosas everyone!' I announced and placed the tray on
the table. The Prasad's tiny balcony looked out on to their
modest lawn and towards the sea in the far distance. It was a
lovely view.

I sat next to Beena and bit into a samosa. The fresh scent
of a nearby tulsi tree filled the air. 'How's the excitement at
home?' I asked her between mouthfuls.

'Oh, *nai pooch* (don't ask),' she turned to me, dismissively
waving her hand. 'It's a nut-house over there and the wedding's a
whole three months away. Navin is flying in the day after
tomorrow. I'll be glad to have him here. After all, it *is* his family.
He can handle the stress for both of us.' As she smiled, I realised
her apparent irritation was but a cover. Inside she seemed to be
happy, content.

I brushed away some crumbs from my lap and smiled,
'You've ended the race way before any of us, you know.'

'Ohhh, the girlfriend thing,' she laughed openly. 'What
little promises we used to make, *na*? We won't get married till
OUR version of Shah Rukh Khan arrives. We will get married
at the same time.' She sighed and memories of nail-filing
and reading romantic novels under the desk in the presence of
the ever-watchful Mr Narayan all came back to me. 'No,' she
continued, 'I mean, it's all good at that age, you know ...'

'I know,' I agreed. I looked at the half-eaten samosa in my
hand. Aunty had made the filling so that all the potatoes had
been mashed in together and were almost indistinguishable from
the other fillings. Green peas stuck out unevenly here and there.
I pushed some of them back in and took to finishing the treat.
Silently, we both turned to listen to the men's conversation.

Uncle was sprawled on his favourite chair, right across from us. It was apparent that he had had a few glasses by now, and was comfortably talkative, a slight lilt to his tone. Shree was on his left, leaning against the window ledge. The window had white metal bars on it and he was holding on to them with one hand behind his back, and had his drink in the other. Vikki was on Uncle's right, about a metre away from me, looking out into the distance, his hands secured on the railings of the balcony and his back turned to his father. I caught a glimpse of Vikki's scar, accentuated by the afternoon light and then looked away.

'My *Chacha*,' said Uncle. 'Puram Singh. Now there was a good man. He was my role model. He was a tailor. You know … tailor?' he acknowledged us and we nodded. '*Haan, thab* what he used to do, he used to gather up all the bits and pieces from his sewing material on the floor, and what?' he suddenly yelled, looking at Shree.

'Good man,' Shree raised his glass and just smiled foolishly at Uncle. Beena and I looked at each other and laughed, shaking our heads. Shree's response, however, seemed to be sufficient for Uncle.

'Correct,' said Uncle. 'He used to make … big … big … sheets. You know, the kind you use to cover yourself at night? Right, Vikki *beta*?'

Vikki kept looking straight ahead and didn't turn around.

'Yeah, very good man,' Uncle continued after a hefty cough. 'Every little piece of cloth, he would sew together, bit by bit. His eyes almost blinded. The light was terrible in the village. Only had kerosene lamp. Yeah. He was my role model. Made sheets for … all the family. Good man. No one should go cold at night. No one. The children, the family. All in a day's work,' he paused suddenly to take another gulp of his drink.

'Good man,' Shree said again, putting his drink away and rubbing his face with his hands in an attempt to get sober again. Even I thought it was a bit too early to be out of it.

'No, no, he used to *finish* the day's work, and then do this at night,' Uncle suddenly announced, laughing gleefully. 'Bloody

good man, like a role model *na* Vikki? Son?' At this, Uncle tried
to get up from his chair, but was unsuccessful, and noisily bumped
the centre table.

Vikki turned around; this time holding the railings behind
him. To me, he seemed a bit embarrassed by the whole exchange.
'He used to beat his wife, Dad,' he said flatly. 'Everyone knew
that.'

'Nonsense!!' Uncle shouted, angrily waving his hands
around. '*Chacha* was a good man. He did everything. He worked.
He sent his children to school. He taught them his trade. He ...
he ...' Uncle paused and looked Vikki straight in the eye. 'He
looked after ... the family. He did a man's duty.'

Trying to reach the samosas, Shree clumsily tipped over his
glass. It fell to the floor but didn't break and he bent to pick it up
then sat, cross-legged on the floor, eating his samosa. Uncle
suddenly subsided into a long, drawn out chesty cough. I winced
uncomfortably. I wondered whether Shree knew what was going
on at all. I looked over at Beena. She was looking shyly at the
floor. Having heard all the commotion, Aunty appeared at the
sliding doors. Uncle could not see her, and she gestured
frantically at Vikki to finish up the drinking and come inside.
Vikki looked at her, but folded his arms and continued the
conversation.

'He had his bad side as well, Dad. I am surprised you call
him your role model. I thought Gandhiji was your role model.'
I couldn't decide from the expression on Vikki's face whether he
was being sarcastic or not.

While shaking his head angrily, Uncle struggled to pour
himself another drink. I looked at Vikki, wondering why he was
provoking his father.

'Bah what do you young people know, eh? You study, you
take the girls out, you dance, dance, dance, you have this ... what
you call? Summer job? Stupid bloody summer job ... all you know
is your books and your summer job and ... what ... nothing ...
what do you know about minding the family, eh? That is a man's

job. You don't know it yet. You will have to learn. Role model. That's why, you need role model. Hmm,' he finished with another sip of his drink. 'Who knows, what kind, eh, what kind of men you mingle with there? Old, smelly professors who cannot see beyond the end of their glasses and who don't know their backsides from their nose. Bah. They have to write a bloody thesis on how to light up a pipe before doing it. Nonsense, you need to be taught how to be a MAN.'

I shook my head and looked down at my hands, concentrating on the many lines on my palms. I wondered at what point idealism died. I then looked up and saw Aunty looking pleadingly at me. I signalled her indicating five minutes and she nodded and walked away. I could understand where her worry lines came from. Meanwhile, Vikki grunted in frustration at his father and said, 'You don't know anything. All you know is the A and B from your home to your office and any detours to your bottle. We have to manage …'

'Don't you DARE speak to me like that boy!' Uncle suddenly yelled, making us all jump 'I put you where you are, you don't question my judgments!' He banged his glass on the table.

'Then what do you WANT?' Vikki asked angrily and my heart leapt at hearing the one question that he had needed someone to answer all his life.

Vikki's tone enraged Uncle even more. With a yell, he got up and tried to walk over to Vikki, only to trip over the table, his weight pushing it noisily along the floor as he fell. He upset the bottles in the process and Shree jumped to salvage them. Frightened, Beena and I got up from our positions. Vikki didn't seem to know how to react.

Aunty came running from the kitchen, '*Bas*. Enough,' she announced and bent to help Uncle up. Beena and I looked at each other, uncertain whether to help or not, but Uncle, leaning on Aunty's shoulder, was able to make his way through the lounge to his bedroom. Aunty's hold on him seemed to be the only support which stopped him from falling over again. We could hear him mumbling angrily to Aunty as he went: 'education ... no use ... disrespect ... money ... role model ... firm hand ... *besharam* (shameless) ...'

After a moment's silence, when everyone decided to settle their emotions, Shree laughed softly and then began singing quietly: '*Badi sooni sooni hai, zindagi yeh, zindagi* ... (Life is so sad ...)'

'Shree! Stop it!' Vikki exclaimed.

'What *yaar*, why do you get provoked by the old man's rage and provoke him back with your own? It's just his way ... he's coping.'

'Coping with what?' Vikki asked, the evidence of suppressed anger in his tone. 'I have done everything he has ever asked of me,' he looked at me as he said this. 'And more.'

I turned away. It was getting too dark to see each other clearly. The sliver of a moon was out, and a sprinkling of stars. The indigo sky was partly cloudy. An unconscious, 'I-told-you-so' expression was the last thing Vikki needed right now, even though I would never have intentionally looked at him in that way.

'No *yaar*,' Shree continued. 'He's old, man. Everything around him is changing. *You* are changing. For many people, it's a scary thing, you know?'

'Still doesn't justify it,' Vikki protested.

'Na man, didn't he just say not to question his judgment, misguided or n—'

'*Abh*, whose side are you on, *yaar*?' Vikki exclaimed angrily. 'And what would you know about all this anyway?'

'Hey, hey, hey,' Shree exclaimed trying to keep his own anger at bay. Shree was sensitive about the absence of his own father.

'Guys,' Beena cut in. 'Cool it. We don't need to carry this any further. We came here to enjoy ourselves. Come on. It's a holiday. We're too young for this, and we have our whole lives ahead of us.'

'*Arreh*, Maharani speaks at last,' Shree smiled and I sighed in relief. Beena laughed, too. 'Your Highness,' he continued, 'come here, sit by us and tell us all about your plans for the big day.'

I appreciated Shree's ability to take things lightly at times like this because any further provocation would have ruined the evening entirely. Beena and I sat down on cushions around the centre table. After a minute's hesitation, Vikki also joined us.

'Chill *yaar*,' Shree addressed Vikki good-naturedly. Vikki sighed and placed his hands on his face, resting his elbows on the coffee table.

'Come on,' I joined in. 'It's just one of those days, one of those things.'

'Mmmhmm,' Vikki responded. All three of us were looking at him now but he had his head down. He laughed softly, then began singing: '*Yeh kahaan, aa gaye hum. Yun hi saath saath chalthe* …' (Look where we have arrived, together …')

All of us laughed in relief, but Shree went a step further. He continued the song, grasping Vikki's hands across the table and pulling them away from his face: '*Teri baahon meh hai Jaanam, meri jismo jaan pighalthe* (I melt in your arms, my beloved).'

Shree's impersonation of a woman embracing her man was hilarious and we all burst into laughter again. This time, it was uncontrollable and provided relief from the evening's strain.

'Everything feels slightly different doesn't it?' Vikki asked when the laughter had subsided. I was making shapes in the frost on a half-empty beer bottle — a heart, a star, a question mark. 'I mean, it's only been three years. I thought I could return. Just return.'

'We are not coming back though, are we?' I asked. 'I mean, not for long. Our home in paradise has become a resort for us. Fiji, next stop. Three weeks 'R&R' and then we are homeward bound, sadly. Either the weather's too uncomfortable for us now, or the temperature too high,' I winked at Shree and he smiled.

'Looks like it's entry into phase three,' said Beena. 'Or at least for me it is.'

I gave her a light hug and said, 'Nothing should keep us apart though. I think it's important, if not wise, to be there for each other over the years.' I rested my head on Beena's left shoulder and looked out at the night sky. 'I think someone famous once said that friends are the family we choose for ourselves. If we let opportunities go by, then we have only ourselves to blame.'

'Well, well, well,' Shree said, clearing his throat and lifting his almost-empty glass. 'Since this is mushy moment number one of many for the night, let's drink to future accountant, future businesswoman, future doctor and future engineer of the century,' he pointed at everyone including himself when he said this and then drank up.

'At least some things don't change,' laughed Vikki, throwing a bottle top at Shree. 'Beena. Soon to be Mrs Kumar,' he said in wonder. 'Do you remember, Beena, you used to be Miss Prim and Proper at school? Always ruling the red margin lines correctly. Exactly three squares on the left of the page. And always ruled at least 10 pages in advance for each class?'

'I remember,' Beena smiled. 'I still do the ledgers — they're all aligned.'

'Ha ha, numerically aligned to your benefit you mean?' Vikki winked at her.

I lifted my head from Beena's shoulder and added, 'And she used to do an extra maths exercise every time we were given homework! Teacher's pet!' I jabbed her in the side and she giggled, pushing me away.

'Now it's kitchen duties and child-rearing,' Shree teased with another flourish of his empty glass. 'Here, here!'

'Oh no, no,' said Beena. 'Navin is adamant about the fact that my career and my family are equally important. We are not rushing into anything yet. We are still young, after all,' she paused, looking around. 'We all are.'

'Yeah,' said Vikki, as Shree burped shamelessly and slapped a mosquito away. 'We are.'

We were quiet for a while. Vikki put his hands on the table and rested his head on it. Beena fiddled with her engagement ring. Shree leaned back and closed his eyes.

'Did the Doc ban alcohol all nights except Saturday, Shree?' I addressed him.

'Hmm? Yeah ... hey,' he opened his eyes in surprise. 'How did you ...'

'You didn't drink on the flight did you?' Now everyone's attention was on Shree.

'What did the doctor say, Shree? You have problems?' Vikki asked seriously.

Like everything else though, Shree rebuffed our questions and concern with humour, 'Oh it's nothing guys,' he answered. '*Daaru peene se liver kharab hotha hai* (Liquor damages your liver). So, the Doc just told me to cut down a bit, nothing more.'

'I guess you'd listen to him then, you haven't listened to us all these years at all,' said Beena hopefully.

'Not tonight,' Shree replied smiling. 'Just not tonight.'

For the moment, everyone let it pass.

I looked at Vikki. He was laughing softly, despite his displeasure. I noticed his scar seemed to disappear when he smiled. I looked past him into the night again. A dog howled softly. Crickets called out to each other noisily. The sounds of the night seemed to somehow be in harmony. Nothing could measure the proximity of people bound together, whether by choice or chance, I realised. No estimation could redefine that tentative bond between father and son — what strengthened or weakened it was a rubber-like, indistinguishable emotional tie. We could try to understand it, but its contractions were beyond amateurish inquiry. Any detective work into the nature of the generational gap were also futile, I realised. City to city, or country to country, the parent-child bond was just as confusing as any. For now, though A to B may be many thousands of kilometres away, we could only be thankful that they were still clearly marked locations on a large and ever-changing map. To nurture and protect these relationships became our duty

'Raksha? Raksha ...'

I blinked my eyes and realised suddenly that Vikki was trying to get my attention. 'Let's go. Dinner's ready.'

I looked around and noticed Beena and Shree were already leaving. Aunty was standing at the glass doors. She smiled faintly at me and I smiled back.

'Raksha?'

I looked back at Vikki. He was holding out his hand. I took it and smiled. 'Yeah, let's go.'

*A rural store, Vunimoli, Labasa, a regular place
for meetings to discuss village affairs.*

CHAPTER TWENTY-ONE

Final Day

Asish Janardhan

IT WAS 23 March, 1989. Out of the corner of my eye, I could see the Air New Zealand 747 rolling in. Three more hours to go. Raj tugged at my leg. He wanted a soda. I pulled his cheeks, gave him some change and off he dashed towards the almost deserted canteen. The Nadi International Airport looked more like an Indian funeral gathering than an airport. Couldn't really blame them; coming to the airport, a rarity in itself, presented the perfect excuse to dress up and 'go out'. You see, most of my family are poor farmers, and the only time they get to venture out is once a month, when they go off to the sugar mills to collect their cane payments, a whole $200.

The final boarding call for passengers was made. Having bid our final farewells, Manju, Raj and I proceeded towards the terminal. I stopped, turned around and looked for Ritesh among the throng. Maybe it was the last time I was going to see my older son …

───────

My name is Ranjit Kumar. My friend once told me that I reminded him of Derek Jeter (I don't know who Derek Jeter is), because the 'jit' in my name is pronounced the same way that his name is pronounced. My first name means 'victor in wars', while my last name translates loosely to 'prince'. It remains to be seen if I come halfway close to being a victorious prince before I die.

Three days ago, I completed my 14th year of living in America. Fourteen years seem to have flown by like 14 seconds I will be a grandfather for the first time in two months. I am still not a legal resident here, however, and my third court hearing (the previous two having been postponed) is scheduled for April next year. I believe I am a legal resident whatever they say, for all that matters in this country is that you abide by the law, pay your taxes and don't have 'bin Laden' as your last name.

I was born in the Fiji Islands, the oldest in a family of four sons and three daughters. I was lucky enough to have completed 10th Standard (the equivalent of sophomore year in American high schools – really, I loathe this particular naming system; how can you be a 'fresh' man when you're stoned half the time?), and my interest in cars landed me a job as a sales and parts clerk at the local Toyota dealership, Asco Motors. I climbed the rungs of the job-status ladder fairly quickly and, in three years, I was made Manager of the Sigatoka Branch.

Manju remained at home, for my average income could feed two families in Fiji. My sons were growing day by day, and I wished that they wouldn't follow in my footsteps and drop out of school early. Raj, the younger one, had asthma, but you could never tell: he was so frisky he was a 'human monkey'. He had a penchant for climbing the highest trees in less than a minute, and he could run in the sand dunes behind our house all day. Ritesh, well, he was more calm and sombre. He was the smarter of the two, but not really athletic. I sometimes felt he really didn't like me; he was detached and more like his own man …

———————

You could almost feel the tension in the air. It had always been there, yet never so blatant. We had a long history of successful coexistence with indigenous Fijians, but sometimes, familiarity bred contempt, as one would expect. The seeds of hatred had been sown long before the Coalition Party came into office. It was going to be only a matter of time before chaos and violence reared their ugly head. And they did.

The first of three military *coups d'état* in Fiji was on 14 May, 1987. A colonel of the Fiji military forces threw out the reigning government by force, and became the head of government, citing the 'good of my people, the *Kai Vitis*' as the reason and motive for his actions. As is usually the case, rioting and looting ensued. Mayhem was the order of the day — many Indians were brutally assaulted, and there were some unreported fatalities. My house was burgled and ransacked, my company truck set on fire, my parents and brothers harassed on their farm in a nearby town. This was the plight of most Indians in Fiji. Worse was to follow … Raj was badly beaten and left to die at his school. It was a miracle that he survived. This was the last straw.

'You have to get out of here, Ranjit, my brother,' said Raymond, my neighbour. He was a proud Fijian, but not so proud of what his fellow countrymen were doing.

'You won't last long here, you and I both know that. Go to America man, the land of freedom and the champion of human rights,' he added. 'That is what their Statue of Liberty represents, and Bush is a good leader.'

There was no other way we could leave except on a tourist visa, and even then one of us would have had to stay behind, as the US Embassy did not offer more than three visas per family at that time. Ritesh had already made up his mind; he was going to stay behind on my dad's cane farm and go to school there. Manju and I didn't know what to do, but we had no other option …

I was overwhelmed by the sheer size of the airport in Los Angeles. I had never travelled like that before, and it was really

jumping into the lion's den. And the people! I had seen white
tourists frolicking in the Fiji sun before, but I did not know what
to make of the 637 other 'types' I saw there!

I made do with my restricted English (it has improved
considerably now) and led Manju and Raj from the airline
counter to the shuttle to the terminal. Throughout, I felt that I
would never fit in, but I knew my journey, and that of Raj and
Manju, was just starting. I had to stay strong, I had to plough on.
The quite-altered face of Manju's uncle was a welcome relief when
we finally arrived in San Francisco. We had made it to America!

I could never have imagined in my worst nightmares the
times that awaited us when we moved in with Jai, Manju's uncle,
and his six-member family in a two-bedroom apartment in
Pittsburgh. The first two weeks were rosy, but the next year and a
half were like a living hell.

We were subject to so much mental abuse that we actually
started believing what they told us we were. Weaker men would
have buckled. Manju and I both worked three jobs (illegally, as
we were still 'tourists') to pay our share of the rent and save
enough money to move out on our own. Raj's asthma worsened,
and he was constantly depressed because he was the last one to be
picked on any team at school.

I missed Ritesh.

In 1990, we finally had an apartment of our own. It was
conveniently located in Antioch and Raj could walk to school
easily. I bought a little Mazda for Manju at an auction so that she
could go off to work without having to depend on me to drop her
off and pick her up each time. Working was a new experience for
her, too; and, among many others, being held at gunpoint at Taco
Bell when working as a cashier is one experience she will never
forget! She was a good wife though, and supported me through
thick and thin. She held us together.

After the first 18 months, Raj had made new friends at
school and he had a new verve about him. What was most

surprising, though, was that he had joined his school wrestling team. He was a skinny little thing at 12 and, what with his asthma problems, I was deeply worried. But I never stopped him. I wanted him to learn and grow and integrate as much as possible, and one of the ways he was going to do that was by taking on new challenges. He was also sounding more and more American, and I had trouble understanding him when he spoke in English.

Our six-month visas had expired long ago, and we were staying over as political refugees. I had paid a hefty sum to the lawyers who fought our case, and they also helped us to get work permits, which had to be renewed every year. I was indeed thankful for this, as the situation back home continued to worsen. It was hard, but I called Ritesh every week with the $10 phone card I bought at the Pittsburgh Indian Store, giving me 23 minutes of talk time. He said he was doing well, but I could never tell if he longed to be with us. I wondered if he missed me. Maybe Raj and Manju, but perhaps not me …

I hoped that, as one of the repercussions of the Persian Gulf War, we would not be deported back to Fiji. I would be glued to the little TV in our apartment, which had bad reception, watching news and images of the war and hoping for a peaceful resolution. It seemed as if I was experiencing firsthand the sheer magnitude and power of America through its military. The coups in Fiji paled miserably in comparison with this battle. It is hard to understand why a war is even given the green light by the world powers, but sometimes it seems legitimate and necessary. Whether or not this one was, I do not have a clear answer.

One of Raj's closest friends, Alvin, also an immigrant from Fiji, was killed during the first Gulf War. I only met him once, and he told me he manned a tank and blew things up all day. Raj himself wanted to join the army, but he didn't have a Greencard …

The differences seem endless between Fiji and America. Sometimes, it even feels unfair to compare the two. The whole meaning of America is so … different. It seems as if this is the only country where one can start from scratch and establish oneself. I also feel very safe in this country, and realise the rights that I have.

I have struggled in this land a lot. And, each passing day, I have had moments when I think of Fiji. Home is where the heart is, but what the heart wants, the heart does not always get. I want to work less and have more money to pay off my debts, a kind of wishful thinking, no doubt, that I'm sure manifests in each one of us.

I find that there is very little 'me' time here, and I am constantly trying to meet deadlines. I have aged faster, and Raj tells me I have a bald patch. The postponement of the court hearings also have drained a lot out of me. Everyone in the world is a slave to time, but none bigger than me. The laid-back approach that I used to have, nurtured and developed through time from being born and bred in the islands, has gone out the window, and punctuality is a new attribute I can say I have.

America to me is a great kaleidoscope. There is so much variety in everything you see, in the people, the food, the cars, the media, sports and even in its seeming obsession with sex! The education system I'm not too sure about, as high school here appears to be a farce. Such a big deal is made out of graduating from high school, you'd be forgiven for thinking that this was the place where PhDs were being offered! I know I might sound hypocritical, having not finished high school myself, but would I be a bandwag-oneer if I said that 'my time was different'? School changed Raj a lot, and wrestling seemed to cure his asthma problems for good. I hate to admit it, and I might sound like I'm contradicting myself, but he has become just what I didn't want him to become — an AMERICAN teenager. The earrings, the bleached cropped hair, the baggy trousers, the friends, the car and the late nights bear testimony to this. I feel as though I 'spared the rod' when I should have used it; discipline was paramount in Fiji. But surely this is not what being an American teenager is all about, or is it?

It seemed like a miracle, but Ritesh finally managed to come over, in 1995. There were a lot of legal wrangles involved, and a lot of risks taken. But he did succeed in securing an International Student visa. As always, he remained distant, and missed Fiji. I have always tried to, and always will, be a good father, but if it's not meant to be, it's not meant to be. My joy, however, knows no end now that he is here. I hope that my younger son takes a few cues from him, because no matter the barrier that exists between us, his maturity and character are to be commended.

Two years ago, I bought my first house in America, for almost $200,000. It's not a mansion, but it's not a hole either. It's just right for the four of us and, with a few improvements here and there, it should be even better. A house is a major investment, and it should help our standing in the court hearing. Somehow, I now feel as if I can hold my head up high. I feel a sense of belonging, an air of acceptance.

Being the person I am, I don't think I will ever fully get the 'hang' of this place. There is many an occasion when I feel out of place, when I search the throng for the familiar face of Manju, when I want to run away. I'd like to consider myself an easygoing individual overall, but sometimes, not being the dominant kind in a particular country can be daunting, not least when it comes to language. I can proudly say, however, that I have become wiser to the world having spent all this time here. 'Refinancing', 'NASA', 'Congress' and 'hustler' are no longer alien concepts to me. Having had to make do practically from scratch initially contributes a great deal to this learning process as well. There abounds a certain sense of sovereignty, knowledge that whatever little I have achieved and acquired through the years has been through my own hard work.

Almost a decade ago, I joined a little (at that time) religious group — the Sri Sanatan Dharm Omkar Ramayan Mandali of Pittsburgh. This was really done out of a need for escapism, a need to get away from each draining work day. I come from a very religious background. *Pitaji* and *Amma* were always holding big *poojas* and religious festive celebrations at our place back in Fiji, so that aspect of their rearing certainly rubbed off on the children, I believe. Our *mandali* now has more than 40 registered families, and it is ever growing. We gather every other Friday at a selected member's house, and hold religious prayers and thanksgiving sessions late into the night. We used to have problems before, as the neighbours would frown at our obnoxiously loud *bhajan* and *kirtan* renditions, but now it seems to have been solved. When they know that a neighbour of theirs is going to play host that Friday night to some 100-odd people, who love to keep them up with their singing, they just decide to go out!

I believe that at least some sense of spirituality is needed in order to live a meaningful life. I try to lead a simple life, I try my level best to do good things every day, and, in return, I ask for forgiveness and the health and wellbeing of my family.

In fact, I am devoted to that 'divine being' so fully now that I attain a state of bliss each morning when I meditate.

In all, I may have worked in more than 15 different jobs before finally settling (hope springs eternal) for my current one. I 'flipped burgers' (as they say here) for quite some time before I moved on to a department store, where I was a warehouse associate, an associate who lifted heavy boxes all day. If there's one thing I aspire to, it's a serious work ethic. I subscribe to the notion that if I'm going to do something, I better put my heart into it or there is no point doing it in the first place. Maybe this is what got me promoted to a supervisory post in mid-2001. I shifted from straining my back all day to overseeing others strain their backs. The pay could certainly have been a little higher though.

Today, I work for Coca-Cola USA, in Benicia, California. I'm a quality control manager and my job entails a little marketing from time to time. But primarily, I attend to the various Coke products that sell at supermarkets and other outlets and deal with displays, orders, promotions and seasonal beverages, among others. The pay is far better than what I was toiling for the previous years, and I even get my own truck to go from store to store and city to city. At first, I used to get lost on new highways and make up some lame excuse as to why I arrived late at a particular store, but now it is our clients who look for excuses to justify their tardiness — I don't need to stop and ask for directions anymore.

As for Manju, she has laboured a lot, too, and endured her fair share of moments when she had given up all hope, but she finally seems to have found something she actually likes. Her limited education from Fiji would have made it hard for her to get a high-status job anyway, and we never really kidded ourselves from the beginning. She works at a large private hospital as a housekeeper, and she gets fairly decent money for it, too. Well, relatively. She has made lots of friends, and looks forward to going to work each day.

Gone are the days of the timid lady who stayed at home and cooked and cleaned for her man. She is now the proud owner of a 2002 Toyota Tacoma truck, her dream car. There seems to be a distinct spring in her step, and her confidence reassures me. Together, we manage to save up a few hundred dollars a month after paying off all our bills. We just might need that money for a rainy day or two — who knows? The advent of August is the most worrying for me, because that is the time when our work permits are renewed. By some twisted turn of fate, if our renewed permits reach our workplaces even an hour late, we will be terminated, and I have seen it happen to many an immigrant.

I am still waiting to meet the man who once proclaimed, 'When you live in America, you mint money', when he came over to our Fiji house from America to meet a relative in our neighbourhood. Frankly, we get these kinds of 'tourists' every so often back in Fiji, who, after having lived for a period overseas, believe that Fiji is the outpost of civilisation. They boast about their fancy houses and luxury cars and 900-thread Egyptian rugs and twin Siamese cats, while we have no choice but to hold our mouths wide open in awe. I fell victim to this, too, as I created this symbolic package of America being a place where one needed custom-made trousers to keep the numerous 100-dollar bills from falling out.

Alas, that is definitely not the case, not for me at least. Sure, there is money to be made, but the more money you make the more expenses there are. There is a common joke here that really typifies the current economic market. They say that when you back your car out of the driveway, you have to take out a bank loan just to pay for the gas that you burnt (a lot!) in doing so. The San Francisco Bay area, where we live, is second only to New York City in terms of cost of living expenses.

But, having said that, I do not think I will be relocating any time soon. I never was the adventurous type, and never will be. I will continue living here till my very last breath. I am settled; I have a house and a decent job. Who knows what struggles I may have to endure if I decide to move house to a cheaper area.

Life, in general, contrary to my initial beliefs, is pretty routine here. Maybe if I was the average thrill-seeking American with 2.5 kids and a debt of $26,000, I would be saying different. For Manju and I, time is divided between work, the *mandali* and babysitting Rohan, our grandson. Even Raj, who always had something new to do each day, has mellowed. He hardly even goes out these days and, at times, I wonder if he is losing his sovereignty. Maybe we are all losing our sovereignty bit by bit, surrendering our individuality and conviction to some outside force.

Raj married his girlfriend in 2001. She is Indian, but then she isn't. You see, she is from Guyana, the land of Ebonics. She does everything Indian, except speak the language. But how can you be of a certain ethnic group and not speak the language? As if talking to *her* in English wasn't enough, now I have to talk to Raj in English, too! Apparently, she has to know everything that goes on, and therefore we cannot speak in our language when she's around. Women certainly are powerful.

Raj's wife is expecting, and I should become a grandfather again in May sometime. Raj is a kid himself; I wonder if he will be able to handle the small matter of starting a family now. And, since he does not have schooling beyond high school, he might find it difficult later on. But, whatever the case, I am always ready to help him out …

Our court hearing is set for April 2004, and I have begun cramming my lines, and so has Manju. If only we had a better command of the language. We do not want to fail at the final hurdle. It's been 14 years and having to go back would be unimaginable, catastrophic in terms of the progress we've all made.

Amid the current war with Iraq, I have the deepest concern for the countless innocent lives that no doubt will be lost. One of those lives might be Ritesh's, now serving with the 101st Airborne Division of the US Army. I last heard his voice two weeks ago, as he prepared to leave for battle for his adopted country. He told me he loved me; that is what I have yearned to hear for 24 long years …

As the sun sets on yet another day, I feel a sense of contentment. I still don't know if I have been a 'victorious prince', maybe far from it. An 'average, hard-working man' will do for me.

*At the Sigatoka market, typical of many rural market towns
selling an array of colourful vegetables: tomato, baigan, bhindi, chillies.*

CHAPTER TWENTY-TWO

Colour My Country

Mosmi Bhim

Colour my country red
Because it is bleeding
Bleeding like the soldiers shot in the mutiny
Bleeding from the wounds
Inflicted on its people

Colour my country blue
Because it is shivering
Shivering like the overtime garment worker,
    walking home alone at night
Shivering from the hatred
It has seen in its people

Colour my country gold
Because it is burning
Burning like the sugar cane torched in the field
Burning out from the waste
Its people have turned it into

Colour my country black
Because it is mourning
Mourning like the farmers evicted from their
    homes of decades
Mourning because it knows
That this damage will never be forgotten

Colour my country white
Because it is innocent
Innocent like the voters choosing the names
    of people they like
Innocent as the lush trees, golden sands and
    smiling sun,
Which have given it the name of paradise

Colour my country grey
Because it is uncertain
Uncertain like the leaders of Fiji who cannot find
unity
Uncertain whether to love
All children fully, or favour its first-born

Colour my country brown
Because it is a mother
Mother, like the Sisters who look after orphans at
    Saint Christopher's Home
Mother, which is why it is still
Looking after these wayward children

Colour my country yellow
Because it is scared
Scared like the parliamentarians held hostage
    from May 19, 2000
Scared of how much more
Destruction it will have to bear

Colour my country orange
Because it is still hopeful
Hopeful like its citizens, migrating overseas
Hopeful that all its people will stop discriminating
Just as she has never discriminated

Colour my country green
Because it is envious
Envious like the parliamentarians, who lost the
    1999 elections
Envious of its neighbouring countries which have not
Experienced such divisiveness of its people

Colour my country silver
Because it is precious
Precious like each coin is, to the beggars on
    the streets of Suva
Precious because without it
Its people will be homeless

Colour my country bronze
Because it is trying
Trying like the Fiji Sevens Team in the
    Hong Kong Finals,
Trying to solve its problems
But with only one-third of its heart.

Temple at Nabila, Nadi

CHAPTER TWENTY-THREE

Searching

Vijay Naidu

ONE HUNDRED AND twenty-five years in geological time is of little consequence, but in human history it can be of massive significance, as seen in the transformation of the human condition globally since the late 19th century. This is a personal reflection on a minute segment of humanity transported more than 6,000 kilometres from India to Fiji and their descendants now spread the world over. It is about a people in search of a place they can call home. The search has taken them far and wide, and into many different situations and interrelationships. From a small Pacific Island country they have traversed the great ocean and, indeed, the globe in this search. Indo-Fijian diasporas exist in England, Hong Kong, Canada, the US, Australia, New Zealand and India. Who are these people and what has driven them to seek homes in these distant places? In order to answer this question, I will traverse the 125 years of their experience. Their story involves the indigenous people of the land, British colonialism, social and economic changes, political development, military coups and the changing immigration policies of Pacific Rim countries.

Imperialism begat colonialism; colonialism begat plantation agriculture; plantation agriculture begat forms of slavery. In the tropical and semi-tropical colonies, slave crops such as cotton and sugar, produced by the sweat, blood and tears of the 'harlots' of the empire, created the wealth of the planters and millers and oiled the machinery of colonialism. In Oceania, Hawaii, New Caledonia, Fiji, Samoa, Papua New Guinea, Solomon Islands, Tahiti and Vanuatu experienced profound demographic, ecological, socioeconomic and political changes in tandem with the expansion of plantation agriculture and, in the case of New Caledonia, mining.

Whereas in the Caribbean indentured labourers from India filled the baracoons emptied by Africans emancipated from slavery in the 1830s, in Fiji they initially supplemented and eventually displaced similarly enslaved Pacific Island Kanaka ('native') labourers recruited from their island homes in the Solomon Islands, Vanuatu and Papua New Guinea. These labourers, recruited from the 1860s on, lived and worked in conditions approximating slavery. Today, the descendants of these pioneer plantation workers live at the margins of contemporary Fijian society as members of impoverished, landless, voiceless and powerless communities.

Until the military coups of 1987, Fiji was a good home for the descendants of the *girmitiyas* and free migrants from India. It appears that on an objective basis Indo-Fijians have fared much better than the descendents of peasants and workers who stayed on in Bihar, Uttar Pradesh and Tamil Nadu. Indo-Fijians have maintained their religions as Hindus, Muslims and Christians, but they have generally lost some of the more socially retrograde practices of their ancestors. Caste has largely disappeared among them and there is no great preoccupation with dowry. In Fiji, the Indians were subjected to racism, being compelled by law at the turn of the 20th century to reside in particular localities. They had limited scope for education, employment and access to social amenities, such as the public library and swimming pool in the urban areas, these being reserved for European use only.

Colonial racism was a form of caste discrimination, but it was ultimately less debilitating then the caste system in India. It must be said that right from the day that indenture contracts began to end, Indian migrants began to move away from farms to create opportunities for themselves and their progeny in non-farm employment. The colonial government set up 'coolie' settlements separate from the residential areas of other 'races' near emerging urban centres. In Suva, Samabula and Vatuwaqa were established for this purpose one mile from the more salubrious white residential areas of the Domain and Tamavua.

Unlike ethnic Fijians, who were compelled to remain in villages closely supervised by their chiefs and the native (later Fijian) administration, Indo-Fijians were left to fend for themselves. Those who chose to cultivate sugar cane as tenants and contractors of CSR were managed closely by the company's field officers, who directed them in what variety of cane to plant, when to weed the fields, the frequency of fertilising the crops and when to harvest the crop. It was the CSR which ensured low rentals on indigenous-owned land and which took the lion's share of the 'super profits' from sugar for its Australian shareholders. Farmers' industrial action over the terms and conditions of the sugar contracts and the share of the sugar profits embittered not only their relations with the company but with the Colonial Government and its allies — whites and chiefs.

Indo-Fijians have been the 'other' in colonial discourse. During the 1880s, indigenous Fijians were strongly advised to keep away from them and not to adopt their 'ill-mannered ways'. Indians were not to stay in the villages and Fijian villagers were not to harbour labourers who ran away from plantations. This was unlawful, punishable by imprisonment. Ethnic Fijians were brought up to regard Indo-Fijians with suspicion and much of this distrust can be attributed to the colonial whites, who greatly feared solidarity emerging among the black people of the colony. Indian and Indo-Fijian farmers' and workers' strikes, their demand for political equality and an end to discrimination, including in pay and uniform in the army, their not being recruited as soldiers in World War II and 'not shedding blood' for Fiji, their adherence to non-Christian faiths, their willingness to toil for long hours in menial work, their entrepreneurship and their rapid population growth were held against them. Negative stereotypes, such as that of the cunning, sly and grasping Indian, were widely held. I remember reading a particularly nasty 1940s travelogue by a white Australian, who compared Indo-Fijians with rats. The famous American writer, James Michener (*Return to Paradise*), likened Indo-Fijians to noisy and squabbling myna birds. Apparently, in his view, the great fault of the Indian was that he never smiled!

Denied access to the handful of government-funded white schools, Indo-Fijian descendants of the *girmitiyas* relied on Christian mission schools and those established by their own communities and cultural associations. Segregated schooling was integral to the Government's divide and rule policies. It is to the credit of a largely illiterate group of people that they devoted so much time and energy to ensure that their children received the education and training that they could never imagine for themselves.

From their humble beginnings as farmers and farm labourers, Indo-Fijians have become skilled workers, professionals and businessmen and women. Although most Indian and Indo-Fijian attempts at business met with limited success, with many bankruptcies, a small group of successful businessmen have emerged among them. Prominent among businesspeople have been the Gujeratis, who have been relatively better educated and connected with their kinsmen and women in India and elsewhere. Together with Europeans, Chinese and some people of mixed ancestry, Indo-Fijians were firmly in the mainstream economy.

In 1987, the National Federation Party–Fiji Labour Party government of Dr Timoci Bavadra was not allowed to fulfil its electoral mandate of instituting pro-poor, pro-labour and small-business programs by the then Colonel Sitiveni Rabuka and his co-conspirators, who belonged to the defeated Alliance Party of Ratu Sir Kamisese Mara. Even though 'Doc' himself was an ethnic Fijian — as was half his Cabinet — his government was seen as 'Indian-dominated', providing expedient justification for the military to overthrow it. For the exclusively ethnic Fiji military, all 'Indians' were enemies. Bavadra, a person of rare integrity, was portrayed as an 'Indian' stooge. When I was detained by the police and military (there was close collaboration between the two) after the September coup, I saw on the military noticeboard a crude caricature of an Indo-Fijian Minister's penis with Bavadra's face on it.

The reinstitution of racially motivated programs began in 1987. These included the use of tax-payers' monies as outright grants and soft loans for exclusively ethnic Fijian endeavours, for example, the Fijian Holdings Limited. Ethnic Fijians and Rotumans were to hold half the positions in the public service and ended up holding some 70 per cent at the middle to lower levels and more than 90 per cent at the upper levels. Provincial considerations crept into the allocation of some of these positions as did political allegiances, kinship and friendship. Cronyism and nepotism became rife in what was previously a largely merit-based system. Corruption became rampant.

It appeared that most ethnic Fijians were swayed by the appeals to racial 'solidarity' and their apparent fear of an 'Indian' takeover of the country. They accepted the argument that 'as Indians controlled the economy', indigenous Fijians should control the Government. The Fijian economy is dominated by foreign transnationals and the State. Mixed in the narrow nationalist sentiments was an evident resentment of the relative material success of Indo-Fijians. Very few ethnic Fijians reflected on why they had not done so well materially or why they were kept outside the mainstream economy for so long.

Sadly, similar sentiments were expressed during and after the 2000 coup. This time around, even more outlandish claims were being made. These included as evidence a garbled fax statement purporting to be an offer by Prime Minister Chaudry to India to colonise Fiji! Another story that was circulated was that the President, Ratu Sir Kamisese Mara, and his close associates had built a tunnel between the President's residence and the Parliamentary Complex in Veiuto along Queen Elizabeth Drive. In the tunnel, the rumour went, there were secret rooms in which the President and his friends drank human blood and ate babies. In this macabre ritual, they were assisted by a Chinese cook and a European doctor!

But I digress. The Rabuka coups, followed by the not-so-civilian coup by the military force against the Peoples Coalition Government, resulted in a massive emigration of Fijian citizens, especially though not exclusively, Indo-Fijians. The country had become by the 1980s near self-sufficient with respect to teachers, doctors and nurses. It had an adequate number of well-qualified engineers as well as skilled workers in many different fields. Thanks to narrow ethnic Fijian nationalism and the willingness of military officers to subscribe to the 'cause', Fiji today has a shortage of professional and skilled people in virtually all fields. Since April 2000, the University of the South Pacific has once again faced a huge turnover of staff. Many departments have experienced staff shortages. Petty bourgeois elements among ethnic Fijian elites targeted Indo-Fijian academics as being 'a cane-belt mafia' during this time, thereby reinforcing their sense of insecurity.

Since 1987, more than 100,000 Fijian citizens have left the country — some 10 per cent of its people. It is surprising that, far from expressing disquiet about this exodus, the ethnic Fijian establishment appears unperturbed by it. Meanwhile, there has been a rapid decline in the quality of health services and public utilities such as water, electricity and roads. Educational standards appear to have been affected by the loss of qualified and experienced teachers.

A few months after I took up my current position in Wellington (as Professor of Development Studies at Victoria University), my partner and I had an interesting encounter with two Indo-Fijian women at Moshim's, the 'Fiji shop' in Porirua. We were perplexed by the variety of flours available and were wondering which was 'sharp' for making roti. As we stood by deliberating, two women, who initially appeared to us by their attire to be Muslims, came close to us and my partner greeted them and asked for help in identifying the flour that we were looking for. With no hesitation, the older of the two women pointed out the 'sharp' to us. She asked where we were from: Fiji, we said. She said that she and her sister were from Fiji, too.

It turned out that they came from a Waimanu Road shoe shop-owning Gujarati family. With their husbands and children, they had migrated to New Zealand in 1987. As we conversed, we realised that we knew the family and that my partner had tutored the younger sister's daughter in the late 1970s. Small world! When we said to them that having been in Wellington for some 15 years, they must know the city well and like it, the older sister responded, 'There is no place like Fiji', with a note of sadness in her voice.

This sentiment is echoed by many ex-Fiji residents. Most Indo-Fijians have a firm affinity with their country of origin. They retain generally favourable and positive memories of where they grew up, their schools and the friends they had. They remember with fondness the relatively stress-free life, the slower pace and the sense of community.

Many concede that Fiji's political problems are not entirely the making of indigenous Fijians and their leaders. They accept that often ordinary ethnic Fijians have been considerate and generous. On many occasions, problems have emerged out of misunderstandings and the failure of Indo-Fijian politicians to adopt more flexible positions on the issues at hand.

For much of my own childhood, I grew up in police barracks and compounds in Nabouwalu, Labasa, Waiyevo,

Nasese, Lautoka and Ba among a very mixed community of people of just about every ethnicity. The compounds were like a big *koro*. It is here that I picked up conversational Bauan Fijian. Children referred politely to adults in the immediate neighbourhood with the putative 'uncle' or 'aunty' irrespective of their ethnicity. Generally speaking, the grown-ups responded as if they were indeed our relatives. My ethnic Fijian friends and their parents were mostly kind and supportive of my siblings and me. We played, fought and made mischief together and were treated even-handedly by the adults. At primary school in Toorak, my favourite teacher was an ethnic Fijian. She was one of the most caring people I have come across. My second-most favourite primary school teacher was a person of mixed European and Islander ancestry. As a young adult, I was fortunate to have a very mixed group of friends, who did not judge me or each other on the basis of ethnicity. I find it sad that in my later life I am confronted with narrow-minded bigotry and racist outbursts by a minority of indigenous Fijians. Even as children, however, we were reminded of our differences — sometimes by the adults and often by children.

My younger brothers and I used to walk some five to six kilometres to school and back each day. It was not unusual for smaller children from the ethnic Fijian government settlement of Draiba located next to the Nasova Police Barracks to tease us with racist slogans. One that has stuck in my mind is '*Kai Idia darawai pani, Kai Viti Kaivalagi*! [Indians wash their bums with water, Fijians are Europeans!]' The same kids when they grew up played games with us and became friends. We would sometimes join together in our fights with school kids from the ethnically exclusive Draiba Fijian School.

Ethnic Fijian nationalists are not inclusive and appear to want to push their agenda of 'Fiji for Fijians' without regard to who they hurt and to the costs. As we know, this form of narrow nationalism has not augured well for post-colonial states that have gone down its road. Some Indo-Fijians have responded with their own brand of racism, which insists that ethnic Fijians are racially inferior people!

For most Indo-Fijians, the politically inspired racism of ethnic Fijians affects their sense of belonging and has to do with a number of factors, material and non-material. At the political level, having relatively little say in decision-making in government for more than 30 years of independence, while being subjected to taxation, is vexing. The military coups generated crises for the country, but they were directed at Indo-Fijians. This fact cannot be easily forgotten, nor can memories of experiences, some rather horrendous and humiliating, which individuals and families underwent during and in the immediate aftermath of the coups. The maintenance of an ethnic army contributes to the insecurity of ordinary Indo-Fijians who remain in Fiji. An openly racist agenda, which was institutionalised in the 1990 Constitution and in other organs of the State, as well as parastatals such as the Fiji Development Bank, have reinforced their sense of unease. After the 2000 coup, there was a repeat in an even more extreme form of various discriminatory affirmative-action programs.

Indo-Fijians have been the primary victims of crime, although these days, in virtually all middle-class gatherings, the conversation invariably shifts to the latest incidents of burglary, home invasion, violent robbery, assaults, rapes and homicides. The ethnic background of the perpetrators of such crimes is predominantly indigenous Fijian. In the pull and push between maintaining the supposed 'Fijian' way of life and the pressure of modernity, indigenous youth have found themselves without the training and skills to enter the labour market and without the business acumen to engage in self-employment. Their marginalisation results in frustration that is expressed in antisocial behaviour, not uncommonly directed at Indo-Fijians. Young Indo-Fijians, who are marginalised, tend to internalise

their frustration and are susceptible to suicide. Stress-related
mental and physical illnesses have afflicted mostly Indo-Fijians.

Indo-Fijians' sense of belonging to Fiji is adversely affected
by their treatment as 'the other', 'the stranger', 'the visitor' or
vulagi. Not having a common name for all of Fiji's people is not
widely appreciated. Fiji may be the only country in the world that
requires its citizens to state their 'race' each time they leave the
country and each time they set foot in it. The 1997 Constitution
adopted 'Fiji Islanders' as a common name, but it has not proved
to be popular. This term is a compromise because of the *Taukeist*
objection for those of other ethnicity using the term 'Fijian'.
A leading proponent for the exclusive retention of 'Fijian' for
indigenous Fijians was the late Sir Leonard Usher, a New Zealand-
born, naturalised Fiji citizen and former spin doctor for the
colonial government. A number of prominent ethnic Fijians, such
as Ratu Sir Kamisese Mara, Sitiveni Rabuka and the late Ratu
Julian Toganivlau, advocated the use of 'Fijian' for all citizens and
keeping the term *I-Taukei* for its autochthonous people. This
remains an outstanding matter in the perception of many.

Sadly, a consequence of 100 years of racial classification
and discrimination has resulted in Fijian citizens other than
ethnic Fijians not recognising their 'nationality'. This is confused
with their 'racial' or ethnic classification. In my experience,
I have found it very common for people to write their ethnicity
in place of 'nationality' when making applications for admission
to a university or when filling in official forms. As they do not
carry 'Indian', 'Chinese', 'Rotuman', 'Part-European' or 'Others'
passports, they cannot be designated as a national belonging to
these categories. The use of the residual and even derogatory
'Others' category is most offensive.

On the material side of things, a critical 'push' factor in the
emigration of Indo-Fijians is that they are not able to have
longer-term security of land tenure. A colleague and friend of
mine used to argue that if one could not own his/her own plot of

land in a country, it was hardly likely that he/she would have a sense of belonging to it. I used to maintain that world-wide relatively few people owned a piece of land and yet most people had a sense of belonging. In recent years, I have changed my mind as more and more former native-land leaseholders have had to move off their farms.

While it is true that leases have a start date and an end date in Fiji, it has been rare during the past 70 years for formal lease arrangements for customary-owned land to be made on the basis of negotiations between a farmer and the landowning group. Under ALTO and ALTA (Agricultural Landlord and Tenants Ordinance/Act), blanket lease approvals were made as a consequence of central government decision-making. With the expiry of agricultural leases since 1997, thanks to the encouragement of Native Land Trust Board (NLTB) officials themselves, many *mataqali* in Macuata, Ba and Nadroga provinces, where sugar cane has been grown, have decided not to renew leases under the Agricultural Landlord and Tenant Act (ALTA). The NLTB, which was set up to administer the commercial leasing of all lands outside 'native reserves', became politicised under the leadership of the late Maika Qarikau. The organisation sought to exert even greater control over indigenous-owned land in a two-step strategy. The first was to urge the landowners not to renew and the second was to organise commercial farming on native land through more direct supervision. In this regard, it openly advocated the abolition of ALTA, which it perceived to be diluting NLTB's exercise of absolute control.

A justification of abolishing ALTA is that it has favoured the tenants over the landlords and that its formula for arriving at rentals is biased against the latter. This is the view of the NLTB, the Great Council of Chiefs, the current Prime Minister and his Soqosoqo Duavata ni Lewenivanua Party-led government. Prime Minister Qarase has adopted the arguments of an expatriate economist, John Davies, on the issue of rentals. He has claimed that the sugar-cane farmers have made a billion dollars during the period of the Lome Convention.[1] Landowners, according to him, hardly received anything. Other authorities, with greater independence, such as Oskar Kurer, have argued that the rent formula has been reasonably fair and most farmers have not become wealthy on the proceeds of sugar.[2] Indeed, studies of the financial situation of farmers indicate that a great majority of them remain heavily indebted.

The people who have gone abroad to Australia, New Zealand, Canada, the US and Britain have generally adjusted very well as immigrants. The initial divisions between pre-1987 migrants and those pushed out by the coups dissipated. Fijian migrants have been among the more educated and skilled immigrants to these countries. They have done well in business, in the professions and as skilled workers. It has not been plain sailing for most of them. They have had to negotiate negative prejudice and outright racism, inter-generational schisms and gender-based conflicts, as well as a range of problems of settling in a new country, including unemployment, depression, alcohol and drug abuse. Families have split up, divorces have increased, some older parents have found themselves on the streets of strange lands overnight; incidents of domestic violence, infidelity and other difficulties continue to affect them. On the whole, however, Fijian migrants have done well abroad. Indo-Fijians have established communities centred on neighbourhoods, temples, mosques and churches as well as on a network of relationships of kinship, friendship, shared interests in sports, culture and even politics.

These overseas communities of Fijians have contributed to a real broadening of the horizons of those who remained at home in Fiji. There are now, for many Fijian people, relatives and friends abroad, places they can stay when they visit or when they need to attend to some medical condition. There are many Fijian people who now regularly go to the various Pacific Rim countries to find short-term employment. Ethnic Fijian women have been going to work as care-givers in the US. Our people abroad provide a loyal niche market for Fijian products: kava, bhindi (okra), baigan, bhaji, nuqa, kawakawa, sabutu, naqari, masala, bhuja and so on. They have donated generously during times of man-made and natural disasters in the country of their birth. They have turned up in large numbers to support our national sports teams. They also visit Fiji from time to time. Indeed, it appears that these days there are as many Fijian people travelling to Fiji as there are travelling from it. It is not unusual for Air Pacific flights to Suva to have on board more Fijians of all ethnicities than tourists. Like tourists, they spend money in the country and generate foreign exchange. It is likely that their dollar goes a lot further within the country's economy then does the tourist dollar. It is not unusual for them to stay longer than tourists.

The Fijian diaspora has contributed positively to Fiji. It has a great potential to help uplift the quality of life of their countrymen and women if given the opportunity. Larger countries, such as Britain, Australia and New Zealand, and more recently China and India, have shown great flexibility in dealing with their citizens abroad. Investments by them have been encouraged. The Chinese growth rate in excess of 8 per cent each year for almost a decade is explainable partially by the willingness of overseas Chinese to invest in and also to put their expertise in the service of China. Countries with diasporas explored and in some cases implemented multi-country citizenship as well as various provisions for easy access. Sadly, in Fiji, the current political leadership, affected by its blinkered ethnic vision, has instituted an immigration bill that will grant dual citizenship only to indigenous Fijians.

It is time that we realised that in the global village ethnic exclusiveness and separatism, the hallmark of our history of which a majority of us are victims, will not lead us to the peace and prosperity that all Fiji's people desire. We need to be inclusive, not only of those in the islands, but of those who have settled abroad and taken a part of Fiji with them. Those who still call Fiji home.

NOTES

1   Davies, John. 1998. 'The causes and consequences of cane burning in Fiji's sugar belt,' *The Journal of Pacific Studies*. 22 (182). pp.1–25; also his *Fiji's Constitutional Dilemma*. Mimeograph. (2000). In my possession.
2   Kurer, Oskar. 2001. 'Land Tenure and Sugar Production in Fiji: property Rights and Economic Performance'. *Pacific Economic Bulletin*. (16) 2. pp. 106–19

Savu Savu Bay, Vanua Levu, beyond the cane belt, is home to large coconut plantations, and is now increasingly a tourist destination.

CHAPTER TWENTY-FOUR

Maarit

Brij V. Lal

BHOLA AUR US ke patni Sukhraji ek din sanjha ke kada gham
se aaye ke aapan ek palia ghar ke poch men sustaat rahin jab un
ke padosi, Nanka, aaye pahuncha. 'Ram Ram bhai,' Bhola se
bolis aur ek lakdi ke baakas pe baith gaye. Sukhraji jaldi se
kitchen men gaye chai banaye jab Bhola aur Nanka gaon ke
chota mota baat kare ke suru karin. Jab Sukhraji teen piyaala chai
laye ke lauti, to Nanka us ke taraf ghoom ke bolis, 'Bhauji hum ek
baat poochi?' Sukhraji bolis, 'Bolo Babu.' Sukhraji gaon ke admi
log ke naam laye ke kabhi nahin pukaare. E gaon ke aadat raha.
Sab roj Babu ya Badkau bole.'Tor Dewa ke saadi kare ke tem hoi
gaye. Aur tum log ke umir bhi din ke din jaat haye. Tum bhi
suno, Bhola.' Bhola chup-chaap sab sunat raha lekin kuch bolis
nahin. 'Bhauji, toke Bhola ke alaawa chaahi koi aur dekh bhaal
kare.' Nanka bada muhchutta, mehra aadmi raha. Okar muh men
lagaam nahin raha.

'Tum log kaahye ke waaste ho,' Sukhraji jhut se jawab
dihis.'Tor bhi to larka hai Dewa.' E gaon ke rishta wala baat raha.
'Kahe nahin tum log bhi is ke baare men kuch karo. Humhi duno
jane ke upar e jimmewari kaahe chorat ho.' Nanka bolis, 'Jon tum
bole ho Bhauji wahi to hum sune maangat raha.' Ek ghoont chai
pee ke Nanka muskiaaye ke aage bolis, 'Lekin ek baat jaroor
haye: samadhin se sab se pahile chaati humai millaib.' 'Arre tu jo

kuch kare maangna karna,' Sukhraji hans ke jawaab dihis. 'Hamaar ladka ke ek accha ghar grihasti wali ladki khoj deo bas.'

Dewa ke bhawwis ke baare men Bhola bahut din se sochat raha, lekin koi se is ke baare men jikir nahin karis. Us ke aadate waysain raha. Bhola ke apne saadi satraa saal me bhaye raha, aur idhar Dewa bees saal ke hoye gaye. Buddhe puraniye bola karat rahin ke aisan umar men saadi nahin kare ke chaahi jab baap beta ke faasla aaja or pota ke rakam rahe. Aur phin kaun jaane kab laṛkan ke e jawaani ke josh kaun taraf kheech lay jaaye. Eka ek Bhola ke khiyaal aaye gaye Asarfi ke laṛka Jhikka ke jon Dhanessar ke laṛki ke saathe badmaasi karis raha. Laṛki bechaari ke chuppe se kahin dusar gaon men bhej dihin. Us ke baad, laṛki ke bhaiyya log Jhikka ke badla utaarin. Ek raat Jhikka Ramayan mandli se lautat raha jab ki okar upar launde toot padin aur khoobe dihin butaraaki. Peet paat ke us ke rasta ke kinaare mohdi men bahaye ke ghare chal dihin. Koi ke pata nahin chala ki oke kaun maaris. Na police ke koi bataais na panchayat ke. E gaon ke aapan kanoon raha. Agar aisen gadbaari me pakdaai gaye koi to peet ke sidha kar det rahin. Jhikka ke jaan to bach gaye lekin u din se okar sab muraahi bhi bund. Dewa seedha saadha laṛki raha, aur Bhola bhi yahi maangat raha ke yahi rakam sab din rahe

Sanjha ke khana khaaye ke baad men Bhola aur Sukhraji Dewa ke baare men baat karin. 'Nanka Babu theeke baat kahis,' Sukhraji kahis Bhola se. 'Ham bhi budhaait haye. Hamaar koi sahaara hoye jaaye ghar men to bada accha baat rahi.' 'Arre wu bhadbhadiya ke baat na biswaas kar tu,' Bhola Sukhraji se sat ke bolis. 'Wu sab ke aisehin bole hai. Okar e aadat haye. Tum to abhi ekdam jawaan ho. Dui teen laṛki aur!' 'Chupp!' Sukhraji sarmaaye ke muh ghumaaye lihis. 'Kahin laṛki sun lihin e baat tab?' Ladṛawe wahi bagal wala room me soote rahin. 'Dheko, hum maangit haye ki e dhandha se kutch chutkaara paaye. Jaai pariwaar men thora ghoomi ghaami,' Sukhraji bole lagi. 'Kuch ke to bahut jamaana bhay nahi mila. Aur ab bahut der na maangit kare. Naati pota hoye jahiyen to e bhi bada sundar baat rahi. Dekho ham log ke umir ke gaon me sab aja aji, naana naani bun gain.'

'Naati potan! Kitna jaldi samay chala gaye,' Bhola apne man men sochis. Us ke aise lagaa jaise okar saadi abhi haaliye men bhay raha. Puraana baat yaad kar ke Bhola ke dil gum hoi gaye. Thora dukh me aaye ke soche laga ke u duno parani aapan jiwan men ketna dukh kaatin. Dui bacche chote men gujar gain, bada pariwaar sab alag alag hoi gayn. Kai pariwaar wale dhoka bhi dihin, garibta bhi moor pe chaae raha. Lekin e sab dukh takleef hote hue bhi, uske aapan chota se pariwaar men koi phutmat nahin bhay. E baat pe Bhola ke bahut ghamand raha. Aur aapan aurat pe bhi uske gaurau raha jon itna sahan kar ke bhi uske saathe aapan jiwan bitaais.'Tummhe yaad hay jab ham log ke saadi bhay raha aur tum ek nai naweli dulhain ban ke e ghar me aae raheo?' Bhola Sukhraji ke yaad dilaais. 'Ka hammen nahi yaad haye!' Sukhraji jawaab dihis. 'Hammen aise lage ki e sab bas kal parso ke baat haye.'

Sukhraji ke maai baap Nangeri nadi ke upaar samundar ke kinaare ke basinda rahin. Huaan u tem ganna ke kheti nahin raha. Sukhraji ke pariwaar huaan badi beemari (1918) ke baad men jaaye ke basin raha. E pariwaar ke baare men bahut log nahin jaanat rahin kaahe ki e log ek kona me rahat rahin. Aur upar se ganna ke kheti bhi nahin karat rahin to dusre se mel milaap bhi kamti raha. Sukhraji ke bappa girmit men Fiji aaye raha. Chiria Tua Tua line men CSR ke ingin driver raha. Otane inke baare men pata raha. Kaise u ingin driver bana, kab Fiji aais, muluk ke kaun gaon se aais, e sab baat ke baare men kuch maloom nahi. Aise inke pariwaar ke bhi itihaas raha. Sukhraji ke maai chote pe gujar gaye rahi. Apne baap ke gujare ke baad, e lag bhag 1930 ke baat haye, pariwaar waale inke dekh bhaal karin. Sukhraji pariwaar me aapan jagha accha se jaanat rahi. Khana pakaye, ghar duaar ke saffaai kare, aur khet men bhi kaam kare. Koi ke ek baat bole ke, taana mare, ke mauka nahin dihis. Sab koi us se kaafi khusi rahin. Pariwaar waale Sukhraji ke bada laar pyaar se paalin.

Agar Bhola Dewa ke baare men soche ke ladka kahun andband na kar bahithe, to ladkin ke maai baap ke upar aur bada jiimewaari raha. Agar pariwaar ke naam kharaab hoi gaye, to is se bada koi badnaami nahi hai. Tem se pahile, larki khoje ke kaam suru hoi jaaye. Pariwaar ke agua aur gaon ke badakawan ke haath men e jimmewaari saunp diya jaat raha.Sukhraji ke tem bhi yahi baat bhaye jab mahila samaaj sanket lihin ki ladki ke saadi ke umar hoi gaye. Aaste se gaon me baat phaila. Bhola ke baare men pata lagaain. Bhola ke lagan baithat raha. Pariwaar bhi bahut accha raha. Un men koi chor, chandaal, badmaas, jehali-pehali nahin rahin. Aur jaat bhi milat julat raha. Ek raha Kurmi and dusra Kori. Baat cheet chala aur kuch din men maarit pakka hoy gaye. Sukhraji ke chekani ke dui saal baad, Sukhraji aur Bhola ke biyah bhawa. Patoh ban ke naya pariwaar men aana koi sahaj baat nahin. Aur Sukhraji to Bhola ke saadi se pahile dekhe bhi nahin rahi. Koi jaana pehchaana nahi raha. Sukhraji apne kandha pe aapan poora pariwaar ke ummid laye ke aais rahi. U e baat accha se jaanat rahi ki chaahe kuch bhi hoi jaaye, u phir laut ke kabhi waapis nahi jaaye paai. Hindu dharam men kanyadaan bahut bada baat hai. Ek baar de diya jaaye to waapis nahi sako leyo. Saadi ke bandhan sada ke liye haye.

Suru suru men kaafi dukh jhele ke pada. Sukhraji thora saanwar rahi aur Bhola aapan maai ke rakam safa. Kabhi kabhi, bechaari ke kariakki kahi ke bulaawen. Bhola ke amma badi kantaain aurat rahi. U girmit men Fiji aaye rahi. Okar dimaag men konchi raha, koi nahin sake jane. U maangat rahi wahi rakam ke rishta-joda jaise muluk men raha: bahu maango saas ke gor ke neeche hamesha raho.'Bhulaai gayo kaise maarat raho hamme ek dam kasaai ke rakam?' Sukhraji poochis Bhola se thoda dukh ke awaaj men. 'Sab koi khai pee ke kahatiya men, aur hammar kaam khatmen nahi. Aur chaar baje sabere roj utho. Khana ek dam budhiya ke pasand ke maango banaao. Thora kuch kamati, kya gaari bakke: chinnar, kutia, haramin, chachundar.' Sukhraji ghoom ke Bhola ke aankhi me taakis. 'Tum hamaar taraf se kabhi ek baat nahin boleo. Kabhi nahin. Hamaar bachaao men kuch to bol deteo. Hum tumhaar aurat raha. Hamaar bhi kuch to haq raha. Chaahe hamaar galti raha chaahe nahin, tum sub roj budhiya ke taraf raheo. Sub roj dulaara beta. Yaad haye jab teen saal tak laṛki nahin bhey to ham ke ka ka bolat rahin? Yaad haye u din jab ham ke ek gaj rassi dihin aur bolin ki jaaye ke latak jao taaki tum dusar saadi kar leo? Tum khade sab sunat raheo lekin ek baat nahin boleo?'

Sukhraji ke purana baat sun ke Bhola ke dil pe bahut chot pahuncha. Aankhi paani se bhar gaye. Sukhraji ek dam such baat kahis. U baat nahin sako kaato. Ab Bhola ka kare, ka bole? Baat to sach haye ki u aapan maai ke baat sunat raha. Aapan maai baap se kabhi muh nahin chalaais, bahut aadar karat raha. U aapan maai ke eklowta beta raha. Aur phir u jamaana men aurat ke kaam raha sab badan ke hukum pe chalo. Nahin, to maar khaao. Aur duniya ke bhi dikhaaye ke ki ghar ke agua kawn haye. Aur mai ke baat bhi nahi sako kaato. Bhola lapak ke Sukhraji ke churiya bhara haath pakdis aur raundhiyaaye ke bole laga. 'U jamaana waisan raha. Beeti baat haye. Lekin aaj dekho. Jo kuch aaj hum log ke paas haye, is men tumhaar poora baraabar ke haath haye: e ghar, e jamin, kheti baari, hum log ke ladkan bacchan, gaon men accha naam. E ham tum saath kamaawa haye. Bhagwaan ke aashirwaad raha to hum tum abhi bahut din saath rahibe.'

Sukhraji ke dil men e baat sun ke thora shanti aais. Aaj pahila baar raha ke u aapan dil ke khaas dukh Bhola se bataais, saccha ghatna sunaais. Bhola ke taraf dekh ke sochis ki Bhola kharaab admi nahi haye. Bhola ke siwaaye okar koi aur raha bhi nahi. Aur aapan pariwaar ke waaste u jaan de ke taiyaar. Aur Bhola ke siwaaye uske koi aur raha bhi nahin.

Lagbagh ek hafta baad, Bhola ke bada bhaiya, Ram Bihari , ghoome aais Tabia. Ram Bihari Wailevu men rahat raha, lekin pariwaar ke khoj khabar hamesha liya kare. Bada bhai hoye ke naate, parwaarik maamla me u sub tem agua rahe. Saadi-biyah, katha-bhandaara men us ke neota hamesha diya jaaye. Pariwaar ke jhanda wahi ke haath men raha. Cha-wa pee-paaye ke baad, Bhola Ram Bihari se bolis 'Bhaiya, Dewa ke saadi kare ke tem aaye gaye haye. Koi accha pariwaar dekh ke baat-cheet chalao.' Bhola ke aapan baat khalaas kare se pahile, Ram Bihari beeche me tapak padis. 'Ham jaanit haye, ham jaanit haye. Parso, markit men hammen Nanka mila raha aur ham se poora baat batais.' Bhola ke dil men thora shanti bhay. 'November ke tem theek rahi. Tab tak dhaan-waan cut jaai aur ganna bhi; thora paisa haath men aaye jaai. Abhi se che mahina haye. Tab tak kaafi cheez batur jaai.'

'Hamme Boca aur Bucaisau ke bagal koi nahin dekhaye haye,' Ram Bihari bolis. 'Ek aad koi hiyaan huaan hoihen, lekin ham ke nahin maloom. Tum to ham ke accha se jaanat ho. Kawn hamme nahin jaane.' Bhola accha se jaanat raha ki use ke bada bhai poora Labasa men naami aadmi raha. Aisan koi bada kaam waala nahin raha jiske Ram Bihari nahin jaanat raha. Gaon ke mandali ke pardhaan, advisory council ke member, Wailevu school ke mukhiya.Bhola apane mane-man sochis ke Bhaiya koi accha pariwaar ke ladki Dewa ke waaste jaroor khoji.

Sukhraji ek aur room ke palla ke peeche se bolis, 'Padhi-likhi larki ke ham log ke na jaroorat haye. Ham log ka karab padhi-likhi larki. Paisa waala pariwaar ke bhi na jaroor haye. Dhani ghar ke larki agar aayee, to bas aapan chaal chalihen. Ham log maangit ek izzatdaar ghar ke larki jon ghar grihisthi samajhe.' Bolte bolte, Sukhraji ke ek aur baat yaad aaye gaye. 'Langdi-looli na rahe, bas. Jaise Guddu ke dulhin badi acchi patoh haye.' Guddu Ram Bihari ke sab se bada larka raha.

Ram Bihari kaafi chalak amdmi raha. Aapan bhalaai sub se pahile. 'Dreketi me koi ke baare men ham suna haye,' Ram Bihari bolis Bhola se. Na Bhola na Sukhraji Dreketi men koi ke cheenat rahin. Huaan ganna-wanna to hot naih raha, bas dhaan-peanut ke kheti se log aapan gujar-basar karat rahin. 'U to ek dam chamar tola hai,' Bhola hans ke bolis. 'Hanso nahin Bhola,' Ram Bihari thora dattiaaye ke bada bhaiya ke rakam bolis. 'Ham huaan kaafi jane ke jaanit haye.' Bhola bhool gaye raha ke Ram Bihari ke sab se badi larki ke saadi Seaqaqa men bhaye raha. Seaqaqa Tabia aur Dreketi ke lag bhag beech men raha. 'Thoda din me dekhna, Dreketi kaise aage badhe haye. Tab Tabia uske saamne garda khai. Kuch din men huaan bhi ganna hoye lagi. Jinke tum chamar samjhat ho, u brahmin ban jahiyen.' 'Khali khelwaar karat raha, bhaiya,' Bhola thora khisiyae ke bolis.

Ram Bihari ke kuch aur pench raha. Agar Dreketi ke taraf ek aur sambandh jut jaat to us ke waaste to aur accha baat raha. Uske ladki ke liye ek aur pariwaar bagle me rahi. Daru-murga ke bahaar. Udhar ke aadmi bada dildaar rahen. Pariwaar ke liye konchi nahin kare ke taiyaar. 'Hamaar bichaar men, Dreketi ke rakam premi jagah aur koi nahin haye,' Ram Bihari gahira awaaj men bolis. Suruwe se Ram Bihari Kallu ke pariwaar ke baare me sochis raha. U pariwaar se is ke jaan-pahichaan raha. Jab e aapan larki ke ghare ghoome jaaye, to udhar bhi chakkar maar dewa karat raha. Khoob khawaai-piyaai hoye. Kallu ke pass paanch larkin rahin, jisme se khali ek ke saadi bhay raha. Ram Bihari Kallu ke aurat Dhaniya se khoob ched-baaji kare, aur Dhaniya bhi khoob aankhi michmichaaye ke bole. Ram Bihari ke khoob chede. Aur aapan admi ke ungri pe nachawe.

Ek din Ram Bihari ghoome ke bahana Kallu ke ghare pahuncha. Ghar ke bagal men kuch jamin parti pada raha. Ram Bihari Dhaniya se muski maar ke kahis, 'Janaaye e jamin bahut din se parti pada haye. Agar khet banaye ke is men makai, urdi boye diya jaaye to accha upaj nikli. Barkha ke mausam bhi bahut door na haye.' Dhaniya jhut se baat pakad lihis. Aankhi nachaaye ke jawaab dihis, 'Batiya to theek haye. Lekin ham ka kari. E gaon men sab bekaar admi hain. Hiyan accha khet jote wala koi haiye nahin. Kaahe nahin tumhai ek aad din ruk ke e sab khetwa jot deo?' E sun ke, Ram Bihari ke dil muskiyaan. Ek aur tem, Dhaniya dillaggi men Ram Bihari se bolis ki hiyaan pe atna gai hain lekin gaon ke aadmi accha se dudh bhi piye nahin jaane. Ram Bihari bada khushi se sochis ki, haan, hiyan accha kaam pate sake! Okar dil maaris kilkaari.

Ek din aise baate-baat men Kallu Ram Bihari ke aapan larki ke waaste larka khoje ke baat chedis. 'Hamaar larki log hamaar ladka hain,' Kallu kaafi ghamand se Ram Bihari ke bataais. 'Jamin ke kaam yehi sab karen hain, khet bhi jote hain aur ghar ke sab kaam bhi yehi log ke haath men haye. Ghar grhasthi ke baare men poora sab jaane hain.' Wahi tem, Ram Bihari ke dimaag men Dewa ke naam turant aais.

'Tumhe u parliwaar se mile ke chaahi, Ram Bihari Bhola se bolis. 'Hum sab koi chale khoi,' Bhola nawab dihis. Dui hafta baad, Mallu ke motor hire karin and gain Dreketi, Bhola, Ram Bihari , Nanka aur Chillar, ek gaon ke puraana dost. Sukhraji bhi maangat rahi jaaye, lekin Ram Bihari minhaai kar dihis. Bhola kuch na bolis. 'Shaadi ke baat cheet chalaana mard ke kam hai,' Ram Bihari ek agua ke rakam bolis. 'Aur kaafi lamba rasta bhi to hai.' Dewa ke bhi nahin poochin. E koi ajab baat nahi raha. 'E to khaali pehala trip hai, beta,' Ram Bihari Dewa ke samjhais. 'Tumhe larki se jaroor mile ke mauka mili jab baat cheet thora pakka hoye jaaye.'

Dreketi men bada accha se khaatir bhaau bhaye. Munni, u larki jekar baat chalaawe ke waaste gaye rahin, cha laye ke bada ijjat se parosis. Ghugri, matar, baarfi-warfi sab ke laaye ke dihis. 'Yahi larki haye, bhaiya,' Kallu bataais sab ke. Munni aapan najar neeche rakhe rahi. Moor pe ujjar orhni raha. 'Bhagwan ke kripa raha to kuch din men larki hum log ke bhi bitiya hoye jaai,' Ram Bihari aapan taraf se hukaar bharis. Agua hoy ke naate, Ram Bihari jyaadaa baat kare aur aapan dhun men must raha. Bhola to waise chuppa aadmi raha, chuppe baith ke sab baat sunis. Ram Bihari jaise maangat raha waise sab kaam pata. Larka dekhe ke baat bhi tai hoye gaye. Teen hafata baad Kallu log Bhola ke ghare aain aur unke bhi khoob accha se khaatir bhaau kiya gaye.

Sab baat-cheet jab pakka hoye waallaa raha tab Dewa
Munni ke dekhis. Kallu, Dhaniya aur Munni ek bahaanaa
banaaye ke Nasea town gayin. Baat to kaafi aage badh gaye raha.
Dewa jaanat raha ki badkawan ke baat kaate nahin sako. Aur
agar larki dekh ke larka naahin kar de to larki waalan ke bada
nichaai hoye jaayee. Gaon me aadmi log baat karihen, kaahe
larki ke naahin kar dihin. Idhar udhar ke phokatiya baat
bakkihen. Phokatiya babaal. Larki dekhe ke roj, Dewa bada soot-
boot me ek patara hariyar terrylene ke pyjama, laal sut aur kariya
joota maare raha. Ek Chaina ke café me pahuchin. Chai aur
bread mangwaain. Jab sab khaye lagin to Dewa Munni ke taraf
dheere se taakis. Munni sarmaaye ke has dihis jub duno ke aankhi
mila. E Dewa ke bahut accha laga. Okar dil me gudgudgudi ke
jhakor maaris. Sukhraji ke bhi larki pasand aais. Subhaau se us ke
laga ke Munni ek aadar waali patoh bani. Maarit maano pakka
hoi gaye.

'Larka ke waaste maange julum saadi,' Nanka Ram Bihari se
bolis jab Ram Bihari ek hafta baad lauta. 'Jon rakam saadi Dewa
ke hoi, waisan saadi e gaon kabhi dekhe nahin hoi,' Ram Bihari
tantanaye ke chaati phulaaye ke bolis. 'Hum poora Wailevu laye
aaib saadi ke waaste. Dekhe waale dekhte rahi jaiyen ki hum log
kaisan pariwaar haye. Aisan tem pe parwaarik ekta bahut jaroori
haye. Maan samaan hoi.' (Aur Ram Bihari ke naam bhi badhi.)
Bhola bhi maangat raha ke aapan sab se bada ladka ke saadi
dhoom dhaam se hoy, lekin duniya ke dekhaye ke waaste nahin. U
maangat raha ki khaas pariwaar aur gaon waalen ke neota daye ke
saadi teen roj men tay-tamaam kar diha jaaye: telwaan, bhatwaan,
saadi. Bephoket ke jyaada kharcha kahe karo. Saadi ke kharcha ke
waaste paisa biyaaj pe le ke padi, aur phir udhar larkan ke school
phees bhi to bhare ke haye. Bhola e sab baat sochis lekin koi se
kuch na kahis. Na maangat raha ki uske koi kanjoos samajhe. Aur
bada bhai ke baat bhi nahin sako kaato.

Saadi bada dhoom-dhaam se bhaye. Kaafi neotaarin aain.
Baratiyan ke laye jaaye ke waaste teen lorry aur dui taxi hire kara

gaye. Udhar Kallu bhi koi kami nahi karis sewa satkaar men.
Julum se julum nachaniya hire karis, aur raat me qauwwali jama.
Nagona-paani bhi raat bhar chala. Rakam rakam ke khana
banwaais: kadhi, poodi, dhall, kaddu ke tarkaari, imli aur
tamaatar ke chutni. Sab baratiyan ke khana majaa pakdis. 'Phir
kab doosar saadi hoi bhayia Bhola,' ek baratiya hasi-majaak men
Bhola se poochis. 'Tum to bhai sona ke khan payee gaye ho.
Aisan pariwaar sab ke mile ke chaahi.'

Sukhraji ke dil poora hafta ek dam bhara raha e baat se ki
saadi ke baad, uske ladka koi aur ke hoye jaayi. Lekin jaun din
baraat lauta, u din, u kaafi khusi rahi. Munni kaafi sundar lagat
rahi: laal sari, haat-gor me mehndi, maang men sindoor, gahana-
gudiya. Munni ke dekh ke Sukhraji ke aapan saadi ke yaad aaye
gaye. Aurat log paisa deye ke dulhin ke muh dekhin. Baad men
baat karihen dulhin ke baare men: uske sundarata, kapda, gahana
gudiya, ketna cheez uske saadi men mila.

Sukhraji ek sas ban gayi: e bat pe uske baht kushi laga.
Munni ke kichdee banaaye men madad karis. E nayi dulhin ke
apne haath ke pakaya pahila bhojan hai. E khali khana ke baat
nahin hai: e gaon aur pariwaar waalen ke dekhaye ke hai ki
dulhin khana banaaye aur ghar ke kaam me kaafi husiaar hai.
Sanjha ke ek khassi Khassi gira, beer aur nagona chala. Accha se
khawaai-piyaai bhay. Teen-chaar roj ke baad door ke pahuna
laute lagin. Gaon waale jhaap ukhadin aur handi-bartan lautara
gaye. Aaste aaste, sab kuch saadi ke pahile ke rakam hoye laga.
Sukhraji Munni ke saathe accha se bartaau kare. Ghar-giristhi ke
kaam dheere-dheere sikhaawe. Agal-bagal ke padosi se
milwaawe, aur saadi-bhandaara me apne sanghe laye jaaye.
Sukhraji ke dil me e bichaar raha ke aaste se ghar ke sab
jimmewari aapan patoh ke haath men saunp de. Lekin okar
sapana poora nahin bhaye. Kuch din baad, ghar men katchkatch
suru hoye gaye. Chota-chota baat pe Munni aapan asli chaal
dekhaaye lagi. Jaise khaali aapan aur Dewa ke kapada dhoye,
khana aapan ghar men akel khaawye. Gaon men ghar ke patoh

log ke kaam rahe ki khana aakhari men khao, lekin Munni ke e baat nahin pasand raha. Munni gos-wos aapan dui parani ke waaste lukuwaaye ke pahile rakh le. Jab kaam ke tem aawe to bole hamaar moor piraaye haye. Bahana nikaale men kaafi aage rahi. Sukhraji Munni ke chaal dekhis lekin suru men us ke bahut fikar nahi laga. U kabhi socchis nahin rahi ke us ke patoh kharaab nikli. Us ke dil men aasra raha ki chota-mota futmat dheere se theek hoye jaayee

Ek din Sukhraji Munni se bolis, 'Beti, hamaar kandha bahut piraaye haye, thora maaalis kar dehiyo?' Munni gurrais, 'Ka bhaye haye toke? Kabhi e kabhi u? Jab se hum e ghar men gor rakkha haye tab se tumhar kuch na kuch piraawa kare. Bas baith ke agora karo ki hum kab tumhaar sewa kari. Ka sochat ho ki hum e ghar ke naukaraani haye?' Aise taana maar ke Munni aapan ghar men jhut se ghus gayee. Sukhraji ke dil men bahut bada chot laga aur u roye lagi. 'Arre Bhagwan, e bilap hamaar moor pe kaise aaye gaye? Hum aisen kaun paap kiya raha ki aaj e bhoge ke para.' Kabhi sapana men bhi nahin sochis rahi ki us ke aapan patoh us se aise muh chalaayee. Us ke saas ke tem, Munni ke maar maar ke chamda utaar diya jaat. Jab Sukhraji Bhola ke Munni ke kahani sunaais, to Bhola thora der kuch soch ke bolis, 'Patoh ke saait koi rakam ke worry hoi jon hum log se bataawe nahin maangat hoi. Hum Dewa se baat karab.'

Dusra din Bhola ke mile se pahile Dewa ke Munni sab baat baaye dihis raha. Dewa jaanat raha sacchaai ka haye. Ghar-baar ke kaam men sab koi haath bataawat rahen. Larke chulha ke waaste lakdi pahaad se laawen, kuaan se paani. Aur okar amma kitichin men khana bannaye men poora madad kare. Phir bhi, kutch na bolis Munni se. Kaahe phokatiya janjhat karo. Us ke dimaag men kutch aur baat rengat raha. Bhola ke dusra larka Tota secondary school me pahila saal men padhat raha. E baat pe Dewa ke bahut jaran lage. U maange Tota ke school chorwaaye ke khet me kaam karaao. Bada kaam-chor admi raha Dewa. Pet ke pani nahin hilaaye maange. Dewa bolis Bhola se, 'Tota ke dekho. U to bahut soot-boot men rahe haye aur hum hiyaan ghaam me din raat pitaayit haye. Kis ke waaste? Tota ke likhaayi-paraahi se hamke kaun faaida? Accha to e haye ki Tota school chor ke kaam men haath bataaye.'

E baat sun ke Bhola chakit hoye gaye. Aaj tak Dewa aapan baap se e rakam kara jabaan men kabhi nahin bole raha. 'Beta Dewa, e sab jagah-jamin tumhaare to rahi. Itna chota jamin men sab ke gujar ka thoro hoye sake. Larkan ke padhaana-likhaana koi sahaj baat nahin haye. Bhagwan ke daya se, padh likh ke aapan haath-gor pe khara hoye jahiyen. Agar hum larkan ke school se chutaaye dihya to Iswar kabhi maaf nahi kari.' Aapn baap ke baat sun ke, Dewa jawaab dihis, 'Hamar ka bhawwis haye?' Us ke yaad aais jab us ke school se nikal ke kaam men lagaawa gaye raha. Dewa padhe likhe men bahut aage raha. 'Jon mauka Tota ke mila, u hamke nahin mila. Agar padhe ke mauka milta, to aaj hum bhi kuch rahit, aaj khet men na dhunnaait.'

'Hum jaanit haye, beta, lekin u tem kuch aur raha,' Bhola samjhaay ke kosis karis. 'Tumhaar maiyya aur hum bahut kuch sapna dekha raha tumhar baare men. Lekin u tem hum log ke chalti bahut kam raha. Bahut bichaar ke sab kutch kare ke padat raha. Jab badkwe bolin ki tummhar school bund karo, to hum log ke baat sune ke paraa.' Dewa ke thora shanti dekh ke Bhola bolis, 'Ham jaanit haye ke tumhaar kandha pe kaafi bojha haye. Kaahe nahin tum aur patoh chutti lay ke Dreketi ghoom aayo. Tum duno parani huaan kutch tem sanghe bitaao. Hum log hiyaan ke kaam sambhaar leb.' Jab Dewa e baat Munni se bataais, to Munni ke dil naache laga. Bolis 'Jetna jaldi, watna accha'.

Teen roj baad, Dewa aur Munni Dreketi rawaana bhain. Dhaniya Munni se ek ek baat khoob ghor ghor ke jakad ke pooche. Pura jar-pullai maange jaane. Munni bataais aapan amma se sab kahani. Bole hamme huaan u kangaal pariwaar men accha nahin lage, bahut dukh-takleef haye. 'Hum log ke kuch kare ke padi,' Dhaniya mane-man sochis. Lekin konchi? Dhaniya aur Kallu apne men baat karin raat ke aur aaste se ek plan

banaain. Sochin hum log ke paas jaroorat se jyada jamin haye.
Kaafi jagah to waise faaltu pada haye. Kahe nahin das bigha
Munni aur Dewa ke naam kar diya jaaye. Is men sab ke faayeda
rahi. Ghar men ek aur marad aaye jaai. Kaam dhanda men bhi
haath bataaye deyi. Aur Munni aapan ghar ke maharani ban jai,
dusre ke naukaraani nahin.

Dusra roj, Kallu Dewa aur Munni se jamin ke baare men
bataais. Munni ke biswaas nahi hoye ki okar takdeer e rakam se
khuli. Doodh, makkhan, malaai sab ek sanghe! Aapan jamin.
Aapan ghar duaar. E Bhagwan ke kya deni haye. Badi khusi
bhayi. Lekin Dewa chuppe raha, kutch nahin bolis. 'Tumhaar ka
bichaar haye beta,' Dhaniya pyaar se Dewa se poochis. 'Jon cheej
tumhaar sasur abhi bolin haye, us men sab ke faayeda haye.
Tumhaar pass aapan jamin rahi, man ke shanti. Aur hum log ke
ek nawa beta mil jaai.'

'Baba ke prastaau to bahut accha haye,' Dewa aaste se jawaab
dihis. 'Hum kabhi sapana men bhi socha nahi raha ki aisan mauka
hamke kabhi mili. Hum maangit thora tem laike ke is ke bare men
accha se bichaar kare.' 'Theek haye beta. Koi hadbadi nahin haye.'
E bol ke Dhaniya chirauri karis ki Munni ke kahe nahin Dreketi
men ek dui haftaa aur ruk jaan deo. 'Hum log ek dusre ke bahut din
se nahin dekha. Dekho bichaari ke. Hiyan kuch din tike se sayad us
ke sahad thora theek hoye jaaye.' Dewa raaji hoye gaye.

Dewa aapan dil men suru se jaanat raha raha ke Dreketi
men us ke kabhi nahin pati. Kaam dhanda men tu wasie dhilla
aadmi raha. Naya jamin safaa karanaa koi sahaj baat nahin haye.
Aur phir ghar-damaad ke jindagi koi jindagi ka thore haye. Aurat
ke lahanga pakad ke chale ke padi. Marad mango marad ke rakam
raho: itna ghamand Dewa men jaroor raha. Aur okar dimaag men
ek aur plan dolat raha. U maangat raha kheti-baari chor ke bus
driver bane. Wahi kaaran se u Mallu ke motor men driving
seekhat raha. Dreketi men kahan driver wala kaam mili.

Dewa jamin ke prastaau aapan maai-baap se bataais. U log
kuch tokin-takin nahin, lekin mane-man men sochin ki Dewa

agar yahin Tabia men rahi ke ghar-baar ke kaam sambhaalat, Dreketi nahin jaat, to accha raha. Ram Bihari ke bichaar alag raha. U Dewa ke bataais jaao. Phir ghoom ke Bhola se bolis, 'Samay badle haye. Pahile ke rakam ab nahin haye. Hum log ke jabaana chala gaye. Kab tak rakhio Dewa ke e ghar men? Ek din u bhi aapan alag ghar-baar banaayee, jaise hamaar laṛka log karin. Time jub ayee to sayad aisan mauka nahin mili.' Dewa sunis aapan badka bappa ke baat, lekin us ke dil se Dreketi bilkul hat gaye raha.

Udhar Dreketi men, Kallu aur Dhaniya aapan pench lagaaye ke suru karin Munni pe. Bataain us ke ki Tabia okar liye faayda ke jagah nahin haye. Dewa ke chote-chote bhaiya-bahin ke dekh-bhaal kare ke padi kaafi saal tak. Dekhte dekhte, sara jindagi beet jaayee. E sab kiske waaste? Jab Munni bolis ki hum log sakit alag rahe, to Dhaniya jhat se poochis: 'Kahan rahiyo? Jamin kahan haye? Ek akkad jamin men ka hoi, kaise gujar-basar kariho?' Dhaniya bolte gaye. 'Han, ek din Dewa ke naam jamin aayee, lekin tab tak nahin jab tak Bhola jinda haye. Okar umar abhi kita haye — pachaas saal? Aur bees saal wait kare ke padi. Tumhaar liye bees saal ke girmit. Socho laṛki! Ketna tem tummhe town jaaye ke mauka mila? Saakhis dekhe ke mauka mila? Naya kapra aapan liye kharide ke piasa diha gaye? Ketna dafe tummhen hum log se aaye ke mile ke mauka mila?'

Ehi rakam, Dhania kaafi der tak badbadaais. Aapan amma ke baat sunte sunte, Munni ke yaad aais kaahe us ke saadi Tabia men bhaye raha. Tabia men saadi kare ke khaas kaaran raha. Plan raha ke huaan jaaye ke u aapan choti bahini log ke liye aadmi khoji; master, policeman, accha naukari wala koi. Munni sochis raha ki u Nasea town jaayi, khoob ghoomi-ghaami pariwaar men. Lekin u sab sapna adhura rahi gaye. Duniya dekhe ke siwaaye, u hian Tabia men ragdaaye.

'Chor do uske,' Dhania Munni ke protsaahan dihis. Munni ke choti bahini log hukaari bharin. Kallu chuppe raha. 'Hum log Social Welfare chalib. Huaan ek Babu ke hum jaanit hay. Hum us ke sab kutch samjhaaye deiib. Tummhen mahina pe accha kharcha mili. Agar Dewa log kharcha nahin bhar paain – aur tum jaano u kangaal log nahin bhar pahiyen – to Dewa ke hiyaan aaye ke padbe kari. Aur tum apan ghar ke boss. Munni sochis ki baat to theek haye. Is men us ke bhalai haye. Jab dui hafta baad Dewa Dreketi lauta Munni ke laaye, to puraana jamin ke baat phir ubhara. Dewa aapan dil ke baat to nahin bataaye sake. Bahana lagaais. Bull, phulaawa kahreede ke paisa lagi. Kahaan se paise batori. Aisan aisan baat.

'U jimmewaari hum log pe chor do beta,' Dhaniya jawab dihis. Dewa ke hichkichaat dekh ke Dhaniya chalte gayee. 'E accha baat haye ki tum aapan chota bhaiya bahini ke baare men sochat ho. Lekin apne baare men, Munni ke baare men, aapan pariwaar ke bare men bhi to kutch socho.' Munni baithi jamin take aur Dhaniya phuta paani ke tap ke rakam aapan waali jhoke chali jaai. 'Tum aapan jindagi aur Munni ke jindagi kahe dusre ke waaste barbaad karat ho beta. Huaan tumhaar liye kutch nahin haye. Hiyaan accha bhawwis haye' 'Abhi nahi, maai, koi aur tem,' Dewa aaste se bolis. U maangat raha e jamin wala baat bund hoye jaye koi hisaab se. 'Tab tak bahut der hoi jaye. Kab tak agoriho?' Dhaniya jawaab dihis. Bolte bolte Dhaniya samajh gayee accha se Dewa ke dil ke baat. 'Chalo ready hoye jaao. Bus aawe wala haye,' Dewa Munni se bol ke uthe laga.

'Nahin, Dewa, tum jaao.' E pahila baar raha jab Dhaniya aapan damaad ke us ke naam us ke muh pe lihis. 'Jao tummhen jahan jaye ke haye. Munni hiaan hum log, aapan pariwaar ke sanghe rahi.' Dewa Munni ke or taakis, lekin Munni aapan muh ghumaye lihis. Dewa akele laut aais. Sochis e chota jhagra haye. Ek din u log aapan galti kabul jaroor karihen. Lekin aise na bhaye. Ek mahina baad, Dewa ke pass ek chitti Shankar wakil ke pass se aais. Us men likha raha ki Munni maange maarit khaarij.

List of Contributors

Ahmed Ali, born in Suva, received his MA in History at the University of Auckland and his PhD on race and constitutional politics in Fiji, at The Australian National University. A former academic at the University of the South Pacific, a Fiji government minister and diplomat, he is currently the Vice President of the Fiji Senate.

Mosmi Bhim was born and raised in Waimanu Road, Suva, and graduated in journalism and history/politics from the University of the South Pacific where she currently works as a program assistant in the START Oceania Secretariat. A former editor of *USP Beat*, she has been associated with the Suva-based Niu Writers Forum.

Praveen Chandra was born in Lautoka, trained as an electrical and electronic engineer in the United Kingdom, and worked at the Fiji Institute of Technology and the Fiji Electricity Authority before migrating to Australia in June 1987. He is a practising electrical engineer in Brisbane.

Saras Chandra was born in Lautoka, graduated in mathematics from London University and after working in the United Kingdom for five years, returned to Fiji until 1987 when he migrated to New Zealand. He lives in Auckland and works as a software engineer and computer systems consultant.

John Connell is Professor and Head of the School of Geoscience at the University of Sydney. Born in England, he has spent most of his professional life working on problems of social and economic development in less developed countries, especially in the South Pacific region. He also works on decolonisation and nationalism as well as urbanisation and migration in the Third World.

Asish Janardhan was born in Ba, raised in Suva and migrated to the United States in 2000 where he lives in Antioch City in the San Francisco Bay Area. He is studying managerial economics at the University of California, Davis and works part-time as online banker in Concord, California.

Kanti Jinna, born and educated in Suva, was the Chief Librarian of the Government of Fiji before moving to Australia in 1984. He currently works at the Australian Bureau of Statistics in the Statistical Publishing Development Section in Canberra. A keen social worker, he is a prominent member of Canberra's Indian community.

John Kelly is a Professor of Anthropology at the University of Chicago. His doctoral research was on *Bhakti* and the spirit of capitalism in Fiji. He has since published path-breaking works on Indo-Fijians, including A *Politics of Virtue: Hinduism, Sexuality, and Countercolonial Discourse in Fiji.*

Vijendra Kumar, born in Martintar, Nadi, began as a high school teacher, but achieved distinction in journalism, becoming the first local-born editor of Fiji's daily newspaper *The Fiji Times*. His tenure as editor coincided with some of Fiji's most turbulent moments in recent times, including the 1977 political debacle and the coups a decade later. He now lives in Brisbane.

Padma Lal was born in Toorak and educated at Mahatma Gandhi High School and the University of the South Pacific. Her doctoral research at the University of Hawaii was on the economics of sustainable mangroves management in Fiji, but she now heads a large Australian-government supported project on the future of the Fiji sugar industry. Some photographs in this book were taken for her project.

Jacqueline Leckie, currently with the Anthropology Department at Otago University, is a Pakeha from New Zealand. Her close association with Fiji began in 1982, teaching history at the

University of the South Pacific. She has several publications on Fiji, including *To Labour With the State: A history of the Fiji Public Service Association*. Her research interests include gender, ethnicity, work and migration. Currently she is writing on madness and colonisation in Fiji.

Vijay Mishra, born in Suva but raised in Nakelo, was educated in New Zealand and has doctoral degrees from The Australian National University and Oxford. He is Professor of English at Murdoch University in Perth and has published widely on the Indian diasporic imaginary and on Bollywood cinema.

Vijay Naidu was born in Suva, raised in various parts of Fiji and educated at Marist Brothers High School and at the Universities of the South Pacific and Sussex. After a long spell of teaching at USP, he is currently Professor and Head of Development Studies at the Victoria University of Wellington.

Mohit Prasad was born in Sigatoka Valley and educated at the University of the South Pacific. A poet and short story writer, he is currently completing his doctoral thesis on Indo-Fijian diasporic identity, literature and popular culture at the University of Western Sydney.

Sushma Raj was born in Labasa and educated at the Universities of the South Pacific and Sydney where she graduated in Geography with a thesis on the Fiji community in the Sydney area. She currently works at the NSW TAFE as acting coordinator in the multicultural education unit, and is working on a post-graduate research project on Indo-Fijians in Sydney.

Shrishti Sharma was born in Lautoka but migrated to Australia after the coups in Fiji. She presently lives in Dunedin, New Zealand where she is a first year Health Science student at the

University of Otago. Her fictional works have been published in the Canberra literary journal *Conversations*.

Annie Sutton was born in Lautoka, grew up in the cane-belt of western Viti Levu and was educated at Cawaci, Levuka in a multi-ethnic and multi-cultural environment. She presently lives in Sydney and is researching a doctoral thesis on identity politics in the Fiji community in her home-town.

Malcom Tester is a retired opthalmic surgeon living in Lismore. He is the moving spirit behind the 'Beam of Hope Project', which seeks to address the problem of diabetes-induced blindness in Fiji. For this philanthropic effort, he was appointed an honorary Officer of the Order of Fiji.

Susanna Trnka teaches Social Anthropology at Auckland University. She was born in England, and has a PhD from Princeton University. Her teaching-interrupted research focuses on violence and Indo-Fijian identity, on racial imaginaries and discourses of citizenship, and on ideas of community.

Christine Weir, English by birth, taught in Fiji high schools from 1976 to 1985 before coming to Australia to do graduate studies. Her doctoral dissertation from The Australian National University was on the history of the Christian industrial missions in the Pacific. She has accepted a teaching assignment at the University of Waikato.

PANDANUS BOOKS

Pandanus Books was established in 2001 within the Research School of Pacific and Asian Studies (RSPAS) at The Australian National University. Concentrating on Asia and the Pacific, Pandanus Books embraces a variety of genres and has particular strength in the areas of biography, memoir, fiction and poetry. As a result of Pandanus' position within the Research School of Pacific and Asian Studies, the list includes high-quality scholarly texts, several of which are aimed at a general readership. Since its inception, Pandanus Books has developed into an editorially independent publishing enterprise with an imaginative list of titles and high-quality production values.

THE SULLIVAN'S CREEK SERIES

The Sullivan's Creek Series is a developing initiative of Pandanus Books. Extending the boundaries of the Pandanus Books' list, the Sullivan's Creek Series seeks to explore Australia through the work of new writers, with a particular encouragement to authors from Canberra and the region. Publishing history, biography, memoir, scholarly texts, fiction and poetry, the imprint complements the Asia and Pacific focus of Pandanus Books and aims to make a lively contribution to scholarship and cultural knowledge.